Journalism Today

Journalism Today

A Themed History

By

Jane L. Chapman and Nick Nuttall

A John Wiley & Sons, Ltd., Publication

Contents

Preface
How To Use the Book and Summary of Sections

The Approach

The idea for this book first evolved from an attempt to identify the major themes facing journalism today, and then to trace their historical roots. We wanted the approach to history to center on these themes and thus, by definition, to be selective. So our starting point has been *to identify current and longer term issues for journalism and society*. We have then elaborated the arguments and presented empirical historical evidence to back them up. All of the FactFiles and Résumés, for instance, predate the twenty-first century.

We selected four themes, and to each we devote a section of the book:

- Journalism and democracy
- Technology, work, and business
- Ethics
- Audience and its impact on journalism.

In the process of historical exploration, we found that we had identified a further four themes that define *modern journalism*, as both significantly different from its forebears and at the same time having a clear familial connection with those antecedents:

- Personalization
- Globalization
- Localization
- Pauperization.

Using the Book

This has been a voyage of discovery to connect past with present as it relates to journalism. We hope that readers will want to share the journey by reading this book cover to cover. It promises to be a fascinating and entertaining journey! Alternatively, the book is also designed to be consulted in sections, or indeed, in chapters and parts of chapters. You can dip in and out, picking names or episodes that seem to stand out from the page, or serve any other purpose that you may have.

Class usage

Class usage is likely to be more systematic than individual usage, so here are some suggestions.

1   This book can be used for *discussion purposes* – students, for instance, can read a section or chapter on a selected theme before attending a class on that theme, or an allied subject.
2   Chapters can also be used for *follow-up work*: the book is clearly divided up so that it will provide background for essays and project work. The "*résumés*," and *case studies* for instance, are intended to be an "aide-memoire" or prompt for further research on the life of the person selected, or the issues involved. In a relatively short book like this it is not possible to provide a complete history of journalism as a chronological transition from A to Z. Rather we have selected case studies that are indicative of those issues still relevant today, and those that also hold the potential for further discrete research as subjects in their own right, using this book as a springboard. The people who have been selected are neither definitive nor unique. Our choice is not exclusive: it is pragmatic to the extent that it is guided by the existence of a body of work (speeches, diaries, books, films, and other reflections) or scholarship – not necessarily on the people themselves and their lives but rather relating to their outstanding contribution to the overall context, enabling readers to investigate in more depth where they wish.
3   The contents of this book do not pretend to be definitive. We realize that other topics and different personalities can offer comparable insights into major events in the world of journalism as much as in the wider world itself.

An Introduction to the Themes

The main themes covered in this book – widening of participation in the public sphere, "nonprofessional" reporting and reporters, globalization of news and news organizations, concentration of ownerships, technological transformations, audience responses to the complexity of multiplatform delivery – are all historical phenomena dating back at least to the eighteenth and nineteenth centuries, often in countries outside the United States and Great Britain. This book traces some of these influences, not as an all-embracing chronological history (for these exist elsewhere), but more as a thematic "potpourri," highlighting in particular those journalistic functions that relate to and interact with wider society. In doing so, we take a long view, stressing continuities as well as change.

The four main sections each attempt a thematic approach that of necessity foregrounds the press and print journalism to a greater extent than its broadcast equivalent. This reflects the much longer history of the printed word itself. Similarly, the examples used throughout attempt to be representative or emblematic of the issues under discussion and there has been no attempt to be all-embracing of either journalism history or ideology.

The Introduction: Uses and abuses of history

The Introduction explains the rationale for our approach and acts as a discursive springboard for the rest of the book.

Part I: Journalism and democracy

Here we explore aspects of the historic relationship between journalism and democracy, first in terms of philosophical milestones such as Magna Carta, John Milton's *Areopagitica*, the writings of Tom Paine and of Jürgen Habermas; then in terms of legal and political struggles for freedom of expression such as the trial of John Peter Zenger, the Haswell case, and the story of Edward Smith Hall, an Australian free speech pioneer. The role of the press in the American Revolution, the First Amendment to the Constitution and other aspects of journalism and democracy (or the lack of it – such as censorship and oppressive laws), as well as challenges from investigative reporting and renegade proprietors, are all discussed. Examples of active political cultures, public debate, the impact of commercialism, and the growth in influence of public relations provide historical illustrations of journalism's good and less auspicious influences on democracy. Critiques of journalism such as the Hutchins Report highlight weaknesses in political coverage and lead on to debates about how journalism can facilitate a new sense of community in the future.

Part II: Technology, work, and business

By tracing historical themes and examples relevant to the evolving relationship between technology and commerce and their impact on the business of journalism, this section explores some of the reasons for the way the news business presently operates. The main trend mapped out here is the continuous march of a business and commercial ethos and the way it has influenced journalism over time. An underlying thread during the late nineteenth century and throughout the twentieth century is the gradual "corporatization" of journalism, that many believe has come to threaten the concept of a "free press."

Part III: Ethics

Journalists have a history of clashing with authority. This can be because they expose the rich and powerful, they antagonize governments or vested interests, or they "get it wrong" for one reason or another and end up in court. The law is one form of constraint but from the late nineteenth century journalists themselves devised various codes of ethics that they hoped all practitioners would adhere to, and in so doing both legitimize the profession and earn the public's trust. This section examines these various ethical codes, from those devised by labor unions and journalists' organizations to those promulgated by proprietors, editors, and individual journalists themselves.

We also draw attention to the ways in which a journalist has to constantly reconcile a variety of ethical standards while doing the job on a day-to-day basis. For it should be remembered that "one very important function is the idea that it [journalism] is seen to bridge a gap between events and audiences, and therefore to mediate experience."[1] It is in the process of mediation that ethical factors become significant, and how they are "played" determines to a large extent how journalists are perceived. Are they trusted? Do they command respect? Answers to these questions are suggested within a historical context that traces the development of ethical codes primarily in Great Britain and America. Major issues studied include privacy and celebrity, the press and royalty, and how fakery, both within the media and from external sources, has at times threatened to undermine public confidence in print and broadcast journalism alike.

Part IV: Audience

Attitudes towards audience have changed considerably over the years – in essence early audiences were self-selective and early newspapers focused on a narrow constituency of readers: "The eighteenth century in England had no 'mass' audience in the modern sense; that was to come only in the next century. But the eighteenth century was modern in the sense that, from that time on, a writer could support himself from the sale of his works to the public."[2] The eighteenth century ushered in the first major development in audience building: the "shift from private endowment (usually in the form of patronage by the aristocracy) and a limited audience to public endowment and a potentially unlimited audience."[3] It is the pursuit of that unlimited audience that has in many respects driven the journalism engine ever since.

Audiences can be serviced, represented, misrepresented, or unrepresented; they can be involved in the process of news production or remain discrete and uninvolved. But there has seldom if ever been an even balance between the producers of news and its consumers, for media tend to be either controlled by hegemonic power, or else act as an expression of counterhegemonic forces that are largely defined by their audiences. This section therefore addresses the argument that journalism has gradually become more democratic and empowering of a better informed and responsive public. But at the same time it rebuts the idea that there has been a continuous trajectory of progress throughout the past toward a glorious present, exemplified by the democratic potential of the internet.

By highlighting some historical examples of different sorts of audience awareness and involvement from the early days of newspapers to the present, it can be shown that a blurring of the boundaries between consumers and producers is a constant *leitmotiv* of journalistic development. The contribution of celebrity, tabloidization, "dumbing down," and increasing personalization of news agendas is also assessed.

Part V: Conclusion

We have allocated the Conclusion a discrete section all by itself. This is because the chapter can be read as a separate exercise in its own right – as the summing-up session for the end of a particular module, program, or series of classes. This chapter contains the ideas to walk away with for the future: we cannot predict accurately – nobody can – but we can provide food for thought. In that respect, we hope we have supplied a satisfying, and also a gourmet experience!

Notes

1 David Berry (ed.), *Ethics and Media Culture: Practices and Representations* (Oxford: Focal Press, 2000), p. 28.
2 Leo Lowenthal, *Literature, Popular Culture, and Society* (Eaglewood Cliffs, NJ: Prentice-Hall, 1961), p. 55.
3 Ibid.

Acknowledgments

With thanks to Macquarie University, Sydney, Australia, where Jane Chapman is an honorary associate of the Centre for Media History and a Visiting Professor. With thanks also to editor Elizabeth Swayze and her assistants for their continuing vision and sound judgment throughout the long project of book writing, and to all the production team at Wiley-Blackwell for their professionalism and efficiency. We are also grateful to our colleagues in the Lincoln School of Journalism for all their encouragement and to Kate Allison for her help with picture/website research.

Introduction
The Uses and Abuses of History: Why Bother With It?

A study of the modern newspaper is meaningless, in the very exact sense of the word, if it is not aware of the historical framework ...
(*Leo Lowenthal,* **Historical Perspectives on Popular Culture**)

When truth is replaced by silence, the silence is a lie.
(*Yevgeni Yevtushenko,* **Soviet dissident**)

Professional journalism is undergoing a reshaping in terms of occupational roles and legitimacy. It is causing a lot of people a lot of pain. Indeed, some commentators believe journalism's very existence is threatened by the potential of internet-based technologies: a potential not only to democratize participation in the public sphere, but also to provide a platform for user-generated content. Against this backdrop of ongoing restructuring of the global news industry and increasing concentration of ownership among transnational corporations, it would appear timely to scrutinize the problems that journalism faces and how our understanding of them might benefit from an examination of the historical dimension.

If we are to understand contemporary and future journalistic forms and allied occupational issues, then we need to appreciate how its various roles and social position have emerged and developed over time. Similarly, we need to have a clear idea of the relationship between the media in a democratic society and that democratic society itself. Robert McChesney and John Nichols visualize the ideal: "Imagine the kind of media that a democratic society deserves; media that bring us a wealth of diverse opinions and entertainment options; media that are held responsible for providing

Jane Chapman and Nick Nuttall, *Journalism Today: A Themed History*
© 2011 Jane Chapman and Nick Nuttall. Published by Blackwell Publishing Ltd.

us with the information we need to function as informed citizens; media where ideas flow in both directions, and where ordinary people routinely have a chance to voice their concerns."[1] As a checklist of aspirations, such values have existed in one form or another throughout the medium's history; but if we want to reimagine or re-emphasize such values then, once again, we have to understand the past.

A historical perspective should be capable of revealing underlying trends, causes, and conditions that might otherwise be neglected. Social histories of the press have shown how institutional and technological factors have shaped news over the last 200 years, reinforcing the doctrine that news is, more than anything else, a culturally constructed category.[2]

Too Much Information!

Today's society suffers from an abundance of information, but this does not necessarily mean that the public can make sense of it. Too much information, if you like, often obscures rather than reveals the truth: "There are times when the historian of the media feels that the best metaphor to use in relation to the recent past is that of 'the thicket'. The technology changes so fast and becomes so obtrusive that broader history is forgotten, and in examining that, not everything converges."[3]

Sophisticated technology and a legally free news media therefore do not necessarily lead to an informed citizenry. And without some historical understanding or perspective, current issues can be misunderstood or deracinated such that their "ancestry" is obscured. This lack of a "communicative competence" enables powerful and vested interests to set the parameters of public debate. In the United States, for example, the way public opinion is formed depends on two factors – firstly, how governments and corporate power choose and define the debate and secondly, the way they influence that debate by setting its frames of reference.[4]

Internet enthusiasts and those optimists who place their faith in the democratizing opportunities offered by blogging and podcasts argue that this traditional power nexus is now being undermined. Certainly there is ample supporting evidence. Some of the most powerful images of the London 7/7 terrorist attacks of 2005 were provided by commuters with their camera phones. Details of the uprising in Burma during 2007 came from bloggers who bypassed reporting restrictions while images of the fighting and demonstrations were captured on mobile phones. Such was the threat that the military leaders imposed an internet blackout to block informational leaks about the violent crackdown. Yet the very ability of the Burmese regime to "pull the plug" should perhaps be considered a powerful corrective to the unbridled optimism of internet enthusiasts.

More recently in 2009 new media allowed the world to connect with the Tehran rebels who supported Mir Hossein Mousavi in the disputed presidential elections in Iran that returned President Mahmoud Ahmadinejad to power. One Iranian graduate, Neda Agha-Soltan, became a "heroine" as well as a martyr, her death from a gunshot wound captured on camera phone and video and beamed around the world. This was one of the first conflicts where Twitter, the social networking website that allows a maximum of 140 characters per "tweet" or message, was also highly influential. As one Twitter message read: "One person = one broadcaster."[5] The Iranian regime's response was to slow down internet speeds to a crawl so "brevity and simplicity were essential." As recorded by journalist Andrew Sullivan: "To communicate they tweeted. Within hours of the farcical election result, I tracked down a bunch of live Twitter feeds and started to edit and re-broadcast them as a stream of human consciousness on the verge of revolution."[6]

These unauthorized broadcasts are symptomatic of the new digital technology flexing its muscles. And already we are seeing the beginnings of a power struggle between those who crusade for total freedom and those who wish to exercise control, whether governments or traditional media conglomerates. Google, for example, is a business that has disturbed the equilibrium of both these power elites. English journalist Henry Porter in an article for the *Observer* described Google as a WWM – a worldwide monopoly – and wrote in April 2009: "Google presents a far greater threat [than other WWMs] to the livelihood of individuals and the future of commercial institutions important to the community." His argument went on to assert that "newspapers are the only means of holding local hospitals, schools, councils and the police to account, and on a national level they are absolutely essential for the good functioning of democracy."[7]

Porter seemed to share his point of view with Rupert Murdoch, although possibly for quite different reasons. From May 2009 Murdoch indicated that he expected to start charging for access to News Corporation's newspaper websites. In August Britain's *Guardian* suggested that he had "dangled a possible lifeline to the struggling newspaper industry by declaring that his titles will start charging for online content."[8] By November 2009, Murdoch had refined his attack by mentioning Google by name: "Rupert Murdoch has underlined his determination to make the internet pay by promising to remove his newspapers' stories from Google."[9] By March 2010, it was confirmed that the UK national newspapers *The Times* and the *Sunday Times* were to start charging for content online in June 2009: "Users will be charged £1 for a day's access and £2 for a week's subscription for access to both papers' websites." News International chief executive Rebekah Brooks "implied in a statement that its other titles, the Sun and the News of the World, would follow."[10]

At the same time, we should not underestimate the desire of governments of whatever stripe – whether the United States after the 9/11 Al Qaeda attacks, Russia after the second Chechen war, the United Kingdom during the IRA bombing campaigns – to exercise some control over news media.[11] The Chinese authorities, for example, have for some time been in conflict with Google over freedom of access to the internet via Google's search engine. Google said it was no longer prepared to comply with demands that it filter web content such as prodemocracy sites behind what has been dubbed the "great firewall of China." Google's stock price fell on the news that it had allowed its internet content provider license to expire. Whether China's attempts to regulate digital technology will survive its own population's desire to circumvent such controls, however, is difficult to determine.

Yet in all the media coverage of the battle between new media forms and entrenched vested interests, as well as the democratizing process inherent in their development and use, few if any observers have made reference to the long history of "citizen journalism" dating back to the eighteenth century, when newspapers often depended on members of the public to act as news gatherers. These early "citizen journalists" were often in the vanguard of new developments in the media, whether the radical press in Great Britain in the first quarter of the nineteenth century, or at an international level acting as foreign correspondents by dispatching accounts of important events in the absence of paid professionals. Such pioneers would surely understand and appreciate the skill and courage with which their descendants communicate the horrors of tyrannical regimes the world over in the twenty-first century.

Egalitarianism doesn't just depend on earth-shattering events to manifest itself, however. *OhmyNews*, for example, is a South Korean online agency which regularly scoops large media operations, employing as it does between 25,000 and 40,000 citizen journalists worldwide (numbers vary) and paying them about $15 a story. Despite allowing anyone to contribute, it attempts to moderate its output by applying some "traditional" journalistic standards to submitted copy. Clearly then, established journalistic criteria are being applied here, but it is the scale and the delivery platform that have changed rather than the concept. One of the themes we examine in this book is how that change has come about and why.

These concerns, still evident in any discussion of online news and other emerging news platforms such as podcasts, blogs, and Twitter, have in fact been the subject of a broad and far-reaching discourse throughout journalism's various checkered and contested histories: news gathering and relations with sources and readers; the political economy of news production and its institutions; definitions of journalism; its values, ethics, and professional identity. In other words, there are certain constants and ongoing themes. The point of these historical analogies is thus not to minimize the importance of current issues in journalism, but rather to remind us of the continuities in media heritage at a time when analysts seem predisposed to inflate the importance – and uniqueness – of current events. We can learn from the past in order to navigate the future.

In order to do so, however, an understanding of context is required. A professional life tends to be lived "in the moment" with little time for reflection or examination of contexts, historical or otherwise. Journalists are aware of being vulnerable to accusations of partisanship when making a controversial value judgment during the process of contextualizing a story. So the temptation to play safe by delivering an arsenal of facts – often making the story less interesting, reducing its political potency, and confusing potential audiences – is often overwhelming. On the other hand, a more partisan writer may well put stories into a context that tries "to find a common thread between them"[12] and in the process alienate "impartial" members of the audience.

The "common thread" provided by history, however, is not a panacea. "It is not always appropriate to learn the lessons of the past," warns media academic Natalie Fenton, "if this is done indiscriminately without taking account of the precise configurations of the present."[13] This is precisely the reason why this study is selective, organized around themes rather than a comprehensive and complete history of journalism. Within these themes, we aim to present as impartially as possible a range of interpretations. But there are gaps. Our history is aimed almost exclusively at perceived contemporary problems in the Western world.

One such problem is the perception that recent media developments, rather than advancing ideas of "community," are reinforcing a pack mentality, whether it's the paparazzi in pursuit of a celebrity or the constant reiteration of the same news stories across radio and television news channels. The lone, intrepid investigative reporter who became an individual hero is largely a thing of the past. The corollary of this is spelt out by British PR magnate Max Clifford who argues that when he began his career, public relations was about promotion. Now the majority of his work is about protection of both celebrities and organizations against the media pack, or the "feral beast," to use a phrase coined by Tony Blair when he was Prime Minister. Clifford considers that today people are "very slow to praise and very anxious to destroy," while Tony Blair argued that in media reporting of politics, attacking the motives of politicians has become more potent than attacking their judgment.[14]

The danger of entrenched viewpoints, from whatever perspective, is their tendency to obscure the wider arguments of history. In fact, there are two contrary ways of construing journalism history that need to be avoided: "gloom and doom" scenarios on the one hand, and the inevitable "march of progress" represented by both emerging press freedoms and new communications technologies on the other. British historians refer to the latter as the "Whig interpretation of press history."[15] Yet these have often emerged as two sides of the same coin. Some industry observers believe that journalism's modern structure has encouraged a dangerous conservatism that, in the case of the United States with its protective First Amendment, was never intended. Noted American journalist Dan Gillmor says, "I don't believe the First Amendment, which gives journalists valuable leeway to inquire and publish, was designed with corporate profits in mind. While we haven't become a wholly cynical business yet, the trend is scary. Consolidation makes it even more worrisome."[16] In Britain the commercial broadcast media have long chafed under what they consider to be the intensely conservative and restrictive "public service broadcasting" doctrine exemplified for so long by the BBC.

There is no question, however, that today's rapid technological changes can be seen as a continuation of socioeconomic trends dating back to the seventeenth century despite differences of scale, character, and emphasis. Scholars have noted how previous communications technologies – the railways, telegraph, telephone, radio, television – changed perceptions of global boundaries and distance, time, and space. The internet and the world wide web, as the latest of these communications technologies, may arguably be the most significant. This prompts two significant questions. Firstly, how does the internet change people's perceptions as media consumers,[17] and secondly, what are the implications for journalists as both users and consumers?

The answers to such questions, we suggest, can be found, in part at least, through an informed appreciation of the cultural, economic, and political functions of the press that emerged during previous technological ages, even if they appear now to be threatened. McChesney and Nichols in their critique of the American media's role in destroying democracy, spinning elections, and selling wars (a paraphrase of their title) point out that some of the endemic problems for political journalism are due to commercial control and the professional code that emerged about one hundred years ago. Therefore, "a rigorous accounting with history offers necessary insights and perspectives on our current situation and points the way out."[18] History, it seems, can go some way toward helping us focus on solutions as well as issues.

One of the most significant of those issues in the current media climate is the plight of traditional newspapers, at both local and national level. They face challenges from expansive local and national radio, 24-hour TV news channels, free newspapers (that encourage readers to think of newspapers as a cost-free product), news delivery via online editions, billboards, and mobile telephony. Revenue streams, meanwhile, are in flux as advertisers migrate to internet competitors such as eBay and craigslist. The print industry has retaliated by attempting to woo readers with free gifts and DVDs. One British national daily has gone so far as to claim that, "The age of podcasts, war-zone bloggers, and countless other online information sources presents newspapers with arguably their biggest challenge ever."[19]

Is this just another example of the traditional doom-mongering that often accompanies dramatic changes in the media landscape? Or is the current turmoil, the digital disturbance of a once peaceful analogue "pond," of a different order from all previous technological upheavals? History suggests that media platforms have regularly reinvented their purpose and user base as new formats and technologies emerge. But what makes the emergence of the online platform such an intriguing challenge is its position as both a rival medium and at the same time a medium for the continuation of the press in a new form.

Newspapers are in the process of reinventing themselves in order to extend their appeal to a generation reared on information delivered electronically. Yet the newspaper crisis should not be exaggerated. In 2006, according to Gavin O'Reilly, President of the World Association of Newspapers, 439 million people still purchased a newspaper every day – an increase of 6 percent over a five-year period. Newspapers remained the world's second largest advertising medium with a 30.2 percent market share.[20] By the following year, the same organization – one that admittedly has a vested interest in selling its image and is clearly benefiting from the burgeoning markets in China and India – was able to report that paid-for titles surpassed 11,000 for the first time in history and that free daily newspaper circulation had more than doubled over five years to 40.8 million copies per day.[21]

Such encouraging statistics, however, cannot hide the fact that transitions can be painful, for new information technologies very often decentralize power, or at least shift the center of gravity, and this fact is not easily conceded by those who are adversely affected. For instance, during the late 1920s and early1930s, print editors saw as one of their roles the provision of news for the new medium of radio. In the USA, they bought into radio stations, and also started their own, but those who did not choose this controlling route depicted the advent of radio news reporting as a threat to democracy and the American Way of Life. In Britain, agreements were made with the fledgling BBC that news would not be transmitted before 6 p.m., thus preserving the press's hegemony over the daily news agenda. In both countries this allowed members of the press to depict themselves as the true, reliable defenders of the public interest.

History as News, News as History

Good journalistic coverage has often provided the first draft of history by enabling the public to understand the meaning of events as they unfold: "It is journalism that ten, twenty, fifty years after the fact still holds up a true and intelligent mirror to events."[22] Award-winning journalist John Pilger quotes T. D. Allman on this point in order to remind us that if journalism discards its role as history's first draft, it promotes "directly and by default, an imperialism whose true intentions are rarely expressed. Instead, noble words and concepts like 'democracy' and 'freedom' and 'liberation' are emptied of their true meaning and pressed into the service of conquest."[23] Thus, according to Pilger, in the 1970s the media by its silence allowed the US to arm the Indonesian dictatorship as it massacred the East Timorese, and to begin secret support for the mujahideen in Afghanistan, out of which came the Taliban and al-Qaida.[24] By the time 9/11 erupted, new publishing tools available on the internet meant that the first draft was being written, in part, by the former audience.

This is just one of the ways that journalism is in the process of being transformed from its former characterization as a twentieth-century mass media structure. The one-way communication model – news as lecture with audience participation confined to the letters pages of newspapers and largely ignored by radio and television – is losing out to a more inclusive discourse that at first just acknowledged the existence of the audience but now actively seeks out that audience and often responds to it. People from the grassroots who may previously have been disempowered are now being listened to. Major players, once again, are forced to adapt, and that process – in which some of the more persistent and important news bloggers such as Glenn Reynolds's *Instapundit* and news aggregation sites such as Matt Drudge's *Drudge Report* actually accumulate considerable influence – needs to be understood.

As the battalions of citizen foot soldiers join journalism's ranks, such questions become more urgent. According to Brian McNair, "The qualities which have been associated with 'good' journalism for centuries – objectivity, analytical skill, interpretative authority, integrity in investigation and reportage, courage in the face of elite pressure – all will increase in value as the number of writers expands into the billions."[25] Yet the intrinsic irony of such predictions is not lost on John Pilger who, with characteristic melancholy, has noted that "as media technology advances almost beyond our imagination, it is not just the traditional means of journalism that are becoming obsolete, but its honourable traditions."[26]

Ways and Means

In a relatively short book such as this we have had to reject the seminal "single year" approach exemplified by W. Joseph Campbell's exclusively American study, *The Year that Defined American Journalism: 1897 and the Clash of Paradigms*. Campbell examines an exceptional 12 months in the history of journalism and argues that there was a clash of "paradigms" between William Randolph Hearst's "journalism of action," the fact-based journalism practiced by Adolph Ochs, and experiments in literary journalism by Lincoln Steffens. While this detailed approach has much to commend it we have opted for a broader overview that is not constrained by dates or by country, while taking periodization and context into account. Besides, for American journalism history there are other candidate years: 1798 with the Alien and Sedition Acts, 1833 and the emergence of the penny press, 1972 and exposure by the *Washington Post* of the Watergate scandal. All of these events appear in the pages that follow, but are approached from the angle of their significance to journalism and society in the present, rather than their importance within a particular chronological year. We have drawn heavily on American, British, and in some cases French history, drawing comparisons between episodes and experiences as a means of enhancing historical insights.

The emergent synthesis of primary and secondary sources adds up to a novel methodological approach. The comparative methodology also makes it eclectic. Readers may find that there are sins of omission, but if this book serves to provide a better understanding and appreciation of the current and historical relationship between journalism and society, then it will have served its purpose.

Notes

1   Robert W. McChesney and John Nichols, *Our Media, Not Theirs: The Democratic Struggle Against Corporate Media* (New York: Seven Stories Press, 2002), p. 11.
2   Michael Schudson, *Discovering the News: A Social History of the American Newspaper* (New York: Basic Books, 1978); Menahem Blondheim, *News Over the Wires: The Telegraph and the Flow of Public Information in America, 1844–1897* (Cambridge, MA: Harvard University Press, 1994).
3   Asa Briggs and Peter Burke, *A Social History of the Media* (Cambridge, UK: Polity Press, 2002), p. 319.
4   Kevin Howley, *Community Media: People, Places, and Communication Technologies* (Cambridge, UK: Cambridge University Press, 2005), p. 20.
5   Andrew Sullivan, "Twitter Ripped the Veil off 'The Other' – And we Saw Ourselves," *Sunday Times*, June 21, 2009, p. 22.
6   Ibid.
7   Henry Porter, "Google is Just an Amoral Menace," *Observer*, April 5, 2009, p. 27.
8   James Harkin, "All The News Fit to Pay For," *Guardian*, August 8, 2009, p. 31.
9   Chris Tryhorn and Bobbie Johnson, "Murdoch Plans to Strip Google of News," *Guardian*, November 10, 2009, p. 25.
10 Mercedes Bunz, "Times and Sunday Times Websites to Start Charging From June," *Guardian*, March 26, 2010. Available online at http://www.guardian.co.uk/media/2010/mar/26/ times-website-paywall, accessed on April 1, 2010.
11 Charles Arthur, "Google Fails to Renew Licence in China," *Guardian*, April 1, 2010. Available online at http://www.guardian.co.uk/technology/2010/apr/01/google-china-licence-expires, accessed on April 1, 2010.
12 McChesney and Nichols, *Our Media, Not Theirs*, p. 19.

13 Natalie Fenton, *New Media, Old News: Journalism and Democracy in the Digital Age* (London: Sage, 2007), p. 12.

14 Andrew Grice, "Blair's Attack Provokes Anger Among Newspaper Editors and Broadcasters," *Independent*, June 13, 2007, p. 5.

15 James Curran and Jean Seaton, *Power Without Responsibility: The Press and Broadcasting in Britain*, 5th edn (London: Routledge, 1997), pp. 10–21.

16 Dan Gillmor, *We the Media: Grassroots Journalism by the People, for the People* (Cambridge, MA: O'Reilly, 2004), p. xv.

17 Hazel Dicken-Garcia, "The Internet and Continuing Historical Discourse," *Journalism & Mass Communication Quarterly*, 1, 75 (1998), 19–27 (p. 23).

18 Robert W. McChesney and John Nichols, *Tragedy and Farce: How the American Media Sell Wars, Spin Elections, and Destroy Democracy* (New York: New Press, 2005), p. xi.

19 Steve Auckland, "The Future of Newspapers", *Independent*, *Media Weekly* special report, November 13, 2006, p. 4.

20 Ibid., p. 6.

21 World Association of Newspapers, 2007. Available online at http://www.wan-ifra.org/, accessed on April 1, 2010.

22 John Pilger (ed.), *Tell Me No Lies: Investigative Journalism and its Triumphs* (London: Jonathan Cape, 2004), p. xiii.

23 Ibid., p. xxvii.

24 Ibid., p. xxv.

25 Brian McNair, "The British Press, 1992–2007," unpublished paper presented at the *Future of Journalism Conference*, Cardiff, September 7–9, 2007, p. 11.

26 Pilger, *Tell Me No Lies*, p. xviii.

Part I

Journalism and Democracy
A Sibling Rivalry?

But such is the irresistible nature of truth, that all it asks, and all it wants, is the liberty of appearing.

(*Thomas Paine,* **Rights of Man**)

1

A Right To Know

The development of a news culture is closely allied to the development of democratic societies. If democracy is, in Abraham Lincoln's words, "Government of the people, by the people, for the people" then journalism at its best exhibits a similar pluralist propensity. Indeed, journalism and democracy can claim a longer marriage than that between journalism and the commercial imperative of media for profit. Yet it is the latter which seems to have taken precedence in the twenty-first century. In the past, the presentation of "diverse" stories and information was useful to the workings of democracy, but by last century's end editors, whether by inclination or circumstance, were increasingly defining news within a business context in order to maintain or increase revenues. News had become commercialized.[1] The process by which this happened is examined in more detail in Part II, but in Part I we examine the implications for democracy.

Who's Right and Who Knows?

"I shall resign the presidency effective at noon tomorrow. Vice President Ford will be sworn in as President at that hour in this office." These words were spoken on August 8, 1974 and brought to an end one of the most bizarre series of events in American history as President Nixon became the only president ever to resign from office. The Watergate scandal, as it became known, was an example of the finest journalism pursued from the highest of motives by men of unquestioned integrity. Richard Nixon, of course, didn't agree.

Jane Chapman and Nick Nuttall, *Journalism Today: A Themed History*
© 2011 Jane Chapman and Nick Nuttall. Published by Blackwell Publishing Ltd.

But how important were the two *Washington Post* journalists, Bob Woodward and Carl Bernstein, in the whole saga of the Watergate break-ins? How significant was journalism in the Watergate story? History is a movable feast, but after 35 years history may already be giving its verdict. To take one example: the internet Wikipedia page, *Watergate Scandal*, is some 7,500 words long. Woodward and Bernstein are referred to only briefly in the main text despite the celebrity status accorded them in the immediate aftermath of the scandal itself. So are we right to assume uncritically that this was a shining example of journalism taking the moral high ground and coming to the rescue of a democracy treated with contempt by a president and a people treated with disdain by the ruling elite? Is it inevitable that our affirmation of one is always at the expense of our faith in the other?

Twenty years later, on October 20, 1994, the UK *Guardian* newspaper published a front-page article by its Westminster correspondent which alleged that a lobbying company, Ian Greer Associates, had paid two Conservative MPs £2,000 a time to ask parliamentary questions on behalf of Mohamed Al-Fayed, the owner of Harrods department store in Knightsbridge, London. This was the first time the names of MPs Tim Smith and more notably Neil Hamilton had entered the public consciousness. Junior Northern Ireland minister Smith resigned immediately, fueling speculation that the allegations were indeed true. But Hamilton and Greer served the *Guardian* with libel writs. Subsequent events led to Neil Hamilton, a junior minister at the Department of Trade and Industry, losing his safe seat at Tatton in Cheshire to journalist Martin Bell. Many political commentators believed the "cash for questions" affair, as it became known, was instrumental in the fall not only of Neil Hamilton but also of John Major's Conservative government and the subsequent election of Tony Blair and New Labour in 1997.

The British media's coverage tended to follow the *Guardian* line. But Neil Hamilton always denied the allegations contained in the *Guardian* article and subsequent newspaper stories. There was an official investigation by Sir Gordon Downey, the Parliamentary Commissioner for Standards, which vindicated the *Guardian*'s version of events. Downey found the evidence "compelling" that Neil Hamilton had indeed been paid large amounts of "cash in envelopes." There the matter might have rested but for the diligent research and enquiring minds of two freelance journalists, Jonathan Boyd Hunt and Malcolm Keith-Hill. Hunt was a former reporter on the regional TV news program *Granada Tonight* and Keith-Hill was an experienced investigative journalist. They had already joined forces to produce a TV documentary (never aired) on the "cash for questions" affair provisionally entitled "From Ritz to Writs."

The conclusions of the Downey Report, at complete variance with the results of their own research for the documentary, led them to pursue the issue with renewed vigor. It was their contention that the whole story was a fabrication, that there never was any "cash" and that Tim Smith, Neil Hamilton, and Ian Greer were innocent of all charges. Hunt and Keith-Hill alleged further that the *Guardian* framed Neil Hamilton with Mohamed Al-Fayed's cooperation and that "when the lobbyist and one of the MPs sued the *Guardian* for libel, for which the *Guardian* was uninsured, its editors, journalists, and lawyers enacted a cynical cover-up."[2]

Yet Hunt and Keith-Hill were unable to get their story published in the press or anywhere else. To combat this, Hunt wrote a book on the affair, *Trial by Conspiracy*, and set up the website www.guardianlies.com as a way of publicizing his and Keith-Hill's investigative work. The world wide web thus became a bona fide outlet for a piece of investigative journalism that might otherwise not have seen the light of day. As the two journalists stated, "This website is undoubtedly the first of its kind in the world. It was constructed to overcome a news blackout enacted by the British media of the two freelances' investigation."[3]

Can we assume from this story that the internet is now a respected and trusted media outlet in its own right rather than just the last resort of cyber-stalkers, ax-grinders, whistle-blowers, or the merely insane? Should we accept it as a legitimate forum for investigative journalism and one that offers a potential corrective to the vast power of a modern media conglomerate? There is no doubt that the internet has become increasingly important to media organizations. The BBC, for example, employs more staff on its website than on its news programming. However, if the internet is to be trusted, it must be possible to distinguish between the legitimate website and the disingenuous. This isn't a problem with the websites of well-known media organizations but for the independent site or newcomer blog issues about trust and truth loom large. For the journalist who has a story to tell and nowhere else to tell it, the internet may well be a boon, but he or she still has to overcome people's natural cynicism when presented with startling "revelations" that have not found a home in a mainstream media outlet.

So, why is it that one of these stories resulted in the two journalists concerned being feted, writing a book, *All The President's Men*, and having a film made of their exploits, while the two journalists telling the other story were only able to publish it on the internet? What does this say about the state of our democracy or, for that matter, the state of our journalism? This chapter will attempt to put these issues into a perspective that takes account of both historical factuality and changing journalistic imperatives.

The motivation behind such stories, however, is always the same: the journalists' sense that the public has a "right to know," that the story is in the public interest and not just of interest to the public. But even more than this perhaps is the broader principle that journalists actually have a duty towards the public. According to the Italian Charter of Duties of Journalists, for example, "A journalist's responsibility towards people always prevails over any other thing."[4] That responsibility includes alerting people to issues, events, situations, and individuals that deserve attention as well as providing them with the information needed to make valid judgments about their rights and responsibilities as citizens. Journalists inform public opinion by reporting, interpreting, and providing background information and context. Journalists serve democracy by pointing out "what, if anything is being done elsewhere, what options exist, what the admitted likely consequences of various actions might be, what choices their (the public's) political leaders are considering."[5]

It was not, of course, preordained that journalists should be the ones to provide such political news and editorial comment. The earliest newspapers, known as *corantos* or *courants* (news books), contained little news. However, the development of the newsbook and the news sheet in seventeenth-century Britain was accompanied by an upsurge in political and foreign "intelligence," or news. This was produced by men who were paid for their labor and it became known as journalism, after the journal or daily newspaper that published their writings. The word journalist entered the language for the first time toward the end of the seventeenth century. Thus the historical role of journalism as supporter of democracy is based on those continuities that the profession has struggled to achieve over the last three hundred years. There are three traditionally linked responsibilities:

1 The presentation of a diversity of informed views on matters of the day including political issues and their interpretation;
2 Watchdog of the public interest, as a guard against politicians and officials who may act in their own interest or threaten democracy rather than serve the public – the notion of the press as a Fourth Estate;
3 An ability to expose untruths and support truth wherever power is wielded arbitrarily, because journalists are, at least in principle, independent from the control of others.

Obviously, by definition, mass communications always relay messages to more people than have a specific need for them. In addition, there have always been (and always will be) journalists and media practitioners who endeavor to contribute to the various forums where public life is scrutinized, for as Walter Lippmann noted, "There can be no liberty for a community which lacks the information by which to detect lies."[6] But as deregulation advances and commercialism becomes more widespread, there has been a marked increase since the end of the nineteenth century in personal "affairs" journalism epitomized by the human interest story. Whether in the arena of sport, business, or entertainment, such stories provide information for people to make sense of their own personal "world" and lifestyle as opposed to their responsibilities as public entities.

Sometimes described as the commodification of culture, where the "consumer is king," this trend has come to symbolize what cultural critics describe as an obsession with the acquisition of personal goods and an equal passion for media-generated entertainment. Fewer people, it seems, are willing to devote time and effort toward the achievement of a common, collective good. Public affairs journalism on matters of national, regional, and local government, whether aimed at the welfare of entire communities, collective private interests, or wider society has in consequence suffered. This democratic "deficit" has left many commentators wondering about the future, in particular how journalism's unique mission can be protected and what the prospects are for any remaining relationship between journalism and democracy.

Résumé
Walter Lippmann

Walter Lippmann was one of the most influential journalists and cultural commentators of the twentieth century. He believed journalists were a link between the governors and the governed and as such had an almost sacred duty to the truth and objectivity, although he understood that all truth was necessarily subjective. He was an elitist and promoted the idea that a "governing class" of experts, specialists, and bureaucrats was needed to safeguard democracy because the notion of a public competent to direct public affairs was a "false ideal."

Lippmann was born in New York in 1889. He studied philosophy and languages at Harvard and graduated in 1909. In May 1910 he wrote to Lincoln Steffens, the "muckraking" investigative journalist, asking for a position on *Everybody's Magazine* "because there is no kind of work that appeals to me as much as yours does."[7] Lippmann soon became one of its editors and Theodore Roosevelt described him as the most brilliant man of his age in all the United States.[8]

He established a political weekly, the *New Republic*, in 1914 and was a member of the US delegation to the Paris Peace Conference of 1919. He also helped to draw up the covenant of the new League of Nations. By then he was a "personality," became an informal adviser to many presidents and wrote a number of significant books on journalism and politics. In 1931 he joined the New York *Herald Tribune* and won the Pulitzer Prize in 1958 and 1962 for his syndicated newspaper column "Today and Tomorrow." He popularized the term "the Cold War" when he published a book of the same name in 1947, and his now famous phrase, the "Manufacture of Consent," was adapted by Edward S. Herman and Noam Chomsky for the title of their 1988 groundbreaking book on the political economy of the mass media, *Manufacturing Consent*. Lippmann died in 1974 in New York.

This relationship is traditionally reflected in the kind of democracy a country enjoys. The North American continent, colonized in the seventeenth century, was in itself a democratic undertaking. Yet the development of the press, mainly because of the sheer size of the continent, has always remained a largely regional affair in the same way that politics at state level can be a more potent force in a citizen's life than federal politics. Similarly a strong state legislature was reflected in a strong regional press clustered around individual states, towns, and cities. Iconic titles of the American press, for example, the *New York Times*, the *Washington Post*, the *Los Angeles Times*, the *Chicago Tribune*, are all named for the cities in which they operate.

These practical continental problems were acknowledged by Founding Fathers James Madison and Alexander Hamilton in the *Federalist Papers* (1787) where they argued that transport engineering and newspapers would unite the nation.[9] Cultural historian James Carey expanded on this simple dictum: "The United States was … the product of literacy, cheap paper, rapid and inexpensive transportation, and the mechanical reproduction of words – the capacity, in short, to transport not only people but a complex culture and civilization from one place to another, indeed between places that were radically dissimilar in geography, social conditions, economy, and very often climate."[10] Carey's acknowledgement of the "radically dissimilar" in the United States has not precluded a vibrant print community, even though transport engineering did little to promote a national press.

Magazines, on the other hand, were more likely to flourish because they operated with more flexible deadlines, weekly or monthly, and broader news agendas which allowed for the vagaries of early transport systems. A good example is *The Nation*, a weekly magazine known as "the flagship of the left," which was first published in 1865 and flourishes to this day. Its early remit was to secure full rights for freed slaves and it still campaigns for traditionally "left-wing" causes. Eventually, modern distribution systems enabled proprietors like Henry Luce to produce magazines that appealed to the broadest possible readerships. His *Time* magazine began publication in 1923 and now boasts a *Time Europe* edition published in London and *Time Asia* based in Hong Kong. Its direct competitor, *Newsweek*, was first published in 1933 but has always trailed *Time* in circulation and advertising revenue. Today it is published in four English language editions and 12 global editions written in the language of the circulation region.

In Britain, the first modern newspapers emerged in the eighteenth century, followed by the concept of "public opinion" and accompanied by ideas about free speech and a free press. Crucially, the beginning of the nineteenth century saw the emergence of a viable national press aided by the early development of mechanized printing presses, the railways, and a national postal service. As a much smaller country distribution was never the issue it was in the USA. And its smaller population encouraged a national press as the main route to profitability.

Magazines similarly were profuse from the early years of the nineteenth century, benefiting from advantageous postage rates and speedy distribution. Today, for example, the UK can boast the largest publishing industry in Europe, with around 3,000 more firms than Germany, the next largest European market. According to Frontier Economics' "Comparative Analysis of the UK's Creative Industries," a report to the Department for Culture, Media and Sport published in 2006, the worldwide journals market, based on data from The Publishers Association, is estimated at £5–7bn and involves around 17,500 publishers and 35,000 journals. Frontier Economics also estimate that the UK has around 25–30 percent of the world market, with a total turnover of £1.5–2bn. Exports account for 60–75 percent of sales for most journals, and for some, the figure will be as high as 85 percent. There are almost 1,300 regional newspapers in the UK. According to the Newspaper Society, they are read by 84 percent of the adult population, compared with the 70 percent who read national newspapers.

The emergence of broadcast media raised fresh concerns in the press and governments on both sides of the Atlantic. In the United States, the Communications Act of 1934 established the Federal Communications Commission (FCC) which ensured that broadcasters acted in "the public interest" in exchange for permission to lease the airwaves. When government exercised some control over broadcast content, there was a substantial amount of news transmitted. But by the time Ronald Reagan became president in the 1980s, news coverage was already dwindling and Reaganomics, as it became known, began the era of deregulation which inevitably accelerated the whole process of decline – in quantity if not quality. In Europe, the survival of public service broadcasting has ensured the tenuous existence of factual programming in the "public interest" – a safety net of sorts for serious journalism.[11] In Britain the BBC was set up, in part, to frustrate the commercial tendencies apparent in American radio. Its acceptance by most people as a "monopoly," indeed its very legitimacy, was in large part a result of its national character. It wasn't until 1967, for example, that the first local radio station, Radio Leicester, began broadcasting. However, in our search for a way forward, we need to go further back in history than the twentieth century to find inspiration.

Magna Carta and Journalism Today

Magna Carta is the birth certificate of liberty. This great charter enshrines the rights of the individual against the state. When disaffected English barons forced King John to sign it in a field after the battle of Runnymede in 1215, they did not realize that this was a document that would enshrine enduring principles. About a third of the world's population is governed according to the principles laid down in Magna Carta: that no person is above the law; that no person may be persecuted by power or imprisoned without fair trial. This latter right – the writ of habeas corpus allowing appeal against unlawful imprisonment – is included within the American constitution. The Fifth Amendment simply rephrased Clause 39 of Magna Carta: "No person shall … be deprived of life, liberty, or property, without due process." Founding Father Alexander Hamilton considered habeas corpus to be the "bulwark" of individual liberty, and condemned secret imprisonment as the most "dangerous engine of arbitrary government."[12] Today, the American Bar Association periodically gathers at Runnymede in Surrey in the UK to rededicate itself to the principles first established there.

Résumés
The Founding Fathers

The Founding Fathers of the United States are generally agreed to be the political leaders who signed the Declaration of Independence in 1776 or those who took part in the American Revolution (War of Independence). American historian Richard B. Morris named seven men as the key Founding Fathers: John Adams, Benjamin Franklin, Alexander Hamilton, John Jay, Thomas Jefferson, James Madison, and George Washington. The following three men are relevant to the present chapter.

Benjamin Franklin

Benjamin Franklin was born in Boston, Massachusetts in 1706. His formal schooling ended at the age of 10 and he was apprenticed to his brother James, a printer. A self-taught polymath, he was a true Renaissance man and became a leading writer, scientist, politician, statesman, and satirist. He is credited with inventing the lightning rod, bifocal glasses, public lending libraries, and the first fire department in America.

As a Founding Father and a diplomat he favored the creation of an American nation and was instrumental in securing the treaty with France and Britain that paved the way for an independent American state. He was Postmaster General in 1775–6 and Minister of Finance in 1778–85. Franklin died in 1790 and his funeral was reputedly attended by 20,000 people.

Alexander Hamilton

Alexander Hamilton was born on the island of Nevis in the British West Indies in 1755. In the American Revolution he joined the New York militia and became aide-de-camp to General George Washington. He was elected to Congress in 1782 but resigned and later founded the Bank of New York. A constitutional lawyer, he became the first United States Secretary of the Treasury and cowrote the *Federalist Papers* with James Madison. In 1802 his rivalry with Vice President Burr resulted in a duel. Hamilton was mortally wounded and died the next day.

James Madison

James Madison was born in Port Conway, Virginia in 1751. He studied at Princeton (then the College of New Jersey) and graduated in two years. He served as the fourth President of the United States, 1809–17, and was responsible for writing most of the *Federalist Papers*, a series of 85 articles that provided a commentary on and interpretation in favor of the Constitution. He is now considered to be the "Father of the Constitution" and was also the author of the United States Bill of Rights. Although always in delicate health, he was the last of the Founding Fathers to die, in 1836.

What has Magna Carta to do with journalism? Quite simply, journalists over the years have had to remind governments of the basic liberties enshrined in its Latin text. For example, Magna Carta states in Clause 29: "To none will we deny or delay right or justice." When Texan millionaire and former presidential candidate Ross Perot put his copy of the charter up for sale in 2007, it was a UK journalist – Ben Macintyre – who, writing in *The Times* of London, called for it to go back on display, and for it to be read again.[13] He argued that this should be done in the light of what was officially referred to as "enhanced interrogation" of prisoners at Guantanamo Bay, the American detention camp in Cuba set up after the destruction of the World Trade Centre in 2001, and also in the light of British legislation that extended the length of the time terrorist suspects could be detained without trial. Clearly today's journalism can learn from history about the preservation and enhancement of democracy. Indeed, the journalism of opposition has always gained much of its legitimacy from the principles enshrined in the Magna Carta.

John Milton's *Areopagitica*

"Let truth and falsehood grapple" said John Milton in *Areopagitica*, his classic seventeenth-century polemic against censorship. Published in 1644 in the midst of the English Civil War, *Areopagitica* is a passionate defense of free expression, unlicensed printing, and freedom of the press. Milton was prompted to pen this pioneer essay after the outrageously hostile reaction he had faced from extremist Puritans who, as the fundamentalist Protestants of their day, had demanded that Parliament reinforce the censorship laws and have Milton's recent pamphlet on the subject of divorce burned. Despite the country's engagement in a civil war, Milton denounced Parliament and demanded the repeal of all censorship. He called his essay "A speech of Mr. John Milton for the liberty of unlicensed printing, to the Parliament of England," and the reference in his main title was to the Aereopagus, the ancient Greek meeting place where Athenian citizens gathered to discuss issues of the day.

For Milton, effective self-government required that people receive information from a diversity of sources, in order that the truth could emerge. English common law at the time considered that truth could be potentially libelous – and thus a dangerous commodity – until in 1720 two London newspaper writers, John Trenchard and William Gordon, using the pen name "Cato," argued that the concept should be reversed: namely, that truth should be a defense *against* an accusation of libel. The impact of this discourse reverberated in the American colonies, where printers, including Benjamin Franklin, republished the work of Cato. In Britain in 1792 the Whig politician Charles James Fox introduced legislation designed to restore to juries the right to decide what was libel and whether a defendant was guilty, rather than leaving it solely to the judge. It is still in force today.

In *Milton's Vision*, historian Theo Hobson describes Milton as the "theorist-in-chief" of liberal Puritanism, but Milton's legacy embraced both moderate and more radical Puritans who "argued there should be no official state religion; they invented the separation of church and state the Americans put into practice in the next century."[14] Thus the First Amendment to the US Constitution specifically prohibits the Congress from making laws both "respecting an establishment of religion" and "abridging the freedom of speech, or of the press." The wording amounted to a blunt way of saying that no law can be passed that allied the state to any religious observance – unlike Henry VIII's legacy in Britain where senior bishops of the Church of England are members of the House of Lords. Similarly, in America no law can be passed to curb press freedom and the media's rights to determine content are unlimited and unfettered by any prior restraint to publication. As Gore Vidal commented, "Milton would have said it more eloquently, but he would have made the same points."[15]

FactFile
The Development of Rights and Liberties

The Putney Debates – 1647

The English Civil War resulted in the defeat of King Charles I at the hands of Oliver Cromwell and his New Model Army. In the immediate aftermath there was a rift between Cromwell, his officers, and the rank and file soldiers of his army over how to deal with the King and how the constitution should operate in the future. Radical elements in the army produced a document, *Agreement of the People*, which called for "one man one vote," religious freedom, equality for all under the law, and ultimate authority to be vested in the House of Commons rather than the House of Lords.

Cromwell invited the disaffected New Agents, as they became known, to debate their proposals before the General Council of the Army. The debates took place in November 1647 at St Mary's Church in Putney, at that time a village on the Thames near London. Much of the debate was about the right to vote. Both sides eventually agreed on a compromise enshrined in a new document, the *Heads of Proposals*. This gave the vote to soldiers who had fought for Parliament in the war but excluded servants and alms-takers (i.e., the poor). The "Putney Debates" provided a platform for the "ordinary man" to make his voice heard and were instrumental in widening the electorate and paving the way for many of the civil liberties taken for granted in democratic societies today.

Bill of Rights – 1689

The Bill was an act of parliament which set out the rights that English citizens and permanent residents were entitled to under a constitutional monarchy. These rights were laid down for all time and still stand today. Some of the main provisions included the following:

- The crown could not usurp the power of parliament by executing laws without its consent
- Freedom of speech in parliament
- Freedom from fine and forfeiture without a trial
- Freedom from cruel and unusual punishment.

The Bill of Rights is still in use on a day-to-day basis throughout the British Commonwealth as well as forming the basis for the American

Bill of Rights and the Universal Declaration of Human Rights. For example, freedom from cruel and unusual punishment is enshrined in Article 5 of the Universal Declaration of Human Rights and Article 3 of the European Convention on Human Rights.

The Universal Declaration of Human Rights – 1948

The Universal Declaration was adopted by the United Nations General Assembly in 1948. It is considered to be the first document that enshrined human rights as universal and applicable to all human beings. Of particular relevance here are Articles 18 and 19:

Article 18: Everyone has the right to freedom of thought, conscience and religion ...
Article 19: Everyone has the right to freedom of opinion and expression ... .

The European Convention on Human Rights – 1950

The European Convention was adopted in 1950 by the countries of Europe to protect human rights and freedoms. The European Court of Human Rights was established by the convention and it is unique because it translates rights enshrined in a treaty into a high degree of individual protection. Articles 8 and 10 relate particularly to privacy and freedom of expression:

Article 8: Everyone has the right to respect for his private and family life, his home and his correspondence ...
Article 10: Everyone has the right to freedom of expression. This right shall include freedom to hold opinions and to receive and impart information and ideas without interference by public authority and regardless of frontiers ...

The ideas enshrined in Magna Carta and Milton's *Areopagitica* became the basis for later defenses of the press and the media in general against censorship and similar attempts to curtail the right to publish. The development of the press as a Fourth Estate of the realm in early nineteenth-century Britain was in many respects an attempt to enshrine these ideas of freedom and impartiality in such a way as to appear to serve rather than oppose the emerging democratic state. According to historian Thomas

Carlyle (1795–1881), it was British politician Edmund Burke who said there were three estates in Parliament – the Lords Spiritual (the clergy), the Lords Temporal (the nobles), and the House of Commons (the commoners) but in the reporters' gallery sat a Fourth Estate which Burke considered more important than the other three.[16] The next chapter examines how the freedom of the press as the Fourth Estate became both *cause célèbre* in the fight for more general freedoms and an excuse for the unscrupulous to pursue personal and political vendettas.

Notes

1 Gerald J. Baldasty, *The Commercialization of News in the Nineteenth Century* (Madison: University of Wisconsin Press, 1992), p. 4.

2 www.guardianlies.com, Rough guide to this website, p. 1.

3 www.guardianlies.com, Website main index, p. 2; See also Jonathan Boyd Hunt, *Trial by Conspiracy* (Exeter, UK: Greenzone Publishing, 1998).

4 Charter of Duties of Journalists, adopted by the National Federation of the Italian Press and National Council Order of Journalists, July 1993. Available online at http://ethicnet.uta.fi/italy/charter_of_duties_of_journalists, accessed on August 10, 2010.

5 Warren G. Bovée, *Discovering Journalism* (Westport, CT: Greenwood Press, 1999), p. 139.

6 Walter Lippmann, *Liberty and the News* (New Brunswick, NJ: Transaction Publishers, 1995), p. 58.

7 Justin Kaplan, *Lincoln Steffens: A Biography* (London: Jonathan Cape, 1975), p. 176.

8 Ibid., p. 177.

9 James Madison, Alexander Hamilton, and John Jay, *The Federalist Papers* (London: Penguin, 1987), Nos. 10, 14.

10 James W. Carey, *Communication as Culture* (Boston: Unwin Hyman, 1989), pp. 2–3.

11 Jane Chapman, *Comparative Media History: 1789 to the Present* (Cambridge, UK: Polity Press, 2005).

12 Madison, Hamilton, Jay, *The Federalist Papers*, Nos. 10, 14.

13 Ben Macintyre, "800 Years On, Still a Great Read," *The Times*, December 14, 2007, p. 21.

14 Theo Hobson, "Oliver Cromwell – a Liberal?" *Sunday Times*, November 9, 2008, para. 4. Available online at http://entertainment.timesonline.co.uk/tol/arts_and_entertainment/tv_and_radio/article5088728.ece, accessed on September 3, 2010.

15 Katrina Borjesson (ed.), *Into the Buzzsaw: Leading Journalists Expose the Myth of a Free Press* (Amherst, NY: Prometheus Books, 2002), p. 6.
16 Thomas Carlyle, *On Heroes, Hero-Worship and the Heroic in History* (Lincoln: University of Nebraska Press, 1966), p. 164.

2

The Road Not Taken

Walter Lippmann categorized the development of the American press as having three phases: firstly, under colonial rule publication was a government monopoly; secondly, the power of political parties helped support a broadening print environment; and thirdly, advertising and a mass circulation financed press independence. While Lippmann's analysis has much merit there is a danger that it oversimplifies the complex and often ill-defined cultural and social changes driven by the press itself and reflected in its pages. Yet there are significant incidents and events which in retrospect can be seen to embody watershed moments in the history of journalism as well as having major ramifications for society as a whole. One such example is the case of John Peter Zenger. It marked one of the points of transition from Lippmann's first to second phase but more importantly it helped define the meaning of "freedom of the press." Political events were soon to entrench that freedom and underpin the growth of party politics played out in the full glare of the nation's newspaper pages.

John Peter Zenger – A Paradigm Shift

In 1733 John Peter Zenger began publishing the *New York Weekly Journal*. It was the first "party" newspaper to appear in the US but, unfortunately for Zenger, his newspaper's politics were in opposition to those of William Cosby, the new Governor for New York Province. After a long campaign to have the *Journal* shut down, Cosby eventually persuaded the New York Justices to issue a bench warrant for Zenger's arrest and Zenger spent eight

Jane Chapman and Nick Nuttall, *Journalism Today: A Themed History*
© 2011 Jane Chapman and Nick Nuttall. Published by Blackwell Publishing Ltd.

months in jail.[1] The ideas enshrined in Magna Carta and Milton's *Areopagitica* became the basis of the defense presented by Zenger's lawyers, who were paid for by Founding Father Benjamin Franklin and other printers.

German-born Zenger had emigrated with his family to America in 1710. He was apprenticed to the royal printer for New York colony from 1711 until 1719 and established his own printing works in 1726. He made a modest living publishing religious tracts but in 1733 he was approached by a lawyer, James Alexander, and asked if he would publish an independent weekly newspaper to be called the *New York Weekly Journal*. Alexander was a founder of the Popular Party which opposed the policies of Governor Cosby. The new paper's chief mission, according to Alexander, was to expose William Cosby and the iniquities of his governorship. Cosby's high-handed behavior had made him many enemies among important and powerful colony members but the reason why Alexander wished to expose Cosby had its origins in a vicious dispute between Cosby and the 71-year-old senior member of the New York provincial council, Rip Van Dam.

Van Dam had served as acting governor for the year between Cosby's appointment and actual arrival in New York. Cosby believed he was entitled to half Van Dam's salary for that period. Van Dam thought otherwise and Cosby filed a suit for the half share. Realizing that no jury would find in his favor, "Cosby designated the provincial Supreme Court to sit as a 'Court of Exchequer' (without a jury) to hear his suit."[2] Van Dam's lawyers challenged Cosby's decision but the three members of the Supreme Court voted two to one in Cosby's favor. The third judge, Chief Justice Lewis Morris, was asked to explain his dissenting vote but rather than write a letter Morris produced a pamphlet which was printed by John Peter Zenger in the *Journal*. Cosby was furious and replaced Morris with James Delancey, a staunch royalist and Cosby supporter.

Subsequent editions of the *Journal* attacked Cosby for a variety of dubious practices and the governor responded by attempting to silence the paper using the law of seditious libel. All his efforts failed and eventually Cosby ordered his attorney general, Richard Bradley, to file "an information" before the Justices which resulted in the bench warrant. While in jail Zenger published an "apology" and managed to keep the *Journal* going with the help of his wife, Anna. The enormous £800 bail condition and the stream of letters he published from jail aroused considerable public sympathy for Zenger. At his trial he was represented by Andrew Hamilton of Philadelphia, considered to be the most skilled attorney in the country.

Hamilton agreed that Zenger had published the words complained of in Lewis Morris's original pamphlet. However, he suggested that if the words were in fact the truth then that was a defense against the charge. (In British and American law today, truth is an absolute defense against an allegation of libel. However, truth was no defense in 1734.) "Not surprisingly, Chief Justice Delancey ruled that Hamilton could not present evidence of the truth of the statements contained in Zenger's *Journal*. 'The law is clear that you cannot justify a libel,' Delancey announced. 'The jury may find that Zenger printed and published those papers, and leave to the Court to judge whether they are libellous'."[3] Hamilton then made the point that leaving the Court to judge whether the papers were libelous "in effect renders juries useless,"[4] much as Charles James Fox was to argue six decades later, in 1792, when his act restored to British juries the right to decide what was libel and whether a defendant was guilty rather than leaving it to the judge. Hamilton's summing up widened the issue to one affecting the liberty of all men under a British government "on the main of America" and their ability to speak and write the truth. The jury returned a verdict of not guilty. As Douglas Linder notes in his account of the incident, "The Zenger trial is a remarkable story of a divided Colony, the beginnings of a free press, and the stubborn independence of American jurors."[5]

The "paradigm shift" represented by Zenger's acquittal is highly significant but also illustrates the problems inherent in paradigm shift analysis – categorization can become too simple and clear-cut, when in fact historical analysis can be quite messy and complicated. So, for instance, Lippmann's second phase lasted for about a hundred years in the US, but for a lot longer in most parts of Europe, where a political press survived alongside a growing commercial one. In Britain, for example, the career of John Wilkes is equally significant in freeing the press from the shackles of government. Wilkes combined careers as journalist and radical politician only to discover, like John Peter Zenger, that the pursuit of one was often inimical to the practice of the other. Wilkes entered parliament in 1757 as MP for Aylesbury in Buckinghamshire. In 1762 he established the radical weekly *North Briton* newspaper which regularly attacked the Prime Minister of the day, the Earl of Bute, who was a close friend of the monarch, George III.

On April 23, 1763, Wilkes published an article in the *North Briton* which criticized King George III's speech at the opening of parliament where he endorsed the recent Paris Peace Treaty with France and Spain that ended the Seven Years' War. The king felt personally insulted and with his ministers decided to prosecute Wilkes for seditious libel. At the court hearing the Lord Chief Justice ruled that as an MP, Wilkes was protected by privilege from arrest on a charge of libel. His discharge was greeted with great popular acclaim and

Wilkes left the court as a champion of liberty.[6] Equally significant in Wilkes's career was his major role in compelling the government to concede the right of printers to publish verbatim accounts of parliamentary debates. *The Times* of London, for example, based its considerable reputation throughout the nineteenth century as a "newspaper of record" on its continuing to publish these verbatim reports long after most other newspapers had ceased to bother.

There were clearly, therefore, some benefits to having a strong and partisan press with a full range and diversity of views. It tended to draw people into participation in the polity. It undoubtedly stirred the passions of political debate and it positively influenced voter turnout in elections. In ante bellum (precivil war) America, for example, voter turnout rose from roughly 25 percent in 1824 to almost 80 percent in 1860.[7] During this phase of press development, where journalists themselves were frequently politicians of one sort or another and as such often funded or edited newspapers, there was no clear distinction between the two roles. At the same time there was seldom any attempt to draw such fine distinctions as might have existed to the attention of readers. Few were aware of or concerned themselves with possible conflicts of interest between the political and journalistic sensibilities of proprietors as would no doubt be the case today.

Journalism and Independence

Zenger's and Wilkes's careers encapsulated the changes in the relationship between the governors and the governed that were to prove fundamental in the move to Lippmann's third phase of press development – the end of direct government and party political influence on the press. In America, the years just before and during the Revolution (1775–83) saw newspapers suppressed, interrupted, and threatened. The *Massachusetts Spy*, published by Isaiah Thomas, was constantly on the verge of being suppressed, from its inception in 1770 until the Revolution itself – its sin being to pursue a radical agenda designed to provoke the British colonial powers. During this turbulent period there was also a scarcity of newsprint, a lack of replacement printing type as it wore out, and extreme difficulty in obtaining foreign newspapers – usually an important source of information.

Newspapers were instrumental in developing a shared reading experience and this experience, whether private or public, was as much a political act as an expression of cultural preferences or social origins.

Inevitably therefore the personal became the political and out of this was born the notion of public opinion. In America this coalesced around the sense of destiny engendered by independence. The Declaration of Independence itself was published by Congress on July 6, 1776 and carried in the *Philadelphia Evening Post*. It was copied by many other newspapers as well as being printed in pamphlets – the most famous being the Dunlap broadsides.

The aim of the newspapers that survived the Revolution was to create a nation out of the still rather loose confederation of states, but many of the pre-Revolution problems had not been resolved. Newspapers were not officially carried through the mails but rather at the discretion of the postmen. The currency of one state was not necessarily accepted in another and the papers themselves were often subject to special state taxes on paper and advertisements. What was inescapable however was the fact that public opinion was growing strongly against all legal restrictions, and for the papers themselves freedom of speech was becoming axiomatic. Thus journalism became important not simply for the reporting of events in the change from colonial to republican rule, but also because it involved the people at large, speaking to and for them: "Journalists as radical propagandists were able to articulate a particular moment in the aspirations of people to be involved in politics."[8]

In Britain, the first attempts to identify and understand public opinion formed part of moral philosopher Jeremy Bentham's work contained in *The Principles of Morals and Legislation*, published in 1781. Bentham attempted to assess the moral content of human action by focusing on its results or consequences.[9] To this end he proposed the principle of utility, its main tenet being the greatest happiness of the greatest number. He described public opinion as a moral sanction against the abuse of power by government over the governed. That such abuse existed was self-evident to early nineteenth-century radicals. William Hazlitt, literary critic and fellow philosopher, for example, had no doubt that "the interests of the government (when once it becomes absolute and independent of the people) must be directly at variance with those of the governed."[10]

The interests of the government were often therefore directly at variance with those of the press, and for most of the eighteenth century were expressed through the imposition of taxes and levies. However, the early decades of the nineteenth century saw the rise of a radical press that became instrumental in the gradual abolition of all government controls. First, the advertisement duty was abolished in 1853; next, stamp duty was abolished in 1855; and lastly, the paper duty was abolished in 1861.[11] These changes resulted in "a period of rapid press expansion, when local daily papers were established in all the major urban centres of Britain."[12]

Yet unlike America, a political press, or at least a press that had political affiliations, hung on in Britain well into the twentieth century. Historian Alan Lee has shown how between 1837 and 1887 the provincial English daily press slowly evolved from one which was highly political – over 97 percent of newspapers were politically affiliated in 1837 – to one which was beginning to assert its independence from party politics as the century closed – just over 50 percent were affiliated by 1887. In London only 10 percent of all newspapers were clearly allied to a particular political party in 1887.[13] This assertion of political independence was to continue into the twentieth century.

Yet politicians on both sides of the Atlantic, regardless of the press's affiliations, were in the process of discovering the capacity of newspapers as a vehicle for persuading electors. Journalists and other writers, from Benjamin Franklin to Alexis de Tocqueville, contributed towards the creation of a climate where the public were open to new political ideas and it was perhaps ironic that in America one of the most influential of these "radical propagandists" would turn out to be the Englishman, Tom Paine.

Résumé
Tom Paine

Tom Paine became a key pamphleteer in the American Revolution and earned a reputation as the greatest political figure of his day. He was born in Thetford, England, in 1737, the son of a corset-maker and from such humble beginnings he produced the eighteenth century's three best-selling books. His pamphlet *Common Sense* (1776) was an instant bestseller and became an intellectual cornerstone of American democracy, prompting hesitant and moderate patriots to join the revolutionary side. It possessed a "republican charisma" and projected a new rhetoric which articulated the emerging egalitarian ethos.[14] Every literate American household knew of Paine's doctrines which were mirrored, within a mere six months, in the Declaration of Independence.

Paine moved to America after meeting Benjamin Franklin in London in 1774, and fought against his native Britain in the American Revolution. He wrote for a number of newspapers. In the *Pennsylvania Journal* of October 18, 1775 he said, "I hesitate not for a moment to believe that the Almighty will finally separate America from Britain. Call it independence or what you will, if it is the cause of God and humanity it will go on."[15] Later, in the same paper (December 19, 1776) he said, "Tyranny, like hell, is not easily conquered; yet we have this consolation with us, that the harder the conflict, the more glorious the triumph."

His words were read aloud to American troops in every military encampment and it is estimated that almost half the population read his pamphlets. His next major work, *Rights of Man* (1791), sold 200,000 copies in three years and inspired working people more than any other radical publication until the appearance of *The Communist Manifesto* in 1848. In the appendix to *Common Sense* Paine had written, "We have it in our power to begin the world over again," words that were echoed almost 75 years later in Marx's famous remark quoted on his tomb in London's Highgate cemetery: "Philosophers have only interpreted the world in various ways – the point however is to change it."

By 1809 *Rights of Man* had sold 1.5 million copies all over Europe. It enjoyed huge sales in Ireland, despite a ban being immediately imposed in Britain. Paine made it known that he sought no profit from the work, so anyone who wanted to reproduce it could do so. He desired a nation that would encourage an "unceasing circulation of (ideas), which passing through its million channels, invigorates the whole mass of civilized man."[16] His writings on democratic government, rebellion, and liberty acted as an inspiration to hundreds of thousands of people in the late eighteenth century, although the importance of Paine's influence arguably lies in the ideological basis that he provided for radical journalism during the nineteenth century.[17] Paine died in New York in 1809.

One of the results of the new political awareness encouraged by people like Tom Paine was that the role of the journalist became more clearly defined. Clashes between newspaper publishers and the authorities in the lead-up to the Revolution provided journalism with a new cultural and social impetus. Political discourse and the newspapers that carried it reveled in a new-found freedom, and the supply of political information became the foundation on which journalism sought to build its occupational legitimacy.[18] Thus the First Amendment of the American constitution specifically identifies the press, freedom of speech, and religion as areas which cannot be legislated against.

This established the idea of "media immunities" – the concept of the media as a vehicle for public communication and as an industry different from any other and therefore worthy of singling out for special treatment in the eyes of the law. However, as the course of media history shows, press freedom is a relative concept. Other legislation can be and often is passed which challenges this absolute principle in areas such as libel, breach of confidence, official secrets, obscenity, and economic competition.

The First Amendment

The Enlightenment-inspired First Amendment to the American Constitution provides the right to hold the government accountable for its actions. "Congress shall make no law … prohibiting the … right of the people peaceably to assemble, and to petition the government for a redress of grievances." The rationale behind such sentiments was that the press would initiate and perpetuate a public discourse. But other factors – largely influenced by the effects of commercialism – have intruded into that "public discourse" over the years, so that "unethical" behavior by many news organizations has been condoned if not celebrated.

There is plenty of evidence that the media frequently acts in a divisive fashion by sensationalizing events, intruding on privacy, and demolishing reputations. This notion of news as a value-free "object" that could be packaged simply to increase its profitability would have been seen as a dangerous and malign aberration by the Founding Fathers. Thomas Jefferson at one point even went so far as to call the press a "pack of liars" who should be thrown into prison.[19] The archetypal case of Anthony Haswell both reflected Jefferson's feelings on the matter and also tested the reliability of the First Amendment. Haswell's triumph, such as it was, revealed the subtle changes in public opinion wrought by the new Constitution.

FactFile
Anthony Haswell and Freedom of the Press

The Haswell incident became an early test of the First Amendment as it related to freedom of the press. British-born Anthony Haswell was a supporter of Thomas Jefferson's Democratic-Republican Party and was appointed by Vermont Governor Thomas Chittenden as the state's first postmaster in 1784. He also began a newspaper which he named the *Vermont Gazette*. The first issue appeared on June 5, 1783 in Bennington, the de facto capital.[20]

Despite Haswell's official appointments, he was a "vigorous critic of President John Adams, his principles, and the policies of his administration."[21] But it was his support for another anti-Federalist printer, Matthew Lyon, that resulted in his arrest and jailing under the Sedition Act of 1798. Matthew Lyon was a member of Congress who was himself found guilty of violating the Alien and Sedition Acts which prohibited malicious writing about the American government or its officials. Lyon published criticism of Federalist president John Adams in his newspaper, *The Scourge of Aristocracy*. He was sentenced to four months in jail and ordered to pay a $1,000 fine. While in jail, Lyon won election to the Sixth Congress.

Haswell supported Lyon in public and organized a lottery to raise the $1,000 needed to release him from prison. It was publication of the details of this lottery that led to Haswell being "arrested, charged, tried, convicted, fined, and jailed by the United States government" under the same Sedition Act.[22] Haswell's trial in 1800 resulted in a $200 fine plus two months in prison. While in prison Haswell was allowed to continue writing for the *Vermont Gazette* and became something of a celebrity. Over a thousand people gathered to celebrate his release from prison.

The Alien and Sedition Acts, passed by Congress in 1798, were in direct opposition to the First Amendment in that they allowed an American citizen to be arrested for what he said or wrote. In 1800 Thomas Jefferson was elected president and pardoned all editors who had been convicted under the Alien and Sedition Acts; the law itself was allowed to expire.

The emerging US democratic system and a press now free from any sense of colonial control still locked horns over the Alien and Sedition Acts but Haswell's legacy is neatly summarized by media academic Jerry Baldasty: "The many legal safeguards for the press in American society are premised on the notion that the press supplies information central to an enlightened electorate, and thus central to democracy itself."[23] In the first half of the nineteenth century a partisan press certainly encouraged political debate in what became a growing democratic discourse, but subservience to advertising revenues in the late nineteenth century began the slow process of undermining the principles of inclusivity that hallmarked such debates.

By the end of the century the participation of the press in democratic debate had become conditional on demographics that encouraged advertising to consumers with money to spend. The poor might have had the vote but they were excluded from this bright new world by their relative poverty. The gradual effect of more advertising and therefore more attention to advertisers' interests, combined with powerful chain ownership, conspired to elevate private commercial gain over a broader public service. This process is analyzed in more detail in Part II.

What was the effect on democracy of this new consumer-orientated news focus? According to Baldasty, "Readers paid little out of pocket for the new newspapers of 1900 but they paid in other ways. They received mountains of 'news' that momentarily entertained but that did not engage them in the reality of their city, nation, or world. In retrospect, inexpensive newspapers were not a great bargain."[24] Political reporting similarly became subject to the vagaries of commercialism. "The biggest speeches are subject to the inexorable laws of space," Moberly Bell, managing director of *The Times* of London, explained to Winston Churchill in 1893. "Statesmen little know that the length of their reports depend on the quantity of advertisements. If we have enough to justify a big paper we shall be able to give you twice as much room."[25]

It is tempting to argue that in the present electronic age information is so freely available that the First Amendment is now an anachronism – no government can possibly undermine press freedom and if it attempted to do so the profusion of media outlets would certainly ensure that if one of them rejected a piece of news, another one somewhere else would surely carry it. Even the role of the press as "gatekeeper," or decision maker about what should be published, is challenged today by the internet and the profusion of other media platforms. According to such arguments press freedom and wider media freedoms were hard won and are not likely to be reversed. Yet if we accept that, in Lord Northcliffe's words, news is what somebody somewhere wants to suppress, then history suggests that vested interests are always ready to subvert those same freedoms in the name of the safety of the realm, collective liberty, commercial sensitivity or other such disingenuous concepts.

Coming of Age – Stages in Press Freedom

In *The Right to Know*, Edward Francis Williams, editor of Britain's former *Daily Herald* from 1936 to 1940, depicted press freedom (in something of a corrective to Walter Lippmann's three phases of press development) as having four main stages. First, early political society is characterized by censorship and licensing but then, as the public appetite for news increases, so does the demand for free expression of opinion. This in turn produces the strong journalistic personality. Initially this takes the form of the editor but gradually publishers and businessmen take over until the final stage – the age of the press as a business – arrives.[26]

This progression toward freedom is often disputed (see James Curran and Jean Seaton's *Power Without Responsibility*) but in so far as it relates to freedom from control by government and political parties there is little to quarrel with. The late eighteenth and early nineteenth centuries in France and Britain were characterized by a constant battle against censorship. Newspapers were started, suppressed, and restarted as part of a "guerrilla war" between the press and the authorities. In Britain, for example, Henry Hetherington published the *Poor Man's Guardian* (1831), a radical weekly paper which constantly drew attention to its refusal to pay government stamp duty. Hetherington said it was "established, contrary to 'law', to try the power of 'might' against 'right'."[27] He was fined on numerous occasions, imprisoned in 1833 and 1836, and had all his printing presses seized and destroyed in 1835.[28]

As the ranks of the "freedom fighters" increased, so Williams's second stage emerges. Now governments found themselves obliged to concede to demands for a free press, and so censorship and licensing, the "taxes on knowledge," were abandoned in favor of more complex but less obtrusive controls on the nature of expression, exemplified by laws on libel, sedition, and contempt. These laws have been refined and modified over the years but laws on the censorship of press content, rather than on the mere physical existence of a newspaper, hung on well into the twentieth century in both America and Britain (see the section on Censorship below).

Résumé
Edward Smith Hall – An Australian Pioneer

There are examples in many countries of pioneering journalists who campaigned for freedom of expression in their newspapers. In Australia Edward Smith Hall was a major contributor toward the achievement of press freedom, representative government, and trial by jury under British colonial rule. In 1826 he launched the *Sydney Monitor* in defiance of the authorities, giving prominence to a letter from a reader stating that it was better for a journalist to be "an inveterate opposer than a staunch parasite of government."[29]

He used the pages of his weekly eightpenny newspaper to campaign against the draconian authority of Governor General Ralph Darling and the use of convict slave labor. He spent more than a year in prison, continuing to edit his paper from jail. He was convicted regularly by military tribunals of criminal libel for exposing the corruption of officials, magistrates, and the governor's staff, and for campaigning for the rights of convicts and freed prisoners. Eventually Governor Darling was recalled to London and free speech was established. By the time of Hall's death in 1861 there were 50 independent newspapers in the province of New South Wales alone, yet most Australians have never heard of Edward Smith Hall.[30]

Throughout this period the role of the press as the Fourth Estate of the realm was being articulated by newspapers like *The Times* of London as a means of legitimizing its establishment role at a time of considerable social upheaval. Although this venerable paper had taken government subsidies in an earlier period, by the mid-nineteenth century it was both profitable and financially independent, and was careful to define the difference between politicians and journalists in its pages by initiating a debate on public opinion. On February 7, 1852, Robert Lowe, MP for Kidderminster and leader writer on *The Times*, argued that the duties of the state and the Fourth Estate were "constantly separate, generally independent, sometimes diametrically opposite." Henry Reeve, *The Times*'s foreign editor, went so far as to declare journalism as "now truly an estate of the realm; more powerful than any of the other estates,"[31] much as Thomas Carlyle had said of Edmund Burke over 10 years previously. Perhaps understandably, British politicians of the time were often worried at the "vile tyranny of *The Times*"[32] and attempted to restrict its reporting – particularly during the Crimean War and its aftermath. Despite such efforts, however, *The Times* "faced the future serenely confident of its authority."[33]

The power of independent and critical expression, hard won by news media over much of the nineteenth century, has now developed to such an extent that today politicians, in their attempts to influence public opinion, have once more made efforts to bypass journalists, using television and radio talk shows and the internet to directly connect with electorates. Thus it seems that freedom of speech has never come easily.

The Editor, the Internet, and the Public Sphere

The rise of the strong journalistic personality of Williams's third stage produced one of the most remarkable and evocative periods in the whole history of the press on both sides of the Atlantic. For the true journalism aficionado the roll call of famous editors' names can still set the pulses racing. By the middle years of the nineteenth century newspapers had largely achieved an independent self-sufficiency via advertising and sales revenues. The stage was set for the emergence of the editor as a "personality" in his own right. Thomas Barnes of *The Times* of London (1817–41) was arguably the first true editor of a daily newspaper. His strengths were a virile and original mind that was attuned to his readers' and the wider public's concerns. His authority was such that a Tory Lord Chancellor acknowledged, "Barnes is the most powerful man in the country."[34] W. T. Stead, editor of the *Pall Mall Gazette* between 1883 and 1889, was sufficiently confident of his position to proclaim in 1886, "Above all, he [the editor] better than any man is able to generate that steam, known as public opinion, which is the greatest force in politics."[35] Kennedy Jones, editor of the London *Evening News*, was credited with leading Alfred Harmsworth into daily journalism. He persuaded Harmsworth to purchase the *Evening News*, which was in dire financial straits. Its later success was instrumental in Harmsworth's decision to publish the *Daily Mail* as his own daily paper. Kennedy Jones became "known in Fleet Street as 'Le Cardinal Gris' of Alfred Harmsworth"[36] and was instrumental in the building up of Harmsworth's newspaper and magazine empire, Amalgamated Press.

The editor–proprietor relationship was less an issue in the American press. Early American editors were often owners of their papers. Nathan Hale assumed the editorship of the *Boston Daily Advertiser* after first purchasing the paper in 1814. He introduced unsigned editorial comment and leading articles, both of which at the time were rare. George William Childs purchased the Philadelphia *Public Ledger* in 1864 at a time when it was losing serious money. Childs changed the editorial policy from Confederate to Unionist politics, raised its advertising rates, and doubled its cover price to two cents.

It was James Gordon Bennett, however, "the pioneer of 'yellow journalism' in America and the first authentic press baron,"[37] who was one of the earliest editor owners to specifically eschew political journalism in his papers. He "believed journalists were fools to think that they could best serve their own purposes by serving the politicians."[38] In 1835 Bennett started the *New York Herald* as a newspaper which viewed news as a commodity to be packaged and sold like any other, ignoring the social responsibility of the press. Bennett wrote, "We disdain all principle, as it is called, all party, all politics. Our only guide shall be good, sound, practical common sense." [39]

At the opposite end of the spectrum was Horace Greeley, for many people the pre-eminent editor of the American press. He began the *New York Tribune* in 1841, as a reliable, trustworthy newspaper in opposition to the sensationalist New York *Sun* of Benjamin Day and Bennett's *Herald*. Always a liberal, politically and culturally, he retained Karl Marx in 1851 as the paper's European correspondent. He stood for the presidency in 1872 but was defeated and died soon after in a sanatorium. Greeley was that relative rarity, the editor who was both loved and respected. Many places – streets, parks, towns, counties, schools, hills – are named for him throughout America.

The major newspaper proprietors of the later nineteenth century and the first half of the twentieth – the press barons – were men who, although often journalists like their predecessors, were more interested in the business of journalism than the writing of it. An entrepreneurial spirit was now more appropriate than a purely journalistic one as the costs involved in starting and running newspapers rose inexorably. Names like Lord Northcliffe and Lord Beaverbrook in Britain and William Randolph Hearst and Joseph Pulitzer in the United States still resonate today. Hearst was variously described by competitors and friends alike as a megalomaniac, a "demagogue, blackmailer, charlatan"[40] and virtually every other derogatory epithet in the lexicon. Lord Northcliffe was known by his enemies as Northoleon. Beaverbrook was "devious and deceitful and never lost the reputation for being a 'shady financier."[41] Pulitzer combined nervous energy with a caustic tongue and was described as being "proud, humourless and irritable."[42]

Each of these "barons" came to symbolize his newspaper in a way that perhaps only Rupert Murdoch has managed in the digital age. As a tribe the press barons were the last of the men who combined the skills of the journalist and the businessman. Since then the commercial imperatives of big business and growing monopoly power have led to the emergence of the global media conglomerate. The idea that a Rupert Murdoch (News International), a Leslie Moonves (CEO of CBS), an Anne Sweeney (President Disney-ABC), or a Jeffrey Zucker (CEO of NBC) might actively edit their own newspapers or news programming is as improbable as it is absurd.

Yet there was a second flowering of the charismatic and powerful editor just before and after World War II as owners regrouped and rethought their journalistic and business strategies for a postwar age. In Britain, Harold Evans of the *Sunday Times*, Donald Trelford of the *Observer*, Guy Bartholomew of the *Daily Mirror*, were all examples of great editorial talent that fell foul of their proprietors and were sacked or eased out. This fall in the power and prestige of the editor is very much a reflection of the failure of journalism to contain and control the rampant commercialism of the modern media conglomerate.

FactFile
Habermas and the Changing Public Sphere

Discussions by scholars about journalism, democracy, and public opinion invariably refer to the theoretical framework provided by German philosopher and sociologist Jürgen Habermas. He wrote of a lost ethical horizon that needed to be rediscovered. In *The Structural Transformation of the Public Sphere* he argued that the "public sphere" emerged in eighteenth-century Europe, was the foundation for civil society, and acted as a forum for citizens to reach agreement through rational debate. Moreover, he contended that "public opinion can by definition come into existence only when a reasoning public is presupposed."[43] His "public opinion" is the concerted opinion of private citizens operating in the public sphere, of which state authority is not a part. It refers to "the tasks of criticism and control which a public body of citizens informally ... practises vis-a-vis the ruling structure organized in the form of a state"[44] and which works as a check on state power.

According to Habermas, a variety of factors resulted in the eventual decay of the public sphere, including the growth of a commercial mass media, which turned the critical public into a passive consumer public. This has produced political apathy, the pursuit of economic and material self-interest, cynicism, and social alienation. And the more commercial the press, the more it becomes a "platform for advertising" and the less it acts as a forum for rational debate.[45]

Habermas's doctrine has received much criticism because of the difficulty of proving completely correct any particular conception of it. Any resurrection of Habermas's public sphere first requires that people are well-informed and second that they are capable of developing a discourse that involves them all – both requirements that in theory at least are capable of being fulfilled by the internet and the world wide web. Testing his hypothesis against actual behavior in, for example, the myriad online information sources now producing both evidential and unverified news outputs on a range of platforms, there is reason to doubt the emergence of his "reasoning public." This is not so much because of any failure of the "public" itself as the failure of any delivery system, so far at least, to both reach and energize the mass of the population.

The irony therefore is that even in information-rich societies deliberative democracy is by no means guaranteed.[46] Thus Habermas's analysis resonates with theorists who are interested in political pluralism, the politics of difference, and the ways in which the media interact with democracy. It resonates particularly, of course, with those for whom the decline of the public sphere is only too obviously a fact and a calamity.

For many who lament the untrammeled power of modern mass media organizations, the fall of a journalism-led news media and the failure of the public sphere, the internet is seen as the "great white hope." Here is a platform that is capable of reaching everyone (or everyone with access to a computer – easier said than done in some parts of the developing world) and that can also instigate debate and argument without reference to race, ethnicity, social class, or nationality. At the same time it is a relatively cheap medium requiring little start-up capital compared with more traditional media platforms. But can the internet guarantee journalistic freedoms? And if it cannot what does that mean for representative democracy? A further problem is that people do not always use their freedoms positively, for the good of society as a whole. Freedom needs to be based on active participation by individuals for the benefit of the whole community. The question then is whether journalism as it is perceived today can serve such altruistic ends.

It may well be that, in the United States, the protection of the First Amendment and the impact of competitive market forces has stimulated a form of journalism that is both uncaring of the individual and detrimental to social cohesion. In Britain on the other hand the power of the libel laws is considered by many to have produced a journalism that is timid and incapable of bringing powerful people and organizations to account. Yet despite such "restrictions" the Enlightenment doctrine of freedom of speech has become a synonym for the greater freedoms inherent in the human condition and a leitmotif of a fair society. Such freedoms are only maintained however by a society that is as vigilant as it is liberal.

Censorship: The Reaction of the Ignorant to Freedom?

Freedom of speech is inevitably contrasted with efforts by governments, and more recently pressure groups and commercial enterprises, to limit that freedom. How a society negotiates the line between such competing freedoms is perhaps a mark of how democratic it really is. This is particularly true in times of crisis and war. Milton composed the *Areopagitica*, his defense of free speech, during the English Civil War. Every time the United States has fought a war, the crisis has prompted some people to call for restrictions on free speech.

Early examples of censorship were inevitably aimed at the press as the dominant medium of communication. Although it may be self-evident when a newspaper or magazine is banned or its journalists silenced, it is far less obvious when self-censorship is practiced. The extent to which journalists are obliged to conform to prevailing commercial cultures by manipulating both news agendas and news values has always been difficult to quantify. And the extent to which such manipulation is culpable in spreading misinformation is similarly difficult to calculate. The danger, of course, is if this occurs without a plurality of media voices to act as a corrective. Journalist and historian Richard Reeves was once asked to define "real news" and answered: "The news you and I need to keep our freedoms."[47] Yet without a plurality of news media it is almost impossible to define the news that *is* needed "to keep our freedoms." To be truly informed, as part of the democratic ideal, it requires journalists who are prepared to stand up and be counted in the cause of press freedom despite the fear of reprisals – losing their jobs or at worst imprisonment for contempt of court.

In both Britain and the US there is a long history of journalists suffering imprisonment, either for publishing in defiance of oppressive laws or more usually in the modern era for refusing to name their sources in court. The perennial issue of press freedom re-emerged in America during debates on such topics as the abolition of slavery when abolitionists were at the forefront of calls for press freedom. In the years 1829–31, for example, two abolitionists were sued for criminal libel for condemning a shipowner and captain for transporting slaves.[48] In 1886 *Baltimore Sun* reporter John T. Morris was jailed for refusing to name the sources for a story he wrote about police corruption and elected officials taking bribes from a gambling syndicate. Marie Torre, a journalist on the *New York Herald Tribune*, was jailed for 10 days in 1958 for refusing to name her sources at a trial when singer Judy Garland sued CBS for defamation. Garland alleged that the broadcaster had defamed her by using quotes from an unnamed network executive. These quotes were gleaned from Torre's *Tribune* column. Torre used the First Amendment as a defense but the trial judge determined that it failed if the information required by the court went to the heart of the plaintiff's claim.[49]

In 1963 two British journalists were jailed for refusing to name their sources in the "sensational" spy trial of an Admiralty clerk. John Vassall was accused of spying for the Soviet Union and sentenced to 18 years imprisonment. Reginald Foster of the now defunct *Daily Sketch* and Brendan Mulholland of the *Daily Mail*, known as the "silent men," were jailed for three and six months respectively.[50] They were hailed as martyrs in the cause of press freedom and found themselves on the front pages of their respective newspapers. Yet perhaps the most notorious case of its kind involved freelance journalist and video blogger Joshua Wolf. He refused to hand over a collection of videotapes he recorded during a demonstration in San Francisco where protestors damaged a police car. He eventually served 226 days in jail before he was released on the order of Judge William Alsup.[51]

Can one be sanguine about such attempts to muzzle reporters? According to media historian David Mindich, "We have had dark times in our history, fought ill-conceived wars, enslaved one group and expelled another, but we have always preserved the workings of a democracy that allows its citizens to speak and protest based on information that has become, for the most part, free and unfettered. In return, the only thing we must do is stay informed."[52] Journalists of all political persuasions have clearly played their part in ensuring not only that information is "free and unfettered" but also that it is communicated to the public regardless of the consequences. Yet is the public playing its part by consuming this information and thereby staying informed? Does it have a duty to do so bearing in mind the roll call of journalists who have suffered while attempting to gather such information? Certainly the roll call is long and getting longer. Websites such as *Reporters Without Borders* (rsf.org) and *The Reporters Committee for Freedom of the Press* (rcfp.org) both list journalists worldwide who have been jailed or suffered in other ways for simply pursuing their calling.

Governments have been no less assiduous in their attempts to control new media as they become part of the news environment. As postal services developed across the United States, the antiobscenity Comstock Act of 1873 made it illegal to send any obscene, lewd, and/or lascivious materials through the mail. These laws applied equally to journalistic material and thus potentially acted as a censor on the press. A striking example of their operation was the father and son team of Edward Bliss Foote and Edward Bond Foote. Both were doctors who published their own magazine, *Dr. Foote's Health Monthly* which sold mainly on subscription. For almost 50 years during the late nineteenth and early twentieth centuries they challenged the use of the Comstock laws.

In 1876 E. B. Foote the elder was charged with violating postal laws for mailing an educational pamphlet advocating the right of families to limit their size through "contraceptics." He was fined $3,500 by Judge Benedict of the US Circuit Court of the southern district of New York. Their magazine became a symbol for a free speech movement. It also supported three radical libertarian organizations – the National Liberal League, the National Defense Association, and the Free Speech League (predecessors of modern civil liberties campaign organizations). Their funds helped the pioneer birth control advocate Margaret Sanger and their magazine was in the free speech vanguard that gradually changed public opinion.[53]

FactFile
The Lincoln–Douglas Debates

In 1858 the American nation was captivated by a series of debates in the contest for one of the Senate seats for Illinois. Democratic Party incumbent Stephen Douglas (also a front-runner for the 1860 presidency) was seeking re-election and was opposed by an upstart contender with only one term's experience in the Congress — Springfield lawyer Abraham Lincoln. Lincoln challenged Douglas to a series of debates throughout Illinois that attracted multitudes. Crowds came from sparsely populated communities all around. In the first of the seven debates, at Ottawa, with a population of only seven thousand, between 10,000 and 20,000 people turned up for the high drama that constituted one of their few forms of entertainment. Quite simply, it was the best show in town, for politics was entertainment and it wasn't until the late nineteenth century that reformers made politics less fun and more puritanical.

There is a certain historical irony in any contemporary comparison with the enthusiasm excited by the Hillary Clinton–Barack Obama primaries, given the fact that this earlier high point of American deliberative politics took place at a time when the entire country still reverberated from the battle over the extension of slavery to new territories. The issue of slavery was of monumental importance to citizens across the nation and the debates in Quincy, Freeport, and Alton drew especially large numbers of people from neighboring states because of this. "Here was a time when people would stand outside for hours listening to detailed, erudite, complex arguments on the nation's most pressing political controversy."[54]

In the days before the invention of spin doctors and PR advisors, the party candidate worked with party editors and "fixers" to smooth out, improve, and elaborate on the candidate's words for the purposes of publication. Newspaper coverage of the debates was intense yet the newspapers on both sides left their rivals untouched, warts and all![55] Thus, interestingly for journalism history, this may have been the first time that some political campaign speeches were reported verbatim.[56] Here was partisan coverage in the interests of democracy, but breaking the rules as later evolved by "objective" journalists, and the public devoured such unmediated political discourse.

Public opinion as a harbinger of change would gather momentum in the twentieth century, aided and abetted by developments in radio and television. The ability of a new medium like radio to influence not only political systems but whole societies was entirely new and produced anxieties in most Western capitalist cultures. Particularly in America in the interwar years, where there was no significant national press, democratic radio worked effectively as the progressive forces of organized labor and the conservative forces of business battled it out over the airways. Not only was there a radio station, WCFL, owned by a labor union and launched in Chicago in 1926, which ran for almost 50 years, but "midcentury listeners throughout the nation could hear a wide array of union sponsored radio programs that promoted labor's political and economic agenda."[57] Despite this apparent diversity Upton Sinclair in his novel *Oil* (1926) described radio thus: "The radio is a one-sided institution; you can listen, but you cannot answer back. In that lies its enormous usefulness to the capitalist system. The householder sits at home and takes what is handed to him, like an infant being fed through a tube. It is a basis upon which to build the greatest slave empire in history."[58] Ultimately the power of corporate America did assert itself once more, much as Sinclair predicted, despite the interventions of the Federal Communications Commission and its creation of the Fairness Doctrine in 1949 which charged holders of broadcast licenses to present controversial issues with honesty, fairness, and balance.

By the end of the 1960s, the influence of radio as a tool of the organized Left had been silenced in the face of desperate calls for less bias and a more open and democratic media. In the 1950s television began to usurp radio as people's preferred broadcast medium. By 1960 the number of TV sets in the US surpassed the number of homes. In an attempt to thwart censorship of the new medium, the National Association of Radio and Television Broadcasters in 1952 adopted a code to regulate broadcast content after concern was voiced about the possible harmful effects of TV on children.[59]

In Britain, the only broadcaster was the BBC and this monopoly led to calls for controls on its output beyond those contained in its charter. In the 1960s conservative public opinion found a champion in Mary Whitehouse, a teacher who railed against the "permissive society" and accused the Director-General of the BBC, Sir Hugh Greene, of being "more than anybody else ... responsible for the moral collapse in this country."[60] In 1965 she formed the National Viewers' and Listeners' Association and began a crusade to "clean up" TV. She obtained more than 500,000 signatures for her "Clean Up TV" petition which was sent to the Queen. Overall her campaign, which goes on despite her death in 2001, has achieved little.

Despite such pressure groups as Mary Whitehouse's there is a tendency for Western societies to become complacent about the consequences of censorship in the media. It invariably takes an eruption of conflict in the area of human rights somewhere else in the world for most of us to suddenly realize that freedom of speech and freedom of the press are still indissolubly linked. In many respects these freedoms are now also being bestowed on the new digital technologies when they are pursuing journalistic functions.

In the 1988 "People Power" uprising in Burma, as many as 3,000 people were killed by soldiers firing on the crowds of demonstrators, yet it took days for the news to emerge. During the "Saffron Revolution" of 2007, in contrast, information from Burma, one of the most closed states in the world, came not only from bloggers and ordinary citizens with mobile phones and digital cameras, but also from exiled journalists in countries such as Thailand and India – whose very existence in exile is a salutary reminder that journalism as purveyor of truth and supporter of democracy is a dangerous job. A more recent example, in 2009, was the furor over the failure of Israel to allow journalists into Gaza during its recent offensive against the Palestinians. The Foreign Press Association successfully petitioned the Israeli Supreme Court for access but was still denied by the military. The sheer fact of this censorship alerted people to the possibility that things were occurring which the world should have known about.

Maybe it is because freedom of speech is considered the most fundamental characteristic of a free society that history is full of bold statements about this right. George Washington, in an address to army officers in 1783 stated, "If the freedom of speech is taken away then dumb and silent we may be led, like sheep to the slaughter." Thomas Jefferson in 1793 was equally clear about the press: "Our liberty depends on the freedom of the press, and that cannot be limited without being lost."

By the middle of the nineteenth century, liberal thinker John Stuart Mill could confidently say in his essay *On Liberty* (1859), "The time, it is to be hoped, is gone by, when any defence would be necessary of the 'liberty of the press' as one of the securities against corrupt or tyrannical government."[61] Hugo Black, a justice of the US Supreme Court until his death in 1971, enunciated similar sentiments when he said, "The Framers of the Constitution knew that free speech is the friend of change and revolution. But they also knew that it is always the deadliest enemy of tyranny." Corazon Aquino, president of the Philippines from 1986 to 1992, who triumphed over the tyranny of dictator Ferdinand Marcos, famously affirmed: "Freedom of expression – in particular, freedom of the press – guarantees popular participation in the decisions and actions of government, and popular participation is the essence of our democracy." So often in such apocalyptic statements the idea of freedom of speech is closely allied to the idea of freedom of the press and journalists are, to that extent, in the front line of the battle for human rights and human dignity.

Notes

1   Douglas Linder, *The Zenger Trial: An Account* (2001). Available online at http://www.law.umkc.edu/faculty/projects/ftrials/zenger/zenger.html, accessed on September 10, 2008, p. 1.
2   Ibid.

3 Ibid.

4 Ibid.

5 Ibid.

6 John Wilkes. Available online at http://www.spartacus.schoolnet.co.uk/PRwilkes.htm, accessed on July 8, 2009.

7 Mark N. Franklin, "Electoral Participation," in Richard Niemi and Herbert Weisberg (eds), *Controversies in Voting Behavior*, 4th edn (Washington: CQ Press, 2001), pp. 83–99.

8 Martin Conboy, *The Press and Popular Culture* (London: Sage, 2002), p. 37.

9 George Boyce, James Curran, and Pauline Wingate (eds), *Newspaper History from the 17th Century to the Present Day* (London: Constable, 1978), p. 21.

10 William Hazlitt, *Selected Writings*, ed. Jon Cooke (Oxford University Press, 1991), p. 6.

11 Alan J. Lee, *The Origins of the Popular Press 1855–1914* (London: Croom Helm, 1976), pp. 46–8.

12 James Curran and Jean Seaton, *Power Without Responsibility: The Press and Broadcasting in Britain*, 5th edn (London: Routledge, 1997), p. 28.

13 Lee, *The Origins of the Popular Press*, pp. 290–1.

14 J. Michael Hogan and Glen Williams, "Republican Charisma and the American Revolution: The Textual Persona of Thomas Paine's Common Sense," *Quarterly Journal of Speech*, 86 (1), 2000, pp. 1–18.

15 John Keane, *Tom Paine: A Political Life* (London: Bloomsbury, 1995), p. 104.

16 Thomas Paine, *Rights of Man* (London: Penguin, 1985), p. 165.

17 Jane Chapman, *Comparative Media History: 1789 to the Present* (Cambridge, UK: Polity Press, 2005), pp. 23, 37.

18 Patricia L. Dooley, *Taking Their Political Place: Journalists and the Making of an Occupation* (Westport, CT: Greenwood, 1997), p. 129.

19 J. H. Altschull, *Agents of Power*, 2nd edn (New York: Longman, 1995), p. 10.

20 Tyler Resch, *Anthony Haswell and Freedom of the Press*, Bennington, Vermont, 2003. Available online at http://www.mediagiraffe.org/docs/haswell_resch_2003.doc, accessed on September 3, 2008, p. 3.

21 Ibid., p. 4.

22 Ibid., p. 1.

23 Gerald J. Baldasty, *The Commercialization of News in the Nineteenth Century* (Madison: University of Wisconsin Press, 1992), p. 143.

24 Ibid., p. 144.

25 Stephen Koss, *The Rise and Fall of the Political Press in Britain* (London: Fontana, 1984), pp. 347–8.

26 Francis Williams, *The Right to Know: The Rise of the World Press* (London: Constable, 1969), pp. 6–9.

27 Henry Hetherington, *The Poor Man's Guardian*, Issue No. 1, Saturday July 9, 1831, p. 1.

28 Henry Hetherington. Available online at http://www.spartacus.schoolnet. co.uk/IRhetherington.htm, accessed on July 11, 2009.

29 John Pilger (ed.), *Tell Me No Lies: Investigative Journalism and its Triumphs* (London: Jonathan Cape, 2004), p. xviii.

30 Ibid.

31 Boyce et al., *Newspaper History*, p. 23.

32 The Times, *The History of* The Times, vol. II, *The Tradition Established* (London: Times Publishing Company, 1939), p. 192.

33 Ibid.

34 The Times, *The History of* The Times, vol. I, *"The Thunderer" in the Making*, (London: Times Publishing Company, 1921), back flap.

35 W. T. Stead, "Government by Journalism," *Contemporary Review*, XLIX, May 1886, pp. 653–74 (p. 661).

36 Special Cable, "Kennedy Jones Dies; Journalist-Politician," *New York Times*, October 21, 1921. Available online at http://query.nytimes.com/mem/ archive-free/pdf?_r =1&res=9A00E6DF1539E133A25752C2A9669D946095D6CF, accessed on October 5, 2009.

37 Piers Brendon, *The Life and Death of the Press Barons* (London: Secker & Warburg, 1982), p. 7.

38 Elizabeth Christine Cook, "Colonial Newspapers and Magazines, 1704–1775," in *The Cambridge History of English and American Literature: An Encyclopedia in Eighteen Volumes*, vol. XV, *Colonial and Revolutionary Literature, Early National Literature*, ed. W. P. Trent et al. (New York: G. P. Putman's Sons, 1907–21), Book I, Ch. VII. Available online at http://www. bartleby.com/ 225/0708.html (para. 29), accessed on October 10, 2009.

39 Frank W. Scott, "Newspapers, 1775–1860," in W. P. Trent et al. (eds), *The Cambridge History of English and American Literature: An Encyclopedia in Eighteen Volumes*, vol. XVI, *Later National Literature* (New York: G. P. Putman's Sons, 1907–21), Book II, Ch. XXI. Available online at http://www. bartleby. com/ 226/index.html#12 (para. 30), accessed on October 10, 2009.

40 Brendon, *The Life and Death of the Press Barons*, p. 126.

41 Ibid., p. 158.

42 Ibid., p. 87.

43 Stephen Eric Bronner and Douglas MacKay Kellner (eds), *Critical Theory and Society: A Reader* (London: Routledge, 1989), p. 137.

44 Ibid., p. 136.

45 Jürgen Habermas, *The Structural Transformation of the Public Sphere: An Inquiry into a Category of Bourgeois Society* (Cambridge, UK: Polity Press, 1989), p. 181.

46   Kevin Howley, *Community Media: People, Places, and Communication Technologies* (Cambridge, UK: Cambridge University Press, 2005), p. 20.

47   John Nichols and Robert W. McChesney, *Tragedy and Farce: How the American Media Sell Wars, Spin Elections, and Destroy Democracy* (New York: The New Press, 2005), p. 36.

48   Amy Reynolds, "William Lloyd Garrison, Benjamin Lundy and Criminal Libel: The Abolitionists' Plea for Press Freedom," *Communication Law and Policy*, 6, 2001, 577–607.

49   Gordon T. Belt, *Jailed and Subpoenaed Journalists — A Historical Timeline*. Available online at http://www.firstamendmentcenter.org/about.aspx?id= 16896, accessed on July 12, 2009.

50   Roy Greenslade, *Press Gang: How Newspapers Make Profits from Propaganda* (London: Macmillan, 2003), p. 176.

51   Belt, *Jailed & Subpoenaed Journalists*.

52   David Mindich, *Tuned Out: Why Americans Under 40 Don't Follow the News* (New York: Oxford University Press, 2005), p. 111.

53   Janice Ruth Wood, *The Struggle for Free Speech in the United States, 1872–1915: Edward Bliss Foote, Edward Bond Foote, and Anti-Comstock Operations* (New York: Routledge, 2007).

54   Michael Schudson, *Discovering the News: A Social History of the American Newspaper* (New York: Basic Books, 1998), p. 133.

55   Harold Holzer, *The Lincoln–Douglas Debates* (New York: Harper Collins, 1993), p. 9.

56   David Zarefsky, *Lincoln Douglas and Slavery: In the Crucible of Public Debate* (Chicago: University of Chicago Press, 1990), p. 54.

57   Elizabeth Fones-Wolf, *Waves of Opposition: The Struggle for Democratic Radio, 1933-58* (Chicago: University of Illinois Press, 2006), p. 1.

58   Upton Sinclair, *Oil* (London: Penguin, 2008), p. 539. Sinclair's novel was the inspiration for the movie, *There Will be Blood*, starring Daniel Day Lewis. The film was nominated for eight Academy Awards, winning best actor for Day-Lewis and best cinematography for Robert Elswit.

59   "'The Shadow of Incipient Censorship': The Creation of the Television Code of 1952." Available online at http://historymatters.gmu.edu/d/6558/, accessed on July 11, 2009.

60   Dennis Barker, "Mary Whitehouse: Self-Appointed Campaigner Against the Permissive Society on Television", *The Guardian*, November 24, 2001.

61   John Stuart Mill, *On Liberty and Other Essays*, ed. John Gray (Oxford: Oxford University Press, 1991), p. 20.

3

Digging the Dirt

When most people are asked to name a journalist, they will usually mention someone who has credentials as an investigative reporter – Bob Woodward, Carl Bernstein, John Pilger, Paul Foot are the names that come to mind. However, when asked to describe exactly what these journalists do, people tend to be less cogent or convincing. Hugo de Burgh offers a straightforward definition in *Investigative Journalism: Context and Practice*: "An investigative journalist is a man or woman whose profession it is to discover the truth and to identify lapses from it in whatever media may be available."[1] There is an immediate question that arises from such a definition however: what is truth? Is truth synonymous with factuality? Or does it have more in common with objectivity? Are facts automatically objective? As a fact can just as easily be false as true, is there anything intrinsically "true" about facts?

Despite such difficult questions, there is no doubt that the general conception of investigative journalism is that it is an attempt to get at the truth, whatever that may be, and that somehow the truth is being concealed. The work of investigative reporters, therefore, carries the potential to extend the influence of journalism within the public sphere, for journalism as part of a media-constituted Fourth Estate provides in theory at least an enormously powerful check against the abuse of power. It does so "by drawing attention to failures within society's systems of regulation and to the ways in which those systems can be circumvented by the rich, the powerful and the corrupt."[2]

With such adversaries it is little wonder that the gains of investigative journalism, as of democracy itself, have been hard won. However, according to Dorothy Byrne, head of News and Current Affairs at Channel 4 Television in the UK, the danger may well be that audiences witnessing the uncovering

Jane Chapman and Nick Nuttall, *Journalism Today: A Themed History*
© 2011 Jane Chapman and Nick Nuttall. Published by Blackwell Publishing Ltd.

of criminality, deceit, corruption, and simple venality are no longer surprised by investigative reporting because "they assume corruption to be endemic."[3] So are journalists culpable in producing a cynical public that neither trusts nor believes its politicians or public figures? Is investigative journalism in fact "the lowest form of newspaper life" as asserted by Bernard Ingham, Margaret Thatcher's press secretary during her years in Downing Street?[4] Or is it more appropriate (and less pessimistic) to suggest, along with the Committee of Concerned Journalists, a consortium of journalists, publishers, owners, and academics worried about the future of the profession, that, "Like a theme in a Bach fugue, investigative reporting has swelled and subsided through the history of journalism but never disappeared"?[5]

I Spy With My Little Eye

One of the earliest examples of investigative reporting and one which already acknowledged its covert nature was an English publication calling itself *The Spie*. In 1644 it announced that it planned on "discovering the usual cheats in the great game of the Kingdome. For that we would have to go undercover."[6] However, it was the Enlightenment, and the new belief that human reason could combat superstition, ignorance, and tyranny, particularly as embodied in religion and the domination of society by a hereditary aristocracy, that provided the impetus for change. As the eighteenth century progressed, there developed an "attraction to scientific method, historical investigation and the questioning of all and every institution in ways that had been known to no other previous civilisation; this was the basis for the idea of impartial evidence and of the reporter as being the one who gathers such evidence."[7] The triumph of reason, originating as a mass of individual opinions, was another factor in the development of an embryonic public opinion.

By the time English radical William Cobbett began his *Political Register* in 1802 and became a strong advocate for parliamentary reform, this nascent public opinion was a major constituent in the radical press's attack on the Establishment. In 1809, for example, Cobbett condemned the use of German troops to put down a mutiny in Ely, Cambridgeshire. He was tried and convicted of sedition and sentenced to two years' imprisonment in London's Newgate jail.[8] By 1817, when the first issue of Thomas Jonathan Wooler's weekly *Black Dwarf* appeared, satire and parody had been added to the weapons a radical press used to gradually eradicate working-class deference to the political elites.

In *The Elements of Journalism*, Bill Kovach and Tom Rosenstiel point out that such pioneer investigative efforts were precisely the reason that the press needed its constitutional freedom, for the press was making transparent the workings of government that people had previously only known about through street and coffee house gossip, or by reading official announcements, often issued as pamphlets and wall posters. In the process of carrying out such investigative reporting, newspapers and periodicals established a role for journalism that distinguished it from other forms of communication. By telling the people what rulers actually did, journalists became "a bulwark of liberty," to use Founding Father James Madison's phrase.[9]

Historically, journalism's role as watchdog has always been seen as a safeguard against tyranny. But equally it has always been legitimate to ask: whose tyranny? Governments have invariably attempted to co-opt dominant media to their cause. Likewise, media owners have seldom rejected the opportunity their ownership offers to pursue personal or business advantage. In 1991 English journalists David Flintham and Nicholas Herbert believed that the British news media were in danger of forfeiting their watchdog role – not so much through their own behavior as through increased legislation and regulation. They suggested there was a danger of the press in particular "throwing in the towel" and questioned with some irony what they saw as supine behavior: "Do we really believe our elected politicians and Government officials to be so infallible ... that the work of the press as an independent guardian of justice and democracy, a platform for debate and the day-to-day recorder of our history, is now redundant?"[10] History of course tells us otherwise – that the struggle to become the "independent guardian of justice and democracy" is both unrelenting and unending.

In its 2008 press freedom index, Reporters Without Borders (RWB), an organization that aims to defend journalists imprisoned or persecuted for doing their job, placed the UK 23rd and the US 36th out of 173 countries. The RWB report for the UK highlighted the jailing of the *News of the World's* royal affairs editor, Clive Goodman, for illegally accessing royal cell phone records. However, it was the use of the Regulation of Investigatory Powers Act, 2000, to search his offices that press freedom campaigners saw as the potentially disturbing trend.

The RWB report for the US noted that the House of Representatives approved the Free Flow of Information Act, known as the "shield law," giving journalists the right not to reveal their sources at federal level. However, the low US ranking appeared to be because it was involved in a war where journalists were "embedded" with the military rather than being free agents.[11]

Despite such criticisms, the finest journalism has always attempted to monitor the powerful – the haves – on behalf of the have-nots in society and to ensure that everybody can access information, not just those who are able to do so because of their privileged position. To this end the world of politics in particular has spawned a long tradition of opposition-supported journals and radical newspapers. From the Letters of Junius in the *Public Advertiser* of the 1770s through Henry Hetherington's *Poor Man's Guardian* (1831) with its fake front page stamp proclaiming "knowledge is power," to the exposure of child prostitution by the *Pall Mall Gazette* of 1885 and most famously the *Washington Post*'s uncovering of the Watergate affair in 1972, there has been a continuous process of discovery and disclosure of the activities of those in power, even if this watchdog role has often been conducted by a so-called "partisan" press. The strong plurality of voices inevitable in a partisan press is always essential to the workings of democracy, even if it also entails a fair degree of rhetoric and special pleading. It should be remembered too that for many journalists the pursuit of that "plurality of voices" has been fraught with danger. Most recently, in November 2009, television journalist Olga Kotovskaya plunged from the 14th floor of a Kaliningrad city centre building one day after winning a court battle to regain control of her Kaskad regional TV channel. Russian journalist, Anastasia Baburova, a freelancer working for *Novaya Gazeta*, was shot dead on a Moscow street in January 2009. Yuri Shchekochikhin, *Novaya Gazeta*'s deputy editor, died of poisoning in July 2003. Igor Dominkov, senior *Novaya Gazeta* reporter was bludgeoned to death outside his Moscow apartment in July 2000. Perhaps most famously, Anna Politkovskaya, and the human rights activist, Natalia Estemirova, were killed in October 2006 and July 2009 respectively for allegedly "upsetting" the oligarchs of the Russian state.

Despite the long history of "shooting the messenger," individual reporters, staffers as well as freelancers, have always been prepared to take risks, personally and financially, in order to expose wrongdoing. Sometimes their revelations, about miscarriages of justice for instance, have helped to make legal history. Don Hale, editor of the *Matlock Mercury* in Derbyshire, England, campaigned for many years to have the case against Stephen Downing – convicted of murdering legal secretary Wendy Sewell in 1972 – reopened. Downing was 17 years old but had a reading age of only 11 when he was convicted. Twenty-seven years after Downing was jailed the Law Lords overturned the conviction.[12]

Social reformers have understood the power of the press to highlight injustice and to mount campaigns for social reform. As early as 1723 James Franklin's *New England Courant* exposed religious institutions in a famous broadside entitled, "Essay Against Hypocrites." Franklin was accused of mocking religion and bringing it into contempt. In 1849 Henry Mayhew wrote what became the first piece of investigative journalism with a series of articles for the London *Morning Chronicle*. He exposed the conditions of the poor through the hitherto unheard voices of beggars, street entertainers, market traders, prostitutes, laborers, and sweatshop workers. Lincoln Steffens's *The Shame of the Cities* in 1904 led to sweeping reforms of local government, while Rachel Carson's *Silent Spring* prompted an international movement for environmental protection. Michael Harrington's work on poverty and his book, *The Other America*, published in 1962, prompted wide-ranging social welfare changes. There were many other striking examples, such as Margaret Sanger's fight for birth control against politicians, church, and censors; Upton Sinclair's undercover work to expose corrupt meat packaging practices that led to the introduction of the Food and Drug Administration; and Ida M. Tarbell's achievement in breaking up the Standard Oil monopoly.[13]

Résumé
Lincoln Steffens

Joseph Lincoln Steffens was one of the muckraking journalists who worked for *McClure's Magazine* before World War I. He represented the American tradition of grass-roots, home-grown radicalism which owes less to ideology than it does to outrage and personality.

He was born on April 6, 1866 in San Francisco and grew up in Sacramento. He studied in France and Germany after graduating from the University of California, where he was first exposed to what were known then as "radical" politics. In 1892 he began working at the New York *Evening Post*. Later on he became editor of *McClure's Magazine*, a political and literary monthly. "With 'Tweed Days in St. Louis,' published in *McClure's* for October 1902, Steffens made his bow as a philosopher of graft and as a muckraker."[14] He became one of a trio of celebrated muckraking journalists who worked for the magazine, the other two being Ida M. Tarbell and Ray Stannard Baker. He published two collections of his articles, *The Shame of the Cities* in 1904 and *The Struggle for Self-Government* in 1906.

In 1919 he visited the Soviet Union and on his return famously said: "I have seen the future and it works."[15] He died in 1936 and according to the *San Francisco Chronicle*, "No other journalist of our time has used his power with more consistent devotion to the principles of human justice."[16]

As well as individual journalists, many newspapers, especially those with radical credentials, were in the forefront of exposing wrongdoing and corruption. Joseph Pulitzer is now remembered less for his part in the "yellow journalism" of the 1890s than for the Pulitzer Prize. But he believed that honest journalists should not be satisfied with merely printing the news; their role was "to protest against the real causes of the prostrate condition of the country – the corruption, the lawlessness, the usurpation and the profligacy of (the) national administration."[17] His paper, the *New York World*, had the courage to question untruths, even when they came from the president himself. In 1908, the *World* ran a story claiming impropriety on the part of President Theodore Roosevelt over funds used to purchase the Panama Canal from its French owners. Next to Roosevelt's comments the *World* printed a disclaimer that stated: "To the best of the *World's* knowledge and belief, each and all of these statements made by Mr. Roosevelt and quoted above are untrue, and Mr. Roosevelt must have known they were untrue when he made them."[18]

Such statements were not likely to endear the newspaper to those it attacked but, as pointed out by media historian David Mindich, the ideal is for a newspaper not to have any friends – that is, people to whom one has to be "nice," for there is a certain freedom in being able to offend anybody and everyone: "Without friends, a newspaper uncovers corruption, vice, and incompetence wherever it finds them." This became something of an obsession for Joseph Pulitzer who displayed a large poster in the *World's* newsroom, "The *World* has no friends."[19]

Résumé
S. S. McClure

Samuel Sydney McClure was born in County Antrim, Ireland in 1857. He emigrated to Indiana with his mother and two younger brothers when he was nine years old and grew up on a farm. He worked his way through Knox College where he established a college newspaper. He founded the McClure Syndicate in 1884. It "would buy authors' works for a price of around one hundred and fifty dollars and then sell the right to print them to various newspapers across the country for five dollars apiece."[20] It was the first successful company of its kind, and was largely responsible for introducing many American and British writers to a national public.

He founded *McClure's Magazine* as a monthly specializing in well-researched and well-written articles and new fiction. At 15 cents an issue, it was less than half the price of competitors like *Harpers* or the *Atlantic Monthly*. By 1898 the magazine had a circulation of 400,000. McClure, however, lacked business acumen and this resulted in him losing control of his magazine in 1912. The last years of his life were spent almost completely out of the public eye. In 1945, he gained some public notice when he was awarded the Order of Merit by the National Institute of Arts and Letters. He died in 1949.[21]

McClure's Magazine, published between 1893 and 1929 could equally be described as a publication with "no friends" – even managing to turn the President, Theodore Roosevelt, from ally into adversary. Its January 1903 issue contained a number of articles on corruption and "the American contempt of law."[22] The issue was a sell-out and Roosevelt "wrote to compliment McClure on his triumph and invite him to the White House."[23] The magazine, however, was also in the forefront of what became known as the "literature of exposure"[24] and by 1906 even Roosevelt was beginning to smart under that same exposure. "'In *Pilgrim's Progress*,' he declared [to a newspaper industry audience], 'the Man with the Muckrake is set forth as the example of him whose vision is fixed on carnal instead of on spiritual things.'"[25]

The analogy, referring as it does to the man with the muck rake in Part II of John Bunyan's *Pilgrims Progress*, is in fact a misrepresentation of the literary allegory. For Bunyan it was the rich who spent their time looking down to "rake" for more riches in the "muck". Thus as journalist Carl Jensen points out: "The term 'muckraker' would more accurately describe the robber barons of Roosevelt's time, not the journalists. John D. Rockefeller was king of the muckrakers, not Lincoln Steffens"[26] Regardless of the President's literary ignorance, *McClure's Magazine* was credited with creating muckraking journalism and counted among its scoops Lincoln Steffens's "The Shame of Minneapolis," Ida M Tarbell's "The Oil War of 1872," and Ray Stannard Baker's "The Right to Work: The Story of the Non-Striking Miners."[27] Part II examines the role of the muckraker in more detail.

The Rise and Fall of Investigative Journalism

The fortunes of investigative journalism have clearly fluctuated over the course of the last two centuries. Perhaps the latest renaissance occurred in the aftermath of the Pentagon Papers exposé and the Watergate scandal. In 1971 the Supreme Court upheld the right of the *New York Times* to publish the Pentagon Papers. They stated in their ruling: "The Founding Fathers gave the free press the protection it must have to fulfill its essential role in our democracy."[28] The press was to serve the governed, not the governors. In other words the justices "accepted that publication of those documents would harm the national interest and might even make the newspaper guilty of a criminal offence. But it was entitled to publish and be damned."[29]

The 47-volume papers detailed the history of United States military involvement in the Vietnam War between 1945 and 1967. They were classified documents and a Defense Department analyst, Daniel Ellsburg, leaked them to the press. The Nixon government tried to prevent their publication. As Richard Nixon himself wrote, "The documents had been illegally turned over to the *Times*, and I believed that the paper acted irresponsibly in publishing them."[30] The *New York Times*, however, began publishing details until a federal court injunction forced the paper to stop. While the *Times* fought the injunction the *Washington Post* began its own series of articles based on the papers after rejecting its lawyer's advice not to publish. Ultimately the Supreme Court found in both papers' favor. As journalist and pundit Bill Moyers later reflected: "The greatest moments in the history of the press came not when journalists made common cause with the state but when they stood fearlessly independent of it."[31]

Just over a year later, in June 1972, the *Post*'s journalists launched into the Watergate investigation, one of the defining moments in modern investigative reporting. Despite further pressure from the Nixon administration to cease inquiries the paper pursued the story until Nixon resigned the presidency. The pressure exerted by the administration was perhaps indicative of the way Nixon operated. *Post* reporters were excluded from covering White House social events; news was fed to its competitor the *Washington Star* "while freezing out the *Post*"; "challenges against the *Post*'s ownership of two television stations in Florida were filed with the Federal Communications Commission" (FCC). The price of *Post* stock fell by 50 percent. Among the challengers – those who proposed to become the new FCC licensees – were "several persons long associated with the President."[32]

Throughout the twentieth century successive British governments, too, have employed a variety of legal weapons to prevent disclosure of what they consider to be secret information. The Official Secrets Acts of 1889, 1911, and 1920, although designed to catch indiscreet civil servants, traitors, spies, and saboteurs were, inter alia, a danger to the proper functioning of the press. In 1930 a reporter on the *News Chronicle* revealed the Cabinet's decision to arrest Mahatma Gandhi. A police hunt ensued and prosecution under Section 6 of the 1920 Act was threatened. It turned out that it was the Home Secretary himself who had leaked the information. Neither he nor the journalist was prosecuted but a precedent had been set. "Over the next 50 years it [the 1920 Act] would be used routinely to deter or punish the disclosure of official information that had nothing to do with security and public safety, but everything to do with saving Governments from embarrassment, inconvenience and unwanted publicity."[33]

After the Watergate scandal investigative reporting underwent something of a renaissance, especially in the US where journalists have traditionally enjoyed greater freedom to publish owing to the rule against prior restraint. Guaranteed by the First Amendment, the rule prohibits government from banning the expression of ideas prior to their publication. The "Watergate effect" undoubtedly redefined the image of reporting – journalists themselves became celebrities and the burgeoning popularity of television on both sides of the Atlantic led to a plethora of investigative-style programs, from CBS's *60 Minutes* and cable TV's Investigation Discovery channel in the US to the BBC's *Panorama*, Granada's *World in Action*, and ITV's *The Cook Report* in Britain. Local TV followed in the US, each with its "I-Team." So much so that the investigative methodology soon became a cliché applied to what would normally have been considered regular journalism. In other words, every trivial injustice became an "investigation" – and with it came a dilution of the skills that regular journalism should have been deploying on the serious issues of the day. "Faux investigations" – that is, TV-style dramatic reporting that hyped a subject of no great consequence to the polity, often celebrity-driven, gradually became the norm.

One of the results of these "faux investigations" is the "diminution by dilution" of television's watchdog role.[34] TV executives have shown less enthusiasm for important investigations that would really challenge political and corporate power. Subject areas such as economics, politics, social welfare, education, corporate power, national security, and the military tend to be bypassed. Exposure of petty criminals, trivial consumer rip-offs, and celebrity entertainment has become the staple diet, while the "big fish," since Watergate, have invariably escaped the hook. Journalistic investigations, on the other hand, based on official investigations such as the Starr Report that formed part of the Bill Clinton/Monica Lewinsky story, are increasing in frequency. One of their attractions is that most of the "leg work" has already been done, but inevitably such investigations rely on the use of unidentifiable sources. The issue at stake here is that while unnamed sources can be authoritative, as was "Deep Throat" in Watergate, they can also be mischievous because they cannot be held to account. Anonymous sources may also become a substitute for meticulous reporting. The press, as its detractors often point out, is not above being fooled into becoming a tool or mouthpiece for various other interests and thus potentially misleading its audience.

Furthermore, investigative reporting is expensive. Reporters who dig around for corruption, incompetence, and injustice still draw a salary while not "filling the space" and, as David Mindich points out, "A newspaper's central business challenge today is how to maintain its integrity and high standards while maintaining profits."[35] At its simplest, the difficulty is that journalism's role as watchdog is rarely synonymous with that of attracting an audience – that is, profit-based ratings – nor is it always compatible with corporate power. In fact, the watchdog role is perhaps more threatened by corporate conglomerates that own media companies as just another part of their portfolio. This can produce conflicts of interest within the organization that undermine the independent, monitoring role of the press.

Sociologists David Croteau and William Hoynes give examples of the impact of corporate control on journalism in *The Business of Media: Corporate Media and the Public Interest*. Their general conclusion is that censorship of the media is now more likely to come from corporations for economic purposes than from governments for purely political ones.[36] Edward Herman and Noam Chomsky identified this trend in *Manufacturing Consent* (1988), noting that the sort of persistence that is required for journalism to act as a Fourth Estate is undermined by a state–corporate nexus that has reinvented the media as an instrument of its own class domination. Part II examines this phenomenon in more detail.

In the process, investigative journalism has often failed to monitor powerful elites adequately or scrutinize potential abuses of such power even though, as media pundit Raymond Snoddy has pointed out, "the availability of inexpensive computers has allowed American journalists to create a new form of reporting – computer-assisted investigative journalism – in which computer-literate reporters ... plough through the electronic records of public bodies."[37] One such reporter was Bill Dedman. He produced a

Pulitzer Prize-winning series of articles in 1989 for the *Atlanta Journal-Constitution* entitled *The Color of Money* using just such methods in order to expose racial discrimination in the lending policies of banks in Atlanta, Georgia. His exposé prompted far-reaching reforms in bank practices throughout the whole of the US. Other threats include the increased use of litigation by large, rich corporations whose weapons used to be limited to PR and advertising; the increased importance of the ratings business; the profit and loss balance sheet; and monopoly ownership. Together with the employment instability created by deregulation of public service broadcasting in most other parts of the world, these concerns have served to encourage a climate of self-censorship by prior restraint.[38]

Yet at the same time there has been a marked resurgence in the work of documentary filmmakers using the cinema rather than the television screen. It is almost as if the make-believe world of the cinema and the big screen provides a less threatening space than the living room for such investigative journalism to flourish. Michael Moore has written a number of high-grossing documentaries. *Roger & Me* (1989) was a muckraking film that took General Motors CEO Roger Smith to task for closing a Buick plant in Flint, Michigan (Moore's hometown) and throwing thousands out of work. This was followed by *Bowling For Columbine* (2002) examining gun crime, high school shootings, and the "violent soul of America." Next came *Fahrenheit 9/11* (2004), a coruscating account of the Bush presidency post 9/11. Next *Sicko* (2007) examined the American health care system and its failures. Other notable filmmakers have included Morgan Spurlock, famous for *Super Size Me* (2004) where he spent 30 days eating only McDonald's food. It documented the dramatic effects on his physical and psychological well-being – weight gain, liver damage, mood swings, and sexual dysfunction. James Miller gained posthumous fame and an Emmy award for *Death in Gaza* (2004) which examined the Israeli–Palestine conflict in Gaza. It followed the lives of three Palestinian children and before filming ended James Miller was shot dead by an Israeli soldier.

Lippmann and Dewey Slug It Out

When Alexis de Tocqueville looked at the state of democracy (and journalism) in early nineteenth-century America, he concluded that the people had found a way, by a combination of community associations, newspapers, and public opinion, to achieve social integration through a celebration of individual freedom.[39] Since then, other thinkers have addressed the question of modern journalism's role through a similar prism. During the interwar years, a period when democracy seemed to be threatened not only by the rise of fascism but also by the complications of modern society such as fast-moving technological change, Walter Lippmann in *Public Opinion* (1922), and John Dewey in *Experience and Nature* (1925) and *The Public and its Problems* (1927), separately wrote about the proper response to the problem of how public opinion could still guide public policy and the role that journalism should play in this endeavor.

Lippmann believed that the answer lay in the fostering of experts (including journalistic experts) to guide public opinion more efficiently. Dewey, on the other hand, believed that process was as important as results and those in power, therefore, had a responsibility to consider how citizens themselves should play the central role in influencing public opinion. He acknowledged, however, that this central role could be facilitated by journalism. In a series of articles and numerous books, Dewey expressed the belief that democracy was too fundamental a value to abandon simply because technology was moving so fast.

Résumé
John Dewey

John Dewey was born in Burlington, Vermont, in 1859. He graduated from the University of Vermont in 1879 and eventually joined the staff at the newly formed University of Chicago in 1894. In 1899 he became president of the American Psychological Association and in 1905 president of the American Philosophical Association. A long and productive academic career generated over 700 academic papers and 40 books.

Dewey wrote extensively on democracy and community, journalism and philosophy and was arguably America's most influential thinker on education in the twentieth century. He was also considered a central figure in American pragmatism although he referred to his own philosophy as instrumentalism.

He believed democracy was more than just the acquisition of voting rights and involved the development of a fully fledged public opinion accomplished through effective communication between the people, experts, and politicians who would be accountable for their actions. John Dewey died in New York in 1952.[40]

In many respects the Lippmann–Dewey debates were won by Walter Lippmann. The projected image of journalism as well as journalists' own perception of their calling is that of an expert class of disinterested observers who monitor and interpret governmental activity in order to enlighten others and hence develop an informed public opinion. Since the 1920s, new aspects of technology from the transistor to the semiconductor chip and digital reproduction have all contributed to making life ever more complex. Lippmann's suggestion that journalists should become better educated to handle this complexity has in fact occurred, often through experts in such fields being co-opted to the ranks of journalism itself. The implication of his ideas – that journalism should lead, not follow, has also proved prescient. Investigative and authoritative journalists are now to be found in most specialist areas, having acquired the necessary expert knowledge to inform and alert the public to the major issues of the day – from global warming and climate change to international defense issues and the credit crunch.

Dewey's thoughts, however, on the need for a democratic media seem equally perceptive in the twenty-first century. More than 80 years ago he recognized that people seldom feel sufficiently engaged in public life. Today this is made worse by the impression that mainstream TV journalism, the platform through which most people gain their news awareness, is talking *at* rather than *with* or *to* people.[41] The result is often a feeling of powerlessness. The public seem to have no control over the political system and this is reflected in the numbers of people in the US who consume no news at all – now 20 percent of the population, up from 14 percent 10 years ago.[42] A University of Chicago study of how news coverage at the time of the 1992 presidential election in the United States shaped people's sense of politics suggested that journalistic emphasis either on irony or on the hopeless complexity of issues contributed to feelings of public disengagement.[43] It remains to be seen whether new technologies like cell phones and the internet, and the opportunities they provide for the amateur citizen journalist, will reinvigorate political engagement.

Impact of Commercialism on Political Coverage

Public disengagement with the political process is not just a result of news complexity. Commercial imperatives are driving news coverage toward less expensive, opinion-based, trivial, and sensationalist content, and in the face of this onslaught, political coverage has suffered. Interest in celebrity, gossip, and crime, of course, is as old as the media itself, because the purpose of newspapers and commercial broadcasters has always been to deliver audiences to advertisers rather than just news to audiences.

So far as political coverage is concerned, ownership by rich press barons from the late nineteenth century onwards in the United States and Europe meant an increase in antilabor union, probusiness coverage and the dominance of right-wing views. According to John Nichols and Robert McChesney: "In community after community, newspapers were in bed with those who owned and controlled the community. In this context partisanship reeked of the heavy-handedness one associates with authoritarian regimes, or to be more accurate, company towns."[44]

During the 1912 US presidential race all three candidates – Woodrow Wilson, Theodore Roosevelt, and Eugene Debs – came out against the corruption and unfairness of the press, such was the feeling that sensational journalism was undermining democracy. Professional journalism emerged from this low point as a self-regulating industry created by owners eager to ward off organized reform. This was the era when, on both sides of the Atlantic, many of the ethical codes of conduct still used today were developed by both individual newspapers and particular job groupings such as editors or reporters. These codes, although voluntary, to some extent enshrined the new professionalism that gave journalists more power to argue the editorial case for public service coverage (see Part IV).

News as spectacle reached new heights with the advent of television. This medium produced a discursive hypertension that could be construed as harmful for journalism and to a lesser extent democracy itself. Firstly, the mediating effect of television both flattens and distorts events in the process of presenting them. One happening or event is as important as the next. Each is supposed to grab our attention through the immediacy of its visual imagery. As more and more spectacles are created there is no hierarchy of importance, little sense of proportion, and even less historical context. The dangers inherent in this lack of historical context are noted by Greg Philo and Mike Berry in *Bad News From Israel*: "One of the key issues to emerge from this research is that for many viewers, their level of interest in news related very directly to their level of understanding of what they were watching."[45]

Television news comprises a series of metonyms from which a viewer constructs "reality." Metonymy is a device whereby a part of something stands for the whole. A single film clip of an event, for example, can only show a moment in time, but from that "moment" a viewer constructs the whole "truth" of the event.

A viewer's perception of events may well be mistaken, therefore, because television by its very nature invariably shows us the dramatic, the spectacular, the unusual, rather than the prosaic, the tedious, or the everyday, which by definition are not newsworthy. "TV's natural tendency is to see the world in shards. It shows us one event with an air of utmost drama, then forgets about it and shows us the next."[46] Politics, however, is about priorities and also very often involves the communication of concepts and values that are not necessarily visual, so do not lend themselves easily to the medium.

One of the ways television solves the problem of communicating concepts and values is through the process of personalization. This is the second of the harmful effects noted above. On the one hand news presenters are shown as authoritative and engaging personalities in their own right, and on the other the people they interview become personalities because of their constant exposure. Thus news is presented as entertainment, like most other aspects of television. The emphasis is on the nature of the encounter, the locking horns of two "personalities" – in front of the House of Commons or the White House – rather than on the issue which is the pretext for the interview.

Furthermore, the issue being investigated may not be of any great importance or relevance to the polity. Out of nearly 500 stories between 1990 and 1994 transmitted in the United States by CBS's *60 Minutes*, hardly a fifth were about the real workings of politics, economics, or long-term issues of national significance. Apart from a rush of interest in race issues following the Rodney King episode in Los Angles in 1991 only one program a year on average dealt with race. Instead, more than a third consisted of celebrity profiles, exposés of small-time scandals, and entertainment industry stories.[47] The role of the media in a democratic society and the tensions between the commercial imperative to sell newspapers and programs and the professional requirement to ensure that citizens are properly informed were evident, however, long before the rise of television. In America they were analyzed in some detail in what became known as the Hutchins Report. In 1942, the President of the University of Chicago, Robert Hutchins, at the behest of Henry Luce, the founder of *Time* magazine, set up a commission of the great and the good to enquire into the state of the American press and "it was in this context that on 28 February 1944, Hutchins announced his intent ' … to discover where free expression is or is not limited, whether by governmental censorship, pressures from readers or advertisers or the unwisdom of its proprietors or the timidity of its management.'"[48]

Résumé
Henry Luce

Henry Luce was born in Penglai City, China in 1898 where his father was a missionary. He moved to America aged 15 and attended the Hotchkiss School in Connecticut. In 1920 he graduated from Yale University where he met Briton Hadden. The two worked together on the *Yale Daily News* and after Luce returned from a year studying at Oxford University he worked with Haddon on the *Baltimore News*. In 1922 they both left their jobs, set up Time Inc., and raised almost $100,000; the first issue of *Time* magazine appeared on March 3, 1923.

Hadden died suddenly in 1929 and Luce assumed total control of the company. In 1930 he launched the business magazine *Fortune* and in 1936 he published *Life*, a picture magazine. *House and Home* followed in 1952 and then *Sports Illustrated* in 1954. By the time of his death, Time Inc. was the largest and most prestigious magazine publisher in the world. Luce's own stock was valued at $100 million. He died in Phoenix, Arizona, in 1967.[49]

The Hutchins Report: *A Free And Responsible Press*

The Hutchins Commission believed that the press was failing in its duty to truly reflect democratic debate. Their report, entitled *A Free and Responsible Press*, called on the press to improve itself in the name of morality, democracy, and self-preservation. The findings of the Commission were roundly rejected by the press itself, which even accused its members of being "Reds."[50] More relevant were the Commission's fears that the freedoms enshrined in the First Amendment were under threat from "newly formed totalitarian regimes in key global positions."[51] By envisaging the press as a forum for the exchange of comment and criticism, the Commission stressed the importance of good journalism to a democracy by describing what good practice *should* involve, by stressing that news stories should be presented with context to enhance audience understanding, and that audiences required "full access to the day's intelligence."[52]

The report, despite being written in a premodern, pretelevision, preinternet language, provides tools that are useful for measuring the performance of current journalism, particularly in terms of a moral language and benchmark standards. It stipulated five minimum requirements for responsible journalism that are still relevant today and remain a fair test of what should be published and how it contributes to the community:

> Today, our society needs, first, a truthful, comprehensive, and intelligent account of the day's events in a context which gives them meaning; second, a forum for the exchange of comment and criticism; third, a means of projecting the opinions and attitudes of the groups in the society to one another; fourth, a method of presenting and clarifying the goals and values of society; and, fifth, a way of reaching every member of the society by the currents of information, thought, and feeling which the press supplies.[53]

Although the report staunchly backed the principles of the First Amendment, which it said should be defended, it was nevertheless widely criticized as having too academic an approach. This particular quality, however, produced some very prescient examples, for instance concerning the way reporting of isolated facts without context can damage race relations. Significantly, this issue was not presented under the guise of "minorities" but rather as "constituent groups," in a bid for unity:

> The country has many groups that are partially insulated from one another and that need to be interpreted to one another. Factually correct but substantially untrue accounts of the behaviors of members of one of these social islands can intensify the antagonisms of others toward them. A single incident will be accepted as a sample group action unless the press has given a flow of information and interpretation concerning the relations between two racial groups such as to enable the reader to set a single event in its proper perspective. If allowed to pass as a sample of such action, the requirement that the press present an accurate account of the day's events in a context which gives them meaning has not been met.[54]

At the time publishers said the Hutchins recommendations would bankrupt them, for if reporters were to provide context, they needed more time for research and writing, and that cost money. Publishers also objected to the idea of public participation in judging journalistic standards, fearing the introduction of government controls over the media. They also dismissed the extension of First Amendment rights to broadcasters.

The report stated that freedom of the press was "in serious danger because of failures, abuses, and derelictions on the part of its most powerful owners"[55] who commanded their empires with little concern for the general public or its opinions. And what Hutchins alleged about the press was equally true of broadcast media. For years a dispute raged between the FCC, television stations CBS and NBC, the National Association of Broadcasters, and Congress concerning the existence of a potential monopoly because the big radio networks controlled so many of the available high-power stations. Finally in 1943 the Supreme Court supported the FCC demand for NBC to abandon one of its two networks, which became the new network ABC. Despite this trend of increasing media concentration, the Hutchins Report backed away from applying antitrust laws to the press, because it considered that this could damage press freedom and could be used "to limit voices in opposition and to hinder the process of public education."[56]

On both sides of the Atlantic after World War II there was a new sense of urgency surrounding the whole issue of control of the news media, prompted in part by the rapidly increasing popularity of television. The Hutchins Report called for a permanent, nongovernmental commission to carry out an ongoing review of the press. In Britain the government established a Royal Commission on the Press which proposed the idea of a Press Council responsible for self-regulation of the industry. In both cases the results were unsatisfactory and in Britain this led to calls for statutory controls on the press. The public service ethic of the BBC was held out as the model. Ultimately, journalists were left in control of their own destiny so perhaps it is incumbent on them to acknowledge the need for self-control at an individual level, translating into self-regulation at an industry level. The age-old responsibility to hold "the rich, the powerful and the corrupt" to account can become the cornerstone of journalism's digital future.

Notes

1 Hugo de Burgh (ed.), *Investigative Journalism: Context and Practice* (London: Routledge, 2000), p. 9.
2 Ibid., p. 3.
3 Ibid., p. 11.
4 Ibid.
5 Committee of Concerned Journalists, "The History of the Watchdog Mission." Available online at http://www.concernedjournalists.org/history-watchdog-mission, accessed on August 12, 2010.
6 Bill Kovach and Tom Rosenstiel, *The Elements of Journalism* (London: Guardian Atlantic Books, 2001), p. 113.

7   de Burgh, *Investigative Journalism*, p. 29.

8   William Cobbett. Available online at http://www.spartacus.schoolnet.co.uk/
PRcobbett.htm, accessed on August 12, 2010.

9   Kovach and Rosenstiel, *The Elements of Journalism*, p. 113.

10 David Flintham and Nicholas Herbert, *Press Freedom in Britain* (London: The
Newspaper Society, 1991), pp. 25–6.

11 Reporters Without Borders. Available online at http://www.rsf.org/-Anglais-.
html, accessed on July 17, 2009.

12 Don Hale, *Town Without Pity: The Fight to Clear Stephen Downing of the
Bakewell Murder* (London: Century, 2002).

13 Carl Jensen,, "What Happened To Good Old-Fashioned Muckraking?" in Katrina
Borjesson (ed.), *Into the Buzzsaw: Leading Journalists Expose the Myth of a Free
Press* (Amherst, New York: Prometheus Books, 2002), pp. 333–50. This outlines
the content that could form a "History of Standard Oil," part 2. It would include:
contributor towards the destruction of rapid transport systems in over 100 US
cities during the 1930s and 40s; a profitable relationship with Nazi Germany;
persistence in inserting lead in gasoline until 1986 when it was banned, despite
knowledge of the public health hazard since the 1920s (p. 344).

14 Justin Kaplan, *Lincoln Steffens: A Biography* (London: Jonathan Cape, 1975),
p. 107.

15 Ibid., p. 255.

16 Ibid., p. 329.

17 John Nichols and Robert W. McChesney, *Tragedy and Farce: How the American
Media Sell Wars, Spin Elections, and Destroy Democracy* (New York: The New
Press, 2005), p. 6.

18 Ibid.

19 David Mindich, *Tuned Out: Why Americans Under 40 Don't Follow the News*
(New York: Oxford University Press, 2005), p. 97.

20 McClure Publishing Company Archives. Available at http://www.lib.udel.edu/
ud/spec/findaids/mcclure.htm, accessed on July 15, 2009.

21 Ibid.

22 Kaplan, *Lincoln Steffens*, p. 113.

23 Ibid., p. 114.

24 Ibid., p. 115.

25 Ibid., p. 150.

26 Jensen, "What Happened To Good Old-Fashioned Muckraking?" p. 348.

27 Ibid., p. 113.

28 Kovach and Rosenstiel, *The Elements of Journalism*, p. 23.

29 Geoffrey Robertson, QC, and Andrew Nicol, *Media Law*, 3rd edn (London:
Penguin, 1992), p. 20.

30 Richard Nixon, *The Memoirs of Richard Nixon* (London: Arrow Books, 1979),
p. 508.

31 Quoted in Nichols and McChesney, *Tragedy and Farce*, p. 36.
32 Carl Bernstein and Bob Woodward, *All The President's Men* (London: Quartet Books, 1974), pp. 220–1.
33 Flintham and Herbert, *Press Freedom in Britain*, pp. 25–6.
34 Kovach and Rosenstiel, *The Elements of Journalism*, p. 120.
35 Mindich, *Tuned Out*, p. 99.
36 David Croteau and William Hoynes, *The Business of Media: Corporate Media and the Public Interest*, 2nd edn (Thousand Oaks, CA: Pine Forge Press, 2005).
37 Raymond Snoddy, *The Good, the Bad and the Unacceptable* (London: Faber and Faber, 1992), p. 160.
38 Jane Chapman, *Comparative Media History: 1789 to the Present* (Cambridge, UK: Polity Press, 2005).
39 Alexis de Tocqueville, *Democracy in America*, ed. J. P. Meyer, trans. G. Lawrence (Garden City, NY: Doubleday, 1969), p. 253.
40 Mark K. Smith, *John Dewey*, 2001. Available online at http://www.infed.org/thinkers/et-dewey.htm, accessed on July 21, 2009.
41 Pew Research Center survey, 2008.
42 Ibid.
43 James Fallows, *Breaking the News* (New York: Pantheon Books, 1996), p. 243.
44 Nichols and McChesney, *Tragedy and Farce*, p. 16.
45 Greg Philo and Mike Berry, *Bad News From Israel* (London: Pluto Press, 2004), p. 257.
46 Fallows, *Breaking the News*, p. 53.
47 Ibid., p. 57.
48 Fred Blevins, "The Hutchins Commission Turns 50: Recurring Themes in Today's Public and Civic Journalism," *Third Annual Conference on Intellectual Freedom*, 1997, p. 1. Available online at http://mtprof.msun.edu/Fall1997/Blevins.html, accessed on September 3, 2008.
49 James L. Baughman, *Henry R. Luce and the Rise of the American News Media* (Baltimore: Johns Hopkins University Press, 2001). Available online at http://www.pbs.org/wnet/americanmasters/episodes/henry-luce/henry-r-luce-and-the-rise-of-the-american-news-media/650/, accessed on August 12, 2009.
50 Blevins, "The Hutchins Commission Turns 50," p. 2.
51 Ibid., p. 1.
52 Mark N. Trahant, "The Hutchins Commission, Half a Century On, II" *Media Studies Journal*, 12, 2, Spring/Summer, 1998, 56–61 (p. 58).
53 Ibid.
54 Ibid., p. 59.
55 Andie Tucher, "The Hutchins Commission, Half a Century On, I", *Media Studies Journal*, 12, 2, Spring/Summer, 1998, 48–55 (p. 49).
56 Ibid., p. 51.

4

Spinning a Good Yarn
and Developing Community

Governments throughout history have sought ways of "managing" the press and other news media. And the extent to which a government is democratic is invariably reflected in the amount of freedom it allows its news media – more of one equates to more of the other. Having said that, eighteenth- and nineteenth-century attempts at such control, in particular of the press, on both sides of the Atlantic have invariably played badly with journalists as well as with their readers. In the absence of such specific regulation for most of the twentieth century, occasional commissions of enquiry and a variety of voluntary controls have been used in an attempt to rein in the worst excesses, in particular, of the tabloid press. In Britain there have been three Royal Commissions on the press and broadcasting since World War II: 1947, 1962, and 1977. In the United States, besides the Hutchins Report, the Annenberg Foundation Trust at Sunnylands in California established a commission on the press in 2004 which examined the role of the press in a democracy. The commission also "searched for ways to allow more voices to be heard and to improve the institution of American free press."[1] So, while governments have been wary of statutory controls, they have gradually developed other more subtle ways of controlling the flow and dissemination of information.

This tighter control has spawned a whole new industry of public relations specialists who have moved into the "corridors of power." Margaret Thatcher, for example, doubled the number of press officers during her time in Downing Street and oversaw a 500 percent increase in spending on the Central Office of Information, which runs the British government's PR departments.[2] Public relations professionals and news agencies now influence news content to an extent hitherto unheard of. The degree to which

Jane Chapman and Nick Nuttall, *Journalism Today: A Themed History*
© 2011 Jane Chapman and Nick Nuttall. Published by Blackwell Publishing Ltd.

journalists are reliant on these sources, as revealed by research[3] and by journalists themselves,[4] now raises a question mark over their role as independent members of the Fourth Estate.

Who Is Telling the Story?

The modern public relations industry in the United States was strongly influenced by Wilsonian progressives who, according to Noam Chomsky, "advocated 'the engineering of consent,' a technique of control employed by responsible men for the benefit of their flock, the ignorant masses."[5] In Britain the rise of media management dates back, as already noted, to the late 1970s and Margaret Thatcher's arrival in power. This was in the wake of the Watergate exposures that rocked the US. But what became a "golden age" for objective professional journalism in America heralded in Great Britain a political culture that has become stylized and promotional in nature rather than purely informational.

Bernard Ingham, Margaret Thatcher's press secretary, became adroit at leaking stories intended to destabilize her rivals. During the same period, marketing and PR companies such as Saatchi & Saatchi were employed to promote the Conservative Party almost as if it were a product. Labour, in turn, championed the "focus group" and "spin." Understandably, spin produced a hostile reaction from journalists who did not enjoy being subject to such levels of manipulation. This hostility manifested itself in stories that highlighted the processes of media management in order to demonstrate the extent to which it had become part of the landscape. In turn, the effect of this was to encourage greater public cynicism about the motives of politicians. It is now part and parcel of the larger crisis within the political system – a crisis of trust brought about partly by the media and partly by politicians themselves in that journalism's culture of cynicism and negativity towards those in power has become, according to some commentators, a danger to democracy.[6]

However, there are still occasions when this cynicism actually benefits open government. In May 2003, two months after the invasion of Iraq, the BBC's defense and diplomatic correspondent Andrew Gilligan alleged on the *Today* morning radio program that a dossier published by the British Government, which set out why Iraq and its dictator Saddam Hussein were a threat, had been "sexed up" to exaggerate Iraq's military capabilities.

It stated no fewer than four times that Iraq had weapons of mass destruction which could be deployed within 45 minutes. A huge row developed between the BBC and the Labour government over this allegation. The "mole" who provided the details to Gilligan, the government scientist Dr David Kelly, was named in the media and and later apparently committed suicide, although there is still some uncertainty about the cause of his death.

Prime Minister Tony Blair ordered an enquiry, to be headed by Lord Hutton. The report, although the most open in British legal history, apportioned most blame to the BBC. Gilligan, it said, "had made 'unfounded allegations' when he said the government probably knew its 45 minute claim was wrong."[7] The Chairman of Governors of the BBC, Gavin Davies; the Director General, Greg Dyke; and Andrew Gilligan himself all resigned. Although Gilligan and the BBC were criticized in the Hutton Report, there was a widespread feeling among British journalists that, despite mistakes, Gilligan had succeeded in exposing failures in the process of government and in intelligence as it related to the issue of weapons of mass destruction. In short, the media carried out one of its major functions of holding the government to account – especially important where, as in this case, parliament had singularly failed to do so.

Anything You Say Will Be Misquoted

The history of public relations is as convoluted and contested as the practice itself. Its relationship with journalism is equally tortuous and challenging. Indeed, according to media academics Denise DeLorme and Fred Fedler: "Journalists seem to treat public relations and its practitioners with contempt."[8] And this hostility seems to have existed for as long as publicists have practiced what some regard as their "nefarious" art. So what is "public relations" and where did it come from? Are journalists themselves partly responsible for the introduction of this cuckoo in their nest? Why are certain kinds of PR identified with "spin"? Is this term inherently derogatory to the whole business of PR and harmful to the cause of journalism and democracy?

According to the British organization the Chartered Institute of Public Relations (CIPR), PR "is the planned and sustained effort to establish and maintain goodwill and mutual understanding between an organisation and its publics."[9] Such an aim may be commendable but it presents major hazards for a journalist who regularly uses PR-generated material.

A journalist, after all, should not be primarily concerned with the relationship between an organization "and its publics." The CIPR Code of Conduct under Principles of Good Practice states: "Fundamentals of good public relations practice are honest and responsible regard for the public interest [and] never knowingly misleading clients, employers, employees, colleagues and fellow professionals about the nature of representation or what can be competently delivered and achieved."[10] These aims are somewhat vague and the clause relating to "never knowingly misleading" makes no mention, except for the anodyne "regard for the public interest," of the ultimate consumer of the PR product – the reading, listening, and viewing public.

The Public Relations Society of America (PRSA) claimed in 1988 that "Public relations helps an organization and its publics adapt mutually to each other".[11] As with its British equivalent, however, this mutuality seems to exist in a vacuum – where for example are truth, impartiality, fairness? In Britain there has seldom been any suggestion that the worlds of PR and journalism might share codes of conduct or membership of the same institutions. Traditionally, as noted by US academics Denise DeLorme and Fred Fedler, British journalists too have been both dismissive and abusive of public relations and its practitioners.

According to journalist Tom Baistow, "the aim of PR is to tell you what it wants you to know and to keep you from finding out what it doesn't want you to know".[12] One of the most striking examples of this is the rearguard action of tobacco companies' PR in consistently denying any relationship between their products and lung cancer. As recently as 2003 the *Observer* newspaper reported that Imperial Tobacco was to "take the unprecedented step this week of denying there is a proven causal link between smoking and lung cancer in the first case against a cigarette firm to go to a UK court."[13]

Yet it cannot be denied that "early reporters and editors were no great paragons of virtue" either. "Many engaged in the very practices (e.g., faking) that they condemned when conducted by PR practitioners."[14] Lord Northcliffe, something of a showman himself, announced that sales of the *Daily Mail* on its first day of publication, May 4, 1896, had topped 700,000 copies. Yet he had no real way of finding out the truth of this statement at such short notice. Equally Northcliffe used stunts to sell his papers as shamelessly as any major corporation. In 1906, for example, the *Mail* offered £1,000 for the first flight across the English Channel and £10,000 for the first flight from London to Manchester. It is difficult to make a distinction between such stunts and the typical work of an assiduous PR practitioner given a similar brief.

Northcliffe's stunts were just one kind of publicity seeking that now seems fairly naive. Today, in contrast, many organizations, whether commercial, governmental, or public bodies, complain that journalists misquote them, get crucial facts wrong or just fail to tell the full story. Hiring a press officer if you're small or a whole PR department if you're big enough can often seem a small price to pay for the chance to communicate your story accurately and with due observance of the facts. Yet despite this, the charge most readily levied against PR today is that it is in the business of distorting information and attempting to disguise unpalatable facts.

Reputation Matters

From a journalistic perspective it is possible to identify three main variations on the PR theme that to some extent have been responsible for giving PR its reputation as a "dark art":

- spin
- pseudo events
- habitual access.

The term "spin" was used for the first time in the 1980s to describe the press agents employed by politicians and governments. The task of these agents was to promote government activity in as favorable a light as possible. An early UK use of the word "spin" appeared in the *Guardian Weekly* in January 1978: "The CIA can be an excellent source [of information], though, like every other, its offerings must be weighed for factuality and spin."[15] The term "spin doctor" appeared about the same time. For example, the following appeared in the *New York Times* in October 1980: "A dozen men in good suits and women in silk dresses will circulate smoothly among the reporters, spouting confident opinions. They won't be just press agents trying to impart a favorable spin to a routine release. They'll be the Spin Doctors, senior advisers to the candidates."[16]

Before even these examples, however, in the lead-up to World War II, Britain's government, headed by Neville Chamberlain, used the techniques of spin to pursue its policy of appeasement toward Hitler and the various fascist tyrannies across Europe. To promote such a policy and ensure a favorable press, Chamberlain used personal emissaries to newspaper editors and proprietors, developed an enlarged Downing Street press office, and exploited the close relationships between government ministers and many newspaper proprietors and editors. Furthermore, as Richard Cockett has noted, "As Chamberlain's pursuance of appeasement became more vigorous and single-minded, he was eager to centralize all government press briefings at Downing Street so as effectively to silence any sounds of dissent in Whitehall".[17] Although the semantics of "spin" did not extend to such conduct at the time, Chamberlain's behavior clearly passed the "duck test" (if it looks like a duck and quacks like a duck ...).

The Techniques of "Spin"

Spin involves interpretation. An event is not allowed to speak for itself, rather it is interpreted by an intermediary – usually a functionary of the organization commonly termed a spin doctor – in order to persuade public opinion in a particular way. Crucially, however, there is the implicit assumption that spin also involves high levels of manipulation, perhaps bordering on deception. Politicians are routinely accused, by their opponents at least, of using spin to manipulate both the media and their audience.

The techniques of spin have been pored over and dissected almost as much as they have been practiced. There are many ways in which a story or event can be "spun" but prominent among them are the following:

- Cherry picking
- The nondenial denial
- Disguising bad news.

Cherry-picking involves presenting information selectively to support a particular position or point of view. For example, an individual instance may be used to confirm a particular position while ignoring those examples that contradict that position. There are inherent dangers in cherry-picking. In the 1992 general election in Britain where the Labour Party had hoped to overturn John Major's Conservative administration, a Labour Party Election Broadcast (PEB) made much of an incident that became known as "Jennifer's Ear." The PEB told the story of two little girls who both suffered from "glue ear" (otitis media with effusion). One girl was forced to wait for treatment on the National Health Service (NHS) because of underfunding (according to Labour) while the other girl went private and was treated immediately. The PEB caused a furor, with the national press spending its time trying to find out who leaked the story rather than on the issue of NHS funding as Labour had planned. Inevitably the Conservative Party produced a number of positive stories about NHS patient care.[18]

The term "nondenial denial" is attributed to Ben Bradlee, the *Washington Post* editor during the Watergate affair. Examples include characterizing a statement as "ludicrous" or "absurd" without saying explicitly that it's untrue, or impugning the reliability of a source rather than the source's allegation. Modern politicians are required to always be "on-message" and ready with a standard denial or rebuttal if needed. Political parties now staff rebuttal units. Ian Hargreaves, a former editor of the *New Statesman*, recalls: "One day, just before dispatching the final pages to the printer, I took a telephone call from the Labour Party's Millbank headquarters, to be told by a well-educated young voice: 'I'm calling from the Millbank Rapid Rebuttal unit. Could you tell me what you are putting in the magazine this week, so that I can prepare a rebuttal?'"[19] News control has reached such levels now that it is common for political parties and governments to issue "prebuttals," getting their rebuttal in before the actual story itself appears.

Disguising bad news can be effected either by including the "toxic" story in a press release that includes a number of major positive stories or by delaying its release so that it can be "hidden" behind a more significant event. In Britain, the Labour government's press officer, Jo Moore, famously sent an email on September 11, 2001 following the destruction of the World Trade Center in New York saying it was a good day to get out any story that the government wanted buried. The criticism of this comment was such that she was forced to resign from her job.

In Britain, the best-known exponents of "spin" are Alastair Campbell, Tony Blair's press secretary between 1994 and 2003, and the publicist Max Clifford who makes a living by fire-fighting celebrities' reputations. Yet for many the word has now become a euphemism for propaganda and has led to wide public distrust of both politicians and journalists. Indeed, if we accept that journalists should serve the interests of their readers, listeners, and viewers then serving up the truth is the essential prerequisite. Truth begets trust and trust is the common currency that connects journalists to their publics.

FactFile
The Pseudo-Event

For most of us, news comprises, on the whole, "occurrences in the real world which take place independently of the media."[20] Pseudo-events on the other hand are those contrived to appeal to the media on the one hand and manipulate public opinion on the other. Deception is intrinsic although that deception is often an absence of relevant information rather than a deliberate peddling of false information. Reporter of the year and *Guardian* journalist Nick Davies in *Flat Earth News* offers a number of examples culled from paperwork that "fell into my hands."[21] "The high-profile rock show, which is really a vehicle to sell men's deodorant; the glossy fashion shoots which are contrived to promote a new car; the Christmas music CD which is themed to sell a brand of sweets."[22] Apart from the anodyne and wearisome nature of such "ideas" the real danger is that people are "sucked into activities and ideas without realizing that they have been created with the sole intention of satisfying some vested interest."[23]

At times the pseudo-event takes on such gargantuan proportions that it resembles the Brothers Grimm or Hans Christian Anderson at their best. In 1998, soap character Deirdre Rachid, played by Anne Kirkbride, a stalwart of Granada TV's *Coronation Street*, set in Weatherfield, a fictitious suburb of Manchester, and at the time the most popular soap on British television, was sent to jail for a fraud she had not committed. This "event" unleashed a major newspaper drive to have her freed. Viewers began a "Free the Weatherfield One" campaign and Granada TV's phone lines were deluged with callers offering their support. A *Daily Mirror* headline read: "Fury as Street's Deirdre is Jailed."[24] A *Sun* front page headlined with a touch of irony, "Blair [Prime Minister at the time] Orders Deirdre Probe." A later *Sun* story offered, "Don't Panic … Deirdre Gets Out in 3 Months." Most of the other national papers, including the broadsheets, ran stories of one sort or another. But these news stories were about a fictitious jailing for a fictitious crime committed by a fictitious person inhabiting a fictitious world. The storyline was in fact devised to boost *Coronation Street's* popularity in a vicious ratings war with the BBC's rival soap, *EastEnders*.

Habitual access is the inevitable result of the ability of large organizations to employ sufficient PR personnel who can "bombard" news media with a constant stream of "stories" about their organizations. Sociologist Herbert Gans researched newsgathering practices in major television and magazine newsrooms and concluded that successful sources were likely to be powerful, well resourced, and capable of supplying a steady stream of information of the kind and at the time a specific news medium required it.[25] As a result these "sources are both 'authoritative' and 'efficient' and they often enjoy 'habitual access' to the news media."[26] Once again the danger is that news media lose their independence once they come to rely on such source material on a regular basis and as Curran has pointed out, "In this way, much of what is perceived as "news" is little more than free advertising."[27]

Thus the more journalism relies on PR output for its stories the more susceptible journalists are to the blandishments of the PR machine. As Nick Davies suggests, "Most PR activity does not involve outright falsehood.... Much more often, however, PR will distort – a gentler, albeit almost equally destructive, art which involves the judicious selection of truths and issues, and the often very skilful manipulation of reporters to persuade them to focus only on those chosen angles."[28] In a world where not only commercial organizations and governments have PR machines but celebrities of whatever kind also employ agents to massage their public image, journalists may be forgiven for believing that PR is the enemy, constantly inserting itself between them and their potential story.

Yet Delorme and Fedler chronicled this as a newsroom phenomenon occurring as early as 1926: "On December 29 ... 147 of the stories in *The New York Times* had been suggested, created, or supplied by PR practitioners. Only 83 had not, with another 26 doubtful. Excluding the doubtful, about 60% of the stories *The Times* published that morning had originated with PR practitioners."[29] Mike Molloy, a former editor of Britain's *Daily Mirror* expresses similar sentiments today. He "claims that PR has taken over from journalism so that the original purpose of newspapers as the primary source of truth has been eliminated. 'We are in a world which is controlled, organised and manufactured by public relations.'"[30] According to this dictum, over the course of the twentieth century, PR has usurped public opinion as the mirror through which journalism is reflected.

An Unholy Alliance

The emergence of what is now described as public opinion was first identified as a phenomenon with the publication of the Letters of Junius in the *Public Advertiser*, a London daily paper, from 1769 to 1772.[31] These anonymous letters were considered to have been instrumental in both the fall of the Duke of Grafton's government and changes in the English libel laws.

The radical press of the early nineteenth century made public opinion its *raison d'être* and it is arguable that this same public opinion, masterfully orchestrated by the press of the day, contributed to the abolition of all government press controls by mid-century. With the rise of the commercial press and the primacy of advertising in the latter part of the century, commercial organizations were quick to realize the importance of influencing public opinion.

In America the dangers of advertising were identified as early as 1860 by Lambert Wilmer in *Our Press Gang*, the "first American book devoted entirely to press criticism."[32] Media historian Hazel Dicken-Garcia draws attention to Wilmer "charging the press with purveying fraudulent and questionable advertising, and with accepting what came to be called 'junkets' and 'freebees.'"[33] The twentieth century has seen the relentless march of this commercial influence. Indeed "newspapers ... adopted the system of selling too cheaply to profit from circulation" alone and this very cheapness made them a more desirable advertising medium.[34] In the UK, the *Daily Mail*, for example, only removed the classified ads and put news on the front page just before World War II and *The Times* of London held out until 1966.

Propaganda, like advertising, aims to influence its audience, but does so by less overt means. Alex Carey examined the role of corporate propaganda in his 1995 book of essays, *Taking the Risk out of Democracy*. He identified three developments of great political significance in the twentieth century: the rise of democracy, the expansion of corporate power, and the growth of corporate propaganda as a means of protecting corporate power against democracy.[35] And this growth of corporate propaganda has at its center the development of the PR company as a separate and independent entity.

Keeping the Wrong Company

Ivy Ledbetter Lee and Edward Louis Bernays are considered the founding fathers of modern public relations. However, the first press agency, the Publicity Bureau, was established in Boston in 1900 by George Michaelis. Soon afterwards in 1902, William Wolff Smith, a reporter for the *Baltimore Sun*, opened his public relations agency in Washington DC and the relationship between journalism and PR was thus established. Smith specialized in defending companies against the unwelcome attentions of muckrakers while himself still working as a freelance journalist. Both these early agencies folded in 1911 after a series of unsuccessful publicity campaigns. Around the same time Ivy Ledbetter Lee, a journalist and newspaper "stringer," joined forces with another former journalist, George Parker, who directed publicity for Grover Cleveland during his three presidential campaigns. They handled publicity for the National Democratic Committee and together founded America's third public relations firm, Parker and Lee, in late 1904. Edward Louis Bernays was a journalist and press agent who set up his PR office in New York in 1919. During his long life Bernays became the acceptable face of PR and *Life* magazine named him as one of the 100 most influential Americans of the twentieth century. In many respects the two faces of PR are exemplified by the attitudes and careers of Ivy Lee and Edward Bernays.

Résumé
Ivy Lee

Ivy Ledbetter Lee was born in Georgia in 1877. He graduated from Princeton and although his first foray into public relations, in partnership with George Parker, failed he went on to become one of the most influential men in the field. His supporters were almost messianic in their fervor. "Fraser Seitel wrote, 'Lee, more than anyone before him, lifted the field from a questionable pursuit (that is, seeking positive publicity at any cost) to a professional discipline designed to win public confidence and trust through communications based on candor and truth.'"[36]

His 1906 *Declaration of Principles* embodied his simple and direct ideas of honest dealing with the press and public alike. Two excerpts from the *Declaration* illustrate Lee's break with PR's somewhat murky past: firstly, "This is not an advertising agency. If you think any of our matter ought properly to go to your business office, do not use it." And secondly, "Our matter is accurate. Further details on any subject treated will be supplied promptly, and any editor will be assisted most carefully in verifying directly any statement of fact."[37]

During World War I, Lee's publicity efforts on behalf of the American Red Cross were universally applauded. "He helped raise $400 million in contributions, recruited millions of volunteers, and established the Red Cross in Americans' minds as the place to turn for disaster relief."[38] He was an inaugural member of the Council for Foreign Relations,

---

established in New York in 1921. However, in the 1930s he worked for the German I. G. Farben chemical conglomerate and this led to accusations that he was anti-Semitic and guilty of spreading propaganda for the Nazi government. Before his role could be properly determined by a Congressional hearing Lee died of a brain tumor in 1934.[39]

Lee's most famous client was John D. Rockefeller who hired him in 1914 to represent his family and Standard Oil after the bad publicity received in the wake of a coal miners' strike that caused 20 deaths at the company's mines in Ludlow, Colorado. Lee believed that PR had a responsibility to the public that was greater than its responsibility to a client and therefore an organization should always tell the truth because eventually the public would find out anyway. Historians credit Lee with the invention of crisis management communications. In 1906, for example, Lee issued what was in effect the first press release after an accident on the Pennsylvania Railroad. He convinced the company that it was preferable for them to divulge information to journalists rather than them hearing it from some other source.

Edward Bernays was the first practitioner to use the techniques of psychoanalysis, crowd psychology, and the power of the subconscious to affect what he called "the engineering of consent." He was a nephew of Sigmund Freud and believed the manipulation of public opinion was a legitimate goal of public relations. Many of his successful campaigns promoted the "lifestyle" associated with a product rather than the product itself, appealing to the aspirational in human nature. He was a proselytizer and taught the first course in public relations at New York University. In 1923 he produced his most significant book, *Crystallizing Public Relations*, which set out the ground rules for the nascent profession. For many, Bernays was the guiding spirit of PR, its most innovative thinker and ultimately its most influential practitioner.

Résumé
Edward Bernays

Edward Louis Bernays was born in Vienna in 1891. His mother was Sigmund Freud's sister Anna. He and his parents emigrated to America in 1892 and Bernays graduated from Cornell University in 1912 with a degree in agriculture. He chose journalism as a career, however, and became a press agent for theaters, concerts, and the ballet.

Bernays was instrumental in drumming up support for American participation in World War I, and after the war he set up as a public relations counselor in New York.

In 1928 he published *Propaganda,* his most important book, in which he argued, contrary to the position of his rival Ivy Lee, that the manipulation of public opinion was a necessary part of a fully functioning democracy. Particular Bernays techniques were the use of third-party authorities and the "tie in" marketing strategy. An example of the first technique was his promotion of bacon sales. He conducted a survey among doctors and reported the results – their recommendation that a hearty breakfast was good for you – to over 5,000 physicians with PR material saying that bacon and eggs was a hearty breakfast. The second technique involved marketing a product through cross-promotion. Thus a radio ad campaign would be linked to newspaper ads and perhaps an in-store promotion in the major outlets for the product. These campaigns could also be timed to culminate during a bank holiday weekend or another public holiday.

In his autobiography Bernays recounted how Josef Goebbels, the Nazi's propagandist in chief, used his book, *Crystallizing Public Opinion* (1923) as a model for his campaign to destroy Germany Jewry. Bernays was as shocked as Ivy Lee had been at suggestions that he could be implicated in Nazi atrocities. Toward the end of his long life he was described as the "father of public relations." Bernays died in 1995, aged 103.[40]

Omens and Portents

Despite the perceived ravages of the PR industry its primary objective was communication. Yet for many writers it was the loss of community that seemed to be the dominant theme post-World War II – from David Riesman's *The Lonely Crowd* (1950) and Richard Sennett's *The Fall of Public Man* (1977) to Christopher Lasch's *The Culture of Narcissism* (1978) and Robert Putnam's *Bowling Alone* (2000). Feelings of loss engendered by such writers have, in turn, sent others on a quest to rediscover community or at least to discuss the conditions under which it could re-emerge. The positivist sociologist Emile Durkheim (1858–1917), who saw in modern individualism the seeds of a more democratic posttraditional community, is probably the most famous. He coined the term "social facts" to describe phenomena that exist as entities independent of the actions of individuals. The internet as a social fact, unlike previous journalistic platforms, has no target community as a primary audience or as a result of its function – rather, it creates communities and what some have called "community fluidity."

FactFile
Neoliberalism's Threat to Community

The High Victorian period before PR had been invented may, in retrospect, be seen as a high watermark of pluralism, both in the press and to some extent in politics. The twentieth century was a litany of retrenchment. The large-scale popular movements of the 1960s – feminism, nuclear disarmament, green politics, environmentalism, industrial solidarity, and other democratizing trends were followed by the neoliberal agenda of the last quarter of the century that undermined this democratic progress. Neoliberalism "questioned the prevailing modes of state regulation. It quickly captured the high ground of public debate by using terms like state censorship, individual choice, deregulation and market competition to criticize the prevailing mix of public and private communication systems."[41] Rupert Murdoch, when he delivered the MacTaggart Lecture at the Edinburgh International Television Festival in 1989, styled this as "freedom and choice, rather than regulation and scarcity."

Apart from elevating the individual at the expense of grassroots collective organizations, this process has also involved the transfer of decision-making power to unaccountable multinational corporations, in the name of "freedom and choice." Reducing the role of government has meant restricted access to decision-making processes for ordinary people – that is, less democracy. Little wonder the spread of formal democracy in areas of the world like Latin America has seemed somewhat hollow, accompanied by feelings of powerlessness – an increasing phenomenon also in the United States.[42]

In the process it is challenging journalism's traditional top-down hierarchy and the professional, normalized values that have been intrinsic to long-established work routines. The web is nonhierarchical, fragmented, and decentered, yet participatory and interactive. So far its democratic potential has been limited by the fact of the "digital divide" between the technological haves and have-nots. Making a phone call is still an aspiration to a majority of the world's population and barely 2 percent have any access to the internet.

Despite this, there is no doubt that the political potential of the electronic world is being understood by more and more politicians, if not their electorates.

Computer-facilitated media platforms such as blogging, podcasts, and streaming news sites have made the whole relationship between those in power and those who report on them more porous (as we shall see in later chapters). The rise of blogging, for instance, as a form of self-publishing, and the availability of cheap digital cameras, are often seen as two-edged swords. Politicians can communicate with their constituents unmediated by any journalistic sensibilities but at the same time are more vulnerable to being found out when they commit errors. One observer, identifying the scandal in 2006 over deputy prime minister John Prescott's sex life as the first big British political story driven by bloggers, suggested that it could be seen either as beneficial to democracy or as "a reckless deskilling of journalism, where rumours are published and reputations besmirched without any supporting evidence."[43] In mitigation, one can point to the sheer ubiquity of the blogosphere and its inbuilt self-correcting mechanism whereby every view has its opposite and every error its reproof.

The combined effect of bloggers, 24-hours news, and online news distribution channels has generally meant a speedier response in holding politicians to account particularly during times of war with its related iniquities. Warblogs, as they are sometimes called, first appeared during the US invasion of Afghanistan in 2001. During the 2003 invasion of Iraq, the pseudonymous "Salam Pax," also known as the Baghdad Blogger, became a celebrity through his "Where is Raed?" blog. He reported on life in Baghdad during the invasion, his friends, the disappearance of people under Saddam Hussein's regime, and his work as a translator. Much of his reporting was a corrective to the standard political line pursued by British and US governments. The significance of blogs has filtered through to the mainstream, although with mixed results. As Paul Bradshaw noted of a recent British ITV effort, "For years journalists accused blogs of being indulgent navel-gazing ego-trips. The ITV News video blog from Afghanistan doesn't do anything to challenge that myth, with little insight, reflection or indeed seriousness. The feeling … is of a lads' jolly."[44]

In the political arena, especially during elections, the use of a candidate's blog, combined with greater profile or "portrait" coverage which concentrates more on the candidate's experiences and feelings than analysis of his or her political program has been referred to in a French context as a shift from information journalism to communication journalism.[45] This trend is certainly reflected in the modern obsession with celebrity culture and the way it constantly challenges boundaries between the public and private spheres. Definitions of what should rightly be in the public domain are formed according to sentiment, taste, and levels of acceptable voyeurism and although the use of public relations to manage and filter such information is not new, the rise of a celebrity culture has endowed it with much greater power and influence.

However, there are key aspects of the internet that weaken traditional ideas of community and citizenship – especially when considering the deliberative ideal. Law scholar Cass Sunstein has pointed out that there are two preconditions for a successful deliberative democracy that are threatened by the internet and the present multiplatform media. Firstly, the concept of deliberative democracy implies that people need to be confronted with ideas and information that they do not agree with or would otherwise choose to avoid. This has always been an important function of the press. A newspaper relies for much of its appeal on serendipity. Thus an article on a seemingly unpopular subject may be positioned next to another more appealing story. There is a chance that readers will look at the "unpopular" story, even if they had not planned to do so. In contrast, electronic usage filters out and personalizes content. Its readers are effectively eliminating the opportunity to engage with "surprise" issues.

Secondly, people need a range of common experiences in order to arrive at an understanding of particular issues. Yet now people as individuals and as groups are becoming polarized within their own narrow realm of knowledge.[46] This contention is supported by various empirical studies,[47] including a 2007 report from Britain's media regulator Ofcom. It voiced concern that the growth of blogging and self-posted video was leading to a narrowing of personal news agendas, with users focusing on single issues of individual and specific interest.

C. P. Scott, veteran editor of Britain's *Manchester Guardian* from 1872 to 1929 once stated: "The function of a good newspaper and therefore of a good journalist is to see life steady and see it whole."[48] This was a plea for a panoramic perspective, the ability to place events within their broader context and to keep them in proportion. To "see it whole" involves an appreciation of connections, causes, and consequences. The internet does not always provide this. In fact Sunstein contends that it has produced group polarization and that this is likely to get worse in the future.[49] Within the public sphere, the internet has enabled people across the globe to communicate, and the anticapitalist campaign, for example, has used this to its advantage. But there is also a danger of the fragmentation of political discourse leading to that very sense of disenfranchisement the internet was supposed to inhibit.

These twin themes of differentiation and personalization have been a feature of news since the nineteenth century, but now the process is referred to as "hyperdifferentiation." According to media historian David Mindich, people who see themselves as individuals within the polity tend to feel powerless, whereas "those who are part of a wider community (our voice/ our vote) tend to see the need for politics and news."[50] He quotes a survey that examined the extent to which news stories use collective words such as crowd, country, humanity, army, as opposed to "self-reference" words such as me, myself, I, mine. Use of the latter has soared over the last 20 years while use of collective words has plummeted. Inherent in this shift of word usage is the potential for a decline in the deliberative aspects of democracies. "The model of deliberative democracy is therefore ultimately replaced by a consumer democracy in which the tendency for fragmentation and atomisa-tion has a real impact on political debate."[51] It is likely that increasing person-alization will have a detrimental effect on democratic processes and people's way of thinking. According to Sunstein, "A market dominated by countless versions of 'Daily Me' would make self-government less workable (and) create a high degree of social fragmentation."[52] Thus news runs the risk of becoming even more personalized, dramatized, polarized, and simplified.

The two preconditions for an efficient democracy are thus potentially threatened by the internet – firstly, that people should be exposed to information that they have not preselected themselves, so that the validity of issues and a range of opinions are both available and, secondly, that people should have a range of common experiences in order to understand specific issues and their implications.

Good Fences Make Good Neighbors

Crusaders still exist, and are still needed to expose wrongdoing, or what Pulitzer referred to as crimes, tricks, and swindles. In carrying out this mission, opinions need to be backed up with empirical evidence. This does not necessarily mean objectivity, but it implies well-researched journalism with an altruistic social motivation and a sense of social responsibility. "Even in the hands of the yellow press mavens at the turn of the century or the tabloid sheets of the 1920s, building community and promoting democracy remained a core value ... Pulitzer used his front page to lure his readers but his editorial pages to teach them how to be American citizens."[53] The best journalists have always understood that their profession needs to be guarded by the collective will rather than run by profit-orientated elites.

This public journalism model involves a range of changes in attitude and approach that goes beyond just listening to the public to also include "giving the public more latitude to set the media's agenda, and redefining news in a manner that focuses less on conflict and negative news and more on building civic capital, reporting ambivalence, and educating the public about the tools of democratic decision making."[54]

So what are the implications of returning journalism to this communitarian sense of democracy, so that like democracy, it becomes journalism by, for, and of the people? Such ideas are being explored by the public journalism movement in the United States which acknowledges the existence of wider cultural influences as, for example, in the Asian sense of community with its values of harmony, respect for authority, social consensus, and stability. These influences suggest that it is not possible to have a community of individualists: thus their message is that "communication forms community."[55] In essence, the media is grounded in the public – as history suggests – and therefore needs to serve the public's right to know. For this to work, people need to become more closely involved with journalism.

The question that naturally follows such arguments is whether new media empower or compromise journalism in its self-declared mission to maintain an informed public. For as political philosopher John Keane has noted, "While it is today generally acknowledged that the accelerating growth of global media linkages has profound implications for journalism, it is much less certain that the whole process has an elective affinity with democratic institutions and ways of life."[56] To forge a public journalism for the twenty-first century, therefore, and particularly one that connects with the institutions it purports to serve, there has to be a public conversation of some sort or another – but how should that conversation be conducted? The formidable nature of the challenge ahead for public journalism can only be appreciated by a greater understanding of how journalism and democracy relate to commercial power, and how that relationship has developed over time.

Notes

1 The Annenberg Foundation Trust at Sunnylands. Available online at http://www.sunnylandstrust.org/programs/programs_show.htm?doc_id=435902, accessed on July 28, 2009.

2   Nick Davies, *Flat Earth News* (London: Chatto & Windus, 2008), p. 86.
3   Justin Lewis, Andrew Williams, Bob Franklin, James Thomas, and Nick Mosdell, *The Quality and Independence of British Journalism: Tracking the Changes Over 20 Years* (Cardiff School of Journalism, Media and Cultural Studies, 2007). Available online at http://www.mediawise.org.uk/files/uploaded/Quality%20&%20Independence%20of%20British%20Journalism.pdf, accessed on September 3, 2010
4   Davies, *Flat Earth News.*
5   Quoted in Robert W. McChesney and John Nichols, *Our Media, Not Theirs: The Democratic Struggle Against Corporate Media* (New York: Seven Stories Press, 2002), p. 18.
6   John Lloyd, *What the Media are Doing to our Politics* (London: Constable, 2004).
7   David Wilby, *Iraq, Gilligan and Hutton 2003* (BBC 2006). Available online at http://www.bbc.co.uk/historyofthebbc/resources/bbcandgov/pdf/hutton.pdf, accessed on August 13, 2010.
8   Denise DeLorme and Fred Fedler, "Journalists' Hostility Towards Public Relations: An Historical Analysis," *Public Relations Review*, 29 (Nicholson School of Communication, University of Central Florida, Orlando: Elsevier Science, 2003), pp. 99–124 (p. 99). Available online at www.sciencedirect.com, accessed on September 11, 2008.
9   *Chartered Institute of Public Relations.* Available online at http://ipr.org.uk/, accessed on April 12, 2009.
10 Ibid.
11 *Public Relations Society of America.* Available online at http://www.prsa.org/, accessed on April 12, 2009.
12 Tom Baistow, *Fourth Rate Estate: An Anatomy of Fleet Street* (London: Comedia, 1985), p. 68.
13 Jamie Doward, "Cigarette Giant to Deny Cancer Link," *Observer*, October 5, 2003, *News* section, p. 4.
14 DeLorme and Fedler, "Journalists' Hostility Towards Public Relations," p. 109.
15 Cited in Gary Martin, "The Phrase Finder: Spin Doctor." Available online at http://www. phrases.org.uk/meanings/spin-doctor.html, 1996–2009, accessed on July 30, 2009.
16 Ibid.
17 Richard Cockett, *Twilight of Truth: Chamberlain, Appeasement and the Manipulation of the Press* (London: Weidenfeld and Nicolson, 1989), p. 15.
18 *Key Issues in the 1992 Campaign.* Available online at http://www.bbc.co.uk/politics97/background/pastelec/92keyiss.shtml, accessed on August 13, 2010.
19 Ian Hargreaves, *Journalism: Truth or Dare* (Oxford University Press, 2003), p. 195.
20 James Curran and Jean Seaton, *Power Without Responsibility: The Press and Broadcasting in Britain*, 5th edn (London: Routledge, 1997), p. 277.
21 Davies, *Flat Earth News*, p. 181.

22 Ibid., p. 182.
23 Ibid.
24 Steve Atkinson, "Fury as Street's Deirdre is Jailed," *Daily Mirror*, March 30, 1998.
25 Herbert J. Gans, *Deciding What's News: A Study of CBS Evening News, NBC Nightly News, Newsweek, and Time* (Evanston, IL: Northwestern University Press, 2004).
26 Denis McQuail, *Mass Communication Theory: An Introduction*, 3rd edn (London: Sage, 1994), p. 225.
27 Curran and Seaton, *Power Without Responsibility*, p. 278.
28 Davies, *Flat Earth News*, p. 159.
29 Delorme and Fedler, "Journalists' Hostility Towards Public Relations," p. 111.
30 Richard Keeble, *Ethics for Journalists* (London: Routledge, 2001), p. 34.
31 The Times, *The History of* The Times, vol. I, *"The Thunderer" in the Making* (London: Times Publishing Company, 1921), p. 21.
32 Hazel Dicken-Garcia, *Journalistic Standards in Nineteenth-Century America* (Madison: University of Wisconsin Press, 1989), p. 166.
33 Ibid., p. 169.
34 Ibid., p. 188.
35 Alex Carey, *Taking The Risk Out of Democracy: Propaganda in the US and Australia* (Sydney: University of New South Wales Press, 1995).
36 Michael Turney, "Ivy Lee Was Decades Ahead of his Colleagues," 2000, Available online at http://www.nku.edu/~turney/prclass/readings/3eras2x.html, accessed on July 26, 2009.
37 Ibid.
38 Ibid.
39 Ibid.
40 Edward Bernays Timeline. Available online at http://www.google.co.uk/searc?q=edward+bernays&hl=en&tbs=tl:1&tbo=u&ei=guJtSpmLNKWEjAe25e2aCw&sa=X&oi=timeline_result&ct=title&resnum=14, accessed on July 27, 2009.
41 John Keane, "Journalism and Democracy Across Borders," in Geneva Overholser and Kathleen Hall Jamieson (eds.), *The Institutions of American Democracy: The Press* (Oxford University Press, 2005), pp. 92–114 (p. 92).
42 McChesney and Nichols, *Our Media, Not Theirs*, p. 22.
43 Patrick Barkham, "How the Net Closed On Prescott," *Guardian*, July 10, 2006.
44 Paul Bradshaw, "War Reporting: Two Online Reports – Spot the Difference," *OJB – Online Journalism Blog*, March 19, 2008. Available online at http://onlinejournalismblog.com/2008/03/19/war-reporting-two-online-reports-spot-the-difference/, accessed on February 7, 2009.
45 C. Brin, J. Charron, and J. de Bonville, *Nature et transformations du journalisme* (Quebec: Les Presses de l'université de Laval, 2004).

46   Cass R. Sunstein, *Designing Democracy: What Constitutions Do* (Oxford: Oxford University Press, 2001).

47   Andrew Kohut, *The Diminishing Divide: Religion's Changing Role in American Politics* (Washington, DC: Brookings Institution Press, 2000). Also see Kevin A. Hill and John E. Hughes, *Cyberpolitics: Citizen Activism in the Age of the Internet (People, Passions, and Power)* (Lanham, MD: Rowman & Littlefield 1998).

48   Mark Hampton, "The Press, Patriotism and Public Discussion: C. P. Scott, the *Manchester Guardian* and the Boer War, 1899–1902," *The Historical Journal*, 44, 1, 2001, 177–97 (p. 177).

49   Sunstein, *Designing Democracy*, p. 65.

50   David Mindich, *Tuned Out: Why Americans Under 40 Don't Follow the News* (New York: Oxford University Press, 2005), p. 99.

51   Martin Conboy and John Steel, "The Future of Newspapers – Historical Perspectives," unpublished paper presented at *Future of Newspapers* conference: Cardiff, September 7–9, 2007.

52   Sunstein, *Designing Democracy*, p. 192.

53   Bill Kovach and Tom Rosenstiel, *The Elements of Journalism* (London: Guardian Atlantic Books, 2001), p. 23.

54   John C. Merrill, Peter J. Gade, and Frederick R. Blevens, *Twilight of Press Freedom: The Rise of People's Journalism* (Mahwah, NJ: Lawrence Erlbaum Associates, 2001), p. 148.

55   Ibid., p. 196.

56   Keane, "Journalism and Democracy Across Borders," p. 113.

Part II

Technology, Work, and Business: Is Journalism More Than Just a Job?

Any sufficiently advanced technology is indistinguishable from magic.
(Arthur C. Clarke)

5

Changing Roles in a Changing World

The Battle of Waterloo took place on Sunday June 18, 1815. Waterloo is close to the Belgian capital Brussels which is 198 miles from London as the crow flies. Eurostar trains do the journey in less than two hours. News of the Duke of Wellington's victory, however, didn't reach London until the following Wednesday – "three mortal days of expectation and suspense!"[1]

Nearly two centuries later, images of the suicide attacks on the World Trade Center in New York on September 11, 2001 were beamed around the world while the attacks were still in progress. New York is 3,471 miles from London. On "Waterloo time" it would have taken 52 days for the news to arrive. Similarly, the London terrorist attacks of July 7, 2005 were recorded by commuters on their mobile phone cameras and sent to the BBC and independent TV newsrooms almost before the attacks were over. These new satellite and mobile phone technologies now ensure that we can be instantly transported to any part of the world where news, as determined by global media organizations, is to be found. Rolling news programs and 24-hour news channels make sure that this news is communicated in real time all the time.

In a modern media environment, therefore, it is almost impossible for journalists not to be aware of the impact of technology on their ways of working and on the different media platforms that publish their work. But it is less easy to determine the extent to which technology, as coercive force, can be disaggregated from the other significant developments that have stimulated print and broadcast media over the past three centuries. Journalism's response to the electronic era, whether it be the rise of broadcasting in the 1920s and 1930s or the "cold type revolution" of the late twentieth century that ushered in the digital age, is both fascinating and instructive. But equally important

Jane Chapman and Nick Nuttall, *Journalism Today: A Themed History*
© 2011 Jane Chapman and Nick Nuttall. Published by Blackwell Publishing Ltd.

to this study is journalism's response to changing patterns of production and consumption – technological, commercial, social, and cultural – that have produced modern market economies and the journalistic hinterland inhabited by the modern media practitioner.

The journalist's clay, if you like, has always been news. As a product it has remained fairly constant – a look at newspapers from almost any era will confirm this – but the journalist is always inventing new ways to mold and manipulate it. The production of news was at first a response to what a small and clearly identified readership wanted. The bewigged businessmen who congregated at Lloyd's coffee shop in eighteenth-century London were interested in financial and shipping news. In the early decades of the nineteenth century, radicals and agitators for social reform fought for press freedom (albeit in a very limited sense) and developed a vibrant radical press to propound their views. In Britain, the mid-nineteenth-century reader was brought up on a diet of sensational crime and human interest stories in a Sunday press that became the blueprint for later commercial success. In any "study of nineteenth-century Britain," noted the press historian, Alan Lee, "there can be little dispute that the context of the whole issue of the press was that of a developing capitalist system, in which, somehow, the press, both as an industry and as an institution had to find accommodation."[2] The American writer Walter J. Fox Jr. felt that this accommodation was not always positive however. "The new popular culture of America," he wrote of the last decades of the nineteenth century, "would be an urban culture, and it would be imposed from above by the new mass-circulation daily newspapers on a populace that had lost touch with its own traditions."[3]

Losing touch with tradition was also the cry of opponents of the New Journalism that swept Britain and America during the same period. As noted in Part I, Alfred Harmsworth (Lord Northcliffe) in Britain and the Yellow journalists William Randolph Hearst and Joseph Pulitzer in America pursued a kind of journalism which favored the "tidbit" of information and the human interest story over the traditional daily fare of political and business reporting. They were harbingers of the burgeoning twentieth-century commercial press and the primacy of the press barons.

In Britain, the country that had led the world with industrialization and urbanization, these new mass-circulation newspapers began to reap the benefits of increased literacy, leisure time, and discretionary income. The Education Act, introducing some state provision in 1870, helped to create this new reading public, variously disparaged as "office boys" by the Prime Minister, Lord Salisbury,[4] and "featherbrained" by poet and critic Matthew

Arnold.[5] "The relationship between paper and reader," according to Alan Lee, "was thus being changed from the ideal one of a tutorial and intellectual nature to one of a market character."[6]

It was during this period, too, that the United States transformed itself into a primarily urban society,[7] and this too was the era when newspapers paved the way for what philosopher and media analyst Douglas Kellner has described as "one of the main trends of contemporary capitalist societies ... the synthesis of advertising, culture, information, politics, and manipulation."[8] This synthesis, essentially commercial and corporatist in nature, led to the creation of news as a product designed to sell newspapers. As noted by Roger Fowler in his examination of news language: "News is not a natural phenomenon emerging straight from 'reality', but a *product*. It is produced by an industry [and] shaped by the bureaucratic and economic structure of that industry."[9] Furthermore, as that structure has become more and more commercial in tone, news has also come to reflect "the financial requirements of the newspaper organization, the vision of its producers, and the day-to-day exigencies of production."[10]

FactFile
The Cold Type Revolution

Fleet Street, as the British press is colloquially known, had for many years been dogged by poor industrial relations. The print unions had a stranglehold on proprietors through so-called "Spanish practices" which, among other things, limited working hours, determined (over) staffing levels, and brought workers out on strike at regular intervals. Journalist Tom Baistow described this as "unsophisticated management that is the prisoner of Lewis Carroll industrial custom and usage, and top-heavy overheads that are the unions' blackmail price of uninterrupted production".[11] By 1986 employers, and particularly Rupert Murdoch of News International, were seeking union approval to new terms which included flexible working, the adoption of new technology, a no-strike clause, and an end to the closed shop.

The print union's response was to call a strike. Murdoch served dismissal notices on all the strikers, effectively sacking over 6,000 employees, and instigated the plan he and his executives had formulated for just such an eventuality. Murdoch had purchased a site at Wapping, part of the old east London docks, and equipped it with the latest computer technology for what everyone believed was to be a new newspaper, the *London Post*. Immediately after the sackings he replaced his workforce with members of the rival Electrical, Electronic, Telecommunications and Plumbing Union (EETPU). They started working at Wapping on his four main titles, the *News of the World*, the *Sun*, *The Times*, and the *Sunday Times*. The print unions began picketing the site and so began the "Wapping dispute."

The government of Margaret Thatcher supported Murdoch's stand and after 13 months, on February 5, 1987, the strike collapsed. Not a single day of production was lost on any of Murdoch's papers. By 1988 most other national newspapers had relocated to Docklands, and had also followed News International in modernizing their printing practices. These practices included offset litho printing rather than the old mammoth rotary presses, input of news stories electronically by journalists themselves using computers rather than the huge lino-type machines of old, and the gradual introduction of color printing. Whereas the old methods used "hot" molten lead to produce the lines of type, the new system sent type from the computer terminal to the phototypesetting machine and was indeed "cold" in comparison. The restrictive practices of the old print unions disappeared with the unions themselves and thus paved the way for the wholesale adoption of digital technology as we know it today.

The demands of this new commercial "tone" infiltrated not just news agendas but also the very DNA of the press itself. It was instrumental in co-opting journalism not to narrow party politics but to the politics of capitalism. Consider for a moment the following: in the Crimean War, fought between Britain and Russia between 1853 and 1856, William Howard Russell, *The Times*'s war correspondent, was able to communicate the horrors of the war and the lack of medical treatment for British soldiers, using the "electric telegraph" for the first time. His reports to a shocked nation effectively brought down the government of the Earl of Aberdeen. A little under a century later, in the run up to World War II, Lord Beaverbrook, owner of the *Daily Express*, was made Minister of Aircraft Production in Churchill's 1940 coalition government. Such an example clearly highlights the power and influence of the press over time, but in diametrically opposite ways.

Traditionally newspaper proprietors were men of the press first and businessmen second. Yet by the middle of the twentieth century the reverse was becoming the norm. Newspapers as businesses had become part of the modern capitalist system and "capitalism is the engine that pulls a long train of ideological coaches, all filled with cultural cargo compatible with financial profit. One of these coaches is the press, a big business enterprise that confines journalism and determines its total configuration."[12] In the 1920s and 1930s, for example, newspapers used a variety of promotional gimmicks to gain readers, from insurance schemes to gifts of pens, tea sets, clothes, kitchen equipment, and even bound sets of Charles Dickens novels, in fact anything that would entice people to take out a subscription. Door-to-door canvassers – often ex-servicemen – were taken on in their thousands to increase sales, and these gimmicks were costing papers upwards of £50,000 a week. These activities had nothing to do with the business of news and everything to do with the need to increase circulations in order to maximize advertising revenue. The audience was now of interest purely in proportion to its numbers.

Yet advertising was a two-edged sword. It might be a wealth creator for the owners of the press but at the same time it acted as a content controller on editors and reporters. "Advertising not only subsidises a paper's cover price," wrote Tom Baistow, "but determines how many pages it will print on a given day: the size of the issue is not decided normally on the amount of news coming in but on the amount of advertising that has been booked."[13] Inevitably news, commercialized as a commodity, followed advertising in becoming primarily valued for its "profitability." By 1880 for example, advertising provided one half of US newspaper revenue. This rose to two-thirds by 1910 and now accounts for two-thirds of the content and 75–85 percent of the income of the average newspaper both in the US and many European countries.[14] And advertising as much as editorial content has taken advantage of and adapted to new technologies. From the classified to the display ad to the television ad break, its ability to generate income has seldom faltered. But now, new technology is seen by many as the enemy – undermining the traditional operating practices of the newsroom and at the same time destabilizing its major income stream through advertising migration to a growing variety of online platforms. Indeed, it is arguable that the press "coach" alluded to earlier is now being derailed by this inexorable advance of modern technology.

The fall in advertising revenues began in the 1960s. In Britain, for example, between 1960 and 1975 the proportion of the popular dailies' revenue derived from advertising dropped from 45 percent to just over 27 percent. More recently this revenue fall has accelerated to the point where many newspapers are questioning their ability to continue. At the same time there has been a consistent fall in newspaper circulations from their high point after World War II. Increased costs of production reflected in higher cover prices and the popularity of television have both been blamed for this fall.

The *News of the World*, for example, was the biggest selling paper in the world in the early 1950s, with a circulation of 8.5m on a Sunday.[15] Today, in comparison, it sells barely 3.5m according to the Audit Bureau of Circulations, and that in a country with a 50 percent increase in population over the same 50-year period. In the US, newspaper sales have held up rather better but overall decline is evident from the 1970s onwards.[16]

Résumé
Lord Beaverbrook

William Maxwell Aitken was born in 1879 in Maple, Ontario, Canada. He was a successful businessman but became caught up in a share-dealing scandal and left Canada for England in 1910. Within the year he was elected MP for Ashton-under-Lyne. In 1917 he bought a controlling interest in the failing *Daily Express* for £17,500, a bargain even then. He proceeded to turn the paper by the early 1950s into the largest selling daily in the world with a circulation of almost four million.

He deployed money and demonic energy in wooing society and politicians and was rewarded with a peerage in 1917 as the 1st Baron Beaverbrook, a name taken from a small village near his boyhood home in Canada. In later life he became a benefactor of many causes, particularly the University of New Brunswick. He died at his home, Cherkley Court in Surrey, in 1964.

If the late nineteenth and early twentieth centuries were the era of commercialization of the press then the late twentieth century can be described as the age of fragmentation. As the range of news outlets multiplied, first with radio and TV, then with cable and satellite, and finally with the digital technology that enabled the world wide web and the internet, so print has lost its monopoly as the only news and advertising medium. Journalists are now using it to report on "new" inventions and technology and thus reflect on their own print medium's growing marginalization. At the same time journalism has responded by ushering in the age of multiskilling and multiplatform working.

How have these multiplying modes of communication influenced what journalists produce? How do these more recent developments compare with the impact of earlier changes in business organization and technology? As media critic James Carey noted with some prescience: "the latest [development] in technology is always the occasion of metaphysical voyages outward in space but backward in time: a journey of restoration as much as of progress."[17] If we accept that technology and commercialism are connected by more than serendipity, and if we also accept as legacy that "the press in the nineteenth century was the most important single medium of the communication of ideas,"[18] then it is clearly necessary to examine how it responded to the myriad changing patterns alluded to here from a standpoint that uses "communication of ideas" as its guiding principle.

Changing Patterns – Funding and Ownership

The commercial expansion of newspapers relied on the development of a financial model that enabled owners to expand without having to answer to a "paymaster." At the beginning of the nineteenth century, there were many small-circulation local and national papers that concentrated solely on politics and business, often owned by individuals or funded by political parties. During the 1830s and 1840s, British newspapers were already demonstrating their profitability. A well-run regional paper selling 1,000 copies a day could make its owner between £1,500 and £3,000 a year (approx. £1.2m and £2.4m today). The *Manchester Guardian*, probably the most prominent regional daily of the time, made nearly £7,000 a year.[19] During this period there was often no formal distinction between ownership, management, editing, and reporting. Indeed the majority of owners were also active editors. Although the role of technology in newspaper development has since become pivotal, in these earlier days a content-led communications revolution could be achieved without any new production breakthroughs.

Yet the beginning of the nineteenth century also saw one of the first technological advances that did in fact require substantial capital. This was the invention of the steam press by Friedrich Koenig. *The Times* of London was the first newspaper to buy and operate a Koenig steam press and in a move which eerily anticipated Rupert Murdoch's behavior at Wapping, John Walter II, *The Times*'s owner, arranged for the parts of the press to be moved from Koenig's premises to Printing House Square "in complete secrecy for fear of an anti-machinery combination within Printing House Square with consequent destruction of the press. There occurred, in fact, a demonstration of compositors, who saw their labour at less demand as a result of the abolition of the hitherto necessary practice of composing duplicate pages."[20]

The newspaper bought two presses in 1814 for a total of £2,800. Each press could print 1,100 sheets per hour,[21] which was a significant advance on mechanical presses like the Stanhope which could print only 250 sheets.[22] Such innovations also pointed to the growing complexity of a substantial newspaper like *The Times*, and John Walter II, in perhaps his most significant innovation, was also the first newspaper proprietor, in 1817, to divest himself of the day-to-day running of his newspaper and entrust it to a separate editor, Thomas Barnes. It was an innovation that tacitly acknowledged that specialist skills were needed to run a newspaper. By the end of the century the editor himself was just one of a plethora of specialists – from news and features editors and subeditors to designers, advertising space salesmen, and graphic artists who reveled in the skills and "romance" of producing a daily or weekly paper.

By 1914, the British journalist William Maxwell described the difference between old and new journalism by comparing the approach of press baron Lord Northcliffe with that of his predecessors:

> The old fashioned newspaper proprietor gave little thought to methods of increasing circulation beyond the intrinsic merits of his journal. He was content to print his paper and let the public take it or leave it. If there was any special organisation for "pushing the sale", nobody suspected it. To-day an army of energetic and ingenious men is busy inventing new means of improving circulation, outwitting and outbidding rivals, securing the support of newsvendors, and attracting the notice of the public and the advertiser.[23]

The shift in emphasis described by Maxwell – from strategic considerations that were content-led to a marketing-led approach – was underscored by the steady increase in the capital needed to start a newspaper. This factor has continued to influence business considerations to the present day with the advent of computers and digital technology. In 1894 Charles Dana, editor of the *New York Sun*, had resisted buying a linotype machine and wished that newspapers did not need advertising but still estimated that a daily paper would need $1m in start-up capital. Costs were relatively higher in Britain than elsewhere during the nineteenth century because of early industrialization, the price of imported newsprint – Lord Northcliffe's Associated Press in 1904 bought huge tracts of land in Newfoundland to reduce paper-making costs[24] – and also because of the dominance of a national press. A London-based paper such as Charles Dickens's *Daily News* cost approximately £27,000 a year to run in 1846, but by the 1870s a London daily cost roughly £270,000 a year to run.[25] The *Daily Mail* demanded £15,000 in start-up costs alone in 1896.[26] In other parts of continental Europe a decentralized press kept entry costs lower, but by the end of the century they were equally high on both sides of the Atlantic.

Résumé
Charles Dana

Charles Anderson Dana was born in Hinsdale, New Hampshire in 1819. He studied briefly at Harvard and in 1846 joined the *Boston Weekly Chronotype*. A year later he joined the *New York Tribune* at the invitation of editor Horace Greeley.

In 1868 Dana became editor of the New York *Sun* and announced in his first editorial that the newspaper would produce "a daily photograph of the whole world's doings in the most luminous and lively manner." Dana's style prefigured modern journalism in being simple, straightforward, and bold. This formula was a success and by 1876 circulation had tripled to 130,000. He died in 1897.

Before advertising became so prevalent, partisan funding from political parties and other organizations provided some security for newspapers, but by the end of the nineteenth century most of these sorts of papers in the US, Britain, and Europe were either threatened or had disappeared. They were replaced by "popular" newspapers with comic strips, fiction, human interest features, and puzzles, but often also "screaming headlines, lurid stories of illicit love, suicide, and graft".[27] This new presentational face demanded huge capital investment for high speed presses, linotype machines, and an organizational structure that prompted Lincoln Steffens to write in 1897 that "The magnitude of the financial operations of the newspaper is turning journalism upside down."[28] As an example, before the launch of the *Independent* newspaper in Britain in 1986, no new quality national newspaper had appeared for 113 years. The costs of starting and sustaining such a newspaper were estimated at more than £20m.[29]

Yet during the twentieth century net investment costs for a newspaper came down as a result of the income from advertising, which was necessary for financial stability. Within this climate, editors were obliged to continue a trend which had first surfaced during the nineteenth century: their papers needed to appeal to as wide an audience as possible in order to retain valuable advertising. Alfred Harmsworth and his brother Harold, Lord Rothermere, understood this. Harold introduced net sales certified by chartered accountants. "Real net sales, achieved after the newsagents' returns had been deducted from copies distributed, were a badge of achievement and influence. They made possible a rate card for advertisers which told them reliably how many readers they would reach for a given expenditure."[30] The Audit Bureau of Circulations (ABC) is its modern incarnation. This innovation by the Harmsworths essentially changed the relationship between newspaper and advertiser and "as political patronage waned and advertising grew, advertisers who patronized the newspaper came to expect advocacy on their behalf. They frequently demanded that newspapers be loyal supports of their business ventures. In short, another illustration of how advertisers propelled the commercialization of news."[31]

A trenchant example of advertising's potential for control was the 1984 clash between Donald Trelford, the editor of the British Sunday newspaper, the *Observer*, and the paper's owner, Lonrho, a multinational conglomerate chaired by "Tiny" Rowland. Trelford published a story about army atrocities in Zimbabwe, where Lonrho earned large profits. Rowland rebuked Trelford and cabled an apology to Robert Mugabe, the Zimbabwean president. When Trelford "rejected the claim of inaccuracy Rowland threatened to withdraw all Lonrho's advertising from the *Observer*."[32] On this occasion Trelford won the day but it is pertinent that Rowland believed the way to "wound" his own paper was to use the advertising threat.

Another aspect of the commercial imperatives driving newspaper expansion was the fundamental change in business form that still carries implications for all media corporations – namely opening ownership to shareholders. "The impact of trading newspaper securities on the stock market has meant that news companies must constantly expand in size and rate of profit in order to maintain their position on stock exchanges."[33] Inevitably this was accompanied by mergers and the further development of chains. In 1894, according to William Maxwell, "the stock exchange list contained not a single newspaper corporation, whereas now [1914] twelve large companies figure in the quotations, and the Stock Exchange annuals mention twenty-six newspaper limited liability companies, all of which, except one, have been registered during the last twenty years."[34] By 1910, 67 percent of the London Metropolitan daily press and 83 percent of the evening press was controlled by three companies; 81 percent of the Sunday press was controlled by just four companies.[35] By 1947 in Britain, there were five major newspaper groups which between them published over 70 percent of the 144 national and local papers then extant.[36] The United States experienced two big waves of newspaper mergers: around 1900 and during the 1920s. By 1929 more than a third of America's total circulation was controlled by 70 chains and journalism as a profession was in many respects marginalized during this period.[37]

The Self-Aware Journalist

In the first half of the nineteenth century, the press began the slow process of job specialization. This resulted eventually in the relatively homogeneous industry we understand today but initially the development of journalism in its diverse forms varied much more according to the culture of different countries. For instance, in France the profession of journalism first emerged from the 1789 revolution when the influence and esteem attributed to *belles-lettres* and the eighteenth-century *philosophes* passed on to journalism. This caused French novelist Honoré de Balzac to comment in 1840 that "public opinion is manufactured in Paris; it is made with ink and paper."[38] The path via journalism to politics that created a new political elite continued in France throughout the nineteenth century, exemplified by the careers of such journalist politicians as François Guizot and Adolphe Thiers. Alexis de Tocqueville considered the desire for office to be "the great, chronic ailment of the whole nation."[39]

In Britain journalism was able to develop as a profession in its own right independent of politics, even if it did lack the prestige of its French counterpart. The radical press of the early nineteenth century had a history of editor-publishers, from Richard Carlile and his *Republican* (1819–26) to William Cobbett's *Political Register* (1802–35), and Henry Hetherington's *Poor Man's Guardian* (1831). John Walter II's political ambitions required that he withdraw from active management of *The Times* in 1818 as "public opinion had not learned to tolerate gentlemen of the Press because it could not consider them gentlemen."[40] The novelist William Makepeace Thackeray felt obliged to adopt a pseudonym when he wrote as a journalist. The *London Review*, as early as 1835, also took the view that men of the press were not gentlemen and that "the Newspaper Press is thus degraded from the rank of a liberal profession ... and the conduct of our journals falls too much into the hands of men of obscure birth, imperfect education, blunt feelings and coarse manners."[41]

Résumé
William Cobbett

William Cobbett is considered the foremost radical thinker of his day. He was an inveterate writer of pamphlets in his native Britain and also in America in the early years of independence, writing under the pseudonym Peter Porcupine. Cobbett was born at Farnham in Surrey, England, in 1763. He joined the army in 1784 but blowing the whistle on military corruption forced him to flee to America. He returned in 1799 and began publishing his weekly *Political Register*, a radical newspaper that fought for electoral and parliamentary reform. It became the main newspaper read by the working classes, selling over 40,000 copies a week. In 1809 he was charged with seditious libel over a piece in the *Register* and sentenced to two years in Newgate prison.

Cobbett saw himself as a champion of the rural way of life at a time when industrialization was on the march. In 1821 he began a series of rides around the country on horseback to see for himself what conditions were like for farmers and laborers. He recorded his experiences for the *Register* and they were collected in *Rural Rides*, published in 1830 and still in print today. He stood for parliament five times and succeeded as member for Oldham in 1832. He died on his farm at Farnham in 1835.

Despite such strictures, the close connection between *The Times* of London and government was a fact of life for much of the nineteenth century. The official history remarks on the "close connexion existing during the 1830s and 1840s between Printing House Square [the paper's London address] and the Privy Council Office, of all departments the one most intimately concerned with the day-to-day machinery of Government."[42] Partly because of this, *The Times*, by 1865, was selling 65,000 copies a day and its income from classified advertisements was such that it could be profitable without government aid.[43] By 1870 *The Times*'s revenue from advertisements was double that from sales.

Yet to some contemporary observers such as the influential liberal thinker John Stuart Mill, the emergence of the commercial press and the professional journalist represented a loss rather than a gain:

> You know in how low a state the newspaper press of this country is. In France the best thinkers and writers of the nation, write in the journals and direct public opinion; but our daily and weekly writers are the lowest hacks of literature, which when it is a trade, is the vilest and most degrading of all trades, because more of affectation and hypocrisy, and more subservience to the baser feelings of others, are necessary for carrying it on, than for any other trade, from that of a brothel keeper upwards.[44]

During this period, even as a pseudo brothel-keeper, the editor was sovereign and small business ruled, with ownership tending to be by individuals or families, especially in provincial towns and cities.

Résumé
John Stuart Mill

John Stuart Mill was born in London in 1806. He was a precocious child, learning Greek at the age of three, and became one of the most significant liberal thinkers and writers of the nineteenth century. Aged 20 he suffered a nervous breakdown but eventually joined the British East India Company as his father had before him.

His most significant works are *On Liberty* (1859) and *The Subjection of Women* (1869). *On Liberty* is a treatise on the extent to which the state can exercise power over the individual. *The Subjection of Women* called for equality between the sexes and proved highly controversial. From 1865 to 1868 he was a member of parliament for City and Westminster. He died in Avignon, France, in 1873.

Towards the end of the century, the social status of journalists was still being contested as it was a period of intense change in the organization of journalism and the press. As Alan Lee notes: "the increasing scale and changing organization of the industry led to a divorce between the working journalist and the proprietor, so that even in the 1880s, when the Institute of Journalists was set up, it was already felt in some circles that it was inappropriate for proprietors to be eligible for membership."[45]The Institute of Journalists received its royal charter in 1889 and its aim was to promote journalism as a profession, but one very much allied to the "respectable" daily press, for the status of journalists was significantly dependent on the status of the audience that they addressed. Sir Walter Besant, who founded the Society of Authors in 1884 to safeguard the rights, especially copyright, of writers, believed that "the only journalism accounted worthy of a gentleman and a scholar was the writing of leaders for *The Times*."[46] On the other hand, a modern press can more properly trace its lineage from the position of the legendary editor of London's *Evening News*, Kennedy Jones, who claimed of John Morley, the departing "gentleman" editor of the *Pall Mall Gazette*, "you left journalism a profession, we have made it a branch of commerce."[47]

Technology – A Space–Time Continuum

Technological developments have moved from the periphery of a journalist's consciousness to center stage, especially in the last half of the twentieth century. Early newspapers only required a printing press and journalists with stout walking boots or a horse. As the industrial revolution gathered pace, the first significant changes to news-gathering procedures occurred. In 1837 Sir Isaac Pitman introduced his shorthand system which, although only a minor technical innovation, has left its mark on journalistic practice. It was adopted because reports and speeches, especially those given in parliament, could be taken down verbatim and with accuracy.

Changing timescales of news production afforded by technological innovation have profoundly altered the relationship between news media and their audiences. During the nineteenth century, it was the norm to report important parliamentary speeches verbatim because they were considered so important. This involved rushing to press with an enormous volume of words. In Britain in 1890, John Pendleton recounted:

> Nearly every daily newspaper had sent out the instruction "Gladstone, first person, verbatim". Twelve, sixteen, even twenty reporters formed the corps of some newspapers; and the half-hour "turns" were suspended for three, five, or ten minute takes, the reporters deftly working hand over hand, section by section; so that when Mr. Gladstone resumed his seat at eight o'clock in the

evening, having spoken since thirty five minutes past four o'clock in the afternoon, nearly the whole of his speech, sent either by telephone or messenger, was in the offices of the London morning papers, and so on the wires for the country. It was an anxious time in many a telegraph office and in many a sub-editor's room, but the speech, which contained 24,700 words, was nearly all in type in Manchester, Leeds and Edinburgh before midnight – before the great statesman who delivered it had emptied his pomatum pot of voice restorative and gone home to bed.[48]

Speed was of the essence. A century earlier, during the French Revolution, newspapers were written with quills and produced by candlelight as revolutionaries worked through the night using wooden, hand-operated printing presses. Almost a century after Pendleton's example, during the May 1968 riots in Paris, student demonstrators used radio to communicate.[49] In Manila "smart mobs" overthrew President Estrada in 2001 by organizing demonstrations via text messages and cell phones.

The importance of the word was equally well understood by radicals and conservatives alike and, with increased speed, expectations and pressures have also increased. Hazel Dicken-Garcia has pointed out that nineteenth-century Americans expected world peace and solutions to the gravest problems to follow the spread of printing and other communications technologies.[50] They were to be disappointed.

The same year that shorthand was introduced – 1837– also saw the introduction of Morse code, invented by Samuel Morse for use with his electric telegraph. Both innovations increased the speed and accuracy of information gathering and dissemination. In that year also *The Times* of London establish a pigeon post from Paris to Boulogne, and William Feathergill Cooke and Charles Wheatstone laid the first electric magnetic telegraph wires alongside the London and Birmingham railway line from Euston to Camden Town. *The Times* was the earliest journal to use the invention,[51] but before long the telegraph, "of all our modern wonders the most wonderful" according to Charles Dickens,[52] was to begin the process of reshaping what we now call "the media." This invention benefited all sorts of businesses by speeding up the communication process. The new telegraphs were, for instance, used by commodity markets in cotton and corn for data on prices and futures trading, by stock exchanges for financial information, by governments for imperial and local administration, and by newspapers for the transmission and collection of news and the exchange of political, cultural, and intellectual ideas.

By 1874 "telegraph lines and cables linked all the continents,"[53] and a new language – cablese – was developed by journalists to counter the high cost of sending cables which were charged by the word. "In cablese, correspondents would write, for example, 'smorning' for 'this morning,' 'ungo' for 'will not go,' and 'protreaty' for 'favored the treaty.'"[54] Newspaper offices had Morse receiving sets and qualified operators around the clock. Such technology was "cutting edge" at the time but is now of course not only long gone but also long forgotten. Are there any lessons here for bloggers, podcasters, texters, and tweeters?

Developments in telegraph and cable technology as they relate to international global communications are also important in the overall expansion of news content and delivery. Although these are dealt with in more detail in Chapter 6, one relevant example here is that of the news agency. America's *Associated Press* and Britain's *Reuters*, for instance, were both products of the new telegraphy and their effect on news-gathering processes was profound. They inevitably selected and processed stories they considered "news" and thus became important in the determination of newspapers' news agendas. Because these agencies supplied a range of different customers, the emphasis had to be on hard facts rather than comment, which gradually led the profession to distinguish between the two. Added to that, the sheer volume of telegraph news demanded a production line system for processing it, yet another reason why news became a commodity, subject to rates and business tariffs.

As well as affecting the gathering of news the telegraph was significant in influencing the 24-hour news cycle. Before the telegraph, each American city had its own "local time," but the telegraph made time zones possible and necessary. These zones were standardized from 1883 onwards, so time became "nationalized" and later "internationalized." At first, usage was purely at a national level, for the engineering challenges involved in large-scale underwater cable-laying were considerable. By the 1890s, however, time and space were becoming a manageable continuum for the first time. The railway and the telegraph ensured an infrastructure for national communications and hence a feeling of inclusivity in large countries such as the United States where this had previously been impossible.[55] What is worth noting, however, is that in the US this major technological development did not inaugurate a robust national press.

In Britain, although a much smaller country, similar time anomalies existed and it was the development of the railways and the need for a standardized timetable that resulted in a common time centered on the Greenwich meridian. Bristol, for example, was only 120 miles from London but had happily existed 11 minutes behind Greenwich Mean Time until the first train from London pulled into Temple Meads station in June 1841. The clock over the old Corn Exchange in Bristol is a reminder of this change. It has two minute hands. The black minute hand shows Greenwich Mean Time and the red minute hand shows Bristol time. The railways were co-opted by newspaper proprietors with some gusto as recorded in the official history of *The Times*: "Some 150 copies of *The Times* of December 11, 1849, were delivered at 1.30 p.m. in Paris on the day of publication. Such an exploit had never before been achieved by any English newspaper."[56] Usually the paper was delivered between twelve noon and one o'clock the day after publication.

Meanwhile, during the latter half of the century Sunday newspapers began to invade the sanctity of the Christian Sabbath. Sunday editions of daily papers had been "accepted in the United States since sabbatarian opposition had been overcome in the 1840s."[57] Joseph Pulitzer produced the *Sunday World* as part of his ongoing Yellow Journalism feud with William Randolph Hearst. In Britain, strictly speaking, the selling of newspapers on Sunday was illegal. However, the law was widely flouted. A curious footnote to Sunday selling occurred in 1899 when Alfred Harmsworth brought out a Sunday edition of the *Daily Mail* in competition with the new Sunday edition of the *Daily Telegraph*. Public protest meetings were held up and down the country and the campaign "succeeded in effecting a collective withdrawal of advertising."[58] The two papers attracted such opprobrium that both were withdrawn. The *Sunday Telegraph* only reappeared in 1961 and the *Mail on Sunday* in 1982.

The desire to colonize every day with some form of news output was clearly an aspiration of the press. But it was only with the advent of broadcast media that the invasion of nighttime began in earnest. As with all new technologies, restraints were placed on its freedom to regulate itself. In Britain at the outset of World War II radio was reduced to one station, the Home Service, and television was closed down for the duration. After the war the BBC resumed with three radio stations – the Home Service, the Light Programme, and the Third Programme – and a single television channel. This channel began broadcasting each day at 3p.m. with an hour-long women's program. It closed down between 4 and 5p.m. Between 5 and 6p.m. there were children's programs followed by a further closedown until the evening schedule began at 8p.m. Transmissions usually ended somewhere between 10.30p.m. and midnight. The closedowns were a response to concerns over television's "intrusion" into the privacy of family life. They allowed time to put children to bed and prepare the evening meal.

These restraints were slowly swept away with the beginnings of commercial broadcasting in 1955. In the US, television schedules were less regulated because there was no national broadcast programming. Most TV stations transmitted round the clock by the 1990s and this entailed new shift patterns for journalists. Breakfast radio and TV programs, for instance, necessitated research and preparation overnight; 24-hour news channels required a constant stream of story updates to keep stories fresh.

The other factor highlighted for the first time by the news agencies was the separation of the observer of a news event from the ultimate producer of that news event as story. Added to that, agencies reconfigured the way stories were told regardless of the story content, and were perhaps the first embodiment of Marshall McLuhan's famous 1960's dictum, "the medium is the message."[59] This separation and reconfiguration has reached its apogee with modern communications technology. Today, for example, information can be generated without any human intervention at all. Computers are programmed to respond by combining discrete packets of data in a variety of ways depending on the manner in which the information is requested. Website browsing, for example, can generate a plethora of unrequested information, usually in the form of advertising, depending on the search criteria used.

Thus the tendency is for computers to proliferate information whereas the earlier electric telegraph reduced it to essentials. Nick Davies in *Flat Earth News* highlighted the dangers, not only for journalists' employment prospects but also for the connection between news and local communities: "Local news coverage [is] frequently supplied by a single journalist monitoring a computerised collection of agency stories and then reading them out twice an hour, often as a pre-recorded link from a regional hub."[60]

If this is increasingly the case then the journalists' role will certainly have changed. At all levels they will have started to become something closer to a functionary and something farther from a defender of freedom and an investigator into wrongdoing. Is this a price worth paying or is it a price that will have to be paid? Are the pessimists right to condemn it as an example of commercial pressures trumping journalistic values? Or are the optimists more accurate when they suggest that this is indeed a new journalism for a new age?

Notes

1   *New York Times*, October 6, 1852.
2   Alan J. Lee, *The Origins of the Popular Press 1855–1914* (London: Croom Helm, 1976), p. 18.

3   Walter Fox, "The Daily Newspaper and Urban Popular Culture." Available online at http://www. netreach.net/~wfox/popcult.htm, accessed on May 12, 2009.

4   Dennis Griffiths (ed.), *The Encyclopedia of the British Press 1422–1992* (London: Macmillan, 1992), p. 184.

5   Matthew Arnold, "Up To Easter," *Nineteenth Century*, XXI, 1887, 629–43 (p. 638).

6   Lee, *The Origins of the Popular Press*, p. 121.

7   Jane Chapman, *Comparative Media History: 1789 to the Present* (Cambridge, UK: Polity Press, 2005), p. 72.

8   Douglas Kellner, *Critical Theory, Marxism, and Modernity* (Baltimore: Johns Hopkins University Press, 1989), p. 132.

9   Roger Fowler, *Language in the News* (London: Routledge, 1991), p. 222.

10 Gerald J. Baldasty, *The Commercialization of News in the Nineteenth Century* (Madison: University of Wisconsin Press, 1992), p. 8.

11 Tom Baistow, *Fourth Rate Estate: An Anatomy of Fleet Street* (London: Comedia, 1985), p. 6.

12 John C. Merrill, Peter J. Gade, and Frederick R. Blevens, *Twilight of Press Freedom: The Rise of People's Journalism* (Mahwah, NJ: Lawrence Erlbaum Associates, 2001), p. 188.

13 Baistow, *Fourth Rate Estate*, p. 37.

14 Robert Picard, "Shifts in Newspaper Advertising Expenditures and their Implications for the Future of Newspapers," paper presented at the *Future of Newspapers Conference*, Cardiff, September 7–9, 2007, p. 1.

15 *News of the World Almanac and Household Guide* (London: News of the World, 1951), p. 285.

16 David R. Davies, *The Postwar Decline of American Newspapers, 1945–1965* (New York: Praeger, 2006).

17 James W. Carey, *Communication as Culture: Essays on Media and Society* (Boston: Unwin Hyman, 1989), p. 8.

18 Lee, *The Origins of the Popular* Press, p. 18.

19 Anthony Smith, *The Newspaper: An International History* (Thames & Hudson: London, 1979), p. 144.

20 The Times, *History of* The Times, vol. I, *"The Thunderer" in the Making* (London: Times Publishing Company, 1921), p. 115.

21 Ibid., p. 116.

22 Ibid., p. 119.

23 William Maxwell, "Old Lamps for New: Some Reflections on Recent Changes in Journalism," *Nineteenth Century and After*, 75 (1914), 1085–96 (p. 1088).

24 Richard Bourne, *Lords of Fleet Street: The Harmsworth Dynasty* (London: Unwin Hyman, 1990), p. 34.

25 Lee, *The Origins of the Popular Press*, pp. 88–9.

26 Griffiths, *The Encyclopedia of the British Press*, p. 184; Stephen Koss, *The Rise and Fall of the Political Press in Britain* (London: Fontana, 1984), p. 368.

27   Baldasty, *The Commercialization of News in the Nineteenth Century*, p. 4.
28   W. Joseph Campbell, *The Year that Defined American Journalism: 1897 and the Clash of Paradigms* (New York: Routledge, 2006), p. 8.
29   Ralph Negrine, *Politics and Mass Media in Britain*, 2nd edn (London: Routledge, 1994), p. 50.
30   Bourne, *Lords of Fleet Street*, p. 79.
31   Baldasty, *The Commercialization of News in the Nineteenth Century*, p. 60.
32   Bruce Hanlin, "Owners, Editors and Journalists," in Andrew Belsey and Ruth Chadwick (eds), *Ethical Issues in Journalism and the Media* (London: Routledge, 1992), pp. 33–48 (p. 42).
33   Ben H. Bagdikian, *Media Monopoly*, 5th edn (Boston: Beacon Press, 1997), p. 24.
34   Maxwell, "Old Lamps for New," p. 1095.
35   Lee, *The Origins of the Popular Press*, p. 293.
36   Viscount Camrose, *British Newspapers and Their Controllers* (London: Cassell, 1947), p. 158.
37   Bonnie Brennen, "Newsworkers During the Interwar Years: A Critique of Traditional Media History," *Communication Quarterly*, 43 (1995), 197–209.
38   Saint-Marc Girardin, *Souvenirs et reflexions politiques d'un journaliste* (Paris: M. Levy Librairie nouvelle, 1859), pp. 55, 76.
39   Alexis de Tocqueville, *Democracy in America*, ed. J. P. Meyer, trans. George Lawrence (New York, Garden City: Doubleday & Co., 1969), pp. 31–2.
40   George Boyce, James Curran, and Pauline Wingate (eds), *Newspaper History from the 17th Century to the Present Day* (London: Constable, 1978), p. 21.
41   Lee, *The Origins of the Popular Press*, p. 105.
42   The Times, *History of* The Times, vol. II, *The Tradition Established* (London: Times Publishing Company, 1939), p. 216.
43   Ibid., p. 354.
44   John Stuart Mill, *The Early Letters of John Stuart Mill 1812–1848*, ed. Frenus E. Mineka (Toronto: University of Toronto Press, 1963), vol. 1, pp. 38–9.
45   Lee, *The Origins of the Popular Press*, p. 127.
46   Philip Elliott, "Professional Ideology and Organisational Change: The Journalist Since 1800," in G. Boyce et al. *Newspaper History from the 17th Century to the Present Day*, pp. 172–91 (p. 179).
47   Quoted in Lee, *The Origins of the Popular Press*, p. 104.
48   J. Pendleton, *Newspaper Reporting in Olden Times and To-day* (London: Elliot Stock, 1890), pp. 103–4, in Martin Conboy and John Steel, "The Future of Newspapers – Historical Perspectives," *Journalism Studies, Special Edition on the Future of Newspapers*, 9, 5 (2008), 650–61 (p. 656).
49   Chapman, *Comparative Media History*, pp. 232–3.
50   Hazel Dicken-Garcia, *Journalistic Standards in Nineteenth-Century America* (Madison: University of Wisconsin Press, 1989).

51 The Times, *History of* The Times, vol. II, *The Tradition Established*, pp. 80–1.
52 Quoted in Asa Briggs and Peter Burke, *A Social History of the Media: From Gutenberg to the Internet* (Cambridge, UK: Polity Press, 2002), p. 135.
53 John Slater, "Technologies of News Gathering and Transmission," in W. David Sloan and Lisa Mullikin Parcell (eds), *American Journalism: History, Principles, Practice* (Jefferson, NC: McFarland & Co, 2002), pp. 350–8 (p. 353).
54 Ibid.
55 Carey, *Communication as Culture*, p. 229.
56 The Times, *History of* The Times, vol. II, *The Tradition Established*, p. 83.
57 Lee, *The Origins of the Popular Press*, p. 229.
58 Ibid., p. 126.
59 Marshall McLuhan, *Understanding Media* (London: Routledge & Kegan Paul, 1964), p. 7.
60 Nick Davies, *Flat Earth News* (London: Chatto & Windus, 2008), p. 68.

6

A New Journalism For A New Age

The history of the press is littered with "new journalisms" – the lurid sensationalism of the nineteenth-century Sundays, the vivid polemics of Yellow Journalism, the New Journalism of the *fin de siècle*, and that other New Journalism initiated by such writers as Truman Capote, Tom Wolfe, and Hunter S. Thompson in the 1960s. All were responses to the need to cultivate and maintain an audience. What should not be forgotten, however, is the role of typographic and stylistic innovation, largely driven by new technologies that provided the "framework" for each of the "new journalisms" as it emerged. This is particularly relevant as the profession moved from the Victorian age into the twentieth century.

Ringing the Changes – Layout and Design Reinvented

Daily newspapers maintained their circulations with a bedrock of subscription sales, a method of financing that, as noted in the last chapter, reached its apogee in the 1930s. Evening papers, in contrast, relied on prominent and arresting headlines on the front page, typically to attract commuters on their way home from work. The late nineteenth and early twentieth centuries saw, for the first time, the methods traditionally used by the evening press invade the dailies. At first this applied in Britain to the popular press rather than the broadsheets but before long only the *Daily Mail* and *The Times* retained classifieds on the front page rather than news. The "sensational" story accompanied a "sensational" presentational style fueled by the urgent need to increase circulations and advertising revenues. There were three factors driving such change – firstly, the economic depression that

Jane Chapman and Nick Nuttall, *Journalism Today: A Themed History*
© 2011 Jane Chapman and Nick Nuttall. Published by Blackwell Publishing Ltd.

gripped America and Britain in the run-up to World War I; secondly, the heating up of competition between newspaper proprietors; and thirdly, the rapid developments in typography and half-tone picture printing.

The financial panic of 1893 came after a decade of exceptional economic growth in the United States and was caused by railroad overbuilding and the shaky finances underpinning such expansion. Many railroad companies went bankrupt, including the famous Atchison, Topeka and Santa Fe. In total over 15,000 companies and 500 banks failed and the resulting unemployment and the loss of life savings turned a once secure middle class into one that couldn't afford its mortgage repayments.[1] The depression helped to keep down newspaper cover prices and advertising rates and the antidote to such dire economic conditions was to go all out for circulation. Joseph Pulitzer, owner of the *New York World*, and William Randolph Hearst, owner of the *New York Journal*, were soon caught up in a battle for the New York reader. Both went in for eye-catching headlines and the "battle" between them produced the sensational style nicknamed Yellow Journalism. The name derived from a regular color comic strip called *Hogan's Alley* in Pulitzer's *World* about a New York "alley kid" who wore a yellow nightshirt.[2]

Résumé
Joseph Pulitzer

Joseph Pulitzer was born in Makó, Hungary, in 1847. He emigrated to the United States in 1864 after being turned down by the Austrian army because of poor health. He settled in St Louis and worked on the *Westliche Post*, a German-language paper. Eventually he bought the paper for $3,000. He championed the "common man" in all his journalism and in 1883, now a wealthy man, Pulitzer bought the *New York World*. It was losing money but Pulitzer soon turned it round by providing a diet of human interest stories with lurid and sensational headlines.

When William Randolph Hearst bought the *New York Journal* in 1896 the stage was set for a circulation war that resulted in what became known as Yellow Journalism. In 1892 Pulitzer offered Columbia University money for a journalism school. The school was set up in 1912, a year after Pulitzer's death. He also set up the Pulitzer Prize which was first awarded in 1917. There are 21 categories, each with a prize worth $10,000. Pulitzer died aboard his yacht in Charleston harbor in 1911.

American historian and journalist Frank Luther Mott defined Yellow Journalism in terms of five characteristics:

- Scare headlines in huge print, often of minor news
- Lavish use of pictures, or imaginary drawings
- Use of faked interviews, misleading headlines, pseudo-science, and a parade of false learning from so-called experts
- Emphasis on full-color Sunday supplements, usually with comic strips (which is now normal in the US)
- Dramatic sympathy with the "underdog" against the system.[3]

Joseph Pulitzer's *World*, for example, deployed headlines such as: "How Babies Are Baked," "Burning Babies Fall From The Roof," and "Lines of Little Hearses."[4] William Randolph Hearst had used similar techniques even before his purchase of the *New York Journal*. A month after buying the *San Francisco Examiner* in 1887, for example, he ran the following headline about a hotel fire: "HUNGRY, FRANTIC FLAMES. They Leap Madly Upon the Splendid Pleasure Palace by the Bay of Monterey, Encircling Del Monte in Their Ravenous Embrace From Pinnacle to Foundation. Leaping Higher, Higher, Higher, With Desperate Desire ... ."[5] Both proprietors used pictures lavishly, exploiting recent developments in halftone printing. During the Spanish–American War in 1898 (the first war precipitated by the media), Hearst's *Journal* stoked up war hysteria by running such headlines as, "Spaniards Search Women on American Steamers." It was accompanied by a picture of a naked woman surrounded by male Spanish officials. It was of course impossible to verify the truth or otherwise of a drawing which was clearly designed to whip up anti-Spanish feeling in his paper's readers.

In Britain a New Journalism appeared that copied some aspects of Yellow Journalism. The emphasis was more on keeping stories simple and readable although Alfred Harmsworth in his *Daily Mail* could be just as jingoistic about the Boer War as Hearst was over the Spanish–American War. Harmsworth's approach to news was of sufficient interest for Pulitzer to invite him to America to edit "the first issue of his New York *World* in the twentieth century."[6] The New Journalism understood that most people approached newspaper texts quite differently from any other reading matter. They wanted the essence of the news, or the story, distilled as quickly and succinctly as possible. So, although the tenets of formula writing had yet to take hold, the principles, those of brevity and clarity, were clearly evident in the journalism promoted by Harmsworth. This brevity also made room for a much wider mix of articles and also allowed for an expansion of advertising, especially as the display ad was coming into its own as a visual enhancement of the page and as a valuable source of revenue.

Résumé
Alfred Harmsworth, Lord Northcliffe

Alfred Harmsworth was of Anglo-Irish stock, and his family moved from Dublin to London when Alfred was two years old. His father was a barrister but was never successful and the family gradually descended into genteel poverty.[7] Once decided on journalism as a career, Alfred began to plot the rejuvenation of his family's fortunes. And it was against this background that *Answers to Correspondents* and ultimately the *Daily Mail* were born.

Harmsworth's early journalistic experience was gained at low-circulation niche magazines such as *Youth* and *Bicycling News*. But, crucially, he was also an occasional contributor to George Newnes's weekly magazine *Tit-Bits*. It was the success of *Tit-Bits* that fueled Harmsworth's ambition to set up a rival magazine and in 1888, aged a mere 23 years, he published the first edition of *Answers to Correspondents*. The contents of the first weekly issue, priced at one penny, included: Strange Experiences, Curious Facts, Tests for the Eyesight, What the Queen Eats, Swindling Advertisers, 100 Jokes. *Answers*, as it became known, was an immediate success. At its height it sold over 200,000 copies a week.[8] Eight years later, in 1896, he published the first edition of his new newspaper, the *Daily Mail*. This, together with *Answers* and the more recently acquired London *Evening News*, formed the bedrock of what was then to become the largest periodical publishing empire in the world, Amalgamated Press. At the height of his success, Harmsworth was launching a new magazine every six months, transferring both the ideas and profits from his periodicals into the world of newspapers. In 1903 he also began the *Daily Mirror* which, although a flop in its first few months, eventually became the biggest selling tabloid in the UK. This success resulted in his ennoblement in 1905 as Lord Northcliffe.

The so-called Northcliffe revolution turned the British press into a business branch of the consumer industry. Northcliffe did not invent popular journalism in Britain – many developments in style and content were influenced by American and French models and change was inevitable, given contemporary economic and social forces.[9] Yet it was Northcliffe who took advantage of these new developments by turning the commercial potential of journalism into a reality. He produced newspapers and magazines that were cheap, entertaining, and at face value free from party political influence. In the process he made a fortune and in 1908 he purchased *The Times* of London, the jewel in the crown of his empire and a tangible symbol of his own political stature.

Northcliffe's empire was essentially a national one but at its zenith he controlled a larger share of Britain's newspaper circulation than did Rupert Murdoch in the 1990s.[10] He suffered a nervous breakdown shortly before his death from heart disease aged only 57.

These trends in layout, design, and format have, by and large, remained as distinguishing features of the newspaper ever since. The use of color, graphics, and images has increased and the tabloids particularly have invested heavily in large-scale "screamer" headlines. More recently the dimensions of newspapers have shrunk – even *The Times* has become a smaller sized paper – but pagination has increased along with the separation of news and features into different sections devoted to specific interests – sport, money, work, travel, and so forth. A recent trend also is for news stories in the broadsheets to become longer as editorial staffs shrink.[11] In Britain, a typical front page of the *Daily Express* in the 1950s might contain 15 or more stories whereas most "broadsheets" today make do with anywhere between two and five.

We're All Professionals Now

Some journalists take pride in describing themselves as hacks. Others are equally insistent that they are members of a profession. Today these polar opposites are being blurred by phenomena such as public relations and citizen journalism. Yet despite this, contemporary journalists can still be identified as an occupational group with an explicit self-image. Work routines in many respects still follow a time-honored pattern – news gathering, interviewing, selecting, writing and recording, editing. The best journalists still insist on a clear demarcation between the "objective" news story and the "subjective" op-ed or polemical feature. Yet such characteristics were not simply imposed or decided upon from above (or below). They evolved in response to the complex and shifting interactions of technology, social and cultural mores, education, industrialization, and changing political environments.

As noted by Kevin Williams, "Prior to the beginning of the twentieth century journalists were part of an 'undifferentiated' literary system, members of a 'loose and informal' collection of writers who plied their trade through a variety of publications."[12] By the 1930s all forms of mass media had expanded to such an extent that those describing themselves as "authors, editors, and journalists" increased threefold between 1891 and 1931; a rate of increase six times that of the whole population. The attempt by journalism to distinguish itself elevated the principle of objectivity to the center of the profession, and in particular in the gathering and processing of news.[13]

Despite this, it is still relevant to ask whether these characteristics are descriptive of a "profession." If you are, for example, an architect, engineer, surveyor, lawyer, or accountant you are said to be practicing a profession rather than just doing a job. As a professional you are licensed or registered in some way, usually after completing a rigorous course of study, in order to carry on that profession. And although you are paid by clients you are never "in their pay." In other words you are required at all times to be impartial between the person employing you and the other party to the contract. In many respects it is this desire of journalists to be seen as impartial that has driven them to present themselves as professionals.

The soubriquet has always been disputed, yet the notion of professionalism has refused to die. In Britain, the Institute of Journalists (IOJ) was set up by Royal Charter in 1890. It consisted "of gentlemen engaged in journalistic work" and was inaugurated "to promote and advance the common interests of the profession."[14] In 1934 the IOJ proposed that, as in other professions, there should be a state register of journalists. Yet according to media lawyer Geoffrey Robinson: "Journalism is not a profession. It is the exercise by occupation of the right to free expression available to every citizen. That right, being available to all, cannot in principle be withdrawn from a few by any system of licensing or professional registration."[15] Although no state register came into being the desire for professional status led to the development of that essential prerequisite of the professional – a set of ethics (see Part III).

In the Britain of the eighteenth century, ethics tended to be a luxury few men of the press could afford. Successive prime ministers, Walpole, Pitt, and North, handed out vast sums of money to tame editors and co-operative writers in exchange for their timely support or helpful silence.[16] In the turbulent years of the America Revolution, newspapers' loyalties tended to follow the tide of battle. "When the colonial forces were in possession, royalist papers were suppressed, and at times of British occupation Revolutionary papers moved away, or were discontinued, or they became royalist, only to suffer at the next turn of military fortunes."[17] Despite this, as newspapers became more dependent on advertising and less on subventions from political, religious, or other organizations (described by some historians as the exchange of one paymaster for another) journalists' writing became depoliticized and increasingly based on "discursive norms of neutrality and objectivity."[18]

The result was a uniformity of journalistic approach rather as Lincoln Steffens described the training he received on E. L. Godkin's New York *Evening Post*: "Reporters were to report the news as it happened, like machines, without prejudice, color, and without style; all alike."[19] Godkin demanded "absolute factuality: humor, pathos, literary flourish and personality belonged only on the editorial page,"[20] and it was Godkin's opposition to individuality in reporting that Steffens ultimately objected to. In Britain, *The Times*'s editorial page, perhaps predictably, outdid even Godkin's strictures and seldom succumbed to "literary flourish and personality." Indeed, there was no signed article in *The Times* until 1884.[21]

Résumé
E. L. Godkin

Edwin Lawrence Godkin was born in 1831 in County Wicklow, Ireland. He graduated from Queen's College, Belfast in 1851 and became war correspondent for the London *Daily News* in Turkey. He covered the Crimean War and was present at the capture of Sevastopol. He arrived in New York in 1856 and in 1865 founded a weekly paper, the *Nation*.

He sold the *Nation* to the New York *Evening Post* in 1881 and became editor-in-chief until 1899. "The paper shunned crime, scandal, or anything that smacked of yellow journalism."[22] Godkin also opposed protectionism, imperialism, and the war with Spain. He suffered a stroke in 1900 and died in Devon, England, in 1902.

So long as newspaper proprietors were willing to accept politicians' bribes, it was difficult to argue the case for professionalism. Yet much later, from the mid-nineteenth century onwards, there were equally powerful arguments deployed against a professional press because now proprietors were perceived as being in hock to commercial advertisers. This difficulty was alluded to by T. P. O'Connor, a member of parliament and founder editor of the London evening newspaper, the *Star* (1887–90): "The theatre manager, the musical impresario, all advertise largely; are the best customers of a newspaper; and there is, of course, the same disinclination in the business of newspapers as in other businesses to fall foul of the best customer."[23]

At the same time arguments about the simple objectivity of factual journalism, the Godkin approach, were challenged by a new breed of journalist personified by editors like W. T. Stead of the *Pall Mall Gazette*, a London evening paper of the period. In his polemic, *The Future of Journalism* (1886), Stead argued that, "Impersonal journalism is effete … for the proper development of a newspaper the personal element is indispensible."[24] T. P. O'Connor was even more certain: "I hold that the desire for personal details with regard to public men is healthy, rational, and should be yielded to."[25] It is arguable whether the "personal element" and "personal details," the basis of the human interest story, heralded the triumph of trade over profession but it does appear that the idea of a professional journalism has faded from the public consciousness. Its supporters seem to have lost their way in a media environment that places more store by size and reach than mere factuality. And as this trend has gathered pace so greater obeisance is paid to the objectivity "god" as the true test of journalism's credentials.

Objective Reporting – Substance Over Style

The concept of "objectivity" therefore would appear to be central to the journalistic sense of professionalism, if not to journalism itself as a profession. But where has this drive for objectivity come from? What is its lineage? There has been some debate among journalism historians about when concepts like objectivity and balance first appeared and whether they were linked to the occupational development of journalism. The increasing emphasis on science in the late nineteenth century and the early commercialism of the penny press have been suggested as catalysts.[26] But what seems more certain is that notions of objectivity are bound up with ideas of independence. Journalism academic Patricia Dooley has noted, for example, how some journalists sought to assert themselves as being different from and independent of politicians as early as the American Revolution (1775–83).[27] *The Times* of London asserted in 1854 that "[Thomas] Barnes [editor] secured the independence of *The Times* by building up corps of expert news correspondents at home and abroad."[28] Yet by the end of the century *Star* editor T. P. O'Connor stated with some vigor: "I like an 'independent' journal as little as the politician who assumes to himself the same adjective,"[29] as if "independent" was a synonym for at best a fence-sitter or at worst a lack of testosterone.

Yet objectivity and independence were the cardinal virtues and the stock-in-trade of another relatively new institution, the news agency. As already noted, all five continents were connected by cable by the end of the nineteenth century and the major news agencies developed in tandem with cable laying. Charles-Louis Havas created the Agence Havas in France in 1835. Associated Press, the major American news agency, was founded as a not-for-profit collective in New York in 1846 and Paul Julius Reuter started his eponymous agency in Germany in 1849. And the changes in the news-gathering process wrought by agency copy have been cited by many as accelerating an already gathering momentum toward all the characteristics of objectivity – simplicity, brevity, factuality. As noted by Raymond Williams in *The Long Revolution*, "The older style was, at its best, that of books; at its worst, what the language textbooks still call 'journalese' ... The desire for compression, to save money on the wire, led to shorter sentences and a greater emphasis on key-words."[30] Certainly the telegraph was as essential to a news agency's style and very existence as the keyboard is to a computer's.

The now universal "inverted pyramid" formula style of writing was another essential feature of agency style, and particularly that of Associated Press. This style of writing copy requires the facts – encapsulated in what is sometimes called the 6Ws: who, what, when, where, why, how – to be presented in the "intro" or "lead" to allow the sale of wire service copy to a range of different clients. Clients could then put their own "spin" or angle on the story. Different skills were required of journalists who were typically used to gathering stories within their own locality and who could also verify their sources. Agency copy first and foremost had to be trusted. And an important part of that trust was enshrined in its objective reporting of events.

However, according to Harlan Stensaas's research into levels of objectivity in American daily newspapers, objectivity was not widely practiced in 1865–74, was common in 1905–14, and normative between 1925 and 1984. Furthermore, his content analysis found that the incidence of objective reporting was not significantly influenced by the introduction of telegraph and wire services.[31]

So whether objectivity can be directly attributed to the influence of news agencies or whether it was a general trend merely accelerated by the advent of such agencies, there is nevertheless little doubt that it was accompanied by uniformity and conformity in both the presentation and the structuring of news. American sociologist Herbert J. Gans suggested in *Deciding What's News* that a range of organizational factors were implicated in the drive for objectivity – the need for journalists to protect their credibility, the assumption that their values were universally valid, and, more recently, a comfortable income that undermined any tendency towards militancy.[32] Thus the creed of objectivity became a form of industry self-defense: it represented a reaffirmation of uniformity of standards at a time when public corruption and Yellow Journalism were each implicated in a moral crisis in the United States in particular.

The idea was further developed between 1900 and 1915 with the establishment of the first journalism schools – Missouri, Columbia, Northwestern, and Indiana. Professional judgment was to be the hallmark of the objective journalist, not the politics of the owner or the whim of the advertisers. The Journalist's Creed, developed by Walter Williams, first dean of the Missouri School of Journalism states, for example, "I believe in the profession of journalism," and "I believe that the journalism which succeeds best ... is stoutly independent."[33] Despite such strictures, however, styles of reporting were still very much affected by the contexts within which they were produced rather than by obscure credos from proto-academic institutions. During the 1920s, for example, when the world was still recovering from World War I and from the impact of the 1917 Russian Revolution, journalist and political commentator Walter Lippmann and fellow *New Republic* editor Charles Merz published a 42-page supplement to the August 4 issue of *The New Republic* called "A Test of the News." This supplement examined more than a thousand editions of the *New York Times* newspaper for coverage of the Russian Revolution. What they discovered was that the paper reported events that had never happened and systematically misrepresented events that had. They concluded that "semi-editorial dispatches" were based on "what men wanted to see."[34] For instance, the *Times* assured readers on 91 occasions that the revolutionary regime was near collapse.

It would seem therefore that the antidote to such "biased" and "opinion-led" journalism would be to pursue with equal ideological fervor the nascent journalism schools' approach to reporting. Here, opposing viewpoints would be represented with the necessary balance by, for example, the use of proportionate quotes and by the presentation with equal weight of "expert" opinion from both sides. Readers could then make up their own minds on the issue. Some zealots would go further, preferring the "bare-bones" approach which leaves no room for comment, whether by quoted "experts" or by journalists themselves. The danger inherent in this approach is that it can lead to a narrowing of ideological disagreements to only two sides and tends "to elevate the dominant viewpoints and ignore the unconventional ones."[35] Such criticism of mainstream journalism was highlighted by Upton Sinclair and echoed many years later by J. Herbert Altschull: "The code of objectivity assists power in the capitalist world to maintain social order and to fix limits to departures from ideological orthodoxy ... It safeguards the system against the explosive pressure for change."[36]

One answer to the "bare-bones" problem was to mix news and interpretation in order to explain and illuminate.[37] According to American sociologist Michael Schudson, the vogue from the 1930s onwards for this kind of "interpretative" journalism by a "professional" press also meant that serious discussion of legislation gave way to entertainment-orientated news reporting, journalists becoming "their own interpretative community, writing to one another and not to parties or partisans, determined to distinguish their work from that of press agents, eager to pass on to younger journalists and to celebrate in themselves an ethic and an integrity in keeping with the broader culture's acclaim for science and non-partisanship."[38] In fact, objective reporting, in so far as it was a trend, has been in decline since World War II. Partly because of interventionist proprietors, partly because of the sheer complexity of a modern statist society, and partly because of the personalization of news agendas, this decline is mirrored by the rise of television as the main source of news for most people.

A lucid example of the dangerous mix of objectivity with a powerful personality was the media coverage of the McCarthy hearings in 1950s America. Senator Joseph McCarthy carried out a witch-hunt of "Communists" in government, the army, and the media. Most famously he accused the *Voice of America* radio station of harboring a Communist element. In the subsequent hearings before a Senate subcommittee, McCarthy's questioning was hostile and laced with innuendo and false accusations. Ultimately none of the charges was ever substantiated. Objective reporting of the hearings, however, resulted in news stories that achieved balance by giving equal prominence to all statements, both those that were true and those that were false. For Senator McCarthy perpetrated many untruths that journalists, reporting objectively, relayed to their publics. So by reporting his words accurately they absolved themselves of any responsibility for the truth.

Sociologist Gaye Tuchman has suggested that claims of "objective reporting" are merely tactical devises used by journalists to guard against criticism.[39] They could safely claim that the task of pointing out a speaker's errors was not the reporter's; it was down to the editor or editorial writers. A contemporary and detailed assessment of the media's handling of McCarthy's accusations concluded that, "Faced with a phenomenon as complex as McCarthyism, the 'straight' reporter has become a sort of straight jacket reporter ... his initiative is hogtied so that he cannot fulfill his first duty, which is to bring clearer understanding to his reader."[40]

The Journalist as Partisan

If the notion of objectivity is fraught with danger, what are the other possibilities? Arguments have been put forward, for example by W. T. Stead, supporting a more "personal" journalism but Stead's detractors have always argued that his "personal" is simply synonymous with partisan journalism and one of the arguments for objectivity is precisely that it is nonpartisan. Yet the differences between the partisan and the nonpartisan are by no means crude or even straightforward. For example, James Gordon Bennett's *New York Herald* of the 1830s and Horace Greeley's *New-York Tribune* of the 1840s both attempted a less partisan approach to public affairs, experimenting with the presentation of context for the news without adherence to a fixed political line, but for all that, they were never neutral.

Frequently historians talk of the "partisan" press as if it were synonymous with the "political" press. Yet many papers were partisan supporters of other causes besides the purely political. Religious and temperance organizations, for example, were hugely popular on both sides of the Atlantic during the nineteenth century. In Britain, the Select Committee on Drunkenness of 1834 "recommended the repeal of the taxes on newspapers on the grounds that the working man would cease to have to resort to the public house in order to read a newspaper."[41] The press, naturally, rallied behind such calls. That having been said, the allure of politics was still powerful enough to draw any number of editors into political activity.

In the US, the Jacksonian era was the high point of the "partisan" press that dominated the antebellum period leading up to the American Civil War. Among the most notable press men were Amos Kendall, editor of the *Argus of Western America* and the *Washington Globe*, who also served as US Postmaster General (1835–40) under Presidents Jackson and Van Buren, and John Norvell, founder of the *Philadelphia Inquirer* in 1829, who later entered Congress as senator for the newly admitted state of Michigan (1837). By the turn of the century there were still roughly 325 different

English and foreign language papers and periodicals published by supporters of the Socialist Party of Eugene V. Debs. The party received hundreds of thousands of votes, boasted 5,000 branches, and its press reached two million readers. Its flagship newspaper *Appeal to Reason* had a readership nearing one million, making it the most successful and powerful of the early twentieth-century socialist newspapers.[42]

FactFile
Appeal to Reason

Julius Wayland (1854–1912) founded *Appeal to Reason* as a socialist journal in 1895. Wayland had trained as a printer and typesetter on the *Versailles Gazette* in his hometown of Versailles, Indiana, and by 1874 he had saved enough money to purchase the newspaper. His success with this title and his conversion to socialism led him to publish in 1893 a radical newspaper, *The Coming Nation*, in Pueblo, Colorado. It quickly achieved a circulation of over 60,000 and became the most popular socialist newspaper in America. *Appeal to Reason* was to eclipse even this success with its mixture of articles and extracts from radical books by people such as Friedrich Engels, Karl Marx, William Morris, Tom Paine, and John Ruskin.

In 1900 Wayland employed Frederick Warren, a familiar figure in left-wing politics, as his coeditor. Warren managed to persuade many high profile progressive writers and journalists – Jack London, Stephen Crane, Helen Keller, Eugene Debs, and Upton Sinclair – to contribute to the paper. It was Fred Warren who, in 1904, commissioned Upton Sinclair to write a novel about immigrant workers in the Chicago meat-packing houses. Wayland gave Sinclair a $500 advance and after seven months research Sinclair wrote *The Jungle*. It was serialized in the paper and helped increase circulation to over 175,000.

As the paper's success increased so did attacks on its coeditors. The paper's offices were repeatedly broken into in an effort to find evidence of criminal activity. In 1912 the *Los Angeles Times* reported that Wayland was guilty of seducing an orphaned girl of 14 who had died during an abortion in Missouri. Depressed by the recent death of his wife and the continuing smear campaign against him, Wayland committed suicide on November 10, 1912. His suicide note said: "The struggle under the competitive system is not worth the effort." After Wayland's death his children won considerable damages after they sued the newspapers guilty of printing libelous stories about their father.[43]

In Britain, one of the most striking examples of a partisan press was the radical, unstamped, and often illegal newspapers of the early nineteenth century. A stamp duty had been introduced in 1712 with the aim not only of raising revenue but also of putting newspapers out of business. Over the next 100 years the tax was increased from a penny to fourpence per copy. Radical publishers, backed by a vociferous working-class campaign, often refused to pay the tax in what became known as the "war of the unstamped," their argument being that it was a "tax on knowledge."[44] However, a partisan press works effectively only so long as there are plenty of different and well-supported newspapers covering a range of opinions, and once the radical press achieved its journalistic objectives, namely the repeal of newspaper taxes, it fell on hard times. From 1868 to World War I, however, as noted by Alan Lee, there was a consistent two-thirds of the provincial daily press that still had either overt or implied political allegiances.[45] In continental Europe also, where newspapers were often owned and run by novelists and other literary figures, a political press survived well into the twentieth century.

Although the economics of newspaper publishing came to favor big business, it would be wrong to assume that commercial concerns ignored politics altogether.[46] William Randolph Hearst's *New York Journal* regularly stated political preferences and gave substantial coverage to the 1897 mayoral elections.[47] The editor of the *Chicago Tribune*, Col. Robert McCormick, a well-known right-winger, hated Roosevelt to such an extent that during the 1936 presidential election campaign he instructed his switchboard operators to answer the phone with "Good Morning, *Chicago Tribune*. There are only 43 [or less] days left in which to save the American way of life."[48] This was echoed by a famous headline in the *Sun* newspaper in Britain in the run-up to the 1992 general election which saw the defeat of Neil Kinnock's Labour party. On the morning of polling day (April 9) the *Sun*'s front page shouted, "If Kinnock wins today, will the last person to leave Britain please turn out the lights."

The inexorable rise of commercialism and big business throughout the twentieth century was inevitably reflected in the media. Mergers and acquisitions in the press were clearly a product of larger economic forces than any trends specific to the press itself.[49] Political leanings, rather than reflecting the ideological position of the proprietor as in the past, now tended to reflect the proprietor's commercial interests. Thus the "personality" of the proprietor was superseded by the "impersonality" of a conglomerate's board of directors and shareholders. The United States experienced two such significant waves of newspaper mergers: around 1900 and during the 1920s.

William Randolph Hearst, for example, created a press empire that straddled the US from coast to coast between the years 1887 and 1934. At its peak it included nearly 40 newspapers including the *San Francisco Examiner*, the *New York Mirror*, the *Chicago Herald-Examiner*, and the *Fort Worth Record*. His move into the magazine market with titles that included *Cosmopolitan*, *Harper's Bazaar*, and *Good Housekeeping* created the largest newspaper and magazine business in the world.

In Britain, by 1919, Lord Northcliffe owned a chain of 31 newspapers including *The Times*, the *Sunday Times*, the *Daily Mail*, the *Daily Mirror*, and the *Observer*, as well as six magazines and two wire services.[50] The contradictions in journalism enhanced by such monopolies were uncovered in the United States by the work of muckraking journalists such as Ida M. Tarbell with her 19-part exposé of Standard Oil for *McClure's Magazine*. Muckrakers sought to expose corruption in government and commerce and were part of the Progressive movement in America around the turn of the twentieth century. They favored economic reform and social liberalism and were always "partisan for the people" which gave them their power and authority (see also Chapter 3).

FactFile
Ida M. Tarbell and Standard Oil

When S. S. McClure, founder of *McClure's Magazine*, decided to investigate oil trusts and in particular the Standard Oil Company owned by John D. Rockefeller, he asked Ida Tarbell to research and write the story because of her first-hand knowledge of the oil industry. Tarbell's father "was a small independent oil operator who was being driven to bankruptcy by Standard Oil's monopolistic practices."[51] Rockefeller was reputedly the world's richest man and was revered and feared in equal measure. Standard Oil had been under federal and state government scrutiny from its formation in 1870 for "allegedly receiving rebates from the railroads and engaging in the restraint of trade."[52]

At the time Tarbell was earning $40 a week for McClure as a staff writer, having previously written a series of articles on Napoleon Bonaparte and Abraham Lincoln which brought her national recognition. She had worked on a variety of magazines, as "annotator" for the *Chautauquan* and then as a writer for the *Daily Herald*. Now she trawled magazine and newspaper articles on Standard Oil and immersed herself in the copious court records relating to civil suits against the company. She carried out a series of interviews with a Standard Oil executive introduced to her by Samuel Clemens

(Mark Twain). This executive gave her chapter and verse on the benefits of monopoly and provided reams of statistics attesting to the company's benign influence. She used this information, however, to develop her critique of Standard Oil's working practices. Eventually Tarbell produced 19 articles for the magazine and the resulting book entitled *The History of the Standard Oil Company* was published in two volumes in 1904.

Tarbell hoped that John D. Rockefeller would be drawn into a debate with her but all he did was command that her name never be mentioned in his presence. Standard Oil mounted a vigorous national campaign to try to discredit the book and its conclusions. Rockefeller donated huge sums to charity in a bid for public support and Standard Oil distributed five million copies of an essay "extolling the benefits of monopolies, and published a book supporting Rockefeller which they distributed free to librarians, ministers, teachers, and prominent citizens throughout the country."[53]

Ultimately his campaign failed and Congress passed the Hepburn Act in 1906 which effectively abolished oil company rebates. That same year a Bureau of Corporations was formed for the purpose of investigating the oil industry. It concluded that Standard Oil had been getting preferential treatment from railroad companies for some time. The Attorney General, Charles Bonaparte, filed a suit under the Sherman Act accusing Standard Oil of "conspiring to restrain and monopolize interstate commerce in petroleum."[54] The company was found guilty and fined $29m. Standard Oil was broken up into 38 separate companies — some still trading today as Mobil, Exxon, Chevron, and Amoco.

Because of her work on the Standard Oil story Tarbell became a beacon for women who wished to pursue a career in journalism. "It was an extraordinary achievement for a woman of her time to single-handedly defeat John D. Rockefeller, the most powerful corporate leader of the time."[55] She carried on writing for a number of different magazines and later joined the Chautauqua lecture circuit but her "muckraking" career was essentially over. She died of pneumonia in Bridgeport, Connecticut in 1944, aged 86.

By the beginning of World War I, however, many of the US papers that had carried articles by well-known muckrakers were now controlled by conservative editors as part of large corporate enterprises. Radical movements suffered from a lack of sympathetic or even accurate coverage in the mainstream press. Negative campaigns against progressive causes meant that it was an uphill task to gain active public support. Although now a famous writer, Upton Sinclair had first-hand experience of mainstream press discrimination and misrepresentation. Sinclair's *The Jungle*, after its success in *Appeal to Reason*, was published in book form in 1906. It epitomized the legislative potential of muckraking journalism in that it publicized the horrendous conditions in the Chicago stockyards and the plight of poor working-class people. It resulted in an investigation that led to the Pure Food and Drug Act and the Meat Inspection Act.

From a journalistic perspective, however, Sinclair's *The Brass Check* (1919) provided the first extensive critique of the limitations of commercial control over journalism and the implications for democracy. The title of the book, which he self-published, refers to the chit issued to patrons of brothels – an analogy to American journalism as prostitute, "a class institution, serving the rich and spurning the poor."[56] In it Sinclair presented his own experiences, bringing to life all the social and economic changes that influenced lifestyles, business organization, national and international politics during the pre-1919 period. He also took the advertising industry to task for its malign influence, as he saw it, on news agendas and news values. It formed part of his broader belief that "Politics, Journalism, and Big Business work hand in hand for the hoodwinking of the public and the plundering of labor."[57]

Sinclair's four-part structural critique of the press in *The Brass Check* can be seen as a forerunner to the now famous propaganda model of the media propounded by Herman and Chomsky in *Manufacturing Consent* (1988). Their central contention is that since the mainstream media depend on advertising revenue to survive, the interests of advertisers come before those of reporting the news. It is possible to argue, therefore, that contemporary media is subject to similar pressures as those detailed in the evidence that Sinclair fastidiously collected over the 12 years before he finally published his exposé.

There was enormous hostility to *The Brass Check*, including threats of libel (although these did not materialize as Sinclair's evidence was watertight). Newspapers refused to review it and the *New York Times* would not even accept paid adverts for it. Ironically, then, the very conditions he sought to expose, critique, and remedy – namely, the suppression of plurality in the news media, structural inequality in the press industry, and the negative social consequences of plutocratic agenda-setting – were the prime factors that "led to the virtual disappearance of *The Brass Check* by the middle of the century."[58] At least Sinclair's hope that his book would find a resonance with future generations of students has been partially fulfilled. A new edition was published in 2003 and it is now available free on the internet.

The circle that writers like Upton Sinclair, Ida Tarbell, and the other muckrakers were unable to square, however, was that between revenue and costs. Newspaper proprietors realized that their survival depended more and more on revenue from advertising rather than cover price. And such revenue came at a price – usually one of editorial obeisance to the sensibilities, at the very least, or to the demands, at the very worst, of their leading advertisers.

Notes

1 Charles Hoffman, *The Depression of the Nineties: An Economic History* (Westport, CT: Greenwood Publishing, 1970), p. 109.

2 David Nasaw, *The Chief: The Life of William Randolph Hearst* (Boston: Houghton Mifflin, 2000), p. 108.

3 Frank Luther Mott, *American Journalism, A History, 1690–1960* (New York: Routledge,1962), p. 539.

4 Michael Emery, Edwin Emery, and Nancy L. Roberts, *The Press and America: An Interpretative History of the Mass Media*, 9th edn (New York: Allyn & Bacon, 2000), p. 257.

5 Nasaw, *The Chief*, p. 75.

6 Richard Bourne, *Lords of Fleet Street: The Harmsworth Dynasty* (London: Unwin Hyman, 1990), p. 34.

7 Piers Brendon, *The Life and Death of the Press Barons* (London: Secker & Warburg, 1982), pp. 110–11.

8 Ibid., p. 112.

9 Ken Ward, *Mass Communication and the Modern World* (London: Macmillan, 1989), p. 40; Peter Catterall, Colin Seymour-Ure, and Adrian Smith (eds), *Northcliffe's Legacy: Aspects of the British Popular Press, 1896–1996* (London: Palgrave Macmillan, 2000), pp. 10–12.

10 Jane Chapman, *Comparative Media History: 1789 to the Present* (Cambridge, UK: Polity Press, 2005), p. 91.

11 Kevin G. Barnhurst, "News Ideology in the Twentieth Century," in Svennik Hoyer and Horst Pottker (eds), *Diffusion of the News Paradigm, 1850–2000* (Göteborg: Nordicom, 2005), pp. 239–62 (p. 245).

12 Kevin Williams, *Read All About It! A History of the British Newspaper* (London: Routledge, 2010), p. 161.

13 Ibid.

14 Cyril Bainbridge, "History of the Institute of Journalists," *Chartered Institute of Journalists* (2007). Available online at http://cioj.co.uk/welcome-to-the-website-of-the-cioj/history-of-the-cioj, accessed on July 10, 2008 (para. 2).

15   David Flintham and Nicholas Herbert, *Press Freedom in Britain* (London: Newspaper Society, 1991), p. 12.

16   Ibid., p. 19.

17   Frank W. Scott, "Newspapers, 1775–1860," in W. P. Trent et al., *The Cambridge History of English and American Literature: An Encyclopedia in Eighteen Volumes*, vol. XVI, *Later National Literature* (New York: G. P. Putman's Sons, 1907–21), Book II, Ch. XXI. Available online at http://bartelby.net/226/1201.html, accessed on August 18, 2010.

18   Jean K. Chalaby, "Journalism as an Anglo-American Invention: A Comparison of the Development of French and Anglo-American Journalism, 1830s–1920s," *European Journal of Communication*, 9, 11 (1996), 303–26 (p. 320).

19   Michael Schudson, *Discovering the News: A Social History of the American Newspaper* (New York: Basic Books, 1978), p. 77.

20   Justin Kaplan, *Lincoln Steffens: A Biography* (London: Jonathan Cape, 1975), p. 56.

21   Stanley Morison, *The English Newspaper 1622–1932* (Cambridge, UK: Cambridge University Press, 1932), p. 287.

22   Kaplan, *Lincoln Steffens*, p. 55.

23   T. P. O'Connor, "The New Journalism," *New Review*, 1 (October 1889), 423–34 (p. 431).

24   W. T. Stead, "The Future of Journalism," *Contemporary Review*, L (November 1886), 663–79 (p. 663).

25   O'Connor, "The New Journalism," p. 428.

26   Schudson, *Discovering the News*; Dan Schiller, *Objectivity and the News: The Public and the Rise of Commercial Journalism* (Philadelphia: University of Pennsylvania Press, 1981).

27   Patricia L. Dooley, *Taking Their Political Place: Journalists and the Making of an Occupation* (Westport, CT: Greenwood, 1997), p. 132.

28   The Times, *History of* The Times, vol. II, *The Tradition Established* (London: Times Publishing Company, 1939), p. 161.

29   O'Connor, "The New Journalism," p. 433.

30   Raymond Williams, *The Long Revolution* (London: Penguin, 1965), p. 219.

31   Harlan S. Stensaas, "Development of the Objectivity Ethic in U.S. Daily Newspapers," *Journal of Mass Media Ethics*, 2, 1 (1986–7), pp. 50–60.

32   Herbert J. Gans, *Deciding What's News: A Study of CBS Evening News, NBC Nightly News, Newsweek, and Time* (New York: Vintage, 1980), pp. 185–6.

33   Walter Williams, *The Journalist's Creed* (Columbia: Missouri School of Journalism, 1908). Available online at http://journalism.missouri.edu/ about/ creed.html, accessed on November 1, 2009.

34   Walter Lippmann and Charles Merz, "A Test of the News," *New Republic*, August 1920 supplement.

35   Warren G. Bovée, *Discovering Journalism* (Westport, CT: Greenwood Press, 1999), p. 122.

36 J. Herbert Altschull, *Agents of Power: The Role of the News Media in Human Affairs*, 2nd edn (New York: Longman, 1994), p. 128.
37 Barnhurst, "News Ideology in the Twentieth Century," p. 258.
38 Michael Schudson, "The Objectivity Norm in American Journalism," in Hoyer and Pottker, pp. 19–35 (p. 32).
39 Gaye Tuchman, *Making News: A Study in the Construction of Reality* (New York: Free Press, 1972), p. 661.
40 Lou Cannon, *Reporting: An Inside View* (Sacramento: California Journal Press, 1950), p. 46.
41 Alan J. Lee, *The Origins of the Popular Press 1855–1914* (London: Croom Helm, 1976), p. 28.
42 *Appeal to Reason.* Available at http://www.spartacus.schoolnet.co.uk/USA appealR.htm, accessed on August 1, 2009.
43 Ibid.
44 Chapman, *Comparative Media History*, pp. 36–9.
45 Lee, *The Origins of the Popular Press*, p. 287.
46 Dan Gillmor, *We the Media: Grassroots Journalism by the People, for the People* (Cambridge, MA: O'Reilly, 2004), p. 4.
47 Gerald J. Baldasty, *The Commercialization of News in the Nineteenth Century* (Madison: University of Wisconsin Press, 1992), p. 7.
48 Andie Tucher, "The Hutchins Commission, Half a Century On," *Media Studies Journal*, 12, 2 (Spring/Summer 1998), 48–55 (p. 50).
49 Edward E. Adams, "Chain Growth and Merger Waves: A Macroeconomic Historical Perspective on Press Consolidation," *Journalism & Mass Communication Quarterly*, 72 (1995), 376–89; Gerald J. Baldasty, *E. W. Scripps and the Business of Newspapers* (Urbana, IL: University of Chicago Press, 1999); S. Elizabeth Bird, *For Enquiring Minds: A Cultural Study of Supermarket Tabloids* (Knoxville: University of Tennessee Press, 1992).
50 Anthony Smith, *The Newspaper: An International History* (London: Thames & Hudson, 1979), p. 165.
51 Carl Jensen, *Stories That Changed America: Muckrakers of the Twentieth Century* (New York: Seven Stories Press, 2002), p. 29.
52 Ibid., p. 30.
53 Ibid.
54 Ibid.
55 Ibid., p. 32.
56 Upton Sinclair, *The Brass Check: A Study of American Journalism* (Urbana: University of Illinois Press, 2003), p. 147.
57 Ibid., p. 153.
58 Ibid., p. xiv.

7

He Who Pays The Piper

Lord Beaverbrook used his newspaper, the *Daily Express*, as a propaganda vehicle to further his political ambitions. In these he signally failed but along the way he helped destroy the career of the then Prime Minister, Stanley Baldwin. In a leader on March 16, 1931, Beaverbrook stated: "The *Daily Express* and the *Daily Mail* are trying to persuade Mr Baldwin to retire and make way for his successor."[1] Baldwin's response came the next day in a now famous by-election speech at the Queen's Hall in London. Thought to have been written by Beaverbrook's former adviser, Rudyard Kipling, in it Baldwin stated that the newspapers of Beaverbrook and Lord Rothermere were:

> engines of propaganda for the constantly changing policies, desires, personal wishes, personal likes and dislikes of two men. What are their methods? Their methods are direct falsehood, misrepresentation, half-truths, the alteration of the speaker's meaning by putting sentences apart from the context … What the proprietorship of these papers is aiming at is power, but power without responsibility – the prerogative of the harlot throughout the ages.'[2]

The kernel of truth in this statement should have surprised no one for when Beaverbrook purchased the *Daily Express* in 1916 he said, "My purpose originally was to set up a propaganda paper, and I have never departed from that purpose all through the years. But in order to make the propaganda effective the paper had to be successful. No paper is any good at all for propaganda unless it has a thoroughly good financial position."[3] In the

Jane Chapman and Nick Nuttall, *Journalism Today: A Themed History*
© 2011 Jane Chapman and Nick Nuttall. Published by Blackwell Publishing Ltd.

twentieth century and the era of the press barons this good financial position was achieved through high circulations and, even more importantly, a healthy income from advertising. Yet the relationship between advertising, politics, and the idea of the press as the Fourth Estate of the realm, that is, its role in a democratic society, is notably complex and contested.

Advertising, Politics and Democracy

By the end of the 1930s, three-quarters of the income of Britain's national dailies came from advertising, and as advertisers increasingly provided the income for newspapers, they were able to exert some control over editorial content. According to many media historians, journalists had effectively swapped one paymaster for another.[4] Press barons of this period, as autocratic as any absolute ruler, were also liable to infiltrate their ideas and views on the matters of the day into their newspapers' pages, at least to the extent that they didn't upset the advertisers. James Curran offers a more ideological attack on the role of advertisers: "[They] made a key distinction between the skilled and poor working class … Once newspapers became identified with the poor, they found it difficult to attract advertising."[5] He cites an advertising handbook of 1921 which warned that papers read by the "down-at-heels" were no places to advertise in and he offers *Reynolds's News* and the *Daily Herald* (two UK papers that both ceased publication in the 1960s) as case studies.

A similar situation existed in the United States. Newspaper advertising revenue tripled between 1915 and 1929, going from $275 million to $800 million while the population increased by only a third from 92 million to 122 million.[6] Such increases in advertising revenues were much to do with the developing ability of newspapers to identify the prosperous amongst their readers. Newspapers in fact sought "affluent consumers 18 to 49 years of age … with above median-family income."[7] While there is nothing intrinsically wrong with a newspaper auditing its circulation into age and socioeconomic groupings, its response to this information is critically significant once the question "How do the mass media strive to reach such people?" is asked. Press critic Ben Bagdikian put it succinctly: "The standard cure for bad 'demographics' in newspapers, magazines, radio and television is simple: Change the content. Fill the publication or the program with material that will attract the kind of people the advertisers want."[8]

FactFile
Advertising, Class, and the *Daily Herald*

The plurality of political reporting in the United Kingdom suffered throughout the twentieth century, particularly with the demise of the *Daily Chronicle* and the *Daily News*, which were amalgamated as the *News Chronicle* in 1930. This paper became the most liberal in Fleet Street and its eventual sale in 1960 to the second Lord Rothermere despite a daily circulation of 1,116,000 was a body blow to left-wing politics. Rothermere absorbed it into his *Daily Mail*.

In 1964 the *Daily Herald* also folded. The Trades Union Congress owned a 49 percent interest in the paper which staunchly supported the Labour Party during the long Conservative ascendancy of the 1950s. On its deathbed it still had a circulation of 1,265,000.[9] This was more than five times the circulation of *The Times* and many Fleet Street editors today would give their eye teeth for such figures. However, its readers were considered the wrong sort of people for stimulating advertising income, and although its share of national circulation was 8 percent, its share of national advertising revenue was a mere 3.5 percent.[10]

It appeared that, whereas the middle classes spent enough money to warrant newspapers with a variety of political stances, the working-class market could not sustain a relatively successful paper based on circulation alone. Between 1960 and 1972 Fleet Street saw the death of the *Empire News*, the *Daily Sketch*, the *Sunday Graphic*, and the *Sunday Dispatch*. They were all publications with working-class readerships and small circulations. Thus they "fell between two stools: they had neither the quantity nor the social 'quality' of readership needed to attract sufficient advertising for them to survive in a deregulated economy."[11]

In Britain, the most blatant and least subtle example of such abuse of power was the attempt by media moguls to use their organizations as alternatives to political parties or as embryo parties in their own right. The culprits in this case were Lord Beaverbrook and Lord Rothermere, the younger brother of Lord Northcliffe. They turned their papers into vehicles for propaganda campaigns against the Conservative Party leadership on the issue of Empire free trade. They put up candidates (unsuccessfully) in by-elections, Beaverbrook for the "Empire Crusade" and Rothermere for his United Empire Party. Beaverbrook's conclusion about press power, and particularly his own, was that "when skilfully employed at the psychological moment no politician of any party can resist it."[12] Rothermere on the other hand was more inclined to assert the power of the proprietor. "The journalist qua journalist must always express more or less the views of the proprietor. Northcliffe, myself and yourself [Beaverbrook] express our own views untramelled [sic] by any one."[13] By 1936 the *Daily Express* was selling 2.25m copies daily – the largest circulation in the world because as Beaverbrook later said, "In an engine of propaganda the engine matters more than the propaganda."[14]

For both Joseph Pulitzer and his arch-rival William Randolph Hearst, the pursuit of political goals was often a simple way of connecting with a readership that supported similar ideas and also advertised in their papers. Hearst's journalists, for example, were given two lists of public figures – those to favor and those to condemn. Furthermore Hearst and Pulitzer were accused of being instrumental in drawing America into the Spanish–American War (1898)[15] through the sensational stories, often untrue, they ran in their papers. Perhaps the most famous example of Hearst's hubris at this time was the comment he is said to have cabled to his artist Frederic Remington who was on the spot in Cuba before hostilities began. Remington cabled Hearst that all was quiet and there would be no war. Hearst responded: "Please remain. You furnish the pictures and I'll furnish the war." Quite clearly for many of the press barons on both sides of the Atlantic circulation and profit came first. Joseph Pulitzer memorably summed up the essence of the approach: "Circulation means advertising, and advertising means money, and money means independence."[16]

FactFile
Forza Italia

The phenomenon of the media organization as substitute for a political party, promoted with such gusto by Lords Beaverbrook and Rothermere in 1930s Britain, was resurrected in Italy by Silvio Berlusconi and his "Forza Italia" movement which made a significant impact in the 1994 general election.[17] Berlusconi is a successful businessman who owns three television stations and a string of other business enterprises. Forza Italia (Forward Italy) was a center-right party and it aimed to attract moderate liberal voters who were, according to Berlusconi, disorientated politically.

Berlusconi used his television stations to promote the party and himself and Forza won the 2001 general election, remaining in power for five years. It used innovative ways of electioneering including stickering, mass mailing of propaganda, SMS messaging, and extensive TV advertising. Toward the end of 2008 the party was officially dissolved and renamed Popolo Della Libertà (The People of Freedom).

Alexander Stille, professor at the Journalism School, Columbia University, offers an insight into the wider significance of the Berlusconi phenomenon:

> The concentration of media, the decline of reading and civic participation, decreasing identification with political parties, the role of celebrity in politics, the appeal of anti-politics, declining unionisation, and the rising gap between rich and poor are growing realities in many advanced capitalist democracies. They create new and troubling possibilities for governments that are run by and for the very few with an enormous media machine at their disposal, who need to win only a tentative nod of approval from an increasingly indifferent and ill-informed public every four or five years in order to continue with their business.[18]

The suggestion here is that media ownership leads to a corrupting influence on the political process. Other commentators have wryly noted that at least it is an Italian who is accused of doing the corrupting rather than a foreigner. American journalist and technology guru Alan Mutter highlights the potential downside of unaccountable media ownership on his *Reflections of a Newsosaur* blog:

> With a growing number of newspapers on the market at a time they most likely will fetch historically low prices, somebody is going to start buying some of them. But don't count on the usual suspects. Start thinking, instead, about such unconventional potential purchasers as the multibillion-dollar investment funds created by countries like Singapore or the sheikhdoms of the United Arab Emirates.[19]

In Mutter's hypothesis, owning a group of widely disseminated publications in the United States would give countries like the United Arab Emirates the extra dividend of a powerful platform for asserting political and commercial influence.

This "independence," however, was not without cost. As advertising became the dominant source of revenue, the economics of advertising-supported newspapers erected a barrier to entry making it almost impossible for small, independent papers to succeed and, indeed, for established newspapers catering for a working-class market to survive. Despite this, in the interwar years in the US there were almost 100 labor-supporting editors – even on conservative papers. This was reflected, for example, in the widespread coverage of the Flint Sit-Down Strike of 1936–7. It became a major national story as General Motors automobile workers at the Flint Michigan plant succeeded in gaining union recognition which led to the unionization of the automobile industry and the formation of the United Automobile Workers Union. In contrast, the1989–90 Pittston Coal strike – the largest since Flint – went almost unreported, partly because by the1980s there were no more than 12 labor-supporting editors.[20] Today there is virtually no labor coverage and what there is tends to be characterized by a "corrosive cynicism" toward politicians and the democratic process,[21] often fueled by what one scholar has called "hyperadversarialism."[22] The other factor that has resulted in such exiguous coverage of labor issues is that "newspapers are also seeking 'to drop or drive away subscribers who represent "demographic targets within markets that are not productive for the advertiser".'"[23]

Fight the Good Fight

The concept of professional journalism was also bound up with the equally beguiling idea that "free markets" were somehow synonymous with democracy. It can be argued, however, that those same commercial factors pursued by the press industries have in fact hindered the use of the medium for the furtherance of democracy. Indeed the pursuit of the free market model is in many respects a grisly example of "the biter bit" and print journalism is now in a fight for its very survival. News organizations around the globe are shedding editorial staff and a number of newspapers in the US are close to bankruptcy. How did the press find itself in this position? There would appear to be three significant factors at work: industry convergence and concentration, the development of broadcast media, and the rise and rise of computer and digital technology.

The twentieth century was the century of media mergers and monopolies. Despite this, overall newspaper circulation in Britain has increased from one in eleven people purchasing a daily paper in 1910 to one in six people in 2009. Overall sales of daily and Sunday papers have doubled over the same period while the population has increased by only 50 percent.

This suggests a vibrant industry. But these figures disguise two factors. Firstly, the high watermark for newspaper circulation was in fact 1955 when daily sales were over 16m compared with 10m in 2009.[24] Secondly, ownership patterns tell a different story. In 1910 in Britain, three owners controlled 67 percent of the morning daily press and four owners controlled 81 percent of the Sunday press. Of these owners, however, only one, Northcliffe, appeared on both lists.[25] By 2009 four conglomerates controlled both 85 percent of the daily and 89 percent of the Sunday press. As James Curran has noted, "This reduced the diversity of the press since papers in the same group tended to adopt similar editorial positions."[26]

In the United States newspaper circulation tells a similar story: it increased by 56 percent during the first half of the century and declined in the second half by 44 percent. Today the top 100 newspapers have a combined sale of almost 37m which is equivalent to one in eight people buying a paper regularly. On both sides of the Atlantic the 1950s were the high watermark of newspaper sales. In Germany, for example, the number of newspaper titles had fallen to 122 in 1976, less than half its postwar peak.[27] This post-World War II period coincided, of course, with the beginnings of popular television broadcasts which also included news bulletins. In the US many newspapers became part of media conglomerates that also owned television stations, magazines, and latterly internet sites. In Britain such mergers have been less marked, mainly because of the anomalous position of the BBC which, although a publicly funded corporation, acts like a media conglomerate in its own right. Rupert Murdoch's News International on the other hand has a dominant position in newspaper production, controlling 38 percent of daily and Sunday circulations, as well as owning Sky TV which is now piped into nearly 10m homes.

Any new means of disseminating information and entertainment tends to destabilize existing media systems. Radio, from the 1920s, was the first new technology that posed a real threat to the press. It couldn't be co-opted to the dominant paradigms that underpinned a newspaper's work routines, news values, and news agendas. Initially of course, it posed a challenge to the historic relationship between the wire services and newspapers but soon the new medium began flexing its muscles. Media theorist Friedrich Kittler has gone so far as to say that "real wars are not fought for people or fatherlands, but take place between different media, information technologies, data flows."[28] The press–radio skirmish was just the first of many that transformed the media landscape in the twentieth century.

Radio was seen, therefore, as a threat in both Britain and the United States. In the US, cross-media ownership became widespread largely because the sheer size of the country tended to insulate regions from each other, reducing competition. For instance, in 1922 *Popular Science Monthly* produced a series of maps that gave the coverage areas for all the main radio stations across the country. The average American may not have been aware of it, but such maps served to illustrate just how local radio transmissions really were. Despite such limitations, it wasn't until 1939 that Associated Press finally lifted its ban on providing news "briefs" to radio stations.

In Britain, the press did not generally favor cross-media ownership. In 1922 there were almost a hundred applications to set up broadcasting stations. But the scarcity of air waves meant some control was needed and this control, rather than governmental, was exercised "by persuading rival manufacturers to invest jointly in one small and initially speculative broadcasting station: The British Broadcasting Company."[29] The BBC was granted a Royal Charter in 1927 and changed from a company to a publicly funded corporation. Its aim was always to be a national broadcaster and as such was always likely to be in competition with the national press. The first Director-General of the BBC, Lord Reith, argued that "it was in the very nature of the medium that it should be available for all, for it 'ran as a reversal of the natural law that the more one takes, the less there is left for others ... There is no limit to the amount which may be drawn off'."[30] This was a prescient argument and one that is used today to highlight one of the major differences (and by implication strengths) of the internet and the world wide web compared with more traditional media.

Such arguments only helped to further alarm members of the press, however, who believed that news should remain their prerogative. In America opposition was split between those who embraced the new medium and those who looked on it as "little more than an experimental toy."[31] Yet despite these different attitudes there were attempts on both sides of the Atlantic to undermine radio's inherent journalistic advantage of immediacy by trying to prevent broadcasters from supplying breaking news. Fear of this advantage was only increased by radio's victory in scooping two major stories on its own: the kidnap of Charles Lindbergh's baby in 1932 and an attempted assassination of President Roosevelt the following year. Perhaps radio's power was best displayed with the spoof broadcast by Orson Welles for CBS's *Mercury Theatre on the Air* slot on October 30, 1938. It was an adaptation of H. G. Wells's novel *The War of the Worlds*. Many listeners believed that the country was being invaded by Martians and that Welles was in fact a journalist "on the spot" reporting the "news." The broadcast caused panic in the vicinity of the "landing" as people fled their homes. There is now a small monument on the spot where the Martians "landed" in Van Nest Park, Grover's Mill, New Jersey.

Despite such oddities and the different ways in which radio developed, with a public service ethos in Britain and a strong commercial bias in the US, the response to radio and the tactics for self-defense employed by the press were similar. In both cases while newspapers lost the arguments radio didn't really affect sales – at least not in the way that television was to do post-World War II. In an attempt to thwart an all-out "war," representatives of the US newspaper and radio industries held a conference at the Biltmore Hotel, New York, in December 1933. The Biltmore Agreement, also known as the Press–Radio Plan, essentially was an agreement whereby broadcasters would no longer gather their own news and in exchange would receive two five-minute bulletins a day, with no sponsorship, from news provided by the press associations.[32] The Biltmore agreement was actually unworkable in that it was never a signed agreement and, despite lengthy consultations with the National Association of Broadcasters which represented independent radio stations, the independents never agreed to the Biltmore program. Thus divisions resurfaced between press supporters of radio and their opponents because "there was just too much money to be made in radio … Those with the means to make the investment in broadcasting were no longer willing to stand aside and let someone else enjoy the profits."[33]

The minority position of the nonprofit, public service radio sector in America provided, if nothing else, a test-bed for new technologies which were deemed unprofitable – AM radio in the 1920s, FM radio in the 1940s, and UHF television transmissions in the 1950s and 1960s. At the first whiff of profitability, however, the commercial juggernauts took over. The "golden age" of radio, when audiences peaked, was in the 1930s and 1940s. By 1935 over 22m American homes had a radio, and cars were being sold with radios in them. During this period "twice as many Americans reported that they'd give up a newspaper before they'd part with their radio."[34] Meanwhile public service radio spawned its own broadcasting reform movement which campaigned, in the end unsuccessfully, for a public service element in the new system.

FactFile
The Broadcast Reform Movement, 1928–35

In 1930s America commercial radio was the *de facto* structure of the emergent industry which was dominated by two broadcasters, CBS and NBC. According to media historian Robert McChesney, the American media system was the result of laws and regulations, together with public subsidies and the granting of operational licenses, all "made corruptly behind closed doors without the public's informed consent." In particular he refers to the granting of monopoly rights to valuable broadcasting spectra and monopoly cable franchises.[35]

The broadcast reform movement challenged this hegemony and posited a noncommercial sector, not so much to replace commercial stations but to act as an alternative and clearly defined "independent" source of news, ideas, and entertainment. "This movement made a strong critique of the limitations of commercial media for a free and self-governing society" concluded McChesney.[36] Between 1928 and 1935 the reform movement attempted to pass legislation to establish a noncommercial radio sector. Although reformers lacked a mass base and exhibited elitist tendencies, they were nevertheless concerned to support free speech through the democratic allocation of broadcast frequencies. Congress considered legislation for permanent regulation in every session from 1927 through to the full passage of the Communications Act in 1934.[37] This Act essentially concluded that commercial stations had ample time for public service programs and there was no need therefore for a "protected" public network.

The defeat of the reformers served to consolidate acceptance of the idea that commercial broadcasting was both American and democratic. McChesney points out that tax codes allowing advertising to be written off as a legitimate business expense "feed the commercialism that has overwhelmed media and society." As regards license holders, "they won a government lottery in which the overwhelming majority were denied the right to even buy a ticket."[38] McChesney has also drawn parallels with the Communications Act of 1995. It represents, he suggests, a logical continuation of this thinking, because it ensures that the infallibility of the market and not public policy will determine the direction that the internet takes.[39]

In Britain the public service ethos had the opposite effect, stifling a commercial sector until the 1970s. By this time television had usurped radio as the most popular broadcast medium and in response to this the first commercial television station, ITV, was launched in 1955. It was to be another nine years before pirate radio, and in particular Radio Caroline, attempted to break the BBC's radio monopoly. Caroline broadcast from a boat moored in international waters three miles off the coast at Felixstowe, Suffolk. It was said the station took its name from Caroline Kennedy, daughter of the US President. Although it was doing nothing illegal, the government responded by passing the Marine Offences Act in 1967, effectively outlawing the pirate stations. Later the same year BBC radio was reorganized and the new Radio 1 played pop music in similar fashion to the pirates. Many of the pirate DJs were then employed by the BBC. Despite this, it wasn't until 1973 that the first on-land commercial radio station LBC (London Broadcasting Company) complete with adverts began broadcasting in Britain. It had taken 50 years for another broadcaster to challenge the BBCs hegemony of the radio waves.

Moving Pictures – How Television Stole the News

According to the most recent figures, half the world's population now spends its leisure time watching television – an activity that even the computer has yet to rival.[40] But equally important, radio industry structures provided the model for the nascent television industry.[41] Television was powerfully democratizing and polarizing, unlike radio which in Britain rather reflected the arrogance and pomposity of the Director-General of the BBC, Lord Reith. As early as 1950 the working-class *Daily Mirror* in Britain said: "Once you have allowed a TV to enter your house, life will never be the same again."[42] The artist Duncan Grant, a member of the Bloomsbury Group, on seeing television for the first time, wrote to Vanessa Bell, "I really think it is the end of civilisation as we know it."[43] In many ways and for many people this was certainly true, although their emphasis was always to be on the "as we know it" rather than "the end of civilisation."

Establishment figures, however, while prepared to accept the BBC, balked at commercial television and mounted a strong rearguard action to try to stop passage of the necessary legislation. They used American TV as their example of all that was wrong with commercial broadcasting. They were further enraged when they discovered that "in the USA the Coronation [of Queen Elizabeth II in 1953] had been shown interspersed with NBC's television chimp, J. Fred Muggs, selling tea. A deodorant had been advertised just before the ritual anointment."[44]

It turned out that in a small country like Britain, however, television created a sense of national unity as people all sat down at the same time to watch the same program. Something of the wartime spirit was evoked by such behavior, enabling people to share a common experience in what were otherwise becoming atomized lives. Personalities were created in living rooms rather than cinemas. Their human scale seemed to make them more real, "more like us," and this helped reinforce the power of the medium to beguile and distract. Lord Reith's dictum was to inform, educate, and entertain. James Curran suggests: "Even with news and documentaries, the pressure to be 'entertaining' – to hold audiences by being immediately accessible and stimulating – overrides other considerations."[45] Notwithstanding, television produced some of the most famous names and personalities of the last half of the twentieth century, many of whom, like Richard Dimbleby in Britain and Edward R Murrow and Walter Cronkite in America, had careers that began in radio and successfully transferred to television. Richard Dimbleby, for instance, reported on the coronation of Queen Elizabeth II and the funerals of King George VI, John F Kennedy, and Winston Churchill. He also introduced the program in July 1962 which showed the first live television signal from the United States using the Telstar satellite.

FactFile
Edward R. Murrow and *See It Now*

America's most famous broadcast journalist, Edward R Murrow, in a speech at the 1958 Radio and Television News Directors Association (RTNDA) annual convention, affirmed his belief that "If radio news is to be regarded as a commodity, only acceptable when saleable, then I don't care what you call it – I say it isn't news." He identified three threats to journalism: commercialism, careerism, and corruption. His World War II broadcasts from London helped establish CBS as the leader in American radio news and he also became famous for his *See It Now* weekly documentary program, in partnership with producer Fred W. Friendly, which ran on CBS television from 1951 to 1955.

Murrow was born Egbert Roscoe Murrow in North Carolina in 1908. He graduated from Washington State College in 1930 and joined CBS as director of talks in 1935. He went to London in 1937 as director of CBS's European operations. His job was to recruit European journalists to broadcast on the CBS network. He recruited William L. Shirer as his opposite number in continental Europe and the two men would become the founding fathers of broadcast journalism in America. Murrow did in fact broadcast from London during the Blitz and became famous for his signature intro "*This* is London," with emphasis on "this" and his equally famous outro, "Good night, and good luck."

The most famous episode of *See It Now*, aired in March 1954, was entitled "A Report on Senator Joseph McCarthy." It exposed the contradictions and falsehoods in McCarthy's arguments about Communist infiltration and the "Red Scare" in American politics. The broadcast was seen as instrumental in the Senator's downfall and provoked thousands of letters and phone calls to CBS which ran fifteen to one in the program's favor. Murrow and Friendly took on a series of difficult subjects, from the dangers of smoking (at a time when television sponsorship was dominated by US tobacco companies), to radioactive fallout from nuclear tests (regularly conducted in the Nevada desert and other places) and a documentary on Egypt and Israel (when the 1956 Suez Crisis sent reverberations around the world).

He brought credibility to radio and TV journalism at a time when they were new and needed to be taken seriously. His statements about values and responsibility show a prescience that still sets the standard for integrity and dedication. He spoke out about his values and where he believed the buck stops in his 1958 speech to the RTNDA annual convention: "The responsibility can be easily placed, in spite of all the mouthings about giving the public what it wants. It rests on big business, and on big television, and it rests at the top. Responsibility is not something that can be assigned, or delegated. And it promises its own reward: good business and good television."[46]

Murrow's principles live on, even if there are fewer practitioners today who are prepared to bite the hand that feeds them by living up to such values:

> Our history will be what we make it. And if there are any historians about fifty or a hundred years from now, and there should be preserved the kinescope for one week of all three networks, they will there find recorded in black and white, or color, evidence of decadence, escapism and insulation from the realities of the world in which we live.[47]

Significantly for the theme of this chapter, Murrow linked good business with good journalism, but they are not always compatible. Despite this, it is difficult to imagine that he would condone many of the practices that masquerade as journalism on mainstream news channels today. Always a heavy smoker, Murrow died of lung cancer aged 57. The Edward R. Murrow Center of Public Diplomacy was established in his honor at Tufts University's Fletcher School of Law and Diplomacy in Massachusetts.

In the 1960s and 1970s broadcasters grew into large media corporations by swallowing up rivals and branching out into other fields. The one area which has grown up independently of them, however, is the computer industry. Microsoft, Apple, Google, and Hewlett Packard are demonstrably separate and different from Time Warner, Disney, and News Corp. Each industry is now beginning to encroach on the other but so far only "round the edges." How long this state of affairs will continue is unclear but undoubtedly there will be attempts at convergence, if for no other reason than that the computer monitor is now used more and more to view the output of both types of corporation.

At an individual level then, as the computer becomes ubiquitous and is used for more and more functions, and in particular for the watching of video content, it may come to be seen as a stage in the development of the moving image rather than an end in itself. Mitchell Stephens argues that the real revolution we are currently experiencing will indeed turn out to be that of the moving image. He points out that even Steve Jobs, cofounder of Apple, said in 1996 that he thought the effect of the computer would not be as profound as the first time people saw a television.[48] TV penetration, for example, reached half of all American households within eight years whereas it took 16 years for the number of households with a computer to go from 8 percent, in 1984, to 50 percent, in 2000. By 2004 both the UK and the US had about 62 percent of households with a computer,[49] whereas 99 percent of households in the US[50] and 96 percent of households in the EU owned a TV.[51]

Newspapers' "Cold Type Revolution"

Few, of course, understood that the "cold type revolution," (see Chapter 5), in effect the first use of modern computer technology in journalism, released newspapers not only from the influence of the print unions but also from the protective cocoon that hitherto had virtually guaranteed their independence as a news platform. The ability of computers to reassemble, store, and analyze information meant that for the first time journalists could do page layout electronically ready for printing, so that new editions could be turned out more cheaply and editorial offices could be separated from printing works. Production costs were thus reduced (short-lived though this was), and this was good news for small-circulation newspapers. But the overall change from being labor intensive to capital intensive was bad news for print workers as large numbers of jobs were lost amid a climate of industrial conflict and worker unrest. Start-up costs were now low enough in the UK to allow a new breed of entrepreneur to operate a paper. In the period immediately after 1986 there were any number of new national newspapers, for example, the *Planet on Sunday*, the *Correspondent*, the *Post, Today*, the *Independent*, the *London Daily News*. Never had so many newspapers used so much newsprint to reach so few readers! None of these papers survived for more than a year or so, with the notable exception of the *Independent*.

Now, a second wave of commercial angst is hitting print journalism, one that is challenging its independence, if not its very existence. Computers and digital technology are beginning to undermine the delicate balance between newspaper production costs and revenue. In Britain it is local and regional titles that are mainly feeling the heat whereas in America it is many of the iconic and revered titles that are now in trouble – titles like the *New York Times* (seriously falling revenue streams), the *Los Angeles Times* (a newsroom half the size it was in 2001), the *Chicago Sun-Times* ($1bn of debt in 2009), the *San Francisco Chronicle* (circulation halved in the year ending 2008 and a consistent money loser). The Tribune Company, owners of the *Chicago Tribune*, the *Baltimore Sun*, and the *Los Angeles Times* filed for bankruptcy protection in December 2008.[52] Such wholesale carnage has resulted in 15,000 journalism job losses in 2008 and another 9,000 by mid-2009.[53]

The main reasons for these difficulties, however, are the same – fewer readers and a loss of advertising revenue. There are fewer readers because of changing cultural habits: the loss of a sense of community which both feeds and feeds off a local paper as much as a regional one, and of course the rise of the internet as a news source that has the benefits of broadcast in its immediacy and of print in its ability to be read and reread at leisure. Similarly, classified ads (most early newspapers placed these ads on the front page, demonstrating their importance), for so long the main source of newspaper revenue, are migrating at speed to the internet. As with music downloads, the prevailing wisdom seems to be "why pay for something if you can get it for free?"

One response to falling circulations and advertising revenues has been the free newspaper. Its premise is that it should generate a higher circulation because it is free and on the back of this will attract more advertising at higher rates. It thus employs a traditional economic model except for the actual cover price. The most intense circulation and turf wars in London and New York, for instance, have been between the "freebies." Interestingly, writing at the beginning of World War I, William Maxwell predicted this phenomenon. In 1914 he wrote:

> We may yet see the newspaper that costs not even a halfpenny, but is the free gift of the great advertisers through a Trust. This is one vision of the commercial journalist. And there are other dreamers who look to the coming of a newspaper which shall know neither party nor advertiser – a newspaper without a cause or a principle. To some people this may seem perfection, but perfection is one of the things that the world can easily dispense with – even in its newspapers.[54]

Yet even free newspapers cannot escape economic reality. Rupert Murdoch closed *thelondonpaper* on September 18, 2009 – almost three years to the day since its launch – after it recorded pretax losses of £12.9m for the year. Associated Newspapers closed *London Lite* on November 13, 2009 for similar reasons. At the same time the only paid-for London evening paper, the 180-year-old *Evening Standard*, became a free paper from October 2009.

The power of the internet and the world wide web has yet to be fully understood but year on year television usage is falling and is being replaced by computer usage. For example in the US about 2 percent of people used the internet for news in 1996 whereas the figure for 2008 is 37 percent. In the same period the numbers of people who regularly read a newspaper fell from 50 to 34 percent.[55] At the same time 37 percent of people thought the internet informative against 20 percent for television. A further 49 percent said that the internet gave them greater control as against only 22 percent for television.[56] In the end, however convergence occurs, the ultimate prize is control of the channels of communication which "bring not only profits … but power to shape the cultural agenda, public opinion, and the nature of social discourse. It is power, to some degree, to determine the way millions of people define and experience reality, and for many, that is a power worth fighting for."[57] The global media conglomerate is one manifestation of such "power" but the way journalists adapt and exploit these new media opportunities must surely be another and, ideally, one that offers a corrective to the excesses inherent in monopoly corporate hegemony.

Notes

1 Anne Chisholm and Michael Davie, *Beaverbrook: A Life* (London: Pimlico, 1993), p. 304.
2 Ibid., p. 305.
3 George Boyce, James Curran, and Pauline Wingate, *Newspaper History from the 17th Century to the Present Day* (London: Constable, 1978), p. 142.
4 James Curran and Jean Seaton, *Power without Responsibility: The Press and Broadcasting in Britain*, 5th edn (London: Routledge, 1997), pp. 7–108.
5 Ibid., p. 35.
6 David Pearce Demers, "Structural Pluralism, Intermedia Competition, and the Growth of the Corporate Newspaper in the United States," in Alan Wells and Ernest A. Hakanen (eds), *Mass Media and Society* (New York: Ablex Publishing Corporation, 1997), pp. 85–108 (pp. 90–1).
7 Ben Bagdikian cited in William S. Solomon, "The Newspaper Business," in Wells and Hakanen, *Mass Media and Society*, pp. 71–84 (p. 73).
8 Ibid., p. 74.
9 Curran and Seaton, *Power without Responsibility*, p. 91.
10 Ibid.
11 Ibid.
12 Chisholm and Davie, *Beaverbrook*, p. 276.
13 Ibid., p. 277.
14 Piers Brendon, *The Life and Death of the Press Barons* (London: Secker & Warburg, 1982), p. 161.
15 The Spanish–American war took place between April and August 1898 in pursuit of the Monroe Doctrine. The Monroe Doctrine was an American policy dating from 1823 which stated that any further European colonization of territory close to the US would be viewed as a hostile act. In accordance with this doctrine the US supported the liberation of the Spanish dependency of Cuba. The war ended with victories for the United States in the Philippine Islands and Cuba. In December 1898 both countries signed the Treaty of Paris which ceded control of Cuba, Puerto Rica, Guam, and the Philippines to the United States.
16 Quoted in Alleyne Ireland, *Joseph Pulitzer* (Charleston, SC: Bibliolife. 2009), p. 115.

17 Paul Statham, "Television News and the Public Sphere in Italy: Conflicts at the Media/Politics Interface," *European Journal of Communication*, 11 (1996), 511–56.

18 Alexander Stille, *The Sack of Rome: Media + Money + Celebrity = Power = Silvio Berlusconi* (London: Penguin Books, 2007). Cited in Granville Williams, "Media For All? The Challenge of Convergence," *Free Press: Journal of the Campaign for Press and Broadcasting Freedom*, 171 (July–August 2009), p. 4.

19 Alan D. Mutter, "Game-Changing Newspaper Buyers," *Reflections of a Newsosaur*, August 17, 2008. Available online at http://newsosaur.blogspot.com/2008/08/game-changing-newspaper-buyers.html, accessed on November 3, 2009.

20 Robert McChesney, "The Rise and Fall of Professional Journalism," in Kristina Borjesson (ed.), *Into the Buzzsaw: Leading Journalists Expose the Myth of a Free Press* (Amherst, NY: Prometheus Books, 2002), pp. 363–81 (p. 370).

21 Brian McNair, "The British Press, 1992–2007," *Future of Newspapers Conference*, Cardiff, September 7–9, 2007.

22 James Fallows, *Breaking the News: How the Media Undermine American Democracy* (New York: Pantheon Books, 1996).

23 Solomon, "The Newspaper Business," p. 74.

24 Peter J. Anderson and Anthony Weymouth, "The Changing World of Journalism," in Peter J. Anderson and Geoff Ward (eds), *The Future of Journalism in the Advanced Democracies* (Farnham, UK: Ashgate, 2006), pp. 17–36 (p. 25).

25 Alan J. Lee, *The Origins of the Popular Press 1855–1914* (London: Croom Helm, 1976), p. 293.

26 Curran and Seaton, *Power without Responsibility*, p. 77.

27 Anthony Smith, *The Newspaper: An International History* (London: Thames & Hudson, 1979), p. 166; Paul Murschetz, "State Support for the Daily Press in Europe: A Critical Appraisal: Austria, France, Norway and Sweden Compared," *European Journal of Communications*, 13 (1998), 291–313.

28 Friedrich Kittler, *Gramophone, Film, Typewriter* (Stanford, CA: Stanford University Press, 1999), p. xli.

29 Curran and Seaton, *Power without Responsibility*, p. 112.

30 Ibid., p. 115.

31 Ibid., p. 111.

32 Jane Chapman, *Comparative Media History: 1789 to the Present* (Cambridge, UK: Polity Press, 2005), pp. 157–8.

33 Gwenyth L. Jackaway, *Media at War: Radio's Challenge to the Newspapers, 1924–1939* (Santa Barbara, CA: Greenwood Press, 1995), p. 34.

34 Bruce J. Evensen, "A History of Responsible Reporting," in Bruce J. Evensen (ed.), *The Responsible Reporter: Journalism in the Information Age*, 3rd edn (New York: Peter Lang, 2008), pp. 11–30 (p. 24).

35   Robert W. McChesney, *Telecommunications, Mass Media, and Democracy: The Battle for Control of U.S. Broadcasting 1928–1935* (New York: Oxford University Press, 1993), p. 381.

36   Robert W. McChesney, "The Broadcast … er … Media … Reform Movement: This is Then and That was Now," paper presented at the annual meeting of the International Communication Association, TBA, Montreal, Quebec, Canada, May 23, 2009.

37   McChesney, *Telecommunications, Mass Media, and Democracy*, p. 5.

38   Robert W. McChesney and John Nichols, *Our Media, Not Theirs: The Democratic Struggle Against Corporate Media* (New York: Seven Stories Press, 2002), pp. 27–8.

39   McChesney, *Telecommunications, Mass Media, and Democracy*, p. 5.

40   Mitchell Stephens, *A History of News: From the Drum to the Satellite* (Fort Worth, TX: Harcourt Brace College Publishers, 1997), p. 11.

41   Chapman, *Comparative Media History*, p. 221.

42   Ibid., p. 207.

43   Frances Spalding, *Duncan Grant: A Biography* (London: Chatto & Windus, 1997), p. 427.

44   Curran and Seaton, *Power without Responsibility*, p. 163.

45   Ibid.

46   Richard D. Heffner, *A Documentary History of the United States*, 7th edn (New York: Signet, 2002), p. 441. Speech given by Ed Murrow to the RTNDA, Chicago, 15 October 1958. The speech is available online at http://www.turnoffyourtv.com/commentary/hiddenagenda/murrow.html, accessed August 19, 2010.

47   Ibid., p. 435.

48   Mitchell Stephens, *The Rise of the Image, the Fall of the World* (Oxford: Oxford University Press, 1998), p. 7.

49   US Census Bureau National Statistics Online, Appendix Table A. Available online at http://www.census.gov/population/www/socdemo/computer/2007.html, accessed on April 10, 2009.

50   The Sourcebook for Teaching Science, *Television and Health*. Available online at http://www.csun.edu/science/health/docs/tv&health.html#tv_stats, accessed on August 6, 2009.

51   Eurobarometer, *E-Communications Household Survey*. Available online at http://ec.europa.eu/public_opinion/archives/ebs/ebs_249_en.pdf, accessed on August 19, 2009.

52   Samuel Chi, *Top 10 Newspapers in Trouble*, RealClearPolitics Media Watch, 2009. Available online at http://www.realclearpolitics.com/mediawatch/2009/02/top_10_newspapers_in_trouble.html, accessed on August 6, 2009.

53 Granville Williams, "Media For All? The Challenge of Convergence", *Free Press: Journal of the Campaign for Press and Broadcasting Freedom*, 171 (July–August 2009), p. 4.

54 William Maxwell, "Old Lamps for New: Some Reflections on Recent Changes in Journalism," *Nineteenth Century and After*, 75, 1085–96 (p. 1096).

55 "Key News Audiences Now Blend Online and Traditional Sources," Pew Research Center, August 17, 2008. Available online at http://people-press.org/report/444/news-media, accessed on August 7, 2009.

56 Frank W. Baker, *MediaLiteracyClearingHouse: Media Use Statistics*. Available online at http://www.frankwbaker.com/mediause.htm, accessed on August 6, 2009.

57 Jackaway, *Media at War*, p. 74.

8

A Power Worth Fighting For

In 1952 Rupert Murdoch inherited the newspaper company started by his father Sir Keith Murdoch. Its main asset was the Adelaide tabloid *The News*. Murdoch junior's first US purchase was the *San Antonio Express-News* in1973. Since then he has built News Corporation into a global company with an operating income of $5.4bn.[1] The search engine company Google, on the other hand, was only founded in 1998, going public in 2004. In 2009 it boasted total assets of almost $32bn and an operating income of $6.6bn.[2] The Millward Brown research agency describes Google as the most powerful brand in the world. It's as if a teenager has come along and taken over the 'hood from all the old grizzled godfathers without even a fight.

It is evident that organizations like News Corporation, Time Warner Inc., and The Walt Disney Company, despite their enormous size and wealth, have to some extent been left at the digital starting gate and are now busily buying up promising internet-based companies like MySpace in an attempt to climb back aboard the digital express. But are they too late? Have they made the possibly fatal mistake of assuming that digital communication is just another technology? History, of course, teaches us otherwise. Many people believed that traveling at over 25 mph on the new-fangled railroad would cause human beings to implode from the effects of the wind on their bodies. Yet the railroad was not really about speed. It changed the social and cultural landscape in ways that its pioneers could never have imagined. The telegraph similarly was not really about speed either, although this was one of its early selling points. It changed the way journalists wrote stories, it changed their news-gathering methods, and in the process it changed newspaper design and content. Ultimately, however, it altered the way journalists *thought* about

Jane Chapman and Nick Nuttall, *Journalism Today: A Themed History*
© 2011 Jane Chapman and Nick Nuttall. Published by Blackwell Publishing Ltd.

their job, something never envisaged by Paul Julius Reuter when he started his carrier pigeon service from Aachen to Brussels in 1850.

The digital era is similarly transforming the media landscape as well as its ideological expression in wider culture and society. This transformation in its initial stages is clearly technology-driven, but ultimately questions about how to monetize webpage content, how to maintain print-based quality in an infinite webscape, or how to control "illegal" file-sharing will all be swept away by the seismic change in worldview that a digital universe will create.

Obama's presidential campaign has been described as the Facebook election and this was responsible, according to political pundits, for the large turnout of young voters and the fact that Obama won 70 percent of the under-25 age group.[3] To better appreciate the psychology of the media organization and its "collision" with computer and digital technology, it is useful to examine the rush to deregulation and consolidation after World War II and how this has made uncomfortable bedfellows of journalism and global capitalism.

Deregulate and Multiply

Globalization and deregulation have always been bigger issues in Britain than in the US or other countries that lack a strong public service broadcasting ethic. Prior to the development of television, media companies were invariably print-based and in Britain there were attempts to maintain a plurality of the press despite the fact that the market was beginning to decree otherwise. The Labour government of Harold Wilson was so concerned that in 1975 Tony Benn, the Secretary of State for Industry, decided to subsidize the *Scottish Daily News*, a paper that operated as a workers' co-operative after Beaverbrook Newspapers closed the *Scottish Daily Express* and made the workforce redundant. The government gave £1.2m so the paper could buy the old Beaverbrook building in Glasgow. Sales were never robust, however, and the paper only lasted six months.[4] There were also suggestions that a paper subsidized by the government was inevitably not to be trusted and was likely to peddle propaganda rather than objective news. This example is confirmation, if any were needed, that a British press that had spent the previous two centuries or more throwing off the yoke of government and other controls was not likely now to succeed by their reintroduction, however laudable the intent.

Yet this has never been the case with broadcast media. In America the default position governing media expansion has invariably favored market-led solutions whereas in Britain, largely because of the power of the BBC, a public-service ethos has, until recently, tended to trump market-orientated solutions. In 1985, the influential Peacock Committee on broadcasting finance was set up by the then Conservative government and although its conclusions favored a free market in broadcasting, there was no clear idea of how this could be achieved. Despite this, it was implicit in the Peacock Committee's approach that "consumers of broadcasting must themselves decide what they want and the price they are willing to pay."[5]

Satellite and cable technology, both in their infancy when Peacock reported, have to some extent achieved this aim, although the position of the BBC in the world of "new media" is still somewhat anomalous and unclear. Put simply, a license fee is payable to watch all television output, not just BBC output, even though the whole fee is paid to the BBC. Thus British consumers must pay a license fee and on top of that a subscription fee if they wish to watch any of the multiple channels supplied by Sky TV or one of the cable companies like Virgin. Yet there is still the seeming impracticality of providing a "transmission system capable of an *indefinitely* large number of channels" as envisaged by Peacock.[6]

One of the prerequisites for such a transmission system is a media corporation with sufficient expertise to create it and sufficient wealth to deliver it – in other words it would be a market-orientated solution. As late as 1965 there were hardly any media companies among the top 300 largest worldwide corporations. By the end of the century, however, there were nine or ten, depending on how you assess their value. This growth was aided by deregulation and abetted by first-wave digital technology (see Chapter 5). Rupert Murdoch's News Corp, which owns Sky TV in Britain and Fox Television in America, illustrates the way in which big business has both taken over the world of journalism on the one hand and left itself vulnerable to the sudden onslaught of second-wave digital media innovations on the other.

FactFile
Rupert Murdoch and News Corporation

Within the satellite world, one empire stands out: that of the digital operator Rupert Murdoch, with his News Corporation and channels such as Sky and Fox television. At the time of writing his business employs 53,000 people, has revenues of $33bn, and reaches an audience of nearly one billion people every day. His fiefdom was built on the modest newspaper holdings in Adelaide, South Australia he inherited from his father. Very soon he controlled seven out of the twelve principal newspapers in Australia's capital cities, and seven out of the ten Sunday newspapers. In Adelaide he now has a monopoly except for just one weekly, and he also owns the printing presses. He is, in fact, responsible for almost 70 percent of Australia's principal newspaper circulation. This has bestowed upon Australia the dubious honor of having the most concentrated press ownership in the Western world.[7]

Murdoch proved masterful at cross-promotion of his various properties, at influencing politicians, and at propagating the sort of tabloid values displayed on Fox Television in the United States and in the *News of the World* and *Sun* newspapers in Britain. The global expansion of News Corp has spread to Japan, India, China, and Latin America and into continental Europe. Murdoch seems to be interested in politics only as a means of either securing business deals or enhancing the commercial environment for News Corp. An example of the former is when he bid for *The Times* and the *Sunday Times* in 1981. Serious concerns were expressed in parliament and demands to refer the deal for official investigation as a monopoly were refused by the then Conservative government. There has always been a suspicion that Margaret Thatcher stopped the referral as a "thank you" for Murdoch's support during and after her election triumph in 1979. An example of the latter is the constant bad press meted out by his British newspapers toward the European Union. The inference seems to be that EU legislation would more likely hamper his entrepreneurial spirit than British laws alone.

Murdoch owns newspapers and magazines in Australia, Fiji, Papua New Guinea, the UK, and the USA. In Britain he owns Sky TV, *The Times*, the *Sunday Times*, the *Sun*, and the *News of the World*. In America he owns the *New York Post* and the *Wall Street Journal*, 20th Century Fox, Fox Television Stations Group, STAR TV, Fox Movie Channel, Fox Sports Net, and Fox Interactive Media. He also owns a range of digital media including MySpace and foxsports.com.

Britain has to some extent been spared this consolidation in the broadcast sector because of the unique position of the BBC. Yet it could be argued that the BBC was formed as a result of the first broadcast "consolidation" in 1922 when the Postmaster General persuaded "rival manufacturers to invest jointly in one small and initially speculative broadcasting station: The British Broadcasting Company."[8] Despite its long history, however, the BBC is not immune to the effects of globalization, for in Britain as elsewhere more and more people obtain their television pictures by either cable or satellite and traditional aerial-provided terrestrial stations are now in a minority. Most recently (2009) "government proposals to 'top slice' the license fee and hand over part of the levy to the corporation's commercial rivals"[9] has produced a concerted campaign of resistance within the BBC itself. While many journalists see the BBC as one of the last bastions of a public service ethic in news and feature production in need of preservation at all costs, others are just as sure that commercial news outlets are the way of the future and they are being hindered by the hegemony of the Corporation with its assured license-fee income.

In the United States, according to the Pew Research Center's Project for Excellence in Journalism (2006), 20 companies now control 68 percent of US daily newspaper circulation, a further 20 companies operate more than 20 percent of all radio stations and 30 percent of local TV stations are owned by 10 companies. The number of households linked to cable systems was 28m in 1982. By 2006 more than 77 million people (approx. 25% of the population) subscribed to cable television and 79 percent of all television reception was via cable or satellite. This contrasts with Britain where 3.5 million people (approx. 6% of the population) subscribed to cable television and only 32 percent of all television reception was via cable or satellite.[10] In the US the three main networks, ABC, CBS, and NBC "have seen their share of the audience cut quite dramatically. Though the networks remain dominant, they have felt the impact of the new media."[11] Most European countries replicate the American statistics, apart from Britain and Italy. The British figures are a stark illustration of the way public service broadcasting and the BBC have had a major effect on the way television is consumed. The relatively small size of the country, enabling good national coverage with traditional aerials, aided and abetted the BBC's hegemony.

FactFile
Cable News Network and the "CNN Effect"

Cable News Network, always known as CNN, was founded in 1980 by Ted Turner. It was the first network to offer 24-hour television news coverage seven days a week. It reaches over 93m American households and CNN International reaches more than 212 countries and territories.[12]

The network has a history of scooping its rivals. On January 28, 1986, CNN was the only network to have live coverage of the launch and subsequent destruction of the Challenger Space Shuttle. The shuttle exploded after lift-off killing seven crew members including Christa McAuliffe, a school teacher from Concord, New Hampshire, who was to have been the first teacher in space. On October 14, 1987, an 18-month-old toddler named Jessica McClure fell down a well in Midland, Texas. CNN was quickly on the spot, and the event helped to make its name.

The first Gulf War in 1991 was a watershed event for CNN. It catapulted the network past the "big three" American networks for the first time in its history, largely due to an unprecedented, historical coup: CNN was the only news outlet with the ability to communicate from inside Iraq during the first hours of the Coalition bombing campaign, with live reports from the al-Rashid Hotel in Baghdad. Such coverage, together with other crises like the Battle of Mogadishu in 1993, led Pentagon officials to coin the term "the CNN effect" to describe the impact of real-time, 24-hour news coverage on the decision-making processes of the US government.

Today CNN is part of the Time Warner media conglomerate and "is struggling to retain viewers against such competitors as the Fox News Channel and 'The Daily Show' with Jon Stewart."[13] In the US it is the number two cable news network after Fox.

Converge or Perish

Convergence can be interpreted in a number of different ways. Sonya Duhe and colleagues offer the following possibilities: "The sharing of news content with other news organisations, sharing of news content with another medium in their own organisation, sharing of staff and promoting other media for which they produce or from which they receive content."[14] One study, which looked at the *Tampa Tribune* newspaper's newsroom as it integrated with a WFLA-TV television channel and the TBO.com website, concluded that convergence did not actually produce "routine cross-platform reporting" but instead inspired a culture of information sharing between the three media.[15]

Multinationals, like Topsy in *Uncle Tom's Cabin*, have "just growed." They have no other evolutionary option. Convergence has been a powerful driver of such growth and has resulted in expansion by both vertical and horizontal integration. Vertical integration is the acquisition of different elements of the production process; for example, News Corp owns the film studio 20th Century Fox and the means of distributing its output via DVD, satellite, and cable. Horizontal integration is the acquisition of companies that operate at similar stages in the production chain; for example, News Corp has acquired a number of newspapers in the UK and the US. It is here that companies seek to maximize their earning potential. Thus a film is expected to spawn a soundtrack, a book, or screenplay, perhaps a video game, an amusement-park ride or even a TV spin-off, as well as appropriate merchandising. The *Lord of the Rings* trilogy, for example, is said to have attracted over $1.2bn thus far in merchandising revenues.[16] Obviously certain genres such as action movies, light entertainment, and sport lend themselves more easily to such exploitation.

Conversely, journalism and public affairs are less attractive unless they also serve business interests. As John Pilger has observed, "We have experienced an expansion of technology but the agenda of the media has shrunk."[17] However, one of the ironies of such developments is that while many of these industries have grown beyond the power of nations to control them, the technologies that have enabled globalization – mainly the satellite and digital sciences – have also enabled minority voices to be heard and to find audiences through the greater accessibility afforded by those very same technologies.[18]

Convergence at the level of personal interaction with this technology is already a reality for many working journalists. Integrated broadband and the "information superhighway," both relatively new in historical terms, allow a journalist's product to be authored once and then delivered electronically with a minimum of repurposing to a variety of different "platforms" – the newspaper page, the website, the blog, the podcast, the radio and television news bulletin, and so forth. At the same time the complete product, whether newspaper, magazine, radio, or television package, can be transported around the globe electronically at the speed of light – the ultimate time machine.

The holy grail of convergence is the linking of all these various "platforms" so they are capable of being accessed through a single device. Digital technology is the key that opens this "box."

Back to the Future?

The word "technology" was first used in the early years of the seventeenth century. The word "journalist" was first coined toward the end of the same century. Since then journalism and journalists have been in the vanguard of those taking advantage of new technologies. Whether the railways (faster and more reliable distribution), the Koenig steam press (faster printing to meet increasing circulations), the rotary press (the final form of the traditional printing press), the electric cable and telegraph (faster and more widespread news gathering), radio and TV (the immediacy of sound and visual images), and finally satellite and digital technologies that have bequeathed the multiplatform universe we inhabit today, each subsequent technological development has been colonized and adapted by the profession and the industry to serve one overarching end – to communicate information that is of a specific kind. It is new, relevant, topical, informative, factual, and, with a bit of luck, surprising or amusing.

While journalism is clearly embedded in technology, it does not necessarily follow that technology determines the nature of journalism. Of course, our understanding of present media is bound to influence how we think about the media of the past, but technology itself may inhibit our understanding rather than enhance it. As noted by Brian Winston: "The storm of progress blows so hard as to obscure our vision of what is actually happening."[19] In fact, a clearer understanding of technological advances can be gained if the development of new media platforms is seen as the product of a constant interplay between social necessity and suppression. This "unwritten law" is Winston's way of explaining the timing of certain invention "take-offs," and how industries develop around particular discoveries. The steam engine was invented around 1765 but it wasn't until 1829 that the steam engine was paired with that other great invention, the wheel, to produce the first mass transit system. The idea of television was suggested in 1877 and patented in 1884, but social factors, and a natural failure to comprehend the power of the moving image, conditioned the technologists' work – both positively and negatively – forcing a "social fit" on such new developments. Thus an invention's radical potential becomes suppressed so that it conforms to pre-existing social conditions. Ultimately, of course, there is little more powerful than a product that can "just hit the taste" of a generation.[20]

Even the internet and the world wide web, ubiquitous as they seem now, were originally considered "elite" technologies. Their radical potential, especially their undermining of the capitalist mantra that everything has a price, is causing consternation among those who have a vested interest in "established" social and cultural norms.

The other major criticism of the internet and its impact on democracy is that such new technologies soon lose their innovative appeal because they end up replicating the traditional structures of power and control that typify corporate agendas.[21] Recent research from the British media regulator Ofcom has shown for the first time a decline in the use of Facebook and other social networking sites by 15–24-year-olds as the age demographic shifts to older groups.[22] To the extent that older people represent traditional structures of power and control then it seems that the innovative appeal of these social networking sites may already be declining.

New technologies also create fear and even journalists are not immune. There is a Luddite tendency hidden in the most progressive mind – the comfort of the familiar and a fear of the unknown – that causes uncertainty and apprehension when traditional work patterns are disturbed. The US press–radio conflict of 1933 is just one such episode. In 1980, the Swedish Journalists' Union made an agreement with media employers that journalists had the right to refuse to use computers and keep on using their old typewriters.[23] Rupert Murdoch's move to Wapping in 1986 was largely because of the intransigence of the print unions and their refusal to accept new print technology.

At an industry level there are three consistent themes that have been examined in this Part II which can be said to have fashioned the visible media ecosystem as it operates today. Firstly, cross-ownership has meant that for the first time news is produced by companies whose main business is not journalism, which throws up the possibility that independent news could be replaced by self-interested commercialism posing as news.[24] Reuter's news agency in the nineteenth century, as well as dealing in news, also diversified into financial information and then stock market prices. It did not, however, buy up electricity companies, retail outlets, or farms, for example, for there is always the possibility of a conflict of interest where journalistic imperatives clash with the commercial instincts of the group's other businesses. Cross-ownership is also evident in the way modern corporations have expanded into different media. Today, most of them own newspapers, magazines, TV and radio stations, and also boast a healthy online presence as well as extensive nonmedia portfolios. In contrast, Lord Northcliffe, despite the size of his empire, headed a predominantly print-based organization, despite opportunities for diversification into the new technologies of radio and film.

Secondly, satellite and internet technologies have changed our perceptions of time and place and produced a news environment that is both fevered and highly competitive. When the BBC produces a news story, for example, it has to be packaged for TV and radio, repurposed for the website within five or six minutes of the story breaking and be accompanied by still pictures and suitable audio or video. Podcasts and entries on journalists' blogs may also be needed to complete the arc of story exposure. The danger of reliance on electronic media alone is that anything or anyone outside its gravitational pull is not just ignored but is actually invisible. Not that long ago, in Ghana before independence, the *Gold Coast Independent* was a respected newspaper which concentrated on news brought to it from all over west Africa by canoe or by hazardous jungle journeys. These were typical newsgathering routines that produced an eclectic mix of hard and soft news stories. And the danger is that we forget at our peril that there are fascinating and important stories that still need the "canoe" to ferry them into the media spotlight.

Thirdly, the sheer scale of media operations is now of an order neither contemplated nor capable of being contemplated by the early pioneers. Today, no one is beyond the media's reach. Whether you are stranded up a mountain, adrift on the ocean, or injured in the jungle you can use your cell phone to "phone home" and call for help. To some extent there is a sense that a "recorded life" is the only authentic life. Interaction with the media is *the* way for a person to validate his or her existence.

Media companies are also willing to invest and sometimes lose vast sums of money in order to dominate their chosen media form, however transient that form may turn out to be. Sony, for example, invested millions in their Betamax video format only to see it lose out to JVC and their VHS system. Rupert Murdoch described himself as a "digital immigrant" and gave this as one of the reasons for his failure to engage with the online world. As a result News Corp paid $580m for MySpace in 2005, both to boost its internet assets and to enhance its legitimacy with the online community. By 2009 however, the chief executive, Owen Van Natta, had made 720 employees redundant and the value of MySpace slumped.[25] In similar fashion, British broadcaster ITV bought Friends Reunited in 2006 for £175m and sold it three years later for a mere £25m, having found it impossible to monetize the site's "potential."[26]

Despite such failures, the second half of the twentieth century was generally a profitable period for the newspaper industry because of economic growth and increasing advertising revenues. Gradually, however, the pressures of increased consumer choice through television and commercial radio began to affect sales and later advertising revenues. London, for example, began the postwar period with three evening papers, the *Evening News*, the *Star*, and the *Evening Standard*. By 1980 there was only the *Standard* left.

By1994 a mere 16 US cities had independently owned dailies in free competition, representing only 1 percent of the country's newspapers. As one journalism educator commented: "This is a business structure designed to shrink the number of readers, even in the best of circumstances. One need not demonize concentration to see this." Monopolies may encourage economies of scale, but many readers lose the habit of reading a daily when there is only one to choose from, whereas audience levels are higher if there is a choice.[27]

The long-standing trends of concentration of ownership and falling circulations and income are now being exacerbated by competition from the internet, facilitated by fast broadband connections. Because of this the classified sections of newspapers are in decline and newspapers' share of total advertising revenue has fallen by one third since 1970.[28] Examples abound that suggest that this is a technology that is coming of age, from the *Drudge Report* that broke the Monica Lewinsky story to the *Huffington Post*, known as *HuffPo*.

The success of such blogs is no doubt in part because of a creeping perception on both sides of the Atlantic (but particularly in America) that newspapers have become boring and are failing to engage with their traditional audience or attract a new one. Reese Cleghorn, past president of the *American Journalism Review*, raised this issue as long ago as 1995: "Newspapers are dull," he said. "They're losing their touch. It's not enough to be modestly respectable, cautiously paced and profitable. For the long term, dull is a downer. I'm missing the snap, crackle, pop."[29]

Journalism has always been buffeted by technological innovation: broadcast has moved from film to video and from tape to digital processes;[30] print has gone from "hot" metal to phototypesetting to computer-aided design technology. Even the internet journalist has to adapt regularly to new software and hardware. All journalists, of whatever persuasion, are coming to terms with accelerating production processes and tighter deadlines. New recruits understand that they must be flexible, multiskilled, and dedicated, not to a specific employer but to the job of being a journalist. For short-term contracts and freelance working are becoming the working mode of choice for many employers. Journalists can look upon this either as a threat or as an opportunity to design their own careers more effectively. News and newspapers matter and the ability to tell the truth about the world is surely a power worth fighting for. The words of Thomas Jefferson have a ring of truth about them when he said: "I would rather live in a country with newspapers and without a government, than in a country with a government but without newspapers."

Notes

1 News Corporation Annual Report, 2008. Available at http://www.newscorp. com/AR2008Flash/NC08.html, accessed on August 23, 2010.

2 Google Financial Tables, 2008, "Income Statement." Available online at http:// investor.google.com/financial/2008/tables.html, accessed on August 23, 2010.

3 Matthew Fraser, "Obama's Win Means Future Elections Must be Fought Online," *Guardian*, November 7, 2008. Available online at http://www.guardian. co.uk/technology/2008/nov/07/barackobama-uselections2008, accessed on November 7, 2009.

4 "Scottish Daily News," *Absolute Astronomy*, 2009. Available online at http:// www.absoluteastronomy.com/topics/Scottish_Daily_News, accessed on November 7, 2009.

5 Ralph Negrine, *Politics and the Mass Media in Britain*, 2nd edn (London: Routledge, 1994), p. 34

6 Ibid., p. 36.

7 John Pilger (ed.), *Tell Me No Lies*, 2nd edn (London: Vintage Books, 2005), p. xix.

8 James Curran and Jean Seaton, *Power without Responsibility*, 5th edn (London: Routledge, 1997), p. 112.

9 Chris Hastings, "BBC Pays Unions to Resist Sharing of Licence Fee," *Sunday Times*, August 9, 2009, p. 4.

10 "Cable TV Subscribers (Most Recent) by Country," 2005. Available online at http://www.nationmaster.com/graph/med_cab_tv_sub-media-cable-tv-subscribers, accessed on March 15, 2009.

11 Negrine, *Politics and the Mass Media in Britain*, p. 180.

12 Christa Robinson, "CNN Leads 24-Hour News Networks with More Viewers than its Competition Combined," August 2000. Available online at http://www. timewarner.com/corp/newsroom/pr/0,20812,667801,00.html, accessed on August 10, 2009.

13 Jeffrey Kanige, "This Date in Deal History: CNN Begins Broadcasting," *Deal Magazine*, May 31, 2006.

14 Sonya Forte Duhe, Melissa Marie Mortimer, and San San Chow, "Convergence in North American TV Newsrooms: A Nationwide Look," *Convergence*, 10, 2 (2004), 81–104 (p. 99).

15 Edgar Huang, Lisa Rademakers, Moshood A. Fayemiwo, and Lillian Dunlap "Converged Journalism and Quality: A Case Study of The Tampa Tribune News Stories," *Convergence*, 10, 4 (2004), 73–91 (p. 86).

16 Filmreference, "The Merchandising Process", 2008. Available online at http:// www.filmreference.com/encyclopedia/Independent-Film-Road-Movies/

Merchandising-THE-MERCHANDISING-PROCESS.html, accessed on August 10, 2009.

17   John Pilger, Speech to the Department of Journalism, London College of Communication, University of the Arts, London, February 15, 2001.

18   Anthony Smith, "Media Globalization in the Age of Consumer Sovereignty," *Gannett Center Journal*, 4, 4 (1990), 1–16.

19   Brian Winston, *Lies, Damn Lies and Documentaries* (London: British Film Institute, 2000), p. 1.

20   George Gissing, *New Grub Street* (London: Penguin, 1985), p. 65.

21   John Nichols and Robert W. McChesney, *Tragedy and Farce: How the American Media Sell Wars, Spin Elections, and Destroy Democracy* (New York and London: The New Press, 2005).

22   Richard Wray and Sam Jones, "It's SO Over: Cool Cyberkids Abandon Social Networking Sites," *Guardian*, August 6, 2009, p. 1.

23   Gunnar Nygren, "The Changing Journalistic Work – Professional Roles and Values," paper presented at the *Future of Newspapers Conference*, Cardiff, September 7–9, 2007.

24   Bill Kovach and Tom Rosenstiel, *The Elements of Journalism* (London: Guardian Atlantic Books, 2001), p. 13.

25   Emma Barnett, "Rupert Murdoch Rules Out Buying Twitter or Selling MySpace," *Daily Telegraph*, July 9, 2009. Available online at http://www.telegraph.co.uk/technology/social-media/5786189/Rupert-Murdoch-rules-out-buying-Twitter-or-selling-MySpace.html, accessed on August 11, 2009.

26   Claudine Beaumont, "Farewell, Friends Reunited", *Daily Telegraph*, August 6, 2009. Available online at http://www.telegraph.co.uk/technology/social-media/5983056/Farewell-Friends-Reunited.html, accessed on August 10, 2009.

27   T. C. Leonard, *News For All: America's Coming-of-Age with the Press* (Oxford: Oxford University Press, 1995), p. 185.

28   Ibid., p. 2.

29   Reese Cleghorn, "Why Are so Many Newspapers Boring?" *American Journalism Review*, July/August 1995. Available online at http://www.ajr.org/article.asp?id=946, accessed on August 10, 2009.

30   Jane Chapman and Marie Kinsey (eds), *Broadcast Journalism: A Critical Introduction* (London: Routledge, 2008).

Part III

Ethics: A Matter of Judgment?

One journalist to another: "If you saw a man drowning and you could either save him or photograph the event ... what kind of film would you use?"

(Anon.)

A long habit of not thinking a thing wrong gives it a superficial appearance of being right.

(Thomas Paine)

9

Private and Confidential?

While journalists are self-evidently communicators, they communicate information from a fairly restricted palette. Cultural demands require that the information they impart is "true," verifiable, and balanced. Historically, therefore, consumers of news are conditioned to believe that what they read, watch, or listen to is the truth. Yet this truth is constantly compromised. For example, consumers of news may be aware that newspapers can often be less reliable than broadcast media in conveying that truth; or that commercial broadcasting in the US has no duty towards impartiality – however that is interpreted – as the British public service broadcasting model espouses; or that opinion and conjecture can be disguised within what appears to be a straightforward news story.

At a manifest level of meaning the information communicated by a journalist may be true, but its ideological basis is concealed. Stories are always told from a particular perspective – for example, Western media tends to be procapitalist with a Euro-American bias. Such perspectives, or media frames, "are principles of selection, emphasis, and presentation composed of little tacit theories about what exists, what happens, and what matters".[1] According to sociologist Todd Gitlin, these frames represent "persistent patterns of cognition, interpretation, and presentation, of selection, emphasis, and exclusion, by which symbol-handlers routinely organize discourse, whether verbal or visual."[2] As a specific kind of symbol-handler, a journalist arranges facts, decides how to tell the story and what to include and exclude, and thus influences what an audience perceives as truth. Donna Halper, in her 2009 paper on censorship in broadcasting, noted how such framing was acknowledged as far back as 1922 when broadcaster "Walter Lippmann

Jane Chapman and Nick Nuttall, *Journalism Today: A Themed History*
© 2011 Jane Chapman and Nick Nuttall. Published by Blackwell Publishing Ltd.

accused his newspaper and magazine colleagues of creating a 'pseudo-environment' in the way they presented interpretations as facts" through oversimplification, "sensationalism or exaggeration, with the end result that the public was often misled."[3] Radio news during this period was, in fact, a more user-friendly medium – even the illiterate could listen to the news every day – and thus more susceptible to the creation of pseudo-environments. Average listeners therefore had "no reason to question what they heard … and … came to trust and rely on what the network newscasts told them about what was going on in the world."[4]

Yet according to philosophers like Umberto Eco the danger of such blind faith in news output does not end there. These "messages," however distorted they may be by the "sender," are further subject to what Eco calls "aberrant decoding" by the "receiver."[5] This is Eco's term for the decoding of a text by means of a different code from that used to encode it. Inevitably such aberrant decoding further compromises the essential "truth" of the message. For instance, a journalist's use of irony may be essential to the story but may equally be misunderstood or missed altogether by some members of the audience, especially those from a different culture. Similarly, dramatic interpretation can often "big up" an event to such an extent that its veracity is compromised in the very process of its communication. Yet for Arthur Schopenhauer (1788–1860), a philosopher who believed art rather than science to be the essence of human endeavor, "Exaggeration of every kind is as essential to journalism as it is to the dramatic art, for the object of journalism is to make events go as far as possible. Thus it is that all journalists are, in the very nature of their calling, alarmists, and this is their way of giving interest to what they write."[6]

Despite this, at its worst there is a sort of Faustian contract between journalist and audience that condones the alarmist tendency alluded to by Schopenhauer. And this bargain is generally impervious to occasional untruths, lack of balance, or presence of bias, especially if media organizations regularly provide an adequate *mea culpa* for their worst excesses. Equally, however, such a bargain can be undermined fatally by a continuous diet of distortion, bias, and untruth – and never more so than when the news agenda is infiltrated with calculated falsehood. As David Berry points out, "the deliberate act of lying requires a 'greater moral condemnation' than the failure to accommodate all aspects of an event through the normal routines of journalistic activity."[7]

Yet the press in particular is littered throughout its history with examples that call into question the probity of its "normal routines." Although the law may be the ultimate check on illegality it is less sure on matters of probity. Thus there has developed over time the sense that journalism is a self-regulating business, even though its ethical dimension has always remained elusive. Although "the word *ethics* appeared in discussions by 1850 . . . it remained rare through the 1880s. Writers generally used the word *moral* when referring to desired journalistic conduct."[8] However, it also became clear that this self-regulation was rather too Humpty-Dumpty-like ("when I use a word it means just what I choose it to mean") for comfort. As an example, the magisterial History of *The Times* newspaper, which runs to over 5,000 pages and seven volumes, doesn't mention ethics or even morals in any of its various indexes.

This chapter and the next one, using selected examples and case studies, attempt to illustrate the shifting sands of ethical thinking over time, as well as raising points of issue relevant to a modern media landscape. It seems appropriate therefore to start with a couple of basic questions: "What *is* journalistic ethics, and how can historical examples help our understanding of current practice?"

Whose Ethics?

One simple answer is that at a purely pragmatic level journalistic ethics can be described as a set of rules that guide journalists' conduct when confronted with dilemmas such as conflict of interest, privacy, and protection of sources. Whether journalism is accepted as a profession or not – and this is still contested territory – abiding by a set of rules, an ethical code if you like, even if it is voluntary, is fraught with difficulties. Yet at first glance it seems relatively straightforward. A journalist has his or her own set of ethical standards and applies them on a daily basis without fear or favor. But typically journalists are subject to at least five different and possibly contradictory ethical disciplines on a day-to-day basis. And each of these may or may not correspond with their own moral compass or with the generally accepted codes of conduct applicable to their media organization.

So firstly, a journalist is guided by his or her own ethical standards that have evolved as the result of a complex interaction between upbringing, religious belief or lack thereof, personal experience, political affiliations if any, and social and cultural conditioning. Not only are these standards unlikely to be replicated in any other individual but also they may be far stricter or conversely far more lax than, for example, national or local guidelines might require.

Secondly, a journalist is likely to be bound, tightly or with some slack, by the ethical standards of his or her editor. And often it is difficult to gauge an editor's ethical compass. Donal MacIntyre, for example, when he worked as labor correspondent for Britain's *Sunday Times*, "had a running battle over his reporting of the miner's strike (1984–5) in which he was regularly pressed by the editor to adopt a less critical attitude towards the National Coal Board and the government."[9] Ultimately he left the newspaper for more congenial surroundings.

Journalist and tabloid editor Derek Jameson, in his autobiography *Last of the Hot Metal Men*, recounts how in 1957 the *Daily Express* was pursuing a story about the singer Shirley Bassey and a rejected suitor named Pepé Davis. Davis had locked himself in Bassey's room at the Cumberland Hotel in London. He then pulled out a pistol and threatened "to shoot unless she promised to love him forever." At one point in the siege Davis fired the gun. Although no one was injured Davis eventually received a three-year prison sentence. According to Derek Jameson's account of the incident:

> in the middle of all the brouhaha, the head of a *Daily Express* reporter appeared upside down outside the hotel window several floors above Marble Arch. His ankles firmly grasped by two friendly photographers, the newsman tapped politely on the window to attract the attention of Miss Bassey and her uninvited guest. "Sorry to bother you," he says politely. "I wonder if I might have a word … "[10]

As Jameson noted, the action of the reporter was "highly intrusive" and it is doubtful if it was in the public interest that the whole affair should be splashed across the pages of a national newspaper. What is undeniable, however, is that the incident was of interest to the public – something a prescient editor would have been well aware of. Jameson the editor makes no comment on the reporter's view of the "stunt." In all such events there is always the likelihood of a clash between the ethical standards of a reporter and those of his or her editor who is determined to "get the story."

Thirdly, reporters have to take into account the ethical standards of their proprietor. These may once again be at variance not only with the reporter's own but also with those of his or her editor. On his acquisition of Beaverbrook Newspapers in 1977, Victor Matthews famously noted, "By and large, the editors will have complete freedom as long as they agree with the policy I have laid down."[11] Failure to take into account such dicta can have serious consequences. Robert Maxwell, best remembered as the proprietor of the *Daily Mirror* from

1984 until his death in 1991, was also known for his hands-on style of ownership. Earlier in his career, in 1975, he invested in a moribund Scottish newspaper group and launched a new paper, the *Scottish Daily News*. The paper failed but during its brief life Maxwell promised further funds so long as they were matched by the workers raising twice as much out of their own wages. As recorded by Joe Haines in his biography of Maxwell, "The National Union of Journalists' chapel (branch) decided that this was, in effect, a wage cut. Its hostility grew when Maxwell contributed a column to the new paper and the chapel committee instructed the editor he was not to print any further contributions from the man who was, in effect, the proprietor but not a journalist."[12] Ten years later Maxwell wrote a leading article in the *Daily Mirror* headlined: "FLEET ST. The party is over." Here he put his case for drastic reductions in the Mirror Group Newspapers' workforce to control the losses at the paper. Inevitably, this edition of the paper was produced and printed by many of the people that Maxwell proposed to sack. This time, however, no attempt was made to muzzle the proprietor despite him once again usurping, however briefly, the role of journalist. Maxwell by this time ruled his empire by a mixture of fear and favor that effectively silenced discontent.

Yet Maxwell's approach should be compared with that of Roy Thomson, the Canadian owner of the *Sunday Times* and *The Times* during the 1960s. He was a famously "hands-off" proprietor and he carried around with him on a piece of paper his "creed":

> I can state with the utmost emphasis that no person or group can buy or influence editorial support from any newspaper in the Thomson group. Each paper may perceive this interest in its own way, and will do this without advice, counsel or guidance from the central office of the Thomson Organisation.
>
> I do not believe that a newspaper can be run properly unless its editorial columns are run freely and independently by a highly skilled and dedicated professional journalist. This is and will continue to be my policy.[13]

Despite the occasional Roy Thomson, the commercial imperatives of powerful owners, more interested in the bottom line than the "top" story, have secured a hold over editorial policy at the expense of both editors and rank-and-file journalists alike.

Fourth in the pantheon of ethical "tripwires" is an appreciation, if not an understanding, of how a newspaper's advertisers might react to a story. The industrialization of the press has meant that the large capital required to start a newspaper and to make it successful must be underpinned by considerable advertising revenue.[14] While it would be invidious to suggest that advertisers are regularly involved in editorial choices, there is evidence that the sensibilities and commercial imperatives of advertisers have to be taken into account.

As noted in Chapter 5, Donald Trelford was editor of Britain's Sunday *Observer* newspaper when he "wrote an article in April 1984 reporting that Zimbabwe's armed forces were torturing and killing their own citizens in the dissident Matabeleland province."[15] This put the owner of the *Observer*, "Tiny" Rowland in a difficult position. His corporation, Lonrho, had major business interests in Zimbabwe and Rowland told Trelford to withdraw the article. Trelford refused and was backed by his staff but, "in the highly publicized row that followed (in which Lonrho reportedly cancelled advertising in its own paper), Rowland had little real choice but to back off."[16] Although Trelford, as editor, "won the day," it was at the expense of advertising revenue. Advertisers would doubtless refrain from classifying any of their attempts at "correcting" news values as having an ethical dimension, but for a working journalist it may prove difficult to place a story that directly calls into question the probity of a significant advertiser.

Lastly, journalists of whatever status always have to acknowledge that their audience – reader, listener, or viewer – is implicated in the complex discourse of ethical assumptions implicit in any news story. All stories involve selection "from the range of possible (and acceptable) interpretations that a social event yields."[17] Inevitably this selection is controlled by media processes that mystify issues of objectivity, bias, and even truth itself. So if readers are willing, for example, to blame a newspaper for publishing a particular story or picture in a way that offends them, they must equally be prepared to "blame" themselves for having "consumed" it. For no story is functionally complete until its meaning is interpreted; that is, until it is "consumed" by being read. As media academic Jason Barker comments: " 'The viewer' and 'the journalist' are both mutable parts of a greater sum of capital arrangements grouped around the ownership, control and circulation of media products."[18]

Conduct and Practice – Making Sense of the Codes

While codes of conduct are largely a twentieth-century phenomenon, control of the press in particular, both overt and surreptitious, has a history as long as the press itself. Before 1695, newspapers and periodical throughout

Britain were subject to state-controlled censorship, first through the Star Chamber and then through the Licensing Order of 1643. Under this Order the names of authors, publishers, and printers had to be lodged at Stationers' Hall and all were liable to arrest and imprisonment for writings perceived as offensive to the government.

Under the greater freedoms of the Restoration, this Licensing Act was allowed to lapse in 1695. Newspapers and periodicals were from that date regulated indirectly by the generally applicable laws of libel, defamation, contempt, obscenity, and sedition. The law of seditious libel, for example, was invoked against Daniel Defoe's "The Shortest Way With the Dissenters" in 1702. Current restrictions on the media include the "criminal laws of official secrets, obscenity, blasphemy, sedition ... and civil laws of libel and breach of confidence; and by the judge-made law of contempt of court."[19]

In the US freedom of the press was guaranteed under the First Amendment of the Constitution. Yet just as in Britain, American newspapers were subject to the general law of the land. Invasions of privacy, for instance, could therefore be treated as trespass, assault, or eavesdropping.[20] The US courts have traditionally been wary of involving themselves in decisions about journalistic taste, decency, or propriety and generally are unlikely to trespass on a journalist's right, enshrined in the First Amendment, to report anything that might be of interest to the public. The 1931 case of Near v. Minnesota, where the court refused to "gag" Jay Near's *Saturday Post* newspaper under Minnesota's Public Nuisance Law (1925), was the first to establish the doctrine that prior restraint was in most cases unconstitutional. Prior restraint is censorship that prevents material from being published in the first place and this is perhaps the most significant difference between British and American law. In Britain an individual can invoke prior restraint by obtaining an interlocutory or gagging injunction from a judge in chambers, thereby preventing the media from reporting a story. More recently British judges have been prepared to grant what have become known as super-injunctions. These not only prohibit the reporting of a story but also forbid journalists from communicating the fact that the injunction itself has been granted.

Many European countries, in contrast with prevailing trends in the US and UK, have traditionally guarded both freedom and privacy more jealously. The world's first freedom of information act was the *Riksdag's* (Swedish Parliament) Freedom of the Press Act of 1766. The tort of privacy was first recognized in France as far back as 1858. Sweden was also one of the first European countries to develop a code and a voluntary body to enforce it.[21] The Swedish Publicists Club was founded in 1874 and the Swedish Press Council was set up in 1916 as an independent body with a remit to hear complaints against newspapers.

Those countries that now belong to the European Union have generally incorporated the European Convention on Human Rights into their domestic legislation. The UK government did so in 1998 and the Act duly became law and thus enforceable in British courts in October 2000. The Convention contains two clauses that deal on the one hand with privacy and on the other hand with freedom of expression. Article 8 states in part: "Everyone has the right to respect for his private and family life, his home and his correspondence." Article 10 states in part: "Everyone has the right to freedom of expression. This right shall include freedom to hold opinions and to receive and impart information and ideas without interference by public authority and regardless of frontiers."

In the United States the earliest code extant was that produced in 1908 by Walter Williams, the first dean of the Journalism School of the University of Missouri. His "A Journalist's Creed" contained eight clauses that each began with the stirring, "I believe." In the UK the National Union of Journalists (NUJ) first produced a code of conduct in 1936 and the Press Complaints Commission (PCC) produced its Code of Practice in 1991. Apart from such industry or "universal" codes, many newspapers and broadcasters produced guidelines for the use of their own journalists. And these codes were bound up with the idea that journalism was a profession, as Walter Williams declared, rather than a mere trade, and as such it had a responsibility to its audience beyond the simple imparting of information.

Codes of Conduct and Privacy

If we accept that news, as Lord Northcliffe said, "is what somebody somewhere wants to suppress. Everything else is advertising,"[22] then invasions of privacy and other "forceful" methods of news gathering can be considered the meat of good journalism. Yet even good journalism needs to be exercised with discretion and principled restraint. In *Media Ethics and Self-Regulation* Chris Frost states, "Invasion of privacy is the issue that probably most concerns the public."[23] As such it is a relatively recent concern and has achieved added piquancy in the latter half of the twentieth century because of the growing media obsession with the lives and loves of celebrities. This is not to deny, of course, that notions of privacy were dear to the hearts of

Victorians. The American philosopher and poet Ralph Waldo Emerson wrote of the British in *English Traits*, "The motive and end of their trade and empire is to guard the independence and privacy of their homes."[24] And this domesticity is enshrined in the well-worn aphorism "an Englishman's home is his castle." In Victorian Britain, however, the idea of the press as an invader of privacy had yet to become part of the public consciousness. For example, during the investigation of a gruesome child murder in Wiltshire in 1860, "A reporter from the *Bath Chronicle* had sneaked into Road Hill House [where the murder occurred] in the guise of a detective, and made notes on the layout. An inaccurate floor plan was published in the paper five days later."[25] There is no record of any action being taken against the reporter or the paper. Today, of course, the PCC Code requires that editors justify intrusions into an individual's private life without consent and the NUJ Code states that no journalist shall intrude into private grief and distress.

So why has privacy become a "hot" issue? There is a sense that print journalists in particular have for years abused their position as news gatherers in order to prompt indiscretions from their quarry, whether by "doorstepping" the rich and famous (i.e., waiting outside someone's door in the hope of obtaining an interview or photograph), inveigling information from the vulnerable, pretending to be someone they're not, or wearing a disguise.

FactFile
Privacy Codes in the United States

The US has more codes "than you can shake a stick at." The lack of a broad spectrum national press has resulted in newspapers developing their own codes to a much greater extent than in Britain or other major European countries. A cursory glance at the major codes, however, indicates that few of them deal with issues of privacy. Walter Williams's "A Journalist's Creed," for example, had no clauses dealing with privacy. Yet the 1910 "Kansas Code of Ethics," adopted by the Kansas Editorial Association, does contain a final clause headed "Bounds of Publicity" and stating: "A man's name and portrait are his private property and the point where they cease to be private and become public should be defined for our association." But even while acknowledging the idea of privacy the code is still ambivalent as to its exact meaning, and in particular the point at which the private becomes public.

The American Society of Newspaper Editors produced its "Canons of Journalism" in 1923, which were revised and rewritten in 1975. It is one of the few codes that refers, however skeletally, to the idea of privacy. Article VI, headed "Fair Play," states: "Journalists should respect the rights of people involved in the news."

The American Newspaper Guild adopted a code of ethics in 1934 as "a symbol of the Guild's concern for the standards of the industry." There is no privacy clause included in its provisions. The Society of Professional Journalists' "Code of Ethics" was formulated in 1973 and a revised version adopted in 1996. It includes a clause that recognizes "that private people have a greater right to control information about themselves than do public officials and others who seek power, influence or attention. Only an overriding public need can justify intrusion into anyone's privacy."

Similarly, codes that relate to broadcasting offer very little guidance on issues of privacy. One of the few that does is the National Public Radio "Code of Ethics and Practices" which came into effect in 2004. In Section VIII, Ethical Conduct in Coverage of News, Clause 7 states: "NPR journalists think carefully about the boundaries between legitimate journalistic pursuit and an individual's right to privacy."

One of the striking aspects of many American newspaper-specific codes, from the *Los Angeles Times*, the *New York Times*, and the *Washington Post* to the humbler *Sacramento Bee* is their concern with the extramural activities and behavior of their journalistic staff. This would more than likely be considered an unacceptable intrusion into the "privacy" of journalists themselves on the other side of the Atlantic.

Premier league soccer players, bishops, actors, a chief of the defense staff, members of parliament, judges, television newsreaders, senior police officers, athletes, minor celebrities – all have resorted to the courts, using a variety of different laws to try to protect themselves from what they see as a rapacious and out-of-control tabloid press. Yet despite an avalanche of discontent, in the last 15 years or so, British governments have repeatedly taken the view that privacy legislation is not the answer. To some extent it can be argued that the British lack of a written constitution has meant that press freedom itself remains "simply an idea, a remarkably powerful and enduring idea, but never, ever, in Britain a fact of law."[26] Considering the lack of clarity on both sides of the argument it is little wonder that the Press Complaints Commission, for example, made 245 privacy rulings in 2007, approximately 20 percent of the total rulings made that year and up from 14 percent in 1996.

FactFile
Privacy Codes in Great Britain

The British press is regulated by two major codes, the National Union of Journalists' (NUJ) Code of Conduct, first formulated in 1936, and the Press Complaints Commission's (PCC) Code of Practice, framed in 1991. The NUJ code has been added to substantially and now comprises 14 clauses. Clauses 5 and 6 touch on privacy. Clause 5 states, "A journalist obtains material by honest, straightforward and open means, with the exception of investigations that are both overwhelmingly in the public interest and which involve evidence that cannot be obtained by straightforward means." Clause 6 states, "A journalist does nothing to intrude into anybody's private life, grief or distress unless justified by overriding consideration of the public interest."

In 1989 the British government set up a Committee on Privacy chaired by David Calcutt QC in response to "public concern about intrusions into the lives of individuals by certain sections of the press."[27] The *Report of the Committee on Privacy and Related Matters* recommended in June 1990 that no privacy law should be introduced. However, Calcutt's subsequent *Review of Press Self-Regulation*, presented in January 1993, took the view that self-regulation of the press had failed and he recommended that "the Government should now give further consideration to the introduction of a new tort of infringement of privacy."[28] Yet in 1995 the Conservative government under John Major stated that "the Government has no present plans to introduce a statutory right to privacy."[29]

The PCC Code of Practice was modeled on the Calcutt committee's proposals and Clause 3 deals in particular with privacy:

i) Everyone is entitled to respect for his or her private and family life, home, health and correspondence, including digital communications. Editors will be expected to justify intrusions into any individual's life without consent.

ii) It is unacceptable to photograph individuals in private places without their consent.

Broadcast media, on the other hand, are subject to a much stricter regime of regulation and control. As noted by media academics Peter Cole and Tony Harcup:

Newspaper journalism in Britain emerged from a print culture that proved resistant to restrictions ... enabling print journalists to carve out for themselves a relatively unregulated space. This is in marked contrast to the much more strict regulatory regime under which broadcast journalists in the UK work, which reflects both the different technologies involved in the development of such journalism (radio and television depended on the limited number of wavebands available, which led to a system of licensing) and the fact that, by the time broadcasting arrived on the scene, the state had got its act together and realised the potential power of the media.[30]

The BBC, as a public service broadcaster, has its own code of ethics, entitled BBC Guidelines.[31] British media organizations in general are regulated by a partly autonomous government agency, Ofcom, which was established as a body corporate by the Office of Communications Act 2002. It has responsibilities across television, radio, telecommunications, and wireless communications services. The BBC is regulated separately by the BBC Trust. Thus broadcast journalists operate under a statutory system of control which effectively reflects a public service ethos regardless of whether the media is commercially or publicly owned. The sanctions are fines or at worst the loss of a license to broadcast.

Private and Confidential

Writing about people is the journalist's stock-in-trade. Specific identifiers, however, apart from relevant context like age or occupation, were seldom part of traditional news gathering routines. A certain level of anonymity, almost by default, was therefore assured of people in the news. A pictorial reproduction, on the other hand, destroyed such anonymity at a stroke. It also initiated a change in the relationship between a person in the news, the journalist, and the reader. For the first time an individual became a recognizable entity. Pictures added flesh to the descriptive bones and in the process, by some sort of alchemy, imbued certain individuals with almost mythical status. Today we know them as celebrities and it is probably true to say that before newspapers were able to take and reproduce images easily and cheaply the "cult" of celebrity didn't exist (with one or two notable exceptions). It is perhaps no coincidence that the use of the word celebrity to mean "famous person" and the publication of the first illustrated newspapers and magazines both date from the mid-nineteenth century. Once the photograph had established itself as a staple of the news diet it was soon realized that the publishing of someone's image was potentially far more intrusive of their privacy than mere words ever could be. And to that extent the newspaper was in part responsible for the very notion of privacy that it then insisted on invading in order to "get the story."

The earliest of the illustrated newspapers in Britain was the aptly named *Illustrated London News* that first appeared in 1842. The "first pictorial daily was the *Evening Illustrated Paper* of 1881."[32] Early illustrations were wood-cuts and early news photographs had to be engraved before they could be printed. The New York *Daily Graphic* published the first halftone reproduction of a news photograph in 1880 and by 1897 halftone photographs could be printed on presses running at full speed. The *Daily Mirror*, begun by Alfred Harmsworth (later Lord Northcliffe) in 1903, was the first morning daily newspaper to proclaim itself a picture paper. It went through a number of incarnations before Northcliffe found the right formula. An early front page, for example, contained news text and two large pictures, one of a traitor and one of an actress. Northcliffe, as usual, was ahead of the curve! The front pages of later editions were entirely picture-based and Northcliffe often interfered in the choice of images. "'Alfonso,' (King of Spain), complained Northcliffe, 'is always smiling. This smile is not news. If you get a picture of Alfonso weeping, *that* would be news!'"[33]

The first movies appeared around the same time as Northcliffe's newspaper revolution and the first permanent cinema, the Nickelodeon, was opened in Pittsburgh, Pennsylvania in 1905. By 1912 actors started to receive film credits, beginning the "star" system that provided a steady stream of images for the emerging picture papers. One of the first feature films, *The Birth of a Nation*, appeared in 1915. It was an American Civil War drama directed by D. W. Griffith and became the first Hollywood "blockbuster," although the French had been making films for some time before World War I.[34] Journalists were not slow to exploit the appeal of the movies by using images of film stars. Inevitably the "perfection" of the star and how he or she looked became a major news value in its own right. By 1921 the wire photo made it possible to transmit such pictures almost as quickly as news itself could travel. However, it was not until the development of the commercial 35mm Leica camera in 1925, and the first flash bulbs between 1927 and 1930 that all the elements were in place for a "golden age" of photojournalism.

At the same time, the "ethics of reproduction" – that is, the manner in which a paper produced its images – became a cause for anxiety as it entered the news mix for the first time. Newspapers increasingly provided images of the notorious, the criminal, the grotesque, and, especially in Britain, members of the royal family. Thus newspapers produced the first personalities – ordinary people in extraordinary situations or, a common complaint today, extraordinary people in ordinary situations. It is an accepted journalistic fact, for example, that a picture of Diana, Princess of Wales, on the front page of a newspaper or the cover of a magazine will boost circulation, regardless of what she is doing and regardless of the fact that she is dead. The twentieth century can rightly be called the century of the image.

Invasions of Privacy

The way that most journalists view privacy issues has to some extent been colored by the attitude of the courts to its supposed breach. There would seem to be a different set of rules for ordinary members of the public compared with so-called celebrities. Yet even the ordinary citizen, who should perhaps be confident in his or her ability to remain private, cannot rely on journalists to respect this privacy. The majority of invasion-of-privacy stories can only be objected to on the grounds of standards, decency, and ethics.

One of the early personalities whose treatment illustrates the fine line between the different handling of the ordinary citizen from the so-called celebrity was William Sidis. Sidis was an oddball genius who became a well-known figure in America in the early decades of the twentieth century. Reputedly he had an IQ between 250 and 300, spoke over two hundred languages, and could learn a whole language in a day. He entered Harvard University aged 11 and achieved notoriety when he was arrested in 1919 for taking part in a May Day parade in Boston. He subsequently became a recluse but in 1937 the *New Yorker* published an article about him – written by James Thurber under a pseudonym – as part of a series that asked what had happened to once-famous individuals, entitled "Where Are They Now?"

Although there had been no attempt to contact Sidis, it described him as living in a shabby apartment in Boston's down-at-heel South End. He was pictured as a loner who had failed to live up to his early promise. Sidis sued the magazine for invasion of privacy, claiming the article was also riddled with inaccuracies and falsehoods. "The article's subtitle, 'April Fool,' neatly encapsulates what the Second Circuit Court of Appeals saw as the piece's condescending and abusive tone toward Mr. Sidis. The magazine focused on the "bizarre ways" in which Sidis's genius was manifested, such as his penchant for collecting streetcar transfers" (he wrote a 300-page treatise on them using the pseudonym Frank Falupa, as well as various other books). According to Dr Abraham Sperling who wrote an article about Sidis in 1945 entitled "A Story of Genius" for *Psychology for the Millions*, "The thought of being considered a public spectacle was positive poison to the soul of Bill Sidis. He refused to have his name attached to any of his later writings and turned down offers of large sums from publishers who would not agree to his use of a pen-name." In 1930 he gained a patent after inventing a perpetual rotary calendar that took into account leap years. Later examination of his life suggests he was probably autistic. "Although the court concluded that the article was 'merciless in its dissection of intimate details of its subject's personal life,' Sidis's privacy claim was rejected."[35]

The court essentially championed the freedom of the press over the individual's right to privacy on this occasion. As noted by Paul Siegel in his examination of the case, the reasons given by the court now seem somewhat limp.

> There are times, Judge Swan wrote, when "the public interest in obtaining information becomes dominant over the individual's desire for privacy." This was surely such a case, the court concluded, in that the *New Yorker* piece had at least the potential for answering a very important question: whether Sidis had lived up to his earlier promise. The answer to that question cannot help but have implications for public policy. After all, how better to determine if society's treatment of child prodigies is for the good than to examine the lives of such persons when they are no longer children.[36]

Judge Swan's argument might now be considered somewhat disingenuous for it is difficult to argue that Sidis had forfeited his right to privacy by any of his own actions. Indeed he had gone out of his way to live a "low-profile" existence, bearing in mind that the years of his "fame" were far behind him. It is also difficult to argue that exposure of his lifestyle and "bizarre ways" was in the public interest. The further argument that somehow his supposed fall from grace could have "implications for public policy" now seems fatuous. We have, of course, become familiar with the "Where are they now?" feature in modern newspapers and magazines. Today it is probably true that journalists are more diligent in their research, having to negotiate agents and PR machines, as well as the celebrities themselves. In part, of course, this is because modern journalism demands that such features are accompanied by pictures and it is difficult to get such pictures without the full agreement of the person concerned. In an age when specially commissioned pictures were still the preserve of film stars, William Sidis had no opportunity to turn down a request for the necessary interview and photoshoot that would now be seen as essential.

Privacy, Breach of Confidence, and Celebrity

The key to the Sidis decision is more than likely that he had once been a "celebrity" and the courts have traditionally maintained that those who live by publicity shall be allowed to "die" by publicity. Such a dictum inevitably brings into sharp focus the difference between the "celebrity" and the ordinary citizen. As far as notions of privacy are concerned the "celebrity" would appear to be at a distinct disadvantage. In 1964, for example, a court in Alabama held that a picture taken by the *Daily Times Democrat* of a woman, Flora Bell Graham, whose dress was lifted by jets of air at a local funfair, did indeed breach her right to privacy. "The court ruled that the photograph, which showed her panties, had no 'legitimate news interest to the public' and upheld an award of $4,166 to the plaintiff for invasion of her privacy."[37] Would the decision have been otherwise if Flora Bell Graham, too, had been a celebrity?

Yet English law, perhaps to ameliorate the lack of any privacy provisions, has according to some "developed a conception of privacy as confidentiality."[38] Examples of "confidentiality" are information communicated between lawyer and client, doctor and patient, husband and wife (secrets of the bedroom), priest and confessor, employer and employee. In these cases the communicating of such information without permission to a third party (a journalist, for example) gives rise to a possible action for breach of confidence. Such an action "is a civil remedy affording protection against the disclosure or use of information that is not publicly known, and that has been entrusted in circumstances imposing an obligation not to disclose that information without the authority of the person who has imparted it."[39]

John Lennon might have thought he was entitled to such privacy when in 1978 he sought an injunction to stop the publication of his ex-wife Cynthia's memoirs of their life together, *A Twist of Lennon*. Yet he was denied an injunction on the grounds that, as their relationship had already been talked about publicly by both of them, he could not now demonstrate that the information was still confidential. There is an assumption here that all the information in the memoir had previously been talked about publicly and as such, although it passed the test of confidentiality, both parties had implicitly agreed to waive their rights.

Yet when supermodel Naomi Campbell sued the *Daily Mirror* in 2002 after it published an article about her attending Narcotics Anonymous for her drugs habit, she won what was described at the time as a "landmark privacy case." The newspaper included pictures of Campbell outside the clinic. However, awarding damages the judge said, "The information clearly bore the badge of confidentiality and when received by the defendants they, Mr Morgan [*Daily Mirror* editor] and the *Mirror* journalists, were clothed in conscience with the duty of confidentiality."[40] So although it was legitimate for the paper to expose the model's drug addiction it had in fact breached her confidentiality by giving details of the treatment itself – in other words the court viewed the information about her treatment as a communication that should have been confidential between doctor and patient.

This ruling was overturned by the Court of Appeal but Campbell took the case to the House of Lords which returned a verdict in her favor saying, in other words, that even a public figure is entitled to privacy where confidential information is involved. Despite her case turning on a breach of confidence rather than any notions of privacy as such, a number of questions remain. To what extent had Campbell forfeited her right to privacy because of her media profile? Was the Law Lords' ruling a privacy law in all but name with all its implications for journalists' news gathering? Why was it decided that taking a picture of Campbell in a public place was not, of itself, an invasion of her privacy? (See Clause 3 of the PCC Code of Practice above.) Why indeed did Campbell go to court rather than appeal to the Press Complaints Commission as would normally be the case?

American courts often treat privacy as an issue "based on the individual's inviolate personality" rather than the concept of confidentiality and "expectations of trust within relationships" recognized by English law.[41] Flora Bell Graham and the "panties" photograph verdict exemplifies such an approach. The court seemed to be saying that the actual invasion of Graham's privacy, with its overtones of smuttiness, while brief, was "information-light" in a strictly journalistic sense. She was entitled, therefore, to a greater degree of privacy than someone with a public profile as part of his or her livelihood.

However, compare this with the case of Carl DeGregorio and CBS television in the same year. In this instance DeGregorio, a building worker, was upset at the station's having included in a story on "Romance in New York" video footage of him walking hand in hand with an unmarried female co-worker. The court surmised that "the perceived novelty of these two hard hats walking in romantic linkage apparently triggered the camera crew's interest."[42] Despite DeGregorio's pleas not to show the video clip in their program, CBS ignored him. He then sued for invasion of privacy. He made it clear, "'It would not look good,'...because he was married and the young woman was herself engaged to be married...In dismissing the claim against the TV network, the court interpreted 'newsworthiness' as broad enough to include 'an exploration of prevailing attitudes towards [romance]'."[43]

The notion that "prevailing attitudes" are in themselves worthy of exploration gives the media, in theory at least, lèse-majesté to do almost anything it likes. And in this case the fact that DeGregorio and the woman were private individuals cut no ice with the court. Neither did the possible ramifications of the ruling itself. DeGregorio was allowed to "die by publicity." CBS presumably felt its decision to invade the privacy of two otherwise anonymous individuals, while initially innocent of any ulterior motive, was vindicated by the court's ruling. The gratuitous decision to show the video clip, however, with the knowledge of its likely outcome for DeGregorio, his female coworker and their families, quite clearly contradicts most codes of ethical behavior. Yet on the surface this story seems to inhabit the same legal territory as that of Flora Bell Graham even though in this instance the court ruled for the defendant rather than the plaintiff.

British courts likewise can be ambivalent in their response to issues of privacy and the media. Famously in April 2003 Michael Douglas and Catherine Zeta Jones won their case against *Hello!* magazine for printing "cheap and tacky" photographs of their wedding at the Plaza Hotel, New York in November 2000. Nonetheless, they lost their claim for invasion of privacy over the paparazzi pictures because the judge, Mr Justice Lindsay, ruled there was no privacy law in the UK. The judge said that the couple's "commercial confidence" had been breached, however, because the official pictures, taken for *OK!* magazine, had commercial value directly related to their being kept secret. Yet despite Mr Justice Lindsay's stricture about the lack of a privacy law, recent cases of alleged intrusion, particularly where the pictures have shown a celebrity naked or seminaked on a beach, have been won in the UK with the award of substantial damages on the basis of Article Eight of the Human Rights Act.

A Royal Flush

Ethics traditionally has concerned itself with journalistic output and the news-gathering process. But what about the stories that are not told? Does a journalist have any ethical accountability for what he or she decides not to write? Can someone's privacy, whatever the circumstances, always trump the public's right to know? The twentieth century offers two stand-out examples of the "not written" story, both of which offer a corrective to *Washington Post* owner Philip Graham's famous "journalism is the first rough draft of history" school of thought.[44] It would take later generations to put the record straight.

No examination of the media's attempts to incorporate something as "mercurial" as the concept of privacy into its voluntary codes can ignore the peculiar position of the British royal family, and in particular its treatment by the press. And the most striking response, or more accurately lack of response, to a royal event did not involve the courts or indeed any other regulatory body. It was the almost total blackout on information during the brief reign of Edward VIII and the unfolding abdication crisis of 1936.

Edward, Prince of Wales, was something of a playboy prince. He had many women friends and in particular he formed an attachment to Wallis Simpson, an American divorcée whose second husband was Ernest Simpson. When Edward ascended the throne in January 1936, as King Edward VIII, he maintained his relationship with Wallis. The British press throughout this period remained silent, even though the story of the King and his married mistress would have been the scoop of a lifetime. At the instigation of the Prime Minister, Stanley Baldwin, Lord Beaverbrook, the proprietor of the *Daily Express*, orchestrated a campaign that resulted in a gentleman's agreement that the national press would keep silent over the King's relationship. However, the "American papers were in full cry. Almost daily articles and photographs appeared showing the two together, while rumour became more and more scurrilous."[45] In the age of the internet, of course, such bipolar "newsworlds" could not exist.

The new King was popular with the people but anxiety grew in court and government circles when it became apparent that his relationship with Wallis Simpson was deeper than one of mere friendship. Initially Wallis's husband Ernest was also part of the King's circle but "little by little the two began to 'shed' Mr Simpson. He was less and less with them, and people of a certain type began giving dinner parties and evening parties 'to have the honour of meeting His Majesty the King and of course Mrs Simpson.'"[46]

Eventually, it became clear that Beaverbrook's "gentleman's agreement" could no longer constrain the press. He telephoned the King on December 1, warning him that the morning papers were set to publish "sensational disclosures" the following day. In particular Geoffrey Dawson, the editor of *The Times*, was ready to publish a critical leader. As a result of this Wallis Simpson was urged to leave the country. She and her entourage fled to the south of France to escape the "hounds of the Press."[47] This was one of the first examples of celebrity-hounding by the press as they chased her across France to Cannes and the villa of her old friend Herman Rogers.

To a modern media, ready to pounce at the first opportunity on any royal story, British editors' willingness to remain silent during the whole of 1936 borders on the mystical. This reticence has been examined over the years, because clearly such a scoop would cement for all time an editor's reputation. No one has put it more eloquently than Brian Inglis, noted journalist and media academic, in his book *Abdication*:

> They [newspaper editors] were afflicted by fears of the unknown. What would the reaction be, should a paper take a chance and spring the story? Obviously its sales for that issue, and probably for the next few issues, would be prodigious, but what thereafter? Suppose the public, though avid for the story when it appeared, thought badly of the paper for having printed it … And what of the advertisers? The weight of official and unofficial disapproval at such an act of lèse-majesté might well lead to the withdrawal of promised advertisements. What, too, of the legal position? A single false step, a misstatement, an unguarded innuendo, and swingeing damages could be expected against the transgressor. No, on the whole, it was safer to wait.[48]

Something of the same mindset remained well into the 1950s when the Queen's younger sister, Princess Margaret, began a relationship with Group Captain Peter Townsend. He was a World War II Battle of Britain pilot and equerry to Margaret's father, King George VI. More significantly however, Townsend was a divorced man. The affair was known about in court circles and the press were also aware of the situation. Yet again, however, there was no overt coverage and the affair remained private until the Queen's coronation in 1953. After the ceremony, while waiting in the porch of Westminster Abbey for her carriage, Margaret was seen by the eagle-eyed press corps to flick off a piece of fluff from Townsend's uniform. This intimate gesture was enough. The foreign press took it as a signal that the relationship was fair game and went into overdrive and this time the British press followed suit. A Sunday newspaper, the *People*, was the first with the story. Royal memories were stirred, however, and Townsend was hastily dispatched as air attaché to the British Embassy in Brussels. Princess Margaret later issued a communiqué to the effect that she had decided – unlike her uncle – not to marry a divorcé.

This was one of the earliest signs that deference to the royal family was slowly being eroded. It wouldn't be long before the postwar generation ushered in the "swinging sixties" and a royal scandal was just as likely to be

reported as any other. Yet a mere seven years later there was a similar episode of press silence – in this case over America's own "royal" family, the
Kennedy clan. During the presidency of John F. Kennedy (1961–3) there
was no mention in the news media about his inveterate womanizing. Even
in as forensically detailed account of JFK's rise as Theodore H White's 1961
book, *The Making of the President 1960*, there was no mention. However, in
the foreword to the 2009 edition Robert Dallek drew attention to this omission: "If White knew about Kennedy's compulsive womanizing, he left it
unsaid, as did all other mainstream journalists at the time; they operated on
the mores of 1960 and confined such information to private conversations."[49]
With hindsight should we ask ourselves whether such a story left "unsaid"
is in fact ethically justifiable? Certainly, no news organization would sit on
such a story today.

There are arguments on both sides – on the one hand many argue that a
politician's private life is no one's concern but his or her own, even though
such information may well be of interest to the public. On the other hand
others argue that a politician's private life cannot be divorced from his or
her public persona – one informs the other – and thus it is in the public
interest to know such information. There can be no hard and fast rule. And
there probably never will be. As a journalist you are entitled to make your
own decisions about what stories to cover and what to pass up. But once
you have a story that is clearly "news," do you not in fact have a duty to
report it, especially if, in your opinion, it is in the public interest that the
facts should be known?

Unquestionably, however, the member of the royal family who epitomized
the fractious and thorny relationship with a rampant, voracious press was
Diana, Princess of Wales. Much of the coverage of her, from the first moment
her relationship with Prince Charles became known, ignored the ethical
standards that the press in particular applied to other public figures. She
initially assumed the iconic role of media "darling" but ultimately, when she
failed to provide the scoops the press required on a regular basis, journalists
began to engineer the scoops themselves. There were many intrusive photographs taken over the years, but the most notorious incident involved pictures of her working out at a gym in Earls Court, London, in 1993.

Rather than the usual paparazzi ploys – staking out a celebrity's home,
waiting outside a nightclub, or the high-speed car chase – the pictures of
Diana dressed in a leotard and cycling shorts in the gym were a set-up from
the beginning. The gym owner, Bryce Taylor, took the photos with a concealed camera and then sold them to Mirror Group Newspapers. They first

appeared in the *Sunday Mirror* and in the following day's *Daily Mirror*. On the plus side the *Mirror* sold 100,000 extra copies on the day the pictures were shown but on the downside some large companies withdrew their advertising in protest. The "democratization" of the royal family was now complete and in many ways the press had come full circle. In the seventeenth and eighteenth centuries royalty was considered fair game. For example, King George III was often lampooned, defamed, and ridiculed in John Wilkes's *North Briton* newspaper; the Letters of Junius, published in the *Public Advertiser* between 1769 and 1772, were often unflattering about royalty. Letter No. 35 (December 19, 1769) noted: "They [the Americans] equally detest the pageantry of a king, and the supercilious hypocrisy of a bishop."[50] From the nineteenth century onwards, once Queen Victoria ascended the throne, such attacks became the exception – in the new commercial world of journalism they were adjudged bad for business! But now, once again, royalty would appear to be fair game.

The issue of privacy, how to define it, how to defend it, its relationship with freedom of speech, all constitute one of the major concerns of modern journalism. Is a person's privacy secure in the hands of journalists' voluntary ethical codes? Or is it so precious a commodity that the only real safeguard is statute law? Digital technology, exemplified by the internet, has further complicated the issue. Notions of universal privacy are now almost impossible to contemplate. The internet is a borderless world in which it can be impossible to determine the origins of a news story. So if anyone wishes to take legal action, under whose jurisdiction should it be taken? Can any law of privacy be sufficiently nuanced to reflect the different positions of the public figure, of whatever kind, and the ordinary citizen? If it can, where should the dividing line be drawn? Ultimately, are we all being forced, whether we like it or not, to become "celebrities" and fulfill Andy Warhol's 1968 prediction: "In the future, everyone will be world-famous for 15 minutes"?

Notes

1 Todd Gitlin, *The Whole World is Watching: Mass Media in the Making and Unmaking of the New Left* (Los Angeles: University of California Press, 2003), p. 6.
2 Ibid., p. 7.
3 Donna L. Halper, "Censorship in Broadcasting's First Two Decades," paper presented at the Joint Journalism Historians' Conference, Marymount Manhattan College, March 14, 2009.
4 Ibid.

5   Umberto Eco, "Semiotic Inquiry into the Television Message," in Toby Miller (ed.), *Television: Critical Concepts in Media and Cultural Studies* (London: Routledge, 2003), pp. 3–19.

6   Quoted in William Maxwell, "Old Lamps for New: Some Reflections on Recent Changes in Journalism," *Nineteenth Century and After*, 75 (1914), 1085–96 (pp. 1093–4).

7   David Berry, "Trust in Media Practices: Towards Cultural Development," in David Berry (ed.), *Ethics and Media Culture: Practices and Representations* (Oxford: Focal Press, 2000), pp. 28–53 (p. 32).

8   Hazel Dicken-Garcia, *Journalistic Standards in Nineteenth-Century America* (Madison: University of Wisconsin Press, 1989), p. 219.

9   James Curran and Jean Seaton, *Power Without Responsibility: The Press and Broadcasting in Britain*, 5th edn (London: Routledge, 1997), p. 87.

10 Derek Jameson, *Last of the Hot Metal Men* (London: Ebury Press, 1990), p. 133.

11 Quoted in Tom Baistow, *Fourth-Rate Estate: An Anatomy of Fleet Street* (London: Comedia, 1985), p. 5.

12 Joe Haines, *Maxwell* (London: Futura, 1988), pp. 377–8.

13 Harold Evans, *Good Times, Bad Times* (London: Weidenfeld and Nicolson, 1983), p. 11.

14 Curran and Seaton, *Power Without Responsibility*, pp. 28–41.

15 Ibid., p. 86.

16 Ibid.

17 Andrew Edgar, "Objectivity, Bias and Truth," in Andrew Belsey and Ruth Chadwick (eds), *Ethical Issues in Journalism and the Media* (London: Routledge, 1992), pp. 112–29 (p. 112).

18 Jason Barker, "'Shock': The Value of Emotion," in Berry (ed.), *Ethics and Media Culture*, pp. 192–207 (p. 204).

19 Andrew Belsey and Ruth Chadwick (eds), *Ethical Issues in Journalism and the Media* (London: Routledge, 1992), p. 6.

20 Ronald B. Standler, "United States Privacy Law," *Privacy Law in the USA* (1998), para 2/2. Available online at http://www.rbs2.com/privacy.htm, accessed on July 16, 2008.

21 Chris Frost, *Media Ethics and Self Regulation* (London: Longman, 2000), p. 97.

22 Quoted in Evans, *Good Times, Bad Times*, p. 10.

23 Frost, *Media Ethics and Self Regulation*, p. 118.

24 Ralph Waldo Emerson, *English Traits* (London: Routledge, 1857), p. 62.

25 Kate Summerscale, *The Suspicions of Mr Whicher* (London: Bloomsbury, 2008), p. 110.

26 David Flintham and Nicholas Herbert, *Press Freedom in Britain* (London: Newspaper Society, 1991), p. 17.

27 David Calcutt, *Report of the Committee on Privacy and Related Matters* (London: HMSO, 1990), p. 1.

28 Sir David Calcutt, *Review of Press Self-Regulation* (London: HMSO, 1993), p. xiii.

29 Department of National Heritage, *Privacy and Media Intrusion: The Government's Response* (London: HMSO, 1995), p. 23.

30 Peter Cole and Tony Harcup, *Newspaper Journalism* (London: Sage, 2010), p. 133.

31 BBC Guidelines are available online at http://www.bbc.co.uk/guidelines/editorialguidelines/edguide/

32 Alan J. Lee, *The Origins of the Popular Press 1855–1914* (London: Croom Helm, 1976), p. 129.

33 Curran and Seaton, *Power Without Responsibility*, p. 46.

34 Jane Chapman, *Comparative Media History: 1789 to the Present* (Cambridge, UK: Polity Press, 2005), p. 103.

35 Paul Siegel, *Communication Law in America*, 2nd edn (Lanham, MD: Roman & Littlefield, 2007), p. 225; Abraham Sperling, "A Story of Genius." Available at http://www.sidis.net/Sperling.htm, accessed on August 24, 2010.

36 Ibid.

37 Standler, "United States Privacy Law," para. 7/3.

38 Neil M. Richards and Daniel J. Solove, "Privacy's Other Path: Recovering the Law of Confidentiality," *Georgetown Law Journal*, 96 (2007), 123–82. Abstract available online at http://papers.ssrn.com/sol3/papers.cfm?abstract_id=969495, accessed on July 29, 2008.

39 Geoffrey Robertson QC and Andrew Nicol, *Media Law*, 3rd edn (London: Penguin, 1992), p. 173.

40 Jessica Hodgson, "Why Judge Backed Campbell in Privacy Case," *Guardian*, March 27, 2002. Available online at http://media.guardian.co.uk/print/0,3858,4382819-105414,00.html, accessed on July 30, 2008.

41 Richards and Solove, "Privacy's Other Path."

42 Siegel, *Communication Law in America*, p. 225.

43 Ibid.

44 In April 1963, Philip Graham, owner of the *Washington Post*, gave a speech to the overseas correspondents of *Newsweek* in London. In it he said: "So let us today drudge on about our inescapably impossible task of providing every week a first rough draft of history that will never really be completed about a world we can never really understand … ."

45 Frances Donaldson, *Edward VIII* (London: Futura, 1976), p. 215.

46 Ibid., p. 165.

47 Ibid., p. 270.

48 Brian Inglis, *Abdication* (New York: Macmillan, 1966), p. 197, cited in Donaldson, *Edward VIII*, pp. 228–9.

49 Theodore H. White, *The Making of the President 1960* (New York: Harper Perennial, 2009), p. xiii.

50 Woodfall's Junius, *The Letters of Junius from the Latest London Edition* (New York: Leavitt, Trow, 1848), p. 209.

10

Fakes, Rakes, and "On The Take"

In the winter of 1990 Britain suffered one of its worst weather events. Known as the Burns' Day Storm it hit on January 25, the birthday of Scottish poet Robert Burns, killing almost a hundred people and causing over £3bn worth of damage. Winds reached over 100 mph. One of the casualties was British actor Gorden Kaye, well-known for the TV show 'Allo 'Allo! He received serious head injuries when part of a wooden billboard blew through the windscreen of his car. Rushed to Charing Cross Hospital in London he was put on life support in intensive care. While Kaye was recovering from emergency brain surgery and only semiconscious, *Sunday Sport* journalist Roger Ordish, together with a photographer, donned doctor's coats and found their way to Kaye's room where they photographed him and attempted an interview. A nurse discovered them and threw them out.

Kaye's agent attempted to obtain an injunction preventing the *Sunday Sport* from publishing its scoop. The paper was known for its salacious and at times semipornographic style but despite this the judge, Lord Justice Glidewell, refused the application ruling that, "It is well known in English law that there is no right of privacy, and accordingly there is no right of action for breach of a person's privacy."[1] The judge did, however, hint that parliament might like to consider passing such a law.

The Fake's Progress

By common consent "faking it" is a betrayal of trust. But how exactly does "faking it" relate to issues of trust? In the *Sunday Sport* story about Gorden Kaye, the two journalists hid their true identity and pretended they were

Jane Chapman and Nick Nuttall, *Journalism Today: A Themed History*
© 2011 Jane Chapman and Nick Nuttall. Published by Blackwell Publishing Ltd.

doctors. The actual story they wrote was largely true but we have no compunction in condemning them for the way they obtained it, regardless of the fact that they committed no crime. So are there circumstances where disguising the fact that you are a journalist might be acceptable? And if so, what are those circumstances? What *is* the standard by which journalists should judge their behavior? Ultimately, if we accept that, as noted by Ian Hargreaves, "the ethic of truthfulness and accuracy is at the heart of the morality of journalism,"[2] and that such "morality" cannot be imposed with pedagogical exactitude through either the law or professional codes, then we can only fall back on the individual journalist – as a first line of defense and as a final arbiter.

Bill Kovach and Tom Rosenstiel have suggested, as one of their nine principles of good journalism, that "Its practitioners must be allowed to exercise their personal conscience."[3] It is difficult to argue with such a principle but it assumes that a journalist's "personal conscience" is a thing well brought up and imbued with a sensibility not dulled by exposure to the vanity, greed, ignorance, and immorality of his or her peers. And it is probably here that journalism practice reflects most clearly the mores of its time and thus today shows a clear ideological separation from some of the traditional patterns of news gathering of previous eras.

Most codes of conduct assume that falsehoods are likely to be perpetrated in error rather than on purpose and once recognized will be corrected "promptly and with due prominence," as the UK Press Complaints Commission (PCC) Code of Practice, Clause 1 (ii) puts it. Yet it is instructive to examine the extent to which newspapers, and more recently broadcasters, either have been duped or have flagrantly distorted events to further, for example, their own political agenda or, more prosaically, circulations and audience. The law is often a blunt instrument when dealing with such events and codes, as we have seen, and largely impotent to either inhibit such behavior before the fact or effect adequate redress afterwards because of their voluntary status. Outside the conscience of journalists themselves, all that remains is general opprobrium or perhaps near financial ruin, as we shall see in one celebrated case.

Newspaper editors are taken as men or women of the world, unlikely to be duped by the proverbial tall story. But at the same time they are always desperate for an exclusive that will raise both the status and the sales of their newspaper. The creative tension caused by this dichotomy not only sets editors apart from their colleagues but also marks them out as people of vision or of clay, often on consecutive days. Some of the more spectacular hijacks of the news agenda have come from external sources, relying on the typical editor's desire for the world exclusive and the front page splash. Yet danger lurks not only from outside the organization but also, at times, from within it. And on these occasions even the most assiduous editor can be caught off guard. History shows us that news media are susceptible to inside attack by hoaxers and fakers just as much as they are from outside sources.

Moons, Balloons, Starrs, and Suns

The early nineteenth century saw a new American penny press that combined serious journalism with entertainment. But sometimes the truth was sacrificed as standards were lowered in a quest for circulation to compensate for the low cover price. A prime example, that in its own way could be described as lunatic, was the "moon hoax." While most hoaxes have a particular journalist as perpetrator and can thus be dealt with fairly easily once discovered, it is not so easy when the perpetrator is the newspaper itself. Here, trust in the paper may be seriously compromised for all time. Such a situation arose at the *New York Sun* during the final week of August 1835, when the first of a series of articles appeared on the front page with the headline: "GREAT ASTRONOMICAL DISCOVERIES LATELY MADE BY SIR JOHN HERSCHEL, L.L.D. F.R.S. &c. at the Cape of Good Hope."[4] The articles, which ran each day for a week, began by triumphantly listing a series of stunning astronomical breakthroughs that the famous British astronomer, Sir John Herschel, had apparently made "by means of a telescope of vast dimensions and an entirely new principle." Herschel, the article declared, had established a "new theory of cometary phenomena," he had discovered planets in other solar systems, and he had "solved or corrected nearly every leading problem of mathematical astronomy." Then, almost as an afterthought, the article revealed Herschel's final, stunning achievement: he had discovered life on the moon![5]

The articles were allegedly reprinted from the *Edinburgh Journal of Science* but Herschel himself was unaware of the articles until much later and had not, of course, made any of the discoveries attributed to him. The whole story was in fact fictitious, an elaborate hoax perpetrated by the newspaper itself. However, the announcement caused enormous excitement throughout America, and the *New York Sun* managed to sell thousands of copies before the public realized it had been hoaxed. The slow speed of communication between Europe and America meant that the veracity of the *Sun*'s claims could not be easily tested. It took weeks for a periodical such as the *Edinburgh Journal of Science* to reach the US. And as public suspicion grew about the articles' authenticity the *Sun* itself

> adopted a stance of innocence, claiming that it had merely published what it had received from Europe and that therefore, if there was a hoax, it was a European hoax. Two weeks after the hoax it righteously declared: "Certain correspondents have been urging us to come out and confess the whole to be a hoax; but this we can by no means do, until we have the testimony of the English or Scotch papers to corroborate such a declaration." (*New York Sun*, 16 September 1835)[6]

The *Sun* also benefitted from the fact that its main rival, James Gordon Bennett's *New York Herald*, had seen its printing works burn down at the beginning of August. Thus the *Herald* could not respond in print to anything the *Sun* might claim. At the end of August the *Herald* resumed publication and was not slow to denounce the hoax. In his column entitled "'The Astronomical Hoax Explained', Bennett noted that 'the town has been agape two or three days at the very ingenious astronomical hoax', and then revealed (or made an accusation) that the true author of the lunar discoveries was … Richard Adams Locke, a Cambridge-educated English reporter who worked for the *Sun*."[7] Although he was a descendant of the philosopher John Locke, he appeared to have inherited none of the latter's moral probity. The defense of the *Sun* to criticism about its coverage of one of the first and most bizarre newspaper frauds in America was telling. The paper claimed it was offering a diversion from the more serious issue of the abolition of slavery which was achieved in Britain by legislation passed in that year.[8]

Moreover, less than 10 years later, in 1844, the same paper published a story headlined "The Atlantic Crossed in Three Days!" This became known as "The Balloon Hoax" and was written by Edgar Allan Poe. According to Poe, a gas-filled balloon had taken only 75 hours to cross the Atlantic piloted by famous European balloonist Monck Mason. The story caused such excitement that a huge crowd gathered in front of the *New York Sun* office, all trying to buy copies of the paper. The story was constructed with exceptional verisimilitude and obviously hoodwinked the paper's editor. Yet should it be considered that buying in a fake story is any less reprehensible that concocting one's own? Although the paper retracted the story two days later, it was symptomatic of the Yellow Journalism pursued by proprietors like William Randolph Hearst and Joseph Pulitzer toward the end of the nineteenth century.

More worryingly, echoes of this readiness to print stories of dubious provenance still afflict journalism today. An example was the British *Sun*'s story of 1986 headlined "Freddie Starr Ate My Hamster." Freddie Starr was a well-known zany comedian who was accused of placing a live hamster between two slices of bread after a gig in Manchester and eating it. It later transpired that the story was a hoax based on hearsay and exploited by Starr's publicist, Max Clifford. When asked some years later if there was any truth in the story Clifford is said to have replied, "Of course not." But he insisted that the story had rekindled Starr's flagging career.

Perhaps more seriously for the *Sun* newspaper and journalism in general was its 1996 Diana fake-tape scandal story, for which it paid a reputed six-figure sum. The front page headline read: "Di Spy Video Scandal" and the strapline: "She's filmed in bra and pants romp with Hewitt" (*Sun*, October 8, 1996). The story was based on a videotape of two "lovers" engaged in horseplay at Highgrove, Prince Charles's country house in Gloucestershire. The man and the woman in the tape, however, turned out to be lookalikes for Princess Diana and her former riding instructor and lover James Hewitt, rather than the real thing. The tape had been bought from "a smart American lawyer" but Princess Diana denied the pictures were of her. The *Sun*'s editor, Stuart Higgins, was forced into a groveling apology to his readers and Princess Diana herself. At the very least the *Sun*'s journalistic skills and procedures must be called into question as it later transpired that a number of other papers had turned down the opportunity to purchase this "exclusive." Stuart Higgins, however, kept his job.

The Empire City Massacre

Mark Twain's journalistic skills were never called into question, however, when in 1863 he fabricated a complete story for the *Territorial Enterprise*, a Virginia City, Nevada, newspaper. He described it later as "a deep, deep satire, and most ingeniously contrived."[9] Mark Twain is world famous for novels such as *The Adventures of Tom Sawyer* and *Adventures of Huckleberry Finn* but in his early days he earned a living as a journalist. He worked for the *San Francisco Morning Call*, the *Daily Alta California*, and the *Sacramento Union*. But it was for the *Territorial Enterprise* that Twain concocted a story of family death and disaster on a truly epic scale. "In 1863 San Francisco newspapers were spilling a lot of ink lambasting mining ventures that were cooking their books, and these same papers were encouraging investors to put their money instead in San Francisco utility companies. But it turned out that many of these utility companies were also cooking their books."[10]

Twain told the story of one man who lost all his money in utility company shares. He went insane and slaughtered his whole family except for his two young daughters. He then rode into town carrying the "reeking scalp" of his wife and collapsed and died outside a saloon. Not surprisingly, the story caused a sensation. It was widely reprinted and taken at face value. The "covenant" between publisher and reader that newspapers do not mislead or print unchecked or unattributable stories was no less potent then than now but it's doubtful whether such a gruesome tale would pass a subeditor's table today without a more careful checking of the basic facts.

Twain's motive was certainly moralistic and probably self-serving. He wished to offer a corrective to the San Francisco newspapers that were promoting the sale of utility company shares in their pages, shares which he believed to be risky investments. His story had to be sensational enough for the paper to print it which, of course, it did. He would no doubt have argued that the means justified the end, but as with all fakery, it broke the covenant of trust that is the bedrock of ethical journalism. There was no official apology offered, however, and luckily for Twain he was forgiven by his editor and did not lose his job, the reverse of which would probably be the case today.

The Pigott Letter Forgeries

So is doing a wrong thing but for the right reasons ethically defensible? *The Times* newspaper certainly believed in such a defense during its dealings with a certain Richard Pigott, a man who nearly bankrupted the paper. From the early decades of the nineteenth century *The Times* was known to readers and critics alike as the Thunderer, because of the often forthright tone of its leading articles. A readiness to take sides on the political issues of the day, however, almost resulted in its demise during the period of Irish agitation for Home Rule toward the end of the century. George Buckle was *The Times*'s editor in 1886 when he took the fateful decision to purchase and publish a set of 10 letters that if genuine would have supported the paper's editorial position of opposition to Irish Home Rule and its main proponent, Charles Stewart Parnell. The events that followed not only called into question the probity of *The Times* itself but also caused severe financial difficulties which affected the paper for decades to come.

Buckle was offered the chance to buy the letters by Irish journalist Edward Caulfield Houston. Houston was already known to Buckle, having free-lanced for the paper in the past. Despite this, Buckle was cautious and initially refused to hand over any money. However, he told Houston that if he managed to obtain the actual documents then the paper would be interested in seeing them. Houston went back to his principal, "a notorious scoundrel called Richard Pigott, who had guaranteed to obtain for Houston material that would incriminate Parnell," and agreed to purchase 10 letters, half of them purporting to be signed by Parnell himself.[11] Houston returned and sold the letters to *The Times* for £1,780 (approximately £100,000 at today's prices).[12] According to the official history of the paper: "The great public importance of the letters, provided they were authentic, was now apparent to Buckle, and it was manifest that their publication in *The Times* would be a political event of the utmost gravity and a momentous contribution to the cause that the paper had at heart,"[13] the cause in question being the defeat of Gladstone's Home Rule Bill for Ireland then before parliament.

As the paper surmised, the letters created an immediate sensation. *The Times* challenged Parnell to sue them. He did nothing and the paper took this as a sign of his guilt. However, Parnell and the Irish members of the House of Commons requested a Commission of Enquiry. The government initially turned down the request but eventually agreed to a judicial commission. *The Times* agreed to co-operate with the commission which ruled that the paper "must make good all the charges contained in the articles."[14] Buckle felt confident the commission would find against Parnell and vindicate the paper. But in February 1889, after 128 sessions, the commission found in Parnell's favor. The letters were indeed forgeries perpetrated by Richard Pigott. Pigott broke down under cross-examination after one of the letters was shown to be a forgery by him, containing as it did many of his characteristic spelling mistakes. Rather than return to the witness box the next day he fled to Madrid where he committed suicide in his hotel room. *The Times* withdrew the letters unconditionally but despite this reverse "did not withdraw the general allegations against Parnellism made in the articles."[15]

Parnell sued *The Times* for libel in the Scottish courts and the newspaper settled out of court for £5,000. On top of this the commission itself cost the paper over £200,000 and for the first time since the beginning of the century the paper went into deficit. It would take a long time for *The Times* to recover both its reputation and its finances.

The Zinoviev Letter

It was another letter with political overtones that caused a furor in the run-up to the general election of 1924. The first Labour government in British history lasted a mere 10 months, from January to October of that year. It was a minority government, however, and Ramsay MacDonald, the first Labour Prime Minister, was forced to call a general election after he was defeated in a Commons vote. Then, on October 25, four days before the election, the *Daily Mail* published a scoop that many believe effectively handed a landslide victory to the Conservatives.

This scoop was the Zinoviev Letter. It had supposedly been written by one Grigori Zinoviev, president of the presidium of the Executive Committee of the Communist International (the Comintern) and Arthur McManus, the British representative on the Presidium. The letter was addressed to the Central Committee of the British Communist Party. It suggested methods to bring about armed insurrection, the development of communist cells in munitions factories and the armed forces, and the possibility of paralyzing all military preparations by what it called the bourgeoisie. In a country already fearful of socialism and communism, the letter was an incendiary device guaranteed to alarm conservative opinion.

Under the headline, "Civil War Plot by Socialists: Moscow Orders to Our Reds," the *Daily Mail* splashed the story over its front page. Yet controversy raged over the authenticity of the letter itself, for it contained errors that led many people at the time to consider it a forgery. It is now generally agreed the letter was a forgery perpetrated by two Russian émigrés working in Berlin.[16] It was originally sent to MI6 by one of its agents in Riga, the capital of Latvia. Subsequent research has shown that the Zinoviev Letter was widely circulated to senior army officers and civil servants prior to the election, the aim being to maximize damage to the Labour government. It is a moot point whether the *Daily Mail* or *The Times*, the other newspaper to publish the letter, believed it a forgery or not. Either way it was probably one of the factors that resulted in the return of a Conservative government under Stanley Baldwin. At this time there were no voluntary controls on the press such as the PCC or even a national labor union so any fallout, political or otherwise, would have been unlikely to have had any effect on the paper or subsequent events.

To a certain extent a newspaper may be forgiven for publishing a false story if it sincerely believes the information upon which it is based is true, or at least true as far as can be verified in the little time deadlines often permit. However, the situation is markedly different when a staff journalist produces fake stories or introduces false detail into a story for his or her own news organization. Notions of truth, factual accuracy, and the duty of journalists, ethically to their media organization and their audience, and morally to themselves, are immediately called into question. Journalists are subject to social and economic pressures that can often conflict, as we have seen, with the notional perfection of purely ethical behavior. Yet the manifestations of fakery are not necessarily capable of only one interpretation.

What A Tangled Web We Weave …

Patricia Smith was a poet, playwright, and Pulitzer Prize-nominated journalist who worked for the *Boston Globe*. In 1998 she admitted to making up people and quotes for her metro column and she was fired from the newspaper. In her final column she wrote, "From time to time in my metro column, to create the desired impact or slam home a salient point, I attributed quotes to people who didn't exist." She continued, "I could give them names, even occupations, but I couldn't give them what they needed most – a heartbeat. As anyone who's ever touched a newspaper knows, that's one of the cardinal sins of journalism: Thou shall not fabricate. No exceptions. No excuses."[17]

The fabrications were discovered during a routine review by *Globe* editors. Following her dismissal the American Society of Newspaper Editors (ASNE) withdrew its Distinguished Writing Award bestowed on Smith the previous April. Part of its statement said, "Everyone in journalism is saddened to learn that Patricia Smith fabricated portions of her work. Appropriately, she resigned from the newspaper. There is no place in journalism for fabrication of any kind."[18] It is difficult to assess the level of Smith's culpability. It would seem that her aim was purely to maintain her profile as a "literary" journalist, someone who possessed a power over words more attributable to the poet or author that she also was. But part of her mea culpa was surely an acknowledgement that the sensational or at least the emotional pull of the "heartbeat," as she described it, was essential to great journalistic writing. In its absence lay her particular ethical dilemma.

Yet within two months of Smith's resignation another *Globe* columnist, Mike Barnicle, was also forced to resign. The "pugnacious writer, who has become an institution in Boston over the course of a 25-year career at the Globe, told TV station WCVB that his resignation was 'the best thing for the paper'." According to *Globe* editor Matthew Storin, Barnicle had fabricated characters in a 1995 column and also lifted portions of a 1986 column from a 1961 book by journalist A. J. Liebling. Earlier that month, however, editor Storin had demanded Barnicle's resignation for plagiarizing jokes from a book by George Carlin without attribution. A public outcry resulted in Barnicle being only suspended for two months without pay.[19] Barnicle admitted only to being "sloppy." One question that can legitimately be asked of these resignations is the extent to which the inclusion of attribution and a note that characters were in fact fictitious would have been (1) journalistically acceptable and (2) ethically sustainable.

Stephen Glass, on the other hand, made up whole events rather than just characters. Glass graduated from the University of Pennsylvania and by the age of 23 he was writing political stories for the left-leaning *The New Republic* magazine. He also wrote for other high-profile national publications. Glass, however, was fabricating much of his material. He made up people, events, and places. He invented quotations and organizations. Many of his articles were total invention from beginning to end. Eventually he was discovered and fired from *The New Republic* in 1998.

In an interview with Steve Kroft of CBS, Glass explained his modus operandi:

> "I would tell a story, and there would be fact A, which maybe was true. And then there would be fact B, which was sort of partially true and partially fabricated. And there would be fact C which was more fabricated and almost not true," says Glass. "And there would be fact D, which was a complete whopper. And totally not true. And so people would be with me on these stories through fact A and through fact B. And so they would believe me to C. And then at D they were still believing me through the story."[20]

Ultimately, fellow journalist Scott Rosenberg's indictment pretty much sums up the "straight" journalist's view of Glass and his behavior. "I can't say I feel much sympathy for poor Glass and his over-booked assignments for high-paying or prestigious publications like *Rolling Stone, Harper's* and the *New York Times Magazine* – where editors presumably fell in love with his great lead paragraphs. Fabricating stories for maximum 'juiciness' is a loathsome enterprise."[21]

FactFile
Faking It

1998: British Channel 4 television had to halt the screening at the last minute of its *Cutting Edge* documentary, "Daddy's Girl," about father–daughter relationships, when it was discovered that one of the father and daughter pairs featured were in fact lovers Victoria Greetham and Stuart Smith. Ms Greetham, 19 years old, admitted that she had hoaxed the television company and its journalists because she wanted to appear on television and become famous.

1997: Another Channel 4 fake controversy erupted over Carlton Television's rent boy documentary, "Too Much Too Young: Chickens." It contained scenes where "clients" of the boys were shown negotiating for sex. These clients were in fact production staff or their friends. Producer Marie Devine admitted lying to Channel 4 about the program. She was banned from working for the channel ever again and Carlton Television, the makers of the documentary, was fined £150,000 by the Independent Television Commission (ITC).

1983: The *Sunday Times*, perhaps the most eminent of British Sunday newspapers, announced the discovery of 62 volumes of Hitler's diaries. It had acquired the rights from *Stern Magazine* whose journalist Gerd Heidemann was said to have received the diaries after they were smuggled out of East Germany. Eminent historian and *Times* director Hugh Trevor-Roper, Lord Dacre, flew to Switzerland and attested the diaries genuine. Doubts were raised almost immediately, however, and it didn't take long before the diaries were shown to be forgeries perpetrated by one Konrad Kujau who was jailed for his trouble. *Stern* editors Peter Koch and Felix Schmidt resigned and Frank Giles stood down as editor of the *Sunday Times*. Its rival newspapers took great delight in ridiculing the paper and Trevor-Roper's reputation never really recovered.

1980: Janet Cooke was a reporter on the *Washington Post* when it published on September 29 her story, "Jimmy's World," about an eight-year-old heroin addict. The story caused consternation among readers and the Mayor, Marion Barry, organized a police search for the boy which proved unsuccessful. Despite this, the *Post* submitted Cooke's story for a Pulitzer Prize and she was awarded the Prize for Feature Writing in April 1981.

However, her previous paper, the *Toledo Blade*, alerted to her success, was perplexed at discrepancies in her résumé and told the *Post*. Confronted by *Post* editors, Cooke confessed that she had not in fact attended Vassar College as she had claimed and the "Jimmy" story was a fabrication. Cooke resigned from the *Post* and returned the Prize. Part of her mea culpa was that the high-pressure environment at the *Post* had corrupted her judgment. Yet this does not account for the falsifications in her résumé which presumably got her the job in the first place.

1972: The foreign editor of the London *Daily Express*, Stewart Steven, revealed that Martin Bormann, Hitler's notorious deputy, was alive and well and living in South America. Simon Wiesenthal, the Nazi hunter, had also claimed that there was strong evidence that Bormann was living in South America. However, six days after the story appeared the *Express* discovered that their picture of Bormann was in fact a photo of an Argentinian schoolteacher. The hoax was perpetrated by a Hungarian journalist and historian, Ladislas Farago. Steven left the paper soon afterwards but eventually occupied the editor's chair at the London *Evening Standard*.

1920: President Woodrow Wilson suffered a debilitating stroke in October 1919 while on a speaking tour. The First Lady and the president's doctor, Admiral Cary Grayson, concealed Wilson's true condition which was very serious. He was paralyzed down his left side and mentally incapable. By 1920 Wilson had made a partial recovery but was far from well and the First Lady "invited Louis Seibold, who covered the White House for the *New York World*, to visit for an interview. Delighted by a chance to get on the front page, Seibold collaborated shamelessly with the scam." He wrote about

> how delighted he was to find the president almost his old self. He joshed with him about running a footrace in a month or two; he would give the president a modest handicap because of his "slight limp." (In fact, Wilson's whole left side remained paralyzed.) Seibold was soon telling even more blatant lies. He said he saw Wilson "transact the most important functions of his office with his old time decisiveness, method and keenness of intellectual appraisement." In fact, Wilson's attention span was about sixty seconds.[22]

Seibold's faked interview won him the Pulitzer Prize for Reporting in 1921 and unlike Janet Cooke 60 years later he never returned it.

One of the most high-profile offenders in the faking it stakes was a journalist named Jayson Blair. He worked for the *New York Times* (1998–2003) and for many years had been faking stories for the paper. He was eventually unmasked while covering a story about a US soldier's family in San Antonio, Texas, coming to terms with their son being reported missing in action during the invasion of Iraq. The senior editor of the local paper, the *San Antonio Express-News*, contacted the *Times* about close similarities between Jayson Blair's article and their reporter Macarena Hernandez's story which had appeared a week or so earlier.

After an internal investigation at the *Times*, Blair was confronted with evidence that he had fabricated quotes and other details in at least 36 stories. The charge sheet concluded that Blair:

> misled readers and Times colleagues with dispatches that purported to be from Maryland, Texas and other states, when often he was far away, in New York. He fabricated comments. He concocted scenes. He lifted material from other newspapers and wire services. He selected details from photographs to create the impression he had been somewhere or seen someone, when he had not.
>
> And he used these techniques to write falsely about emotionally charged moments in recent history, from the deadly sniper attacks in suburban Washington to the anguish of families grieving for loved ones killed in Iraq.[23]

Blair resigned and the *New York Times* took the unprecedented step of publishing a front page 7,000 word apology acknowledging that the affair marked "a low point in the 152-year history of the newspaper." Executive director, Howell Raines, and the managing editor, Gerald Boyd, both resigned in the wake of the scandal. According to some they had been instrumental in fast-tracking Blair's career.

> Blair's editor Jonathan Landman told the Siegal committee – a committee of 25 staffers and three outside journalists led by assistant managing editor Allan Siegal – he felt the fact that Blair was African-American played a large part in his initial promotion to full-time staffer. "I think race was the decisive factor in his promotion," he said. "I thought then and I think now that it was the wrong decision."[24]

There is some debate about the probity of the US press being greater than that of its UK counterpart. The evidence is mixed but the general lack of a "tabloid" culture in America and a cursory glance at American newspapers, exemplified by such journalism as the *New York Times*'s front page apology, suggests that their papers are certainly less sensationalist, more considered and, it has to be said, often much duller than their British equivalents.

Doctoring Documentary

While it is perfectly permissible for a newspaper to "be partisan," that is, to support a particular political viewpoint, it is expressly forbidden in the UK for a broadcaster to do likewise. The BBC, as a public sector broadcaster, is required by its charter to remain impartial and this is also the case with commercial networks. American television is less tightly regulated and it is quite clear that an organization like *Fox News*, for example, despite its "We report, you decide," strapline, generally supports a Republican worldview.

Yet despite this public service remit, it was Britain's Carlton Television which was involved in the production of two award-winning documentaries in 1994 and 1996 that were subsequently found to be full of faked material. In October 1996, "The Connection" purported to expose a new heroin trafficking route from Colombia to the UK. However, according to Independent Television Commission (ITC) chairman Sir Robin Biggam, much of "what was offered as evidence used to substantiate this was fake," and Carlton was guilty of "a 'wholesale breach of trust' with the viewers."[25]

The absolutist position is that to document anything other than truth is a derogation of the journalist's prime function. As noted by media analyst David Berry, "There should not be any ethical dilemma between economic considerations and the pursuit of truth once a journalist posits the truth as fundamental to journalistic practices."[26] Thus lies are indeed "damned lies" and cannot be justified either morally, technically, or commercially because they are a "breach of public trust."

Conversely there is the relativist position that what you don't know can't harm you – for example, not knowing that a scene is a reconstruction rather than the "real thing" does not necessarily invalidate the point the documentary maker wishes to make. The "necessarily" is of course crucial and many documentary makers believe that they themselves should be required to justify their decisions rather than be bludgeoned by what is seen as an inflexible code. Thus they have argued that the only restraint on documentary practice should be grounded in the common law rather than an ethical code produced by regulators.[27] However, the common law, in Britain at least, is notoriously "flexible" and often at the mercy of a capricious judge and therefore perhaps no more capable of safeguarding ethical standards than regulators.

Having said that, the Independent Television Commission (ITC) found the program makers guilty of breaching its code as follows:

- Evidence for a new heroin route to the UK does not exist.
- The programme-makers did not risk their lives as claimed.
- The cartel leader was not the person interviewed in the programme and the "secret location" for the interview was the producer's hotel bedroom.
- Actors pretended to be drug-runners and the heroin shown was in fact sweets [candy].
- A drugs "mule" seen apparently boarding a plane destined for London had never left Colombia.[28]

The ITC code had lengthy sections on impartiality, fairness, and privacy and the charge sheet above clearly indicted Carlton Television under each of these three sections (the functions of the ITC have now been subsumed into the Ofcom Broadcasting Code as of July 25, 2005). Carlton was fined £2 million by the ITC.

However, two years previously, in 1994, Carlton Television had aired another documentary by the same producer, Marc de Beaufort, in its *Network First* series. "Inside Castro's Cuba," winner of two international awards, included an interview with Fidel Castro. The *Guardian* newspaper alleged in June 1998 that this interview had been faked, as film clips of Castro talking to camera and passed off as a one-to-one interview were from archive footage provided by the Cuban government. Castro's personal cameraman, Roberto Chile, who gave the footage to Carlton, was quoted as saying the interview was "false." Despite this, the ITC (British television watchdog) found that no such claims were made in the program or in on-screen trailers.

Media Literacy

In a complex world of multiple media platforms, a media-literate population is seen as essential to a fully functioning democracy. Media literacy has been defined by Ofcom, the independent media regulator and competition authority for the UK communications industries, as "the ability to access, understand and create communications in a variety of contexts."[29] In the United States a similar definition was adopted by the National leadership Conference on Media Literacy in 1992: "to access, analyse, evaluate and communicate messages in a variety of forms."[30] It would seem that "understand" and "evaluate" are the key words here and understanding is clearly undermined by journalists or media organizations knowingly, or indeed unknowingly, presenting the false, the hoax, or the fake as unmediated truth. Thus an important component of media literacy must be the ability to discern one from the other. This is relevant not only so the media can be held to account but also so that an audience can determine its response to media outputs, whether it be belief, skepticism, cynicism, scorn, or mirth. The dangers of failure, as David Berry notes, are firstly a predisposition to "doubt the validity of statements" and secondly to cultivate a culture of indifference. "The *culture of indifference* emanates from the belief that morality is temporarily suspended because of the widespread acceptances – in this case – of dubious news practices by sections of the reading and viewing public."[31]

Audiences today are confronted by a plethora of different media, and consumption patterns are constantly shifting. Often one medium subverts another. Many films, for example *The Paper* (1994) and *Sweet Smell of Success* (1957), offer a cynical view of journalists, describing journalism as "cutthroat" and journalists as "ruthless and unscrupulous." Television programs like *NewsRadio* (CBS, 1995–9) or the UK sitcom *Drop the Dead Donkey* (Channel 4, 1990–8) presented the news media as comic or incompetent and regularly satirized historical events. Yet modern audiences, although "satire savvy," often have only a tenuous grasp of historical fact and may easily confuse the satire with the "truth" of the events themselves. In the absence of any ethical controls with "bite" (statutory or otherwise), demands on an audience's media literacy thus become greater than ever before.

The history of the press in particular is one where overt controls were gradually replaced by covert ones. But unquestionably the press was always seen by politicians as a powerful ally and a dangerous foe. Codes were devised to both encourage good journalism and suggest the boundaries within which it should be practiced. Today, codes deal with such issues as ethnicity, race, gender, disability, coverage of suicide and other sensitive issues, as well as how journalists should behave both at work and privately. While the UK's National Union of Journalists (NUJ) Code of Conduct is a prime example of a "bottom-up" code, one devised and adopted by working journalists, the PCC Code of Practice and the various codes relating to UK broadcast media are "top-down" codes – devised and imposed by proprietors, editors, and other controllers of the media. American newspaper codes appear to be hybrids – produced by management on the one hand who provide guidance on such issues as staff expenses and relationships between staff and the media organization, and produced in consultation with the staff on the other hand when dealing with issues such as journalistic ethics, staff behavior, and extracurricular activities.

Ultimately, however, all these codes are voluntary. And in the absence of clear legal guidance, especially in Britain, there are calls at regular intervals for codes to become statutory. Yet this call for statutory controls is in part a response to the perceived behavior of journalists themselves and like it or not, ethical standards are ultimately in the hands of those journalists who do the job on a day-to-day basis. It is their sensitivity, their integrity, their commitment to doing the right thing that will determine how journalists and the industry they work in are judged.

David Blundy was a foreign correspondent who had worked for the *Sunday Times* Insight team and then joined the now defunct *Sunday Correspondent*. In 1989 he was covering the civil war in El Salvador and had "gone out into the action one last time, when other journalists would have been content to file from the comfort of their hotel room, to put a final definitive top on his copy."[32] A sniper's bullet hit him and he died soon afterwards in hospital. Blundy's death at 44 shocked the press corps as he was a much-liked and respected colleague. At his memorial service, his old *Sunday Times* boss Harry Evans said of him:

> He was one of those reporters who give what we call the freedom of the press its moral energy. That moral energy is renewed whenever journalism enables people to make free, informed choices ... The whole of ethics is based on the presumption of free will and the freedom to make choices.... David was in the front line of truth – not so much because he exposed himself to danger as that he never ceased to expose himself to doubt ... Is my story accurate? Is it clear? Is it fair? Is it boring? David naturally doubted whether he met the tests he set himself. But he did, in deceptively simple prose.[33]

If anything demystifies ethics and offers a simple and straightforward riposte to those who cynically deride journalists and journalism Evans's eulogy is it.

Notes

1   Roy Greenslade, *Press Gang: How Newspapers Make Profits from Propaganda* (London: Macmillan, 2003), p. 540.
2   Ian Hargreaves, *Journalism: Truth or Dare* (Oxford: Oxford University Press, 2003), p. 225.
3   Bill Kovach and Tom Rosenstiel, *The Elements of Journalism: What Newspeople Should Know and the Public Should Expect* (New York: Crown Publishing, 2001), p. 12.

4   Alex Boese, "The Great Moon Hoax of 1835," *Hoaxipedia* (2008). Available online at http://www.museumofhoaxes.com/moonhoax.html, accessed on March 22, 2010.

5   Ibid.

6   Ibid.

7   Ibid.

8   Jane Chapman, *Comparative Media History* (Cambridge, UK: Polity Press, 2005), p. 34.

9   Alex Boese, "Empire City Massacre," *Hoaxipedia* (2008). Available online at http://www.museumofhoaxes.com/hoax/Hoaxipedia/Empire_City_Massacre/, accessed on August 14, 2008.

10 Ibid.

11 Oliver Woods and James Bishop, *The Story of* The Times (London: Michael Joseph, 1985), p. 137.

12 The Times, *The History of* The Times, vol. III, *The Twentieth Century Test* (London: Times Publishing Company, 1947), p. 48.

13 Ibid., p. 45.

14 Woods and Bishop, *The Story of* The Times, p. 144.

15 Ibid., p. 150.

16 Gill Bennett, *A Most Extraordinary and Mysterious Business: The Zinoviev Letter of 1924*, Historians, LRD History Note No.14 (London: Foreign & Commonwealth Office, 1999). This paper was published in January 1999 by Gill Bennett who was chief historian at the Foreign Office.

17 "Boston Globe Columnist Resigns, After Admitting to Fabricating People and Quotes," *Jet*, June 19, 1998. Available online at http://findarticles.com/p/articles/mi_m1355/is_n6_v94 /ai_21246923/, accessed on March 31, 2010.

18 "ASNE Withdraws Award to Globe Columnist Patricia Smith," *American Society of Newspaper Editors*, July 1, 1998. Available online at http://204.8.120.192/index.cfm?ID=1393, accessed on August 25, 2010.

19 "Boston Columnist Resigns Amid New Plagiarism Charges," *CNN*, August 19, 1998. Available online at http://edition.cnn.com/US/9808/19/barnicle/, accessed on August 25, 2010.

20 Steve Kroft, "Stephen Glass: I Lied For Esteem," *CBS 60 Minutes*, August 17, 2003. Available online at http://www.cbsnews.com/stories/2003/05/07/60minutes/main552819.shtml, accessed on March 30, 2010.

21 Scott Rosenberg, "Hacker Heaven, Editors' Hell," *Salon, 21st Century, Let's Get This Straight*, 1998. Available online at http://archive.salon.com/21st/rose/1998/05/14straight.html, accessed on August 5, 2008.

22 Thomas Fleming, "Fakery in American Journalism," *History News Network*, June 2, 2003. Available online at http://hnn.us/articles/1474.html, accessed on March 30, 2010.

23 "Times Reporter Who Resigned Leaves Long Trail of Deception," *New York Times*, May 11, 2003. Available online at http://www.nytimes.com/2003/05/11/

national/11PAPE.html?ex=1367985600&en=d6f511319c259463&ei=5007& partner=USERLAND, accessed on March 30, 2010.

24 Kristina Nwazota, "Jayson Blair: A Case Study of What Went Wrong at The New York Times," *Online NewsHour*, December 10, 2004. Available online at http://www.pbs.org/newshour/media/media_ethics/casestudy_blair.php, accessed on March 30, 2010.

25 BBC News, "Carlton Fined £2m for "Faked" Documentary," *BBC News*, December 18, 1998. Available online at http://news.bbc.co.uk/1/hi/uk/237715. stm, accessed on August 11, 2008.

26 David Berry (ed.), *Ethics and Media Culture: Practices and Representations* (Oxford: Focal Press, 2000), p. 33.

27 Brian Winston, *Lies, Damn Lies and Documentaries* (London: British Film Institute, 2000).

28 BBC News, "Carlton Fined £2m for "Faked" Documentary."

29 "Media Literacy Audit – Report on Adult Media Literacy." Available online at http://stakeholders.ofcom.org.uk/market-data-research/media-literacy/ medlitpub/medlitpubrss/medialit_audit/, accessed on August 26, 2010.

30 Sonia Livingstone, "The Changing Nature and Uses of Media Literacy," *Media Culture-Online*, July 2003, para. 8. Available online at http://mediaculture-on-line.de/fileadmin/bibliothek/livingstone_changing_nature/livingstone_ changing_nature.html, accessed on September 10, 2010.

31 Berry, *Ethics and Media Culture*, p. 36.

32 Quoted in Peter Chippindale and Chris Horrie, *Stick it up Your Punter* (London: Heinemann, 1990), p. 341.

33 Ibid., p. 342.

Part IV

Audience: Citizen Consumer or Consumer Citizen?

If you don't read the newspaper, you are uninformed; if you do read the newspaper, you are misinformed.

(*Mark Twain*)

11

Finding an Audience

He was first pictured in long shot walking toward the camera holding his wife's hand and dressed in a smart suit. Telephoto lenses on tripods were strapped to car roofs. Television cameras from all the world's broadcasters were trained on him as he walked by. It was late afternoon and the sun shone warm on everyone. A roar went up from the crowd. He shook people's hands, smiling all the time, and then climbed into a waiting car. The cavalcade drove at walking pace through the people clamoring to see him and touch the car. The crowd was put at half a million. It was 4p.m. on February 11, 1990. The most famous political prisoner in the world, Nelson Mandela, had just walked free from Victor Verster Prison in Paarl, South Africa, after being incarcerated for 27 years. The live television coverage reached a worldwide audience estimated at one billion. It was described as a historic moment and part of that "history" was clearly to do with the numbers of people watching the event worldwide. Such large audiences are usually only achieved with what might be termed "staged" events such as Mandela's release. The largest television audience ever, for example, was the 2.5 billion people who watched Princess Diana's funeral.[1]

The concept of "audience," whether readers, listeners, or viewers, has clearly changed dramatically since the first readers of "corantos" or news books in seventeenth-century London perused their few pages in offices or coffee shops. What is undoubtedly true, however, is that audiences have always been manipulated in one way or another and the extent to which they are aware of that manipulation is the extent to which they collude in it. In the television coverage of Nelson Mandela's release from prison, for example, there were a number of shots of a crowd disturbance

Jane Chapman and Nick Nuttall, *Journalism Today: A Themed History*
© 2011 Jane Chapman and Nick Nuttall. Published by Blackwell Publishing Ltd.

and looting by some black youths. Questions could legitimately be asked about why these shots were included, and what particular purpose was served by such coverage on a day when black people in particular had cause to rejoice. What is evident, nonetheless, is that a sense of the "audience" clearly played a part in the editorial decisions resulting in such coverage as much as the particular prejudices or sensibilities of the media organization itself.

An Audience with the Media

In less frenetic times, when newspapers were one of the few means of communicating information on a regular basis, proprietors depended for their income on cover price – which often precluded the poor and laboring classes – or subventions from political parties, religious groupings, or wealthy individuals. For example, Robert Walpole, Britain's first Prime Minister (1721–42), "spent £50,000 on secret hand-outs to the press in the last ten years of his administration."[2] President Andrew Jackson (1829–37) "had no less than fifty-seven journalists on the official payroll."[3] From 1789 to 1799 John Walter "received during these years an allowance from the Treasury of £300 a year in 'reward for the politics' of *The Times*."[4] To suggest that such support was altruistic is probably stretching credulity. So audiences, to some extent, were incidental to early journalistic endeavors. Proprietors generally had a clear idea who they were writing for and could be reminded if necessary. The first American newspaper, *Publick Occurrences*, was an early casualty of a proprietor's failure to fully comprehend his potential audience. It was published in Boston by radical bookseller Benjamin Harris in 1690 without express permission of the Crown. It was suppressed after just one issue by a royal authority, represented by the Governor of Massachusetts, already aware of and fearful of the power of the press.[5]

A newspaper's cover price was also elevated by government stamp duties. The tax was first imposed on British newspapers in 1712 and gradually rose from a penny until the 1815 Stamp Act increased it to fourpence a copy. Few people could afford to pay sixpence or more each day for a newspaper, so the tax restricted circulations to people with fairly high incomes. Inevitably such newspapers tended to reflect the opinions of this predominantly middle-class and moneyed audience. The editor of the *Manchester Guardian*, A. P. Wadsworth, pointed out in a paper to the "Manchester

Statistical Society in 1955, 'Newspaper Circulations 1800–1954', that much of the history of the British press in the first half of the nineteenth century derived from the conviction that 'the lower orders were not to be trusted' and that newspapers should be kept from them."[6] In contrast, during the 1830s, the American penny press happily "sold a product to a general readership and sold the readership to advertisers."[7] This commercialization of newspapers forced editors to appeal to a wider audience which inevitably included the "lower orders," and also to recognize the greater economic power of nonpartisanship: "Why talk to half the town with party slogans, reasoned the editors, when you can reach them all with sensationalism and/or balanced reports?"[8]

Today there are many varying audiences for the media, and they tend to be well-documented and studied by advertisers and media executives alike. This has not always been the case, however. The cultural form of a newspaper was defined during the eighteenth century and its definition of news has been transmitted with little quibble to broadcast media and to the ever-increasing array of platforms offered by digital technology. Only slowly did notions of audience impinge on the journalistic sense of what constituted news. As such, journalism's "reach" has always been contingent – on the availability of the organs of communication and on the subtle and inchoate interactions of society and culture as manifested through the media audience itself.

Locating an Audience

One of the earliest attempts to "locate" an audience, to give it some sort of shape or size, to assess its "reach," was instigated by *The Times* of London in 1792. This was because "some artful and insidious reports have been lately circulated, tending to deprecate the character and sale of the paper."[9] The paper swore an affidavit before the Lord Mayor of London attesting to sales of 17,304 for the week beginning December 3, 1792. Although not directly aimed at its advertisers, such data was obviously considered necessary to the continued health of the paper. And as the official history of the paper notes: "It was the ambition of newspaper proprietors then, as now, to fill the paper with advertisements."[10]

It would be wrong, however, to suggest that the measurement of audience was anything but a haphazard affair during most of the nineteenth century. It tended to be the province of "snake oil" salesmen making hugely inflated claims for a newspaper's circulation that could neither be substantiated by the owner nor verified by the readers. In the 1890s, as noted in Chapter 5, Lord Northcliffe's brother Harold Harmsworth (later Lord Rothermere) was the first proprietor to realize the significance of a newspaper's readership. By independently auditing sales figures Harmsworth "monetized" his readers and "sold" them to his advertisers, although at this stage not so much to increase his advertising revenue as to protect it. It would be another half century before systematic audience surveys were produced on a regular basis. In Britain, for example, the first such survey was not commissioned until 1937.[11]

Yet the importance of "audience" has grown as the importance of the media and journalism has grown. And in the process our understanding of audience has matured. Early audiences were significant mainly for their size but as surveys became more sophisticated the kind of audience – socioeconomic grouping, gender, age, buying power, and other factors – became equally important. As Lord Rothermere was interested in the size of his readership so later press barons were equally interested in the kind of readership their publications attracted. And it was advertisers first and foremost who required this more specific information. "The discovery of advertising," noted the official history of *The Times*, "was bound ultimately to revolutionize the Press by changing the balance of power from the directly political to the directly commercial."[12] One of the casualties of this change, as already noted in Chapter 7, was the *Daily Herald* newspaper. Despite a relatively large circulation it failed because, in large part, it attracted the wrong kind of readership or audience.

This raises a number of crucial issues that go to the heart of the relationship between news media and the people they serve. For example, has the kind of audience a publication or broadcast station attracts now become more important than the quality of its news output? Can we say that "market forces succeeded where legal repression had failed in conscripting the press to the social order"?[13] Indeed, has the pursuit of "audience" deformed news agendas and news values to such an extent that news media no longer report the world as it is but rather report the world according to their advertisers? One instance in a long list is the way the *Sun* newspaper in Britain regularly covers stories that do not appear in rival publications. For example, on April 8, 2009, the paper "launched a best sideburns contest, 'inspired by *X-Men Origins: Wolverine*, starring Hugh Jackman.'"[14] This contest offered a £5,000 prize for the best sideburns as chosen by Jackman. As reported in the satirical magazine *Private Eye*:

Jackman then popped along to the Sun's offices to take part in a charity abseil – the cue for more gratuitous puffery. Finally it fell to Robin Galloway [a *Sun* reporter] to crowbar a plug into a feature about Twitter. "If you're following *X-Men* hero Hugh Jackman you'll know he wants Twitterers to tell him about their favourite charities – and the most passionate tweet will see him donate £100,000 of his own money to that good cause," Galloway sighed admiringly. "*Wolverine* has certainly sparked Tweetmania."

Why this interest in such a bad film, *Private Eye* asks? Then, answering its own question, "No £5k prize for guessing the answer: it's produced by the Dirty Digger's [Rupert Murdoch] Twentieth Century Fox."[15]

Murdoch, of course, is also the owner of the *Sun* newspaper and the suggestion here is that this story was manufactured purely to plug the product of another Murdoch company. In the process, it could be argued, both the *Sun*'s news values and its news agenda were hijacked for purely commercial purposes.

FactFile
News Values

News values were first codified in the work of two Norwegian sociologists, Johan Galtung and Mari Ruge, in the *Journal of International Peace Research* in 1965. They analyzed a series of international news stories and developed their key hypothesis that the more news values an event satisfied, the more likely it was to be reported.

They were not the first to try to identify what has become known as news values, however. As early as 1695, a German writer, Kaspar Steiler, wrote about news values in his book, *Zeitungs Lust und Nutz*, roughly translated as *Uses and Gratifications of Newspapers*. Steiler listed importance and proximity – nearness to home – as news values. He also identified events that were dramatic and negative. In 1922 Walter Lippmann produced his own analysis of news values in *Public Opinion*.[16] He suggested that stories about influential institutions, dramatic escalation of damage, and serious civil disorder such as strikes and major demonstrations were more likely to be reported.

Galtung and Ruge identified 12 news values: frequency, threshold, unambiguity, meaningfulness, consonance, unexpectedness, continuity, composition, reference to elite nations, reference to elite people, personification, and negativity.[17] Later theorists have from time to time taken issue with this list and attempted to bring it up to date. Most recently, New Zealand sociolinguist Allan Bell in *The Language of News Media* made a number of additions – competition, co-optation, prefabrication, and predictability –[18] and in 2001 Tony Harcup and Deirdre O'Neill listed the following values as being important in stories covered by the British press: power elites, celebrity, entertainment, surprise, bad news, good news, magnitude, relevance, follow-ups, and media agenda.[19]

Herbert J. Gans in 1980 offered a distinctly more American focus on what he called "Enduring values in the news" and suggested the following eight clusters: ethnocentricity, altruistic democracy, responsible capitalism, small-town pastoralism, individualism, moderatism, social order, and national leadership.[20] More broadly, Denis McQuail produced a list of "primary news values in Western media" in *Mass Communication Theory* that offered a clearer focus on modern mass media: scale of events, closeness, clarity, short timescale, relevance, consonance, personification, negativity, significance, drama, and action.[21]

Digital media and online news platforms are already affecting news values, as the distinction between producers and consumers of news, evidenced by the growth, for example, of citizen journalism begins to redefine how news is sourced and shaped. Never truer perhaps is the journalist's eternal cry, "Watch this space!"

Do such expansions of the news agenda reflect an acknowledgement of the importance of audience or are they merely a cynical exercise in manipulation? Is advertising therefore the most powerful indicator of the economic health or otherwise of a democracy and its news media? Is the audience in effect ancillary to the organic flow of news events transmitted as and when they happen because event and audience share less and less the same temporal frame of reference? Bound up in such questions is the need to understand the tensions implicit in commercial news media and their ability or otherwise to serve a citizenry that is both sophisticated and increasingly cynical.

Are You Sitting Comfortably?

The tensions implicit in serving such an audience and the way audiences interact with news output have been the subject of much theorizing. Although it is not appropriate here to examine such theories from a comparative perspective, some understanding of how an audience and the media it consumes interact at a philosophical or metaphysical level is a necessary prerequisite for the more pragmatic analysis of audience contained in this chapter.

Audience research is a complex and often mysterious discipline which has been studied from a variety of perspectives. In an attempt to bring some order to this brief overview the following four categories are offered as a way of examining some of its complexity:

- Effects studies
- Uses and gratifications
- Encoding/decoding
- Ethnographic studies.

David Morley offers a useful and concise overview of audience research: "the history of studies of the media audience can be seen as a series of oscillations between perspectives which have stressed the power of the text (or message) over its audience and perspectives which have stressed barriers 'protecting' the audience from the potential effects of the message."[22] Effects studies is a major example of the first of these positions. Often described as the "hypodermic syringe" model, the argument here is that an audience is "injected" with a particular message by the media that will cause it to react in a certain way. Of necessity, this is a simplistic description of an approach where "the media ... were credited with considerable power to shape opinion and belief, to change habits of life and to mould behaviour."[23] Political conservatives thus viewed the media as being responsible for the breakdown of what they saw as traditional values while those of the left blamed the media for undermining the political sensitivities of audiences by offering them "bread and circuses," that is, distraction and entertainment.

The Frankfurt School of Social Research produced the most powerful studies of the relationship between mass media and mass audiences from a left-leaning perspective. Rooted in the work of Theodor Adorno and Max Horkheimer, the School's thesis is often deeply pessimistic of mass media and its effects. Colored no doubt by the rise of Nazism in their native Germany, they described a society that had become "atomized" by the breakdown of traditional family and societal ties. In the process people were more susceptible to external influences such as mass media propaganda and manipulation. In Morley's words, "Implicit here was a 'hypodermic' model of the media which were seen as having the power to 'inject' a repressive ideology directly into the consciousness of the masses."[24]

As Hitler rose to power in Germany during the 1930s, many of the Frankfurt School members emigrated to America. Their influence on media studies indirectly led to a distinctly American school of media research – one that rebelled against the pessimistic theoretical models propounded by Adorno, Horkheimer, and others as failing to reflect the plurality of American society. Almost as an antidote to such theorizing, American research developed its own empirical approaches to audience studies – "American researchers, such as Herta Herzog, Robert Merton, Paul Lazarsfeld and, later, Elihu Katz began to develop a quantitative and positivist methodology for empirical audience research into the 'Sociology of Mass Persuasion.'"[25] Such research established that consumers of media were not just passive victims of media cultures. Notably, Merton, Katz, and Lazarsfeld "developed the concept of the 'two step flow' communication, in which the influence of the media was seen as crucially mediated by 'gatekeepers' and 'opinion leaders', within the audience community."[26] Out of such developments was born a "new perspective on media consumption – the 'uses and gratifications' approach largely associated in the United States with the work of Elihu Katz and, in Britain, with the work of Jay Blumler, James Halloran and the Leicester Centre for Mass Communications Research, during the 1960s."[27]

Put simply, the uses and gratifications approach on the one hand looks at how people use the media and on the other hand studies what gratifications the media offer them. The researcher can analyze a "text" – a news story for example – and cite examples of each use and gratification it takes care of. Examples of such uses and gratifications are: to be amused, to satisfy a need to be well-informed, to understand the world, to experience vicariously history being made. Surveys can be employed listing a series of statements that relate to particular uses and gratifications an audience member might enjoy while watching a particular television program or reading a newspaper story. Such surveys are of necessity guides only to mass audience behavior but are often potent transmitters of the way people respond to a particular example of media output. As Morley notes, "Uses and gratifications did represent a significant advance on effects theory, in so far as it opens up the question of differential interpretations."[28]

Serious limitations in uses and gratifications approaches eventually led to the development of the "encoding/decoding" model by the sociologist Stuart Hall at the Centre for Contemporary Cultural Studies at Birmingham University in Britain. The Centre was founded in 1964 and Hall's model attempted to synthesize aspects of previous theories and research paradigms. Hall's model "represented the media text as located between its producers, who framed meaning in a certain way, and its audience, who 'decoded' the meaning according to their rather different social situations and frames of interpretation."[29]

Hall's model has continued as something of a definitive methodology for audience research although more recently there has been a rise in the use of ethnographic research of audiences in a domestic setting and in particular focusing on television viewing habits. Ethnography studies people's behavior in their own particular milieu – for example, in the workplace or in the home. Originally it developed a rather bad reputation as it was associated with time-and-motion study. However, modern ethnographic methodologies are particularly interested in how people as audiences respond to media output within a domestic setting.

Most of these audience studies either look at the audience as a totality or as individuals. More recent research, whether theoretical or empirical in tone, has understood that an audience cannot really be treated in either fashion. In fact, according to Denis McQuail, "The audience is now little more than a metaphor drawn from another context – that of the theatre and live performance – which bears little relation to the diverse realities of modern communications media."[30] Richard Sennett in *The Fall of Public Man* identifies this difference as "the paradox of visibility and isolation" where one "sees more and interacts less."[31] Thus a mass media audience sees more but interacts less than a traditional audience at live events, for example, in theaters and concert halls. Sennett charts the history of live audiences and suggests that "the mass media intensify the patterns of crowd silence which began to take form in the theatres and concert halls of the last [nineteenth] century, intensify the idea of a disembodied spectator, a passive witness."[32]

Sennett goes on to describe how the logic of passivity built into electronic media, together with the paradox of visibility and isolation in such communication has serious implications for the political process. "When twenty million people watch a politician give a speech on TV," he suggests, "he has usually to treat them all as belonging to one category, that of citizen."[33] He can only appeal to distinct groups in the most general terms – "'To those of you under thirty, I would like to say ...' and so on."[34] In other words he has to treat his audience on "peculiar terms of equality." This requires the message to be bland enough to appeal to a mass audience of equals. Thus any ideological content is of necessity "hollowed out" and this inevitably leads to broadcast media's tendency to concentrate on the person rather than the message.

Modern society is sufficiently diverse in ethnicity, race, class, and income, that it presents a major stumbling block to a mass media desirous of appealing to society *en masse*. Little wonder then that the ability to find ways of quantifying the diversity of an audience became the holy grail of audience research. Little wonder too that finding ways of appealing to that diversity has become so important. Sennett was writing in the 1990s before the birth of modern digital technology and its interactive services. He suggested then that, "The complete repression of audience response by the electronic media [in comparison with live audience interaction in a theater or concert hall] creates the logic of the interest in personality."[35] But now audiences can email their thoughts, phone the studio, press "red" buttons, and vote for particular performers or choices in a variety of programs on television and radio. BBC Radio 4, for example, has a Saturday evening news program called *IPM* that follows the regular *PM* news program. It is entirely driven by topics emailed in by listeners – the "I" standing for interactive. Is it the case that, turning Sennett's logic on its head, this interactivity will signal the death knell of the "interest in personality," rather as citizens who can now e-petition the White House or Downing Street on a particular issue are generally indifferent to the personality of the politician involved? Or is it the case that this interactability will only reinforce an audience's interest in the subtler interstices of a personality's life?

Regardless of the answers to such questions, the traditional audience "problem" has always been the inability to understand or quantify its diversity. Now the additional problem facing news media is to try to discover how representative of the whole that diversity, exemplified by the phone callers, letter writers, emailers, texters, and tweeters, really is. This problem is often identified as the dilemma of audience atomization.

The "Connected Up" Audience

Journalists have traditionally responded to their audience by professing that their first allegiance is always to the citizen. In research surveys 70–80 percent of all journalists attach their first loyalty to audience, over and above family, employers, and their profession.[36] However, allegiance to audience implies a knowledge of that audience – or at least an acknowledgement that it exists in a form that journalists believe they can communicate with. More generally, audience-centered thinking can be traced through the rich history of press/reader interactions and more recently in the stylized and mediated relationship between broadcast media and their myriad audiences.

The task of newspaper owners had traditionally been to produce readers, not just news, so the latter had always been tailored for a specific readership in an attempt to both influence it and/or create profit. As notions of the profession of journalism developed, ethical considerations became more important. By the time the American Society of Newspaper Editors was founded in 1912, its code of ethics claimed: "Independence: Freedom from all obligations except that of fidelity to the public interest is vital."[37] Such a statement represents a strand of thinking that links audience to professional objectivity and detaches it from any political allegiance – at the time deemed necessary in order to appeal to the widest possible range of people. This principle was exemplified by Adolph Ochs, when on the first day of his ownership of the ailing *New York Times* in 1896, he expressed his "earnest aim to give the news impartiality, without fear or favor, regardless of party, sect, or interests involved." It was also, in part, a reaction to the sensationalist journalism of Hearst and Pulitzer, and the implication was that the needs of the audience would come before immediate business or political considerations.

FactFile
Joe and Jolene Sixpack

Journalism has never been an exact science, and one particular study demonstrates a typically "instinctive" but inherently unscientific approach to audience by an American regional newspaper. In 2000 media sociologist and historian Randall S. Sumpter observed editors at work in a large daily paper in the capital of an American Southwestern state (unnamed in the research). He identified a major problem they faced at budget meetings: "How to select stories for page one that would attract the maximum readership from a dwindling unknown audience courted by other media."

Sumpter found that one editor required his reporters to lunch once a month with people who were not routine story sources and then report back the conversations. Editors "grudgingly accommodated the news construction uncertainty generated by unknown readers." They made their assessments of newsworthiness by having conversations in and outside of meetings with colleagues and family, and by imagining typical local readers and "imaginary interlocutors."

One employee interviewed for the study (with a working wife and two children) invented a similar couple with children whom he called "Joe and Jolene Sixpack." According to the profile he created, these people, as typical target readers, were interested in education, disliked waste in government, watched some TV, and didn't have a lot of time. So they always tended to ask, "Why should I care?"

Another editor at the same paper provided the example of a plane that crashes at 5 p.m. and kills a hundred people. "We don't want to give them (readers) a story that says it happened. We want to answer the question whether it can happen to them." As for Joe and Jolene Sixpack, Sumpter discovered: "You need to tell them why they should care in every story. And, uh, they're folks who like a good laugh so that if you can give them something that's kind of light, that's good … Bring them stories that matter to them because they just don't have much time."[38] Joe Sixpack also happens to be the byline of award-winning Philadelphia *Daily News* beer reporter and author, Don Russell.

Such thinking took it for granted that notions of "impartiality" were likely to generate the largest possible audience. But more sophisticated readings of audience gradually established that no "single" audience as such existed and that a newspaper's impartiality was unlikely to be a bell-wether of success. New thinking about the relationship between audience and media began to recognize that first, individual audience members themselves have conflicting interests and needs and second, until the advent of the digital age those audience members were often unaware, in an ideological sense, of the existence of a like-minded community and, even if they were aware, lacked the wherewithal to interact with it.

A Moveable Feast

One of the ways underrepresented or unrepresented groups in society have traditionally reacted to a sense of exclusion is by establishing their own newspapers or other publications in a bid to improve public awareness of their particular standpoint. In the early days of the press, set-up costs were low enough to do this. Improved technology from the mid-nineteenth century onwards, however, meant that high-cost sophisticated printing presses and greater investment were both needed. The *News of the World* "stated in its first issue (1 October 1843), 'It is only by a very extensive circulation that the proprietors can be compensated for the outlay of a large capital in this novel and original undertaking.'"[39] Only more recently has self-publishing,

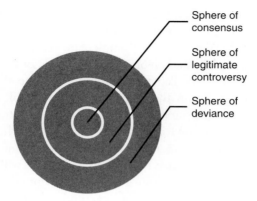

Sphere of
consensus

Sphere of
legitimate
controversy

Sphere of
deviance

Figure 11.1   Spheres of consensus, legitimate controversy, and deviance

via the internet, once again become economically viable for smaller organizations and groups of people. But even if such groups are able to create a space of their own, it is invariably on the mainstream news media's terms. Thus mainstream news media both prescribe and proscribe.

In his book about the media and Vietnam, *The Uncensored War* (1986), Daniel C. Hallin suggested that in trying to understand the inherent complexity of prescribing and proscribing it might be "useful to imagine the journalist's world as divided into three regions, each of which is governed by different journalistic standards."[40] He illustrated his ideas using the "doughnut" diagram shown in Figure 11.1[41] The sphere of consensus is the "region of 'motherhood and apple pie'."[42] Here are grouped all those social "objects" which are generally agreed to be uncontroversial – for example, Lincoln was a great president, anyone who works hard enough can succeed in America. Within this region Hallin writes, "journalists do not feel compelled either to present opposing views or to remain disinterested observers."[43]

The sphere of legitimate controversy is the area that most journalists inhabit on a day-to-day basis. Here is found reasoned debate on the major issues of the day – for example, party political matters and political news agendas as defined by Washington or Whitehall. In Britain it is exemplified by the early morning news program, *Today*, on BBC Radio 4, that sets the news agenda for the day. In the US, "perhaps the purest expression of this sphere is *Washington Week* on PBS [Public Broadcasting Service], where journalists discuss what the two-party system defines as 'the issues'."[44] As noted by Hallin, "Within this region, objectivity and balance reign as the supreme journalistic virtues."[45]

The sphere of deviance is "the realm of those political actors and views which journalists and the political mainstream of the society reject as unworthy of being heard."[46] Hallin offers the example of the Federal Communications Commission (FCC) guidelines on broadcasting: "It is not the Commission's intention to make time available to Communists or to the Communist viewpoints."[47] In Britain, on the other hand, if you think the monarchy should be abolished, or if you believe the BNP (British National Party) is a great political party, or if you think that the English should have the right to bear arms, you are likely to "experience the press as an opponent in the struggle for recognition,"[48] and there is little chance your views will be reflected in the mainstream news. Journalism becomes a "boundary-maintaining mechanism" by "exposing, condemning, or excluding from the public agenda those who violate or challenge the political consensus."[49]

The boundaries between the three spheres are both fuzzy and mutable but in each case, according to Jay Rosen, it is "journalists [who] affirm and enforce the sphere of consensus, consign ideas and actors to the sphere of deviance, and decide when the shift is made from one to the other."[50] In the process audiences are deemed to be a part of the consensus when, in fact, this is often not the case.

Jay Rosen brings Hallin's "doughnut" analogy up to date by contrasting traditional "Big Media" with the online world. In the past, the press in particular "was able to define the sphere of legitimate debate [controversy] with relative ease because the people on the receiving end [the audience] were "atomized" – meaning they were connected "up" to Big Media but not across to each other."[51] Now, like-minded people can locate each other and exchange information, share opinions, and start to comprehend their number. In the process they may well "establish that the 'sphere of legitimate debate' [controversy] as defined by journalists doesn't match up with their own definition."[52] Rosen concludes by suggesting that

> In the past there was nowhere for this kind of sentiment to go. Now it collects, solidifies and expresses itself online. Bloggers tap into it to gain a following and serve demand. Journalists call this the "echo chamber," which is their way of downgrading it as a reliable source. But what's really happening is that the authority of the press to assume consensus, define deviance and set the terms of legitimate debate or controversy is weaker when people can connect horizontally around and about the news.[53]

Audience atomization – being connected "up" to Big Media but not across to like-minded others – is thus overcome and crucially, in the process, the terms of the debate are invariably changed. "You don't have to use the tone of the conventional mainstream media, which is attempting to be impartial and slightly aloof," says former television journalist Nick Booth, now "a key figure in ... 'the "blogging community'." "I'm not going to control the editorial process ... I'll just give them access to the medium and access to the audience."[54]

Despite such progress, a lack of recognition and public visibility for certain people or groups can still be seen as an ongoing difficulty: "The most important political problem facing us in the 21st century may well be that large groups of disenfranchised people (migrants and immigrants, lower-income groups, for example) do not feel included in the body politic, and do not feel that their issues and concerns are addressed by traditional political institutions or prestige news and media outlets."[55] Arguably, disenfranchisement for such groups can now be said to include the inability to access the internet with a good broadband connection.

If You Want an Audience Start a Fight

It has been proposed that the current media landscape consists of a mainstream characterized by an elite sphere dominated by establishment sources ranging from politicians to corporate managements and representatives of nongovernmental organizations. Another older response to this mainstream hegemony can be characterized as the development of "a number of alternative spheres as forums in which marginalised groups debate different issues in different ways and strive to gain access to, and representation in, the mainstream."[56] Put simply, we live in an age when marginalized groups and subcultures of whatever sort are no longer prepared to be ignored or subsumed within the hegemony of the mainstream media.

One response to this question of inclusion and exclusion has been elaborated by feminist thinker and philosopher Nancy Fraser in a critique of Habermas's theory of citizenship in the public sphere (see Chapter 2). According to Fraser:

> Members of subordinated social groups – women, workers, people of color, and gays and lesbians – have repeatedly found it advantageous to constitute alternative publics. I propose to call these *subaltern counterpublics* in order to signal that they are parallel discursive arenas where members of subordinated social groups invent and circulate counterdiscourses to formulate oppositional interpretations of their identities, interests and needs.[57]

In this process of struggling for cultural recognition, such groups often act as participants as well as their own audience, crossing between mainstream and alternative communication media in a way that implies a reasonable level of fluidity between the two. When Jann Wenner started *Rolling Stone* magazine in 1967, its circulation was small and restricted largely to San Francisco and the Bay area of California. Its audience was equally a small community of music lovers, flower power hippies, and West Coast drop-outs. Over time as the cultural interests of this group grew so did the magazine's circulation. Yet in its heyday *Rolling Stone*, without changing its editorial stance or its political position – that is, without attempting to move from its location in Hallin's sphere of deviance – became part of the mainstream. In other words the sphere of legitimate controversy itself moved its borders to accommodate the interloper in the best traditions of left-field journalism.

Ornebring and Jonsson echo aspects of Nancy Fraser's critique in their four-point analysis of "alternative" public spheres,[58] all of which have historical precedents:

1   *Location*: discourses that take place in alternative media outlets such as specialized journals and the internet;
2   *People*: other participants can be discerned than those who normally dominate media discourse;
3   *Content*: debate centers on different issues than the ones commonly discussed;
4   *Methodology*: ways of discussion differ from those commonly adopted by mainstream media, such as citizen participation.

Such alternative public spheres, as discrete entities, can be seen as problematical on a number of levels, however. They assume a mainstream media environment that is immobile, lacking in fluidity, unchanged, and relatively stable. This has seldom been the case in the past. Specialist journals, for example, often initiate debate on issues which then mutate as mainstream media take them over – journals like *Nature* and *Scientific American* are both good examples.

The radical press in Britain and the US in the early decades of the nineteenth century is a powerful example of an alternative *location* – unstamped and often illegal newspapers – published and read by *people* who seldom found voice in the mainstream media because the *content* – working-class emancipation, parliamentary and electoral reform – was seldom dealt with positively in the mainstream press. Yet "one of the most important, and least remarked, aspects of the development of the radical press in the first half of the 19th century was that its leading publications developed a nationwide circulation."[59]

In America, titles such as the *Mechanics Free Press* and the *Working Man's Advocate* became extremely popular, and by the end of the nineteenth century "working-class newspapers proliferated in cities across the country. Between 1880–1940, thousands of labor and radical publications circulated, constituting a golden age for working-class newspapers."[60] It is difficult, therefore, to support notions of rigid differentiation between mainstream and alternative media audiences, especially from a historical perspective. As political, technological, social, and cultural mores changed over time so journalism and journalists reflected such changes – by adapting news-gathering techniques, writing styles, and, perhaps most importantly, their sense of the "sphere of legitimate debate" as embodied in news agendas and news values.

Letters to the Editor

Early newspapers had neither readers' letters nor editors. A newspaper's "sphere of legitimate debate" was the private concern of the proprietor and those few readers who shared his views or whose interests, commercial or otherwise, the paper served. Yet letters played as important a part in eighteenth- and nineteenth-century public life as they did in private relationships. London postal deliveries, instigated by William Dockwra in 1680, ensured that "letters were sent out for delivery, to the Inns of Court or places of business ten or twelve times a day, and to other places according to distance, from four to eight times."[61] Men of letters, often the social and cultural arbiters of their age, assumed importance in a society where most people could neither read nor write. These men wrote letters to newspapers but also produced pamphlets and letters that addressed the citizen directly on issues of the day.

One of the earliest examples of such writing were letters written by John Trenchard and Thomas Gordon. They were published under the pseudonym Cato in the *London Journal* and the *British Journal* between 1720 and 1723. Their theme was freedom of speech and freedom from tyranny. All 144 letters were later collected and published as *Essays on Liberty, Civil and Religious* and in this form were to influence the ideals of the American Revolution (War of Independence). *Letters from a Farmer*, written by

Pennsylvania lawyer John Dickinson between 1767 and 1768, argued that taxes imposed by the British parliament designed to raise revenue rather than regulate trade were unconstitutional because the colonies were sovereign regarding their own internal affairs. The 12 letters were widely read and reprinted amongst the 13 colonies and although not published in any journal they nevertheless made Dickinson famous. The Letters of Junius (1769–72) are perhaps the most celebrated example of letters written to a newspaper, in this case the London *Public Advertiser*. The letters dealt with similar issues to Cato and "The Farmer" but with heightened invective and a more scurrilous tone (see Chapter 4).[62]

A characteristic of early letter writing was its anonymous nature. The right to lambast, praise, or satirize anonymously, intrinsic to a free press and to free speech was, for example, central to the 1735 trial against John Peter Zenger, which began with an anonymous essay (see Chapter 2). This anonymity was part of an accepted tradition that saw newspaper journalism in particular written without the benefit of bylines. It wasn't until 1884, for instance, that a signed article appeared in the pages of *The Times*.[63] By the turn of the twentieth century, however, editors were developing a growing antipathy towards anonymity in all its forms. Despite some reactionary opinions, the "impersonal view was seen to be relatively impotent."[64] Ordinary people increasingly took pleasure in the reflected glory of their thoughts being echoed by an authority who signed his articles. Newspapers validated their untutored opinions and this forged a new kind of bond between readers and their daily newspaper. Today most papers will reject any letter for publication if it is submitted anonymously.

Letter writing, by definition, was always the preserve of the educated. And in a society that lacked a means of delivery (the uniform penny postage only began in Britain in 1840 and postage stamps were first issued in the US in 1847), newspaper proprietors developed other marketing strategies to attract and retain an audience. Chief among these was the question-and-answer format. Although the interaction was fairly pedestrian compared with today's fast-paced communications, it struck a chord with readers. The *Athenian Mercury*, published in 1691 by John Dunton, was one of the first of these popular question-and-answer journals. It was significantly different from its rather sober predecessors. As the historian John Feather noted: "The question-and-answer journal remained popular for a number of years, and the *Athenian Mercury* found a number of imitators, such as the *British Apollo*; indeed, in the late nineteenth century the young George Newnes revived the form for one of his first forays into popular journalism, *Tit-Bits*."[65] In the *British Apollo* (1701–11), a twice-weekly journal, the editor said he would "endeavour to answer all Questions in Divinity, Philosophy, the Mathematicks, and other Arts and Sciences, which appear fit and worthy to be answer'd."[66] By the time George Newnes published *Tit-Bits* in 1881, the nature of the questions had changed. The first issue offered a prize of one guinea for the best tit-bit of information and a prize of "ten guineas for the person answering correctly the largest number of questions" during a three-month period.[67]

All these publications were relentless in their courting of the reader, whether as "correspondent" asking questions or offering answers to other readers' queries. Significantly, this democratization of the reader bore no resemblance to the interplay between newspapers and readers' letters in the traditional daily press. These letters were usually expressions of opinion from informed and didactic sources, or else were expressions of support for, or disagreement with, the paper's position on some weighty issue. Contributions to *Tit-Bits* and its competitors on the other hand were quite different. Often informative and factual, they generally dealt with "inconsequential" matters to do with etiquette, modes of dress, and domestic issues. Replies were "so worded as to make every simple letter-writer imagine that he or she was the peculiar care of the editor to the exclusion of all others."[68] As an incentive to purchase, this individualization of the reader within the context of a shared experience was powerfully addictive. The *History of The Times* acknowledged this in its comments on *Tit-Bits*: "No space was given to politics; but while the mass of *Tit-Bits* consisted of scissors and paste, original contributions from readers were invited."[69]

Résumé
George Newnes

George Newnes was one of a quartet of journalists whose entrepreneurial spirit led to the development of the New Journalism at the end of the nineteenth century – the other three being C. Arthur Pearson, founder of the *Daily Express* in 1900, W. T. Stead, and Alfred Harmsworth.

Newnes was born in 1851 in Matlock Bath, Derbyshire. In 1867 he began work in the "fancy goods" trade working in London and Manchester. His publishing career began in 1881 when he founded the weekly magazine *Tit-Bits*. The story of the genesis of *Tit-Bits*, while having an apocryphal ring, is still instructive. Newnes apparently read "tit-bits" from the newspaper aloud to his wife over tea each day. Her pleasure inspired him to create a paper designed for her consisting only of such tit-bits.[70]

George Newnes became W. T. Stead's partner in the *Review of Reviews* but, their opinions on journalism being very different, the partnership only lasted a few months. Newnes then started the *Strand Magazine* in 1892 with the promise of a picture on every page. This venture was another success, not only because of the visual excitement generated but also because Newnes secured and serialized the Sherlock Holmes stories being written by Arthur Conan Doyle. Newnes also founded *Country Life* and the *Westminster Gazette*, an evening paper printed on green paper to "rest the reader's eye."[71]

He is credited with making "great use of the anecdote as a means of conveying information and practically introduced it as a standard journalistic form."[72] He was knighted in 1895 and in his final years became something of a philanthropist. He died in 1910 from complications associated with diabetes.

The traditional newspaper, as it slowly developed a measure of financial security, began to expand its staff and this in turn led to the early stages of job specialization. Adam Smith's *Wealth of Nations* had been published in 1776 and the "division of labor" as a means of increasing productivity began to take root in all manner of industries. Thus the editor, as an organizer of these growing staffs rather than as a journalist, began to appear. The word was first used in Britain, in the context of running a newspaper, in 1803. Before that, newspapers were run by proprietors or managers. John Walter Junior, for example, became sole manager and editor of *The Times* of London in 1803 but by 1807 had decided to devolve his editorial duties to a "specialist."[73] In 1817 Thomas Barnes was appointed editor of the paper and became the first such person to occupy the editor's chair in the sense that we understand it today.

The editor naturally became keenly interested in the way his paper was perceived and the "editorial" or "opinion" column developed as an early form of "brand awareness." Known also as the leader, it encouraged readers to respond to the paper's opinions and this led to the expansion of the letters page as a useful way of gauging readers' reactions to the paper's views on the issues of the day. The editorial and letters pages thus became a special place for community discourse, a forum for public deliberation. Yet it was not publicly owned; it was a private sphere directed by the editor and journalists who controlled access, allocated space, and decided on the topics for debate. Not all participants had equal freedom to say what they wanted. Rather, as A. J. Liebling noted, "Freedom of the press is guaranteed only to those who own one."[74]

The editor's role developed throughout the nineteenth century as he gradually took responsibility for both the economic prosperity of his title and also its political and commercial direction. Circulations during this period also increased despite the fact that there were no catchy headlines, no real page design, few if any half-tone prints – in fact nothing to relieve the dense columns of small print and the often variable quality of the writing. The main reason for rising circulations, identified in particular by Benedict Anderson in *Imagined Communities*, was that newspapers offered readers a sense of community. "The obsolescence of the newspaper on the morrow of its printing," Anderson observed, "creates this extraordinary mass ceremony: the almost precisely simultaneous consumption ('imagining') of the newspaper-as-fiction."[75] Anderson described this as a particularly vivid example of an "imagined community" and then noted, "At the same time, the newspaper reader, observing exact replicas of his own paper being consumed by his subway, barbershop, or residential neighbors, is continually reassured that the imagined world is visibly rooted in everyday life."[76]

This shared experience was significant also for those who were either unable to read or were too poor to purchase a newspaper regularly. Readers shared the newspaper as a social experience, often by reading sections aloud to each other in public places such as bars, coffee houses, working-men's clubs, and salons. The setting for this performance of reading was an important part of the newspaper experience – and this was an act of audience empowerment that reinforced social relationships with fellow citizens. There were papers for every imaginable cause – temperance, antislavery, women's rights, workers' rights, employers' solidarity, religious groups – and every political faction. Equally there were papers that appealed across the whole range of social and cultural classes. "For women, for blacks, and for many citizens of humble status, the reading of news was one position of power that seemed within reach."[77]

Résumé
C. P. Scott and the *Manchester Guardian*

Charles Prestwich Scott was born in 1846 in Bath, Somerset. He was a nephew of the *Manchester Guardian*'s founder, John Edward Taylor. At Oxford he took a first in Greats (Classics) and the following year, 1870, he went to Edinburgh to train on the *Scotsman*. He joined the *Manchester Guardian* in February 1871 and became editor in 1872. He was elected MP for the constituency of Leigh, North-East Manchester, in 1895 and also became president of the Manchester Liberal Federation. Despite being based in Manchester, Scott became an influential figure in Liberal circles where he supported women's suffrage and reform of the House of Lords. He retired from Parliament in 1906 to concentrate on running the paper which he had purchased on the death of its owner.

In a famous essay composed to mark its centenary in 1921, Scott set out his guiding principles on the role of the newspaper. Accurate news reporting was the first duty and he coined the now famous phrase: "Comment is free, but facts are sacred." Scott remained editor until 1929 and died in 1932. He was succeeded by his youngest son, Ted. His middle son, John, took over on Ted's early death and he also founded the Scott Trust that now owns the Guardian News and Media group of companies. The newspaper dropped the "*Manchester*" from its title in 1959.[78]

Nothing could alter the fact, however, that the power to decide what people read always rested ultimately with the editor. He became the fulcrum around which a newspaper's "take" on the world expressed itself – through its news-gathering policies just as much as its leader columns. In the US, pioneers such as Horace Greeley, editor of the *New York Tribune*, Samuel Bowles, editor of *The Republican (Springfield)*, George William Childs, editor of the *Philadelphia Public Ledger*, Whitelaw Reid, editor of the *New York Herald Tribune*, and Ben Bradlee, editor of the *Washington Post* all shaped their newspapers to cater for a particular readership that was defined in large part by its political allegiance and social status.

In Britain, similarly, pioneering editors such as Thomas Barnes and John Thadeus Delane of *The Times*, W. T. Stead of the *Pall Mall Gazette*,

T. P. O'Connor of the evening *Star*, and C. P. Scott of the *Manchester Guardian* forged their newspapers around a broad set of political principles that were often inferred rather than declared. T. P. O'Connor's *Star*, for example, was "a project to popularize democracy rather than politics."[79] Thus there was a clear difference between, on the one hand, the aspiring professional classes and Establishment figures that *The Times* of London catered for and, on the other hand, the perspiring laboring and working classes who favored the entertainment and sensational stories provided by popular papers such as *Reynolds's Weekly* and the *News of the World*. Yet in each case these pioneers, whether reformers, reactionaries, polemicists, or essayists found a ready audience for their ideas and once found they each played that audience its favorite tunes.

Notes

1 Guinness World Records, *Guinness World Records 2008* (London: Guinness World Records Limited, 2007).
2 Francis Williams, *The Right to Know: The Rise of the World Press* (London: Longmans, 1969), p. 8.
3 Raymond Snoddy, *The Good, the Bad and the Unacceptable* (London: Faber and Faber, 1992), p. 161.
4 The Times, *The History of The Times*: vol. 1, *"The Thunderer" in the Making* (London: Times Publishing Co., 1935), p. 51.
5 Williams, *The Right to Know*, p. 18.
6 Ibid., pp. 7–8.
7 Michael Schudson, *Discovering the News. A Social History of the American Newspaper* (New York: Basic Books, 1978), p. 25.
8 David T. Z. Mindich, *Tuned Out: Why Americans Under 40 Don't Follow the News* (New York: Oxford University Press, 2005), p. 96.
9 The Times, *The History of The Times*: vol. 1, p. 34.
10 Ibid., p. 25.
11 Jean K. Chalaby, *The Invention of Journalism* (Basingstoke, UK: Palgrave Macmillan, 1998), p. 177.
12 The Times, *The History of The Times*: vol. 1, p. 20.
13 James Curran and Jean Seaton, *Power Without Responsibility*, 5th edn (London: Routledge, 1997), p. 9.
14 "Media News," *Private Eye*, May 1–14, 2009, no. 1235, p. 9.
15 Ibid.
16 James Watson, *Media Communication: An Introduction to Theory and Process* (New York: Palgrave Macmillan, 2003), p. 117.

17 John Galtung and Mari H. Ruge, "The Structure of Foreign News", in Jeremy Tunstall (ed.), *Media Sociology: A Reader* (London: Constable, 1970), pp. 259–98.

18 Allan Bell, *The Language of News Media* (Oxford: Blackwell, 1991). His additions to Galtung and Ruge are: Competition: commercial pressure to get a story first; Co-optation: a story mildly related to a major story can be interpreted and presented together with the major story; Prefabrication: if a story is already written and available via press releases, wire copy, etc; Predictability: more likely to be covered if it is a prescheduled event.

19 Tony Harcup and Deirdre O'Neill, "What Is News? Galtung and Ruge Revisited," *Journalism Studies*, 2, 2 (2001), 261–80. Harcup and O'Neill's revisited list is: The power elite: stories concerning powerful individuals, organizations, or institutions; Celebrity: stories concerning people who are already famous; Entertainment: stories concerning sex, show business, human interest, animals, an unfolding drama, or offering opportunities for humorous treatment, entertaining photographs, or witty headlines; Surprise: stories with an element of surprise and/or contrast; Bad news: stories with negative overtones such as conflict or tragedy; Good news: stories with positive overtones such as rescues and cures; Magnitude: stories perceived as sufficiently significant either in the numbers of people involved or in potential impact; Relevance: stories about issues, groups, and nations perceived to be relevant to the audience; Follow-ups: stories about subjects already in the news; Media agenda: stories that set or fit the news organization's own agenda.

20 Herbert J. Gans, *Deciding What's News: A Study of CBS Evening News, NBC Nightly News, Newsweek, and Time* (New York: Vintage, 1980), pp. 42–57.

21 Denis McQuail, *Mass Communication Theory: An Introduction*, 3rd edn (London: Sage, 1994), pp. 270–1.

22 David Morley, "Audience Research," *The Museum of Broadcast Communications*. Available online at http://www.museum.tv/eotvsection.php?entrycode=audi encerese, para. 1, accessed on August 26, 2010.

23 McQuail, *Mass Communication Theory*, p. 328.

24 Morley, "Audience Research," para. 2.

25 Ibid., para. 3.

26 Ibid., para. 5.

27 Ibid., para. 6.

28 Ibid.

29 McQuail, *Mass Communication Theory*, pp. 100–1.

30 Ibid., pp. 283–4.

31 Richard Sennett, *The Fall of Public Man* (London: Faber and Faber, 1993), p. 284.

32 Ibid., p. 283.

33 Ibid., p. 284.

34 Ibid.

35 Ibid., pp. 284–5.

36 Bill Kovach and Tom Rosenstiel, *The Elements of Journalism* (London: Guardian Atlantic Books, 2001), p. 52.

37 John B. Thompson, *The Media and Modernity: A Social Theory of the Media* (Oxford: Polity Press, 1995), p. 247.

38 Randall S. Sumpter, "Daily Newspaper Editors' Audience Construction Routines: A Case Study," *Critical Studies in Media Communication*, 17, 3 (2000), 334–46 (p. 338).

39 Curran and Seaton, *Power Without Responsibility*, p. 30.

40 Daniel C. Hallin, *The "Uncensored War": The Media and Vietnam* (Berkeley: University of California Press, 1989), p. 116.

41 Ibid., p. 117.

42 Ibid., p. 116.

43 Ibid., p. 117.

44 Jay Rosen, "Audience Atomization Overcome: Why the Internet Weakens the Authority of the Press", *Pressthink*, January 12, 2009. Available online at http://journalism.nyu.edu/pubzone/weblogs/pressthink/2009/01/12/atomization.html, accessed on August 9, 2009, para. 4.

45 Hallin, *The "Uncensored War,"* p. 116.

46 Ibid., p. 117.

47 Ibid.

48 Rosen, "Audience Atomization Overcome," para. 8.

49 Hallin, *The "Uncensored War,"* p. 117.

50 Rosen, "Audience Atomization Overcome," para. 13.

51 Ibid., para. 18.

52 Ibid.

53 Ibid., para. 19.

54 Stephen Moss, "Stop Press," *Guardian*, April 3, 2009, section G2, p. 7. Available online at http://www.guardian.co.uk/media/2009/apr/03/local-newspapers-journalism-democracy, accessed August 30, 2010.

55 Henrik Ornebring and Anna Maria Jonsson, "Tabloid Journalism and the Public Sphere: A Historical Perspective on Tabloid Journalism," *Journalism Studies*, 5, 3 (2004), 283–95 (pp. 284, 294).

56 Ibid., p. 285.

57 Nancy Fraser, "Rethinking the Public Sphere: A Contribution to the Critique of Actually Existing Democracy," in Craig Calhoun (ed.), *Habermas and the Public Sphere* (Cambridge, MA: MIT Press, 1992), p. 123.

58 Ornebring and Jonsson, "Tabloid Journalism and the Public Sphere," p. 286.

59 Curran and Seaton, *Power Without Responsibility*, p. 19.

60 Karla Kelling Sclater, "The Labor and Radical Press 1820–the Present: An Overview and Bibliography," *The Labor Press Project* (2008). Available online at

http://depts.washington.edu/labhist/laborpress/Kelling.htm (para. 2), accessed on August 22, 2009.

61 Herbert Joyce, *The History of the Post Office from its Establishment Down to 1836* (London: BiblioBazaar, 2008), p. 37.

62 Cato (95–46 BC) was an opponent of Julius Caesar and a supporter of republican principles at a time when Caesar was appropriating all power to himself. The Junius of the Letters of Junius is now thought to refer to Lucius Junius Brutus, founder of the Roman Republic in 509 BC (not to be confused with Marcus Junius Brutus (85–42 BC) – one of the conspirators who killed Julius Caesar). Another suggestion is that the name derives from the Roman poet Juvenal who was believed to also carry the Roman name Junius.

63 Stanley Morison, *The English Newspaper 1622–1932* (Cambridge, UK: Cambridge University Press, 1932), p. 287.

64 J. D. Symon, *The Press and its Story* (London: Seeley, Service, 1914), p. 106.

65 John Feather, *A History of British Publishing* (London: Routledge, 1988), p. 107.

66 *The British Apollo*, February 13, 1708, p. 1.

67 *Tit-Bits*, October 22, 1881, no. 1, p. 16.

68 Symon, *The Press and its Story*, p. 253.

69 The Times, *The History of The Times*, vol. III, *The Twentieth Century Test* (London: Times Publishing Company, 1947), p. 94.

70 Margaret Beetham, *A Magazine of her Own? Domesticity and Desire in the Woman's Magazine, 1800–1914* (London: Routledge, 1996), p. 122.

71 Dennis Griffiths (ed.), *The Encyclopedia of the British Press 1422–1992* (London: Macmillan, 1992), p. 435.

72 "Sir George Newnes Dead," *New York Times*, June 10, 1910. Available online at http://query.nytimes.com/mem/archive-free/pdf?_r=1&res=9F01E6D 71530E23 3A25753C1A9609C946196D6CF, accessed on November 12, 2009.

73 The Times, *The History of* The Times, vol. II, *The Tradition Established* (London: Times Publishing Company, 1939), p. 164.

74 A. J. Liebling, *The Press* (New York: Ballantine Books, 1961), p. 30.

75 Benedict Anderson, *Imagined Communities: Reflections on the Origin and Spread of Nationalism* (London: Verso, 1991), pp. 34–5.

76 Ibid., pp. 35–6.

77 Thomas C. Leonard, *News For All: America's Coming-of-Age with the Press* (New York: Oxford University Press, 1995), p. 32.

78 C. P. Scott. Available online at http://www.spartacus.schoolnet.co.uk/JscottCP. htm, accessed on August 8, 2009.

79 *The History of The Times*, vol. III, *The Twentieth Century Test*, p. 96.

12

How Audiences Rewrote the Script

In his seminal text, *Democracy in America* (1831), Alexis de Tocqueville alleged that "The inhabitants of the United States have, then, at present, no national literature. The only authors who I acknowledge as American are the journalists. They are indeed not great writers, but they speak the language of their countrymen, and make themselves heard by them."[1] On first reading it might be thought that de Tocqueville was damning with faint praise but on reflection it is clear he was just acknowledging a journalist's greatest gift – to be able to speak in the "voice" of his compatriots.

Yet, as we have seen in the last chapter, the idea of "countrymen" as a single audience has become highly contested territory. The nineteenth century saw the rise of special interest groups and also an increasing proclivity for audiences to coalesce around such vague notions, at the time, as shared ethnicity, gender, and class. People began to see themselves as inhabiting a number of different "spheres." It is now understood that, for example, gay women, black chief executives, blue-collar politicians, even the ubiquitous "housewife," all have to inhabit multiple worlds and the idea that a homogeneous mainstream press might fulfill all, or indeed any, of their needs has gradually become unsustainable.

In particular, women, ethnic minorities, and the "working classes" have all at some point laid claim to special treatment by society, either the desire to be acknowledged for themselves, or the desire to receive equal rights under the law and/or the constitution. Part of this struggle has inevitably involved a fight for press and later, broadcast media representation, both to increase overall awareness of their minority interests and also to promote

Jane Chapman and Nick Nuttall, *Journalism Today: A Themed History*
© 2011 Jane Chapman and Nick Nuttall. Published by Blackwell Publishing Ltd.

positive media images of them as individuals and as groups. These efforts have led to "alternative" newspapers and magazines and to a broader minority "footprint" in the mainstream press in particular. By criticizing traditional authority and power, disenfranchised or underrepresented people have used the press to communicate their need for a more prominent place in society. Yet the danger with any such group, as we shall see, is that it becomes self-defining and thus lends itself to stereotyping or being represented, for example, solely by its class, age, gender, or ethnicity – what is sometimes referred to as the "cage" of identity.

Other Voices, Other Rooms

On May 4, 1884, more than 70 years before Rosa Parks fueled the civil rights movement by refusing to give up her bus seat to a white man [in Montgomery, Alabama], 22-year-old Ida B. Wells spurned a segregated train car to sit in the ladies' coach. After she was forcefully removed from the coach, she exited the train, hired an attorney and sued the Chesapeake & Ohio Railroad Company on the grounds that blacks were relegated to the smoking car when the law called for separate and equal public accommodations. A court awarded her $500 in damages.

"Darky Damsel Gets Damages," reported the *Memphis Daily Appeal* on December 25, 1884. While the state supreme court reversed the circuit court ruling in 1887, the experience helped launch the career of a fearless journalist who unflinchingly put her livelihood and life on the line to confront racial injustice. After writing about her legal battle in a religious newsweekly, *Living Way*, Wells would for another four decades use journalism as a weapon against the virulent racial bigotry sweeping the South.

In 1889 her *Living Way* columns under the pen name Iola were nationally circulated in black newspapers.[2]

This story, told by Pamela Newkirk, illustrates the dichotomy of ethnic representation in the mainstream press. The headline in the *Memphis Daily Appeal* plays fast and loose with notions of ethnicity (Darky) and femininity (Damsel) in order to belittle the positive aspects of the story. Such responses, common at the time, were clearly an important factor in the continuing development of an ethnic press in the United States.

The first black American newspaper, *Freedom's Journal*, was launched in 1827 at a time of national debate over the expatriation of African Americans to Africa. The paper was strongly antislavery and anticolonial, aiming to counteract the negative depiction in other newspapers of blacks as inferior. It was, in effect, "the first serious foray into media criticism."[3] The other aim of the founders, the Reverend Samuel Cornish and John Brown Russworm, was to provide coverage of issues that were being ignored, with the effect of rendering the black population invisible. Thus, most of New York's daily newspapers, with the notable exception of the *Albany Argos*, had failed to even mention the emancipation of New York State blacks on July 4, 1827.[4] Like many other eighteenth- and nineteenth-century nonestablishment newspapers, *Freedom's Journal* was short-lived, but its significance was disproportionate to its two-year life cycle. Between 1827 and the signing of the Emancipation Proclamation in 1863, 40 black newspapers were established in northern states, eight of them in New York City alone.

In the southern states the struggle to communicate could be dangerous: Elijah Lovejoy's abolitionist weekly, the *St. Louis Observer*, was put out of business twice by proslavery gangs. On the third attempt to set up his press, Lovejoy was killed by a mob. Similarly, the hugely popular and influential former escaped slave, Frederick Douglass, founder in 1847 of the *North Star* in Rochester, New York, had his house burned down and his newspapers destroyed. The weekly antislavery paper was read in other parts of the United States, Europe, and the West Indies, a fact that has prompted the claim that it influenced both black and white opinion more than any other newspaper before or since.[5] The journal capitalized on his personal fame by renaming itself *Frederick Douglass' Paper* in 1851 and continued until Abraham Lincoln was elected to the White House and the South seceded from the United States Union in 1860.

By the early twentieth century, as African Americans moved from rural to urban centers in increasing numbers, most cities with an African-American population developed a vibrant African-American press. The foremost newspapers were "the *Chicago Defender*, the *Detroit Tribune*, the *Pittsburgh Courier*, and the (New York) *Amsterdam News*."[6] However, as most cities had daily newspapers aimed at the general public the "idea of an African-American newspaper was to give African-Americans the news through the lens of their own eyes."[7]

The *Reflector*, for example, was an African-American newspaper printed in Charlottesville from 1933 to 1935. Its editor was an African American, Thomas J. Sellers, and he stated that the paper was for "race lovers" but also for those with a "keen sense of loyalty to worthwhile negro endeavors."[8] In the fourth issue his editorial stated: "We attempt to create civic pride." But more presciently he went on to assert: "the 'Open Forum' is your medium of protest, of expression of opinion; the society column is a log of your social activities; each part in the paper is yours; no single column, no certain page, the entire paper is yours."[9] Yet however worthy the aims of the ethnic press, it should be borne in mind that "the 'primary motivation' of African-American newspaper proprietors was 'not uplift, but profit.' In addition, from a social standpoint, these newspapers were a source of pride for the African-American community and a focal point for African-Americans to stick together and fight the constant oppression they were under."[10]

Today in the United States it is not uncommon for large cities to support a variety of newspapers aimed at specific ethnic, racial, or religious groups. It would appear that the mainstream press, despite its ubiquity, cannot address minority issues in a way that satisfies minority audiences. In New York, for example, a recent study entitled *Ethnic* by the Project for Excellence in Journalism 2008 asked the question: "What would a reader or viewer of the major ethnic media, Spanish-language, learn or not learn about a particular event compared with what is offered in English?"[11] The issue examined was the 2007 debate on overhauling immigration law that had failed to make progress in the Senate. The study found that "Hispanic audiences turning to native-language news, especially the broadcast programs, heard a much different side of the bill's defeat."[12] More specifically, the coverage in the Spanish-language media was more emotional, less political, and dealt with the effects on "everyday people." One other finding was that Hispanic communities "differ greatly in their individual cultures, nationalities and ethnicities"[13] as much as did white or black communities.

By comparison, the ethnic press in Britain lacks a high national profile and is centered mainly in London. *Black Voice* (1970–99) was the organ of the Black Unity and Freedom Party (BUFP), a radical left-wing grouping, and the paper documented the many abuses black people suffered, including "police brutality." The party disbanded in 1998 and with it the paper. Other publications have included Joseph Harker's *Black Britain*, Arif Ali's *West Indian World* and *Caribbean Times*, and the *Weekly Journal*. *African Voice* is a weekly that styles itself as "Britain's No. 1 African Newspaper."[14] Launched in 2001, it has a circulation of 25,000 and as its title implies is aimed squarely at the African Diaspora. The weekly *New Nation*, published by Ethnic Media Group, was launched in 1996 and became Britain's best-selling black newspaper. Its parent company went into administration at the beginning of 2009 and *New Nation* was relaunched after being bought by African Media Enterprises.[15]

The most significant newspaper of the UK ethnic press, however, is *The Voice*, originally published in Brixton, south London. It is a national weekly tabloid aimed at the British Afro-Caribbean community and was founded by Jamaican-born Val McCalla with a grant from the Greater London Council in the aftermath of the Brixton race riots of 1981. It campaigns for black people and issues relevant to minority groups nationwide. It has become a breeding ground for many significant and high-profile black journalists in both TV and print including Rageh Omaar and Martin Bashir. Val McCalla died in 2002 and the paper was bought in 2004 by the Gleaner Company, a long-established Jamaican-based newspaper group.

A Racing Certainty

The rise of the sporting press is one of the most significant examples of minority interests gradually infiltrating the mainstream press. The earliest magazine devoted to the whole gamut of sporting activity was the monthly *Sporting Magazine* published in London from 1792 to 1870.[16] Unusually, readers were encouraged to contribute material and the proprietor, John Wheble, insisted on complete accuracy, much as he did with his own reporters. It set the tone for such magazines, mainly covering field sports such as coursing, hunting, racing, fly-fishing, cock fighting, and cricket. In 1822 Robert Bell founded *Bell's Life in London*, a weekly that soon became Britain's leading sporting newspaper. By the 1860s *Bell's Life* itself was facing competition from *The Field* (1853–present), *Sporting Life* (1859–1998), and the *Sporting Times* (1865–1932) in what was becoming a lucrative market.[17]

In the United States, newspapers had sporadically covered sport since the 1830s: "first cricket and particularly horse-racing, then prize fighting by the 1850s . . . and baseball in the 1870s."[18] Many baseball journals were short-lived, however. The *Ballplayers Chronicle* was the first weekly devoted entirely to baseball but lasted only a year (1867), as did the *New England Base Ballist* (1868). This weekly called itself an "Advocate for the National Game, Field Sports and the Drama."[19] The *National Chronicle* succeeded the *Base Ballist* with a more diversified look at "American Sports and Amusements" but again lasted little more than a year. Despite this, baseball was clearly understood by mid-century to be the national game even though most of the publications boasted only local circulations. The first full-time sports reporter for a daily paper was Henry Chadwick, the "Father of Baseball," who was employed by James Gordon Bennett in 1863 to cover baseball for the *New York Herald*.

In contrast, Michael Oriard in his book *Reading Football* draws attention to the extensive coverage of (American) football in the daily press of the late nineteenth century. When Joseph Pulitzer purchased the *New York World* in 1883 "one of his initial acts as publisher was to create the first separate sports department, headed by its own 'sporting editor.'"[20] This in particular and the New York daily press in general "had an impact on college football … greater than television's effect on professional football in the 1950s and 1960s."[21] Oriard goes so far as to suggest that "the late nineteenth-century daily newspaper 'created' college football to an even greater degree, transforming an extracurricular activity into a national spectacle."[22]

By comparison, the English game, with its working-class roots, flourished regardless of newspaper coverage either locally or nationally. In both countries, however, the end of the nineteenth century was a pivotal period. "By the mid-1890s both the quality and quantity of the football coverage in the daily papers in New York, Philadelphia, and Boston were staggering: front-page, full-page, several-page accounts."[23] In Britain sports news became firmly ensconced on the back pages of most daily newspapers, especially after the Football League was established in 1888.

Coverage was further boosted by the introduction of the football pools in 1923 which gave the average supporter a chance to win huge sums of money each week. Most sports now have their own monthly magazines such as football's *FourFourTwo* and athletics' *American Track and Field*. The remains of the sporting press are now almost entirely devoted to horse and greyhound racing. The *Racing Post* is the only print-based paper now in circulation in Britain. It was started in 1986 as a competitor to *Sporting Life* which itself ceased print publication in 1998 and is now entirely web-based.

The Study of Perfection

The earliest magazine devoted to women was the London-based *Lady's Magazine* (1770). This was followed in 1798 by the *Lady's Monthly Museum*, "launched by 'A Society of Ladies,'" and in the new century John Bell started *La Belle Assemblée* (1806). These three magazines, which merged in 1832, were aristocratic rather than popular but "established the woman's magazine as the genre we understand today."[24] The first American example of a popular women's magazine was *Godey's Ladies Book* (1830–98). According to Tracy Seneca, "While there had been American publications for women, *Godey's* was the first successful one, and the first to approach the now standard format."[25] It included short stories and poetry, addressed personal issues, and included job advertisements. Importantly, "readers could become involved in the course and nature of the publication"[26] because much of the content was reader-generated. It also included fashion plates but it was not until Ebenezer Butterick published the *Delineator* (1863–1937) "that fashion magazines really came into existence".[27] Later examples are the now-famous *Ladies Home Journal* (1883–present) and *Good Housekeeping* (1885–present) both of which used reader's letters, questionnaires, and product "quality guarantees" as ways of maintaining reader involvement.

Women's magazines, however significant or commonplace, were an alternative space that essentially reinforced female domesticity within a developing consumer-orientated environment.

Newspapers like Britain's *Women's Penny Paper* (1888–90) used women to write about women but enjoyed little success and the *Women's Penny Paper* is now best remembered for its support of the suffrage movement, where it found its most faithful audience. The first issue established its territory as "inaugurating a new feature in journalism" because "there appears to be as yet no bold and fearless exponent of the women's cause in the Press."[28] Yet the position of such a journal was always anomalous. It supported women's suffrage but was at pains to point out how "the special contention of the advocates of Woman Suffrage is the value of *womanliness*" (emphasis in original).[29] It could ridicule the manly woman "with her hair cut short" and "her billy-cock hat" while at the same time attempting to gain accommodation in the Press Gallery of the House of Commons, then an all-male bastion that the paper failed to breach.[30]

FactFile
La Fronde

The radical and feminist inclinations of French women manifested themselves in some of the earliest examples of "alternative" political newspaper and magazine communications anywhere in the world, especially during the late 1830s and the 1840s. Yet it was not until the "Belle Epoque" (1897) that a mass daily newspaper was launched by and for women. *La Fronde* was the brain child of actress and journalist Marguerite Durand, and was reputedly financed by the banker Gustave de Rothschild as a Dreyfusard paper at the time of the Dreyfus Affair (that rocked France with the issues of antisemitism and army corruption that it raised). Apart from the night janitor, the daily was staffed entirely by women, even down to the typesetters and printers. The *frondeuse* tradition of journalism had originated during the seventeenth-century rebellion against chief minister Mazarin, and literally meant a "slingshot" a female David against the male Goliath. In the words of the weekly *L'Illustration* (January 15, 1898), the paper provided "not feminist theses, but exclusively feminine opinions on politics and the news of the day."

To show its sense of equality the paper dated each edition according to a variety of different calendars – the Jewish calendar, the French Revolutionary calendar, the Gregorian. In its first week *La Fronde* sold 200,000 copies a day but then went down to 50,000. Eventually financial problems reduced it to a monthly and it closed for good in March 1905, although it was briefly revived by Durand in 1914 and 1926. The problem of identity for *La Fronde* was that it appeared neither feminist nor feminine. Attempts at presenting readers with a diversity of female representation led to confusion over the approach women's journalism should take. Nevertheless, *La Fronde* was said to be the newspaper for school teachers, usually better educated than the majority of women, and one of Durand's aims was to raise public consciousness of the ways in which female identity was represented in French culture. The paper's initial impact shows that female readers were open to a variety of journalistic provision, including discourses on the "New Woman."

Ultimately it was the mainstream media, influenced by the New Journalism of the *fin de siècle*, that demonstrated an ability not only to appeal to women readers but also to commodify them and turn them into consumers equally as susceptible to advertising blandishments as men. Feature articles and women's pages became popular and advertising aimed at female consumers increased in importance.[31] In Britain, the *Daily Mail* was the first popular newspaper to include elements that would appeal directly to women. "The Daily Magazine" appeared in the first issue and was subheaded, "An Entirely New Idea in Morning Journalism." The jaunty typeface drew attention to the lighthearted nature of the page and "A note from the Editor" confirmed that it was "a practical attempt to provide something more than mere news" and furthermore "the style of the 'Daily Magazine' is to be entirely different to the other parts of the paper."[32] Magazine writers and novelists were featured and although the "magazine" was "designed to interest both sexes" Alfred Harmsworth was at pains to point out that "movements in woman's world … are as much entitled to receive attention as nine out of ten of the matters which are treated of in the ordinary daily paper. Therefore, two columns are set aside exclusively for ladies."[33]

Seven years later, in 1903, Harmsworth started the tabloid *Daily Mirror* as a paper specifically for women. In a similar manner to *La Fronde* in France, his paper too was staffed mainly with women journalists. However, the paper failed in its first three months and all the women were sacked and replaced by more experienced male reporters from the *Daily Mail*. Harmsworth had identified an "alternative" public sphere but had misunderstood its requirements. Women did not want their own daily paper, "or at least the respectable, socially aspiring conservative women he sought did not,"[34] especially if it served up a diet of trivia and domestic content that could be obtained from magazines elsewhere. Harmsworth complained bitterly: "It's taught me that women can't write and don't want to read."[35]

For critics such as novelist and essayist Matthew Arnold there were many dangers inherent in any "alternative" public sphere. Arnold believed that culture was the pursuit of "sweetness and light," a "study of perfection"[36] and a necessary bulwark against anarchy. The "great aim of culture," he believed, was to set "ourselves to ascertain what perfection is and to make it prevail."[37] His distinction between traditional "old" journalism as "organs of reason"[38] and the New Journalism as "feather-brained"[39] was a factor that, according to Margaret Beetham, "implicitly mobilized the vocabulary of gendered identity."[40]

New Journalism, whether because of Arnold's strictures or not, did become inescapably bound up with notions of the feminization of the press. This provided a new lexicon in which those attributes that were deemed to distinguish the female from the male were similarly employed to distinguish the New Journalism from the Old. New Journalism was intimate rather than authoritative; it stressed the personal note in its reporting and, moreover, focused much more on the lives of "ordinary" people rather than pursuing the "heroic" public figure. New Journalism provided a colloquial patois that neither patronized its readers nor assumed intellectual pretensions and this change in tone from a "tutorial and intellectual nature" (see Chapter 5, p. 101) signaled the beginnings of that revolutionary move away from the paradigm of the male didactic to that of the empathetic female so marked in twentieth-century journalism.

In the process, female journalists were often portrayed in disparaging tones, from the "Jennie Jot-it-down" or "Rita Rite-it-up" with her "complete absence of such adult literary ingredients as grammar, style and common sense,"[41] to the "manly" woman who seemed to come in for particular opprobrium. "If there is anything the [Englishman] hates and ridicules," wrote a correspondent to the *Girl's Own Paper*, "it is a masculine, unwomanly woman."[42]

Much of this anxiety was precisely because women were beginning to carve out careers for themselves in various branches of the profession. The New Woman, who aspired to a measure of independence, whether in education, career, sexuality, political or cultural activity, was a pivotal figure around which much of this anxiety coalesced. "Perceived to have ranged herself perversely with the forces of cultural anarchism and decay,"[43] she embodied much of the doubt and anxiety of the *fin de siècle*, from the perceived danger to religion of Darwin and his *On the Origin of Species*, to economic liberalism and the free trade ethos challenged by socialism and the rise of labor, or the cultural decadence of the aesthete, symbolized by Oscar Wilde, as a threat to notions of Victorian maleness and manhood.

FactFile
Le Petit Journal

Le Petit Journal was a tabloid-style newspaper published in Paris between 1863 and 1944. It was founded by Moïse Polydore Millaud and at the height of its popularity had a circulation of one million copies a day. Millaud understood that appealing to women readers made good business sense and also that a paper needed to be both attention-grabbing and readable. It was "nonpolitical" – that is, unaligned and thus exempt from the legal deposit and possible fines for offensive content at a time of censorship. It sold on the streets (as opposed to annual subscription sales) for 1 sou (5 cents) and outsold its nearest rival four times over. In 1884 an illustrative Sunday supplement, with a now iconic all visual front page, was introduced.

At a time when the political journal on both sides of the Atlantic was in decline, Le Petit Journal, full of human interest, domestic subject matter, and the all-important serial novel – aimed at an expanding female readership – can be seen as a countercurrent to such newspapers as the *Women's Penny Paper* in Britain and *Truth* in America which, as much because of their content as their target readership, were largely marginalized as "feminist" products. Le Petit Journal's appeal to a female audience was unashamedly mainstream. It can reasonably be construed as an extension of the democratic mandate, but at the time patronizing "feminized" content was seen by contemporaries as a form of immoral depoliticization of the press. It was feared that such content would have a corrupting influence on the potentially impressionable and irrational female reader.

In fact, the paper's style amounted to a form of conservative feminization. A contemporary account described Le Petit Journal's approach as one that aimed to articulate what everyone was thinking, even if this meant being bold enough to appear stupid.[44] An assessment of the demand for the paper points to the fact that women and peasants had to be encouraged to read and that Le Petit Journal "obliged the latter to become interested in current affairs."[45] Proprietor Moïse Millaud referred to his readership as "les petits gens" [46] – the ordinary folk – but nevertheless applied a great deal of marketing flair to the task of promotion.

Alfred Harmsworth (Lord Northcliffe from 1905) was much impressed by the French paper's high circulation and successful business model, and he seriously picked the brains of the proprietors during a number of visits to their premises (and much socializing with them), immediately prior to the launch of The Daily Mail. In fact, he lifted the word feuilleton, serialized novel, for use as a heading in his paper, acknowledging the appeal of fiction to the female reader. There is evidence that Northcliffe's various stunts owed much to the ideas of Le Petit Journal. In 1891, for example, Le Petit Journal created the Paris–Brest–Paris cycle race and in 1894 inaugurated the first motor car race, the Paris–Rouen Horseless Carriage Competition (Concours des Voitures sans Chevaux). Anglo-American scholarship tends to claim erroneously that The Daily Mail was the first daily paper to reach a mass circulation of one million, when in fact Le Petit Journal hit this target in 1887 – nine years before the Daily Mail was founded.

In 1914, looking back on his coverage for the *Daily Mail* of The Hague Peace Conference in 1899, journalist William Maxwell wrote: "I was bombarded for several days with telegrams urging me to 'describe the doings of the ladies!'" He responded that if they wanted this sort of coverage they should send "a society reporter" to replace him. Eventually the editor intervened and instructed Maxwell to continue taking the business seriously. Nevertheless, Maxwell concluded from this episode that "'The ladies' have exercised a subtle and powerful influence on journalism."[47]

Agent Provocateur

There is a stark difference between the visual appeal of newspapers from the early nineteenth century and the *fin de siècle*. Conventions of layout and style were only gradually established and it was the weekly rather than the daily press that became the seedbed of innovation. The *Illustrated London News*, for example, published in 1842, was the world's first illustrated weekly. Costing sixpence, the magazine had 16 pages and 32 woodcuts. Mid-century saw the growth of the populist Sunday press in Britain with *Lloyds Weekly Newspaper* (1842), the *News of the World* (1843), and *Reynolds's Weekly Newspaper* (1850). These papers combined woodcut illustrations with sensationalist reporting of crimes and scandal.

By the end of the century the telegraph and an expanding railway network both ensured a quicker and more extensive circulation of information at a time when page space was also under pressure from the increased demands of advertising. Printing technology had advanced significantly, but not to the extent that a daily paper could print any number of pages and still be available for distribution the following morning. This combination of circumstances ensured that the full, often verbatim "report," the mainstay of the serious paper, gradually became truncated and turned into what became known as a "story" – something that could be chopped about to fit the available space by that newly invented newsroom journalist, the "subeditor."

As news styles developed, so also did ways of handling audiences. Decisions about what should be sacrificed and what should be published, as well as decisions about what version of events best suited a particular audience, all formed part of an emerging philosophy that was gradually formalized around concepts such as news agendas and news values. The "audience design"[48] of the newspaper began to reflect its readers' expectations as well as the paper's own cultural and political inclinations. This "compact" gradually underpinned its news agenda and became a powerful articulation of a paper's promise to its readers, in both its reporting and its opinions. On launching the *Daily Mail*, for example, Alfred Harmsworth instructed his staff to write in a plain, clear style for his lower-middle-class readership and later, in his account of the paper, attributed the *Mail*'s success to its brevity and "compactness."[49]

For the historian, the memoirs of proprietors, editors, and journalists are also a rich source of information on specific journals' intentions regarding potential audiences. But particularly in the nineteenth century, the launch prospectus also provided an opportunity for a newspaper to summarize its ideas about readership and the overall direction of its editorial policy. The subscriber system that was so popular in the United States and European countries like France for much of the nineteenth century reinforced the importance of the prospectus as a means of drawing people into a given community. Agents collected names with a pledge to pay – a technique also used in the US to fund public halls, churches, and even canals and railways.

In the early precommercial press, a form would be passed around, like a petition, and the resultant list of loyal readers then sent off to the printer. The word "subscriber" suggested a mutual commitment by journalists, publisher, and readers to the ideas contained in the prospectus. Politicians used the practice to raise party awareness at a time when this was ill-defined by modern-day standards: "The recognition by readers that they formed a community of the like-minded was one of the achievements of political journalism."[50]

In the United States, a country with a dispersed and often difficult-to-reach population, subscription sales, especially for antislavery, women's rights, and socialist publications were often crucial to survival. Such sales depended on the enormous efforts of agents who traveled thousands of miles across the country, giving speeches at public meetings, introducing new ideas, and publicizing the newspapers that communicated these ideas. In the struggle to extend audience reach and newspaper appeal, many of these agents became personalities in their own right. Feminist Abby Kelley's lectures added seven hundred supporters to an abolitionist paper in one summer.[51] Another agent sold more than 100,000 subscriptions for socialist papers during 20 years across 17 states. By 1913 *Appeal to Reason* (see Chapter 6) had an army of agents in every state and a circulation close to one million.

This was clearly a national network of readers, but subscriptions also created groups of like-minded folk in local communities. The significance for the creation of the audience, therefore, was not simply one of reader volume. Subscriptions were often generated as a result of negotiations on price and editorial policy among clubs of readers. During the 1880s, for example, the *Ladies' Home Journal* gained 90 percent of its subscriptions through clubbing plans "as it sounded its call for domesticity."[52] By the turn of the century the *Ladies' Home Journal* was the most popular women's magazine in the US and published the work of muckrakers such as Jane Addams, who went on to win the Nobel Peace Prize.

By the second half of the nineteenth century, however, according to Jean Chalaby, public discourse was fast disappearing, being replaced by a com-modified journalistic discourse.[53] Individual newspapers were developing their own particular lens "through which reality was refracted, and one that provided each particular newspaper's claim to authority and authenticity."[54] For many newspapers there was little more authoritative and authentic than the human interest story and such journalism found a public ready and eager to read it.

All Human Life Is There

Michael and Edwin Emery and Nancy L. Roberts have suggested that whenever the needs of the masses are ignored by the established organs of communication they are eventually met by a journalism of "sensationalism."[55] In support of this argument they quote some of the key dates in media history: 1620, when the first "corantos" or news sheets, reporting on the important events of the Thirty Years' War, were produced by Dutch printers for the English market; 1833, when the penny press was introduced; the 1890s, when New Journalism redefined popular newspapers; and finally 1920, the year in which the first American radio stations to seek a regular public audience were launched. In Britain one could reasonably add the Sunday press of the 1840s to this list of key dates for "sensationalism."

Defenders of more traditional journalism on both sides of the Atlantic complained that human interest stories were neither instructive nor useful. But the American penny press in particular was aimed specifically at a nonelite public who were open to a journalism that entertained, amused, and startled and one, moreover, that sold for one penny what generally cost six cents. The most noted example of the penny press was Benjamin H. Day's daily *New York Sun* with its motto, "It Shines for All." Founded in 1833, two years before its main competitor the *Herald*, its ideal reader according to Day was the "common man" and its "reports of police court activities and its witty treatment of news made it a success."[56] The *Sun* and the *Herald* were the only two papers to survive from over 30 penny papers begun over the next decade.

Most newspapers in the early nineteenth century cost six cents and were distributed through subscription. Day had noted how previous attempts to introduce a penny press had failed but thought he could succeed by aug-menting subscription sales by also selling direct to the public using street vendors. Previously, subscriptions had been $6 to $10 a year, which was more than a weekly wage for a skilled worker. Subscription sales also tended to be more suitable for stable, financially secure, professional middle-class workers. However, industrialization and urbanization were leading to a change in previous notions of class and status as popular culture began to reflect life in the expanding cities.

Day's price cut meant new immigrants to the cities could afford to buy a paper for the first time; and the street vendors meant that a community of readers who would identify themselves with the newspapers' views had to be encouraged by catchy headlines and entertaining news every day, especially for the journey to and from work. But as James Crouthamel has pointed out in his study of the New York *Herald*, the emergence of a press aimed at a wider audience and selling at a lower price was also due in large part to technological developments enabling a mass circulation to be produced more quickly and cheaply.[57]

The penny press from 1833 onwards can therefore reasonably be said to represent the start of the integration of journalism into a capitalist framework that, according to Ralph Nerone (1987), was the key change in American press history.[58] Henceforth, journalism developed along commercial lines and the penny press according to some interpretations represented a new democratic world where notions of public and private were being redefined. Other readings argue that it was part of the long tradition inherited from popular broadsheets and ballads. Either way, the writers of the penny press "were spokesmen for egalitarianism ideals in politics, economic life, and social life through their organization of sales, their solicitation of advertising, their emphasis on news, their catering to large audiences, and their decreasing concern with the editorial."[59]

Thus the conception of what constituted news was changing and this was clearly evident by 1835 with the launch of the New York *Herald*. Founder James Gordon Bennett introduced "extras" (special editions), a letters column for readers to comment on the paper, an increase in crime reporting, sports news, and a financial section. Bennett stated that the function of a newspaper was "not to instruct but to startle." Yet this pursuit of the sensational did not preclude the paper being a staunch supporter of the Democratic Party during the American Civil War. During the Jacksonian "antebellum" era, politics for the "laboring classes" was also beginning to win recognition as by 1850 property ownership and tax requirements were eliminated, resulting in almost all white males having the right to vote. The public sphere was now gradually being extended to the lower middle classes.

By 1841, when Horace Greeley founded the *New York Tribune*, the "common man" audience was pursued by way of campaigns and crusades rather than through sensationalist reporting. So much so that Greeley's *Tribune* became America's most influential newspaper from its inception until the 1870s and Greeley himself was considered the greatest editor of his day. Greeley's paper reflected a certain ease Americans felt with their socio-economic system, unlike, for example, the readers of Britain's radical press. And unlike that press, the *Sun* was full of advertisements including a new "wanted" section but contained no information for the financial classes other than a small amount of shipping news and nothing in the way of radical politics. Benjamin Day copied the idea of crime reporting from the successful reporting of Bow Street Police Station in London. The appeal was nonpartisan, although one study has drawn attention to the wide coverage given to the women's rights movement.[60] When Day sold the paper to Charles Dana in 1868, the *Sun* hired its first female reporter, Emily Bettey, and in 1880 hired what is taken to be the first fashion editor in America, Eleanor Brainerd.

Another response to the "craze" for sensation, on both sides of the Atlantic, was the police journal. The ultimate voyeur's delight, it became extremely popular with its "true crime" content. It asked readers to report crime and even offered rewards for information leading to a conviction. The American *National Police Gazette* was founded in 1846. Despite its title, this weekly was a purely commercial publication, neither sanctioned nor produced by the police. Its editor for most of the nineteenth century was Richard K. Fox, who filled it with celebrity gossip, lurid murders, outlaw cowboys, and sport, particularly boxing. It was also famed for its woodcuts and later photographs of scantily clad strippers, burlesque performers, and prostitutes. At its peak it boasted a weekly circulation of over 150,000.

In Britain, the *Illustrated Police News* covered similar territory to its American counterpart. It was founded in 1864 as one of the earliest British weekly tabloids and contained melodramatic and sensational stories of murders, violent crimes, and also hangings. In many respects it was a descendant of the execution broadsheets of the eighteenth century. It became famous for its detailed and salacious coverage of the Jack the Ripper murders in the East End of London in 1888. The British *Police Gazette* was, in contrast, an official organ of the Metropolitan Police. It began in 1772 as the *Quarterly Pursuit* but changed its name in 1828. It contained woodcuts and descriptions of stolen property, details of offenders "escaped from justice," and pictures of wanted men and women. All these journals were extremely popular and reinforced the trend towards sensational crime reporting that became a hallmark of the penny press in America and the Sunday press in Britain.

Despite Greeley's example, it was another half century before the press in general developed aggressive campaigning strategies, supporting popular causes as much for self-promotion as moral indignation. Campaigns were designed to either raise or change public opinion but could often mask an editor's or proprietor's own particular prejudices or political viewpoint. By the 1890s, Joseph Pulitzer's New York *World* and William Randolph Hearst's *New York Journal* were locked in a circulation war that saw sensationalism reach new heights (see Chapter 6 on Yellow Journalism). Now the aim was to "act" rather than just talk on behalf of the audience ("While Others Talk the Journal Acts," went Hearst's tagline). These "acts" included obtaining a court injunction to prevent a city franchise being given to a gas company and legal actions against alleged abuses in government and by corporations.[61]

Despite the obvious abuses perpetrated by Yellow Journalism, such aggressive stances can also be interpreted as providing "an alternative public sphere, where a grassroots-based populist critique against established corporate and governmental elites could come to the fore."[62] Both Hearst and Pulitzer understood that any "populist critique" gained immeasurably from the power of the human "voice" with its ability to add verisimilitude to a story, so much so that Hearst in particular regularly faked his paper's more sensational interviews.

Can I Quote You On That?

In so far as news gathering requires a journalist to talk to people, often informally, the interview must be considered as old as journalism itself. But until the middle of the nineteenth century the interviewee "voice" was largely absent. Newspapers consisted of descriptive prose and verbatim transcriptions of speeches and other proceedings, interspersed with some interpretative content. The subtext was clear – journalists knew best what to give their readers and in the process assumed a certain benevolent autocracy. Sociologist Michael Schudson describes how American political journalists began to see their role as "involving some fundamental translation and interpretation of political acts to a public ill-equipped to sort out for itself the meaning of events."[63]

Candidates for having produced the first "real" interview are numerous. Edmund Yates introduced a "Celebrities at Home" feature for his periodical, the *World*, in 1874, an innovation swiftly copied by rivals (in passing, one of the earliest uses in this context of the word "celebrity"). Yet almost a decade earlier, in 1865, George Augustus Sala of Britain's *Daily Telegraph* had interviewed Napoleon III and a year later Garibaldi during the Austrian campaign of 1866. Alfred Austin of the London-based *Standard* interviewed Bismarck in September 1870. These early examples follow a predictable pattern that "involves a number of separate notions: the journalist has personal contact with the great man, discusses some matter of public moment, and makes the fact of the interview plain in his published report."[64]

This approach is clearly evident, for example, in Austin's interview with Bismarck. The "personal contact" in this case was fortuitous – "I had the luck yesterday morning to fall in with the royal cortege."[65] The matter of "public moment" was the German advance on Paris and the interview contained six direct quotes, only two of which, however, concerned matters relating specifically to the conflict. While his story, taking up one whole column of the newspaper, was clearly dependent upon the interview taking place, this dependence was minimal. There is no real sense of a dialogue and no exposition of character to mark it out as significantly different from the journalism that surrounds it. As in virtually all early interviews it is the powerful and influential who are privileged; it is great or significant events which are reported, and the tone is authoritative and institutional rather than personal.

Without doubt it was W. T. Stead, when editor of the *Pall Mall Gazette*, who popularized and democratized the interview. In *Victorian News and Newspapers* Lucy Brown makes the point that "where Stead ... was an innovator was in the systematic use he made of the interview."[66] But while this is certainly true it would seem parsimonious to suggest this was his only innovation. His particular contribution also relates to the kinds of people he interviewed and the way he manipulated his material. His approach signaled a clear break with the past and the work of journalists like Yates, Sala, and Austin.

Stead's interviews often *were* the story. The whole essence, the *raison d'être* of the article, was the fact that the interview took place. The kind of information imparted was not authoritative in content or tone, but was often subjective; Stead used the interviewee's words rather than reported speech, invariably enhancing characterization and atmosphere; his subjects were ordinary people, the ubiquitous "man in the street," and they were not caught up in momentous events, except in the way the journalist and newspaper manipulated the resultant copy. The tone of Stead's interviews was therefore personal rather than institutional, approximating much more closely to everyday speech and speech patterns. For example, he quoted one brothel madam as saying, "Vot is it you a doin to that von leetle girl?"[67] Such examples display, for the period, a remarkable flexibility in the use of language in a journalistic context. All these characteristics of Stead's journalism are perhaps best exemplified in the "Maiden Tribute of Modern Babylon" series of articles.

FactFile
Audience Reaction to W. T. Stead's
"Maiden Tribute of Modern Babylon"

On Saturday July 4, 1885, British journalist W. T. Stead, editor of the *Pall Mall Gazette*, warned his readers that on the following Monday he would "publish the report of a Special and Secret Commission of Inquiry" into child prostitution and trafficking in London. The *Pall Mall Gazette* was an evening paper that had a small but influential readership (it sold about 12,000 copies a day)[68] and Stead had been editor since 1883. He also suggested that "those who are squeamish … will do well not to read the *Pall Mall Gazette* of Monday and the three following days."[69] This was a classic teaser tactic copied from the Sunday press and ratcheted up the sense of anticipation for the "Maiden Tribute of Modern Babylon," as the story was headlined.

Stead had managed to buy a girl, Eliza Armstrong who was just 13, from her mother and then sell her to a house of ill repute before revealing his ruse and handing her into the care of the Salvation Army. His "Maiden Tribute" documented "in lurid detail how poor 'daughters of the people' were 'snared, trapped, and outraged, either when under the influence of drugs or after a prolonged struggle in a locked room'."[70] Stead was prosecuted and spent three months in jail because he had not secured the consent of the girl's father before "buying" her and stating in public that he had "abducted" her. His experiences and the whole issue of child prostitution were reported at length with the passion of a revivalist preacher.

With subheadings such as "How Girls are Ruined," "The Confessions of a Brothel Keeper," and "the Violation of Virgins," followed by "How Annie Was Poisoned," "I Order Five Virgins," and "You Want a Maid, Do You?" the story caused public outrage and many readers and advertisers canceled their orders for the paper. W. H. Smith, the newsdealer, refused to carry it so Stead employed newspaper boys and volunteers to sell it on the streets. Playwright George Bernard Shaw telegraphed Stead and sarcastically offered to act as a paperboy by selling a thousand copies at street corners.[71] By the third installment crowds besieged the newspaper's offices, some in outrage and others clamoring for copies that were selling at premium second-hand prices.

The enormous stir and public debate culminated in a mass demonstration in London's Hyde Park (estimated at 250,000)[72] and the passing of the Criminal Law Amendment Act of 1885 to increase the age of consent from 13 to 16 years. The *Pall Mall Gazette* lost revenue but increased circulation. In fact, the furor generated by the "Maiden Tribute" stimulated "grass-roots political activity: throughout Britain, social purity groups and vigilance committees were organized to oversee the local enforcement of the act."[73] Some of these vigilance committees attacked public theaters and music halls and forced "police crackdowns on solicitation and brothel-keeping."[74] More remarkably, the effects of Stead's emotional appeal were felt throughout the British Empire, "in the form of age-of-consent (marriage) laws" and eventually to "official prohibitions against liaisons with 'native' women."[75]

Most of Stead's interviews were with victims and this set the tone for the first phase of interview journalism. According to recent research into interview subjects, however, there is now evidence of a clear shift from the victim or other actor in a story to the official source or expert. A century ago there were hardly any outside experts in stories and

> an official source turned up in only one of every four stories. Today, fully one fifth of the actors or victims have disappeared from the average story, replaced by experts and officials, and outside experts appear in one fifth of stories … From the perspective of the reader, the landscape of grey text had become depopulated beyond what these average figures suggest. The results show why other studies have found that persons have been vanishing from the front pages.[76]

The rise of the expert is closely tied to the rise of the public relations industry with its penchant for firing off press releases and ensuring that suitable "experts" are available to offer "expert" opinion in a digestible soundbite format (see Chapter 4). Press relations officers are now to be found in industry and commerce, including the world of entertainment, central and local government, charities, pressure groups, government agencies, the emergency services, and most other public bodies.

Today, the kind of stories broken by W. T. Stead and others are becoming ghettoized as "investigative journalism." In many newsrooms and features departments this sort of investigative journalism is perceived as a "luxury" and is the first target for cuts in the modern mania for downsizing editorial staffs. Thus the interview, for all its democratizing zeal, may have had the opposite effect – that of cutting off the true democratic voice of the "man in the street." In the process the human interest story has been reduced to the "Look at What Docs did to my Granny Boobs!"[77] or the "I Chose My Own Testicles"[78] variety, a kind of journalism that has become all-pervasive, mainly because it is politically nonthreatening and journalistically cheap to produce.

A useful comparison is the French press, where the use of the interview was slow to take off. French politicians in particular were reluctant to grant interviews, preferring to write articles themselves and have their speeches reported verbatim. In 1965 France's leading regional daily, *Ouest-France*, established a research and development department with people paid to think about the content of the newspaper and especially what the readers thought of it, with quantitative and qualitative studies about readership, layout, and editorial strategy. Such audience research came within a framework of traditional suspicion of the concept of "marketing." French newspapers had always believed that progress was connected to editorial content and the social, cultural, and political ideas expressed in the paper.[79] According to this argument, the French press is less sensational and more serious and ideologically driven in a way that would be unthinkable in Britain and the United States.

Historian James D. Startt, for example, suggested that "during the era of the New Journalism, "good journalism" remained alive,"[80] the inference being that there coexisted both an "elite" and a "popular" print culture and that New Journalism, commercially sound though it may have been, was by definition not "good journalism." Nevertheless, its influence is clear on both sides of the Atlantic. The development of a discursive environment that included concerns about audience not only was new at this time but also had serious ramifications for the development of media strategies throughout the twentieth century both in print and the emerging broadcast news media.

Notes

1   Alexis de Tocqueville, *Democracy in America*, ed. J. P. Meyer, trans. George Lawrence (Garden City, NY: Doubleday, 1969).

2   Pamela Newkirk, "Ida B. Wells-Barnett: Journalism as a Weapon Against Racial Bigotry," *Media Studies Journal*, 14, 2 (2000), 26–31. Available online at http://www.hartford-hwp.com/archives/45a/317.html, accessed on September 2, 2009.

3   Pamela Newkirk, *Within the Veil: Black Journalists, White Media* (New York: New York University Press, 2000), p. 39.

4   Ibid.

5   Ibid., p. 41.

6   Adam Friedman et al., "The Reflector: History of African-American Newspapers." Available online at http://www2.vcdh.virginia.edu/afam/reflector/newspaper.html, accessed on September 2, 2009.

7   Ibid.

8   Adam Friedman et al., "The Reflector: Adult Years of T. J. Sellers." Available online at http://www2.vcdh.virginia.edu/afam/reflector/newsellers2.html, accessed on September 2, 2009.

9   Adam Friedman et al., "The Reflector: This Is Your Newspaper." Available online at http://www2.vcdh.virginia.edu/afam/reflector/8.26.1933.paper.soc1.html, accessed on September 2, 2009.

10 Friedman et al., "The Reflector: History of African-American Newspapers."

11 Project for Excellence in Journalism, *Ethnic* (New York: State of the News Media, 2008). Available online at http://www.stateofthemedia.org/2008/narrative_yearinnews_ethnic.php?cat=6&media=2, accessed on September 2, 2009.

12 Ibid.

13 Ibid.

14 Ola Ogunyemi, "The News Agenda of the Black African Press in the UK," *Journal of Black Studies*, 5, 37 (2007), 630–54.

15 Owen Amos, "*New Nation* Saved From Closure After Buyer Is Found," *Press Gazette*, February 25, 2009. Available online at http://www.pressgazette.co.uk/story.asp?storycode=43173, accessed on September 1, 2010.

16 "Newspapers," in *Georgian Index*. Available online at http://www.georgianindex.net/publications/newspapers/news_sources.html, accessed on August 27, 2009.

17 Alan J. Lee, *The Origins of the Popular Press 1855–1914* (London: Croom Helm, 1976), p. 127.

18 Michael Oriard, *Reading Football: How the Popular Press Created an American Spectacle* (Chapel Hill: University of North Carolina Press, 1998), p. 58.

19 *New England Base Ballist – A Weekly Journal, an Advocate for the National Game, Field Sports and the Drama,* in Historic Baseball Newspapers. Available

online at http://www.oldjudge.com/archive/20090416/historic/, accessed on September 1, 2010.

20   Oriard, *Reading Football*, p. 59.

21   Ibid., p. 57.

22   Ibid., pp. 57–8.

23   Ibid., p. 57.

24   Margaret Beetham, *A Magazine of Her Own? Domesticity and Desire in the Woman's Magazine, 1800–1914* (London: Routledge, 1996), p. 17.

25   Tracy Seneca, "The History of Women's Magazines: Magazines as Virtual Communities." Available online at http://besser.tsoa.nyu.edu/impact/f93/students/ tracy/tracy_hist.html, accessed on August 31, 2009.

26   Ibid.

27   Ibid.

28   "Our Policy," *Women's Penny Paper*, October 27, 1888, Issue 1, p. 1.

29   *Women's Penny Paper*, January 26, 1889, p. 5.

30   Ibid., March 22, 1890, p. 258.

31   Jane Chapman, "A Business Trajectory: Assessing Female Influence and Representation in Europe's First Mass Circulation Daily Newspaper," in Angela Kershaw and Maggie Allison (eds), *Parcours de femmes – Twenty Years of Women in French* (Oxford: Peter Lang, forthcoming, 2011).

32   *Daily Mail*, May 4, 1896, p. 4.

33   Ibid.

34   Richard Bourne, *Lords of Fleet Street: The Harmsworth Dynasty* (London: Unwin Hyman, 1990), p. 33.

35   Maurice Edelman, *The Mirror: A Political History* (London: Hamish Hamilton, 1966), p. 5.

36   Matthew Arnold, *Selected Prose*, ed. P. J. Keating (London: Penguin, 1987), p. 205.

37   Ibid., p. 207.

38   Ibid., pp. 258–9.

39   Matthew Arnold, "Up to Easter," *Nineteenth Century*, XXI (May 1887), 629–43 (pp. 638–9).

40   Beetham, *A Magazine of Her Own?*, p. 122.

41   Patricia Marks, *Bicycles, Bangs, and Bloomers: The New Woman in the Popular Press* (Lexington: University Press of Kentucky, 1990), p. 85.

42   Wendy Forrester, *Great-Grandmama's Weekly* (London: Lutterworth Press, 1980), p. 34.

43   Linda Dowling, "The Decadent and the New Woman in the 1890s," *Nineteenth Century Fiction*, 33 (1978), 434–53 (p. 440).

44   Jules Lermina, *Dictionnaire universelle illustré biographique et bibliographique de la France contemporaine … Par une société de gens de lettres et de savants*, sous la direction de J. Lermina (Paris, 1884–5).

45   Ibid.
46   Michael B. Palmer, "Some Aspects of the French Press During the Rise of the Popular Daily" (PhD thesis, Oxford University, 1972), p. 93.
47   William Maxwell, "Old Lamps for New: Some Reflections on Recent Changes in Journalism," *Nineteenth Century and After*, 75 (1914), 1085–96 (p. 1090).
48   Allan Bell, "Language Style as Audience Design," in Nikolas Coupland and Adam Jaworski (eds), *Sociolinguistics: A Reader and Coursebook* (London: Macmillan, 1997), pp. 240–50.
49   Alfred Harmsworth, "The Making of a Newspaper," in Arthur Lawrence, *Journalism as a Profession* (London, Hodder & Stoughton,1903), p. 12.
50   Thomas C. Leonard, *News For All: America's Coming-of-Age with the Press* (New York: Oxford University Press, 1996), p. 48.
51   Ibid., p. 50.
52   Ibid., p. 52.
53   Jean K. Chalaby, *The Invention of Journalism* (Basingstoke, UK: Palgrave Macmillan, 1998), p. 66.
54   Donald Matheson, "The Birth of News Discourse: Changes in News Language in British Newspapers, 1880–1930," *Media, Culture & Society*, 22 (2000), 557–73 (p. 561).
55   Michael Emery, Edwin Emery, and Nancy L. Roberts, *The Press and America: An Interpretative History of the Mass Media*, 9th edn (Boston: Allyn & Bacon, 2000).
56   "*New York Sun*," *Encyclopaedia Britannica*. Available online at http://www.britannica.com/EBchecked/topic/412540/New-York-Sun, accessed on September 13, 2009.
57   James L. Crouthamel, *Bennett's New York Herald and the Rise of the Popular Press* (Syracuse, NY: Syracuse University Press, 1989).
58   Ralph Nerone, "The Mythology of the Penny Press," *Critical Studies in Mass Communication*, 4 (1987), 376–404.
59   Michael Schudson, *Discovering the News: A Social History of the American Newspaper* (New York: Basic Books, 1978), p. 60.
60   Sylvia D. Hoffert, "New York City's Penny Press and the Issue of Women's Rights, 1848–1860," *Journalism Quarterly* (1993), 70, 656–65.
61   Emery et al., *The Press and America*, p. 249.
62   Henrik Ornebring and Anna Maria Jonsson, "Tabloid Journalism and the Public Sphere: A Historical Perspective on Tabloid Journalism," *Journalism Studies*, 5, 3 (2004), 283–95 (p. 290).
63   Michael Schudson, "The Politics of Narrative Form: The Emergence of News Conventions in Print and Television," *Daedalus*, 111(1982), 97–112 (p. 99).
64   Lucy Brown, *Victorian News and Newspapers* (Oxford: Clarendon Press, 1985), p. 160.

65 Alfred Austin, "An Interview with Bismarck," *Standard*, September 13, 1870, p. 4.

66 Brown, *Victorian News and Newspapers*, p. 162.

67 W. T. Stead, "Maiden Tribute of Modern Babylon," *Pall Mall Gazette*, July 7, 1885, p. 3. Available online at http://www.attackingthedevil.co.uk/pmg/tribute/, accessed September 2, 2010.

68 Frederic Whyte, *The Life of W. T. Stead*, 2 vols (London: Jonathan Cape, 1925), vol. 1, p. 288.

69 W. T. Stead, "Notice to our Readers," *Pall Mall Gazette*, July 4, 1885, p. 1.

70 Judith R. Walkowitz, *City of Dreadful Delight: Narratives of Sexual Danger in Late-Victorian London* (London: Virago, 1992), p. 81.

71 Jane Chapman, *Comparative Media History: 1789 to the Present* (Cambridge, UK: Polity Press, 2005), p. 77.

72 Walkowitz, *City of Dreadful Delight*, p. 82.

73 Ibid.

74 Ibid., p. 83.

75 Ibid.

76 Kevin G. Barnhurst, "News Ideology in the Twentieth Century," in Svennik Hoyer and Horst Pottker (eds), *Diffusion of the News Paradigm, 1850–2000* (Göteborg: Nordicom, 2005), pp. 239–62 (p. 249–50).

77 Caroline Reid and Nilufer Atik, "Look at What Docs Did to My Granny Boobs," *Best*, September 15, 2009, p. 24.

78 Neil Palmer, "I Chose my Own Testicles," *Guardian*, *Weekend* magazine, July 1, 2006, p. 12. Available online at http://www.guardian.co.uk/lifeandstyle/2006/jul/01/familyandrelationships1, accessed September 2, 2010.

79 Jean-Marie Charon, *La presse en France de 1945 à nos jours* (Paris: Seuil, 1991), p. 270.

80 James D. Startt, "Good Journalism in the Era of the New Journalism: The British Press, 1902–1914," in Joel H. Wiener (ed.), *Papers for the Millions: The New Journalism in Britain, 1850s to 1914* (Westport, CT: Greenwood Press, 1988), pp. 275–98 (p. 293).

13

Watching and Listening

An early "dummy" edition of the *Daily Mail* dated February 22, 1896 carried the front page headline, "The Man of the Moment" above a drawing of Leander Starr Jameson. The picture caption read "God bless you, Dr. Jameson! Here's your country's love to you!"[1] Jameson was popularly known as Dr Jim or the Doctor and became notorious after the failure of the Jameson Raid in December 1895 which was one of the precursors to the Boer War (1899–1902). Jameson had put together a force of about six hundred men who crossed into the Transvaal, southern Africa, in a bid to overthrow the Boer government. His plan was to make a three-day dash to Johannesburg and trigger an uprising by the British expatriate workers (*uitlanders*) who were in a majority of two to one over the mainly Dutch-origin Boers. Jameson and his private army were forced to surrender, however, and the leaders of the raid were shipped back to England to face trial.

Jameson's arrest caused a sensation in London. A telegram from the German Kaiser congratulating President Kruger and the Boer government on their success was leaked to the press and this caused a storm of anti-German feeling. Jameson was lionized by the press and London society. An edition of the *Daily Mail*, dateline February 26, 1896, carried a four-decker headline: "DR. JIM / Extraordinary Scenes in Bow-Street Court / CHEER UPON CHEER / Special Descriptive Reports of the Opening Proceedings in the Great Trial."[2] Such coverage was, to say the least, unusual. It is one of the earliest examples of the media responding to public opinion and also feeding off it. Jameson was produced as an antidote to the perceived German "menace" and, despite his raid's failure, he became a bona fide hero in the

Jane Chapman and Nick Nuttall, *Journalism Today: A Themed History*
© 2011 Jane Chapman and Nick Nuttall. Published by Blackwell Publishing Ltd.

absence of any more suitable candidate. His celebrity status, however, was based on his public deeds and persona rather than any revelations about his private life. Invasions of "privacy" were still a step too far for most news organizations.

In the past this kind of celebrity status had been accorded specific individuals because of what they did or did not do, but without a universal press to "domesticate" them ("Dr Jim," for example) and keep them in the public eye this status always tended to be temporary. Once the interview became a legitimate and accepted journalistic form, however, people's "voices," muffled though they still were in the early decades of the twentieth century, began to flesh out the rather unemotional and detached forms those "in the news" had hitherto assumed. Once allowed to speak, of course, such voices were impossible to silence. They pushed ajar the door to the "private" world that had been beyond the interest or indeed the imagination of journalists and newspaper proprietors for most of the nineteenth century. More than that, these intimate worlds were responsible for broadening the audience appeal of newspapers when, for the first time, they were subject to real competition from an emerging broadcast media. Yet despite this it would still take most of the twentieth century for this private world to metamorphose into the all-pervasive "celebrity culture" reported obsessively in the media today.

Everyone Is Entitled To My Opinion[3]

It was inevitable that serious readers and cultural critics alike disliked this "new" journalism for it was yet another assault on their hallowed traditions. Already the increased use of pictures and the arrival of display advertising were transforming the pages of newspapers like the *Daily Mirror* in Britain and the *New York World*. Together with the new human interest element, they began to squeeze available space and the loser in this "space war" was political and economic affairs, the traditional male-orientated subjects that had been the bedrock of professional journalism. As noted by Kevin Williams, "A content analysis found that 'the *Daily Mail* and the *Daily Mirror*...reduced coverage of political, social and economic affairs during the inter-war period. Most strikingly the *Daily Mirror* halved its public affairs coverage.'"[4] Newspapers like *The Times*, however, showed no comparable change.

This development, slow though it was in the early years of the twentieth century, also reflected, if only for economic reasons, the growing awareness of a need to extend audience reach to people whose reading skills, available time, and attention span would have been challenged by a verbatim court report of some 33,000 words in the manner of *The Times* of London. It was perhaps inevitable, therefore, that journalism began to be seen as a reflection of class rather than purely social or cultural interests. The focus on the interview can be seen as part of this class "struggle." It resulted in a broadening of the news-gathering process, both vertically as it gradually drew in all classes and social groupings as worthy of study and horizontally as it democratized human experience – moving it beyond the traditional male boundaries of politics, the law, finance, war, and empire.

The inevitable corollary of exposure was fame or notoriety and once the interview began to explore emotions and opinions – with hindsight another inevitability – certain types of interviewee began to achieve what would now be described as celebrity status. One obvious example was that of Charles Lindbergh, the pioneering aviator whose baby, Charles, Jr., was kidnapped and murdered in 1932 in what the newspapers described as "the crime of the century." Such was the media attention on Lindbergh that he and his family eventually moved to Europe in 1935. Predictably over time this sort of media attention led to a backlash in which celebrities attempted to reassert some control, if not on the amount of media coverage, at least on the way their image was projected and exploited by the media. How does this exploitation work? Is it a simple two-way transaction of the "I'll scratch your back if you'll scratch mine" variety? Or are there other more sinister undercurrents at work that color the resultant story in ways unknown to the audience?

Celebrities are not numerous but as an overexposed minority they benefit from privileged access, via the media, to the public sphere. Thus when a "star" becomes associated with specific projects or roles, the media becomes complicit in the exploitation of the commercial potential. This complicity between celebrity news and monetary goals dates back to the very early days of the Hollywood studios and their star system. A film was easier to sell if it was connected with a celebrity and a celebrity was easier to sell if he or she had a film "vehicle" behind which any private life "abnormalities" could be concealed. Rock Hudson, for example, was huge box office in the 1950s and 1960s, being voted "Star of the Year" and "Favorite Leading Man." He was constantly photographed and filmed in the company of beautiful women. Hudson, however, was a homosexual at a time when this was considered box-office poison. He even got married to stave off questions about his sexuality. The personality of the star could thus be exploited in a carefully controlled commercial environment.

Yet another aspect of that exploitation was the use by the media of ghost writers, a mild form of deception that reflected the low opinion of many journalists who had little time for celebrities as a breed. According to Hamilton Fyfe, former editor of Britain's *Morning Advertiser, Daily Mirror*, and *Daily Herald*, writing in 1949: "Rarely had the celebrities, whose views the deluded public thought it was reading, anything whatever of their own to say. Most of them signed anything that was put before them. They were glad of the money and they liked the publicity."[5]

This all amounts to the much-lauded capitalist virtue of creating added value, what sociologist Edgar Morin calls the "royal jelly" of celebrity.[6] Like bees, celebrities produce a royal jelly, but in this case it's clothes, accessories, and other lifestyle products that ordinary people can also acquire, so long as they are prepared to pay for them. The star system thus acquires symbolic importance as an expression of the possibilities for individual achievement under capitalism. Media-generated promotional events such as award ceremonies, television chat show appearances, and marketing offers of the "You too can ... " variety all offer a hermetically sealed star "product" with a ready-prepared private life exploited in "through the keyhole" features and interviews. These have become so ubiquitous that now whole magazines are devoted to celebrity lifestyle coverage.

The dark underbelly of this trade, however, is that it often masks the machinations of the celebrity or perhaps more significantly the celebrity's agent. Before the interview, a "contract" will be produced that lists the subjects the celebrity won't talk about. It can be as specific as listing particular events or individuals who are off-limits. After the interview, this contract will authorize the celebrity and his or her agent to have sight of the finished article and make any alterations, deletions, or other adjustments they may require prior to publication. The sanctions for failure to abide by these requirements can be refusal to allow publication and/or blacklisting of the magazine or newspaper as far as future stories about that particular celebrity are concerned. If we accept that the resultant coverage "is a powerful example of how the media portrayal and *construction* of celebrities shape the way in which audiences understand and make sense of the social world,"[7] then any misrepresentation or falsification in that portrayal is just as serious as it would be in more traditional news categories.

These new themes, which produced the personal as the litmus test of popular culture, have been interpreted more positively by Edgar Morin as an overflowing of the novelistic genre into mass culture with its themes of love, adventure, and private life, for instance.[8] Mass culture has a historical tendency to center on the search for individual happiness and its failures, so tabloid narratives, in particular, began to follow individuals (frequently celebrities) with human interest stories that plotted alternate peaks and troughs of happiness and sorrow or presented uplifting parables of triumph over tragedy. In this interpretation, "fame is part of a Western ideal of personal freedom. Today's celebrity culture is based on rewarding self-improvement and efforts towards self-development, rather than being a consequence of hierarchical privilege and elite networks."[9] It was only a matter of time, therefore, before audiences desired their own measure of "fame" as an expression of "personal freedom."

FactFile
Leo Lowenthal and Celebrity "Idols"

Leo Lowenthal was born in Frankfurt in 1900. His childhood was overshadowed by the turbulent years of the Weimar Republic and in 1926 he joined the newly formed Frankfurt Institute for Social Research. He became its leading expert on the sociology of literature and mass culture. Along with many of his Institute colleagues including Theodor Adorno, Max Horkheimer, and Herbert Marcuse, he left Germany after Hitler's assumption of power and settled in the United States.

Lowenthal worked for many years at the University of California, Berkeley. He wrote extensively and his publications were collected in the 1980s and published in both German and English. One of the most notable is *Literature, Popular Culture, and Society*[10] which contains a content analysis of "biographies of popular heroes found in two American magazines: *Collier's* and the *Saturday Evening Post*."[11] He classified these biographies depending on whether they dealt with political life, business and the professions, or entertainment. He found that the number of biographies increased over time but that those devoted to political life and business decreased while those devoted to entertainment increased. As noted by Levin et al., "During the opening decades of the twentieth century ... Americans heaped adulation on "idols of production" (Lowenthal, 1961). These were the industrial tycoons who served as role models for the countless citizens who accepted a secularized version of the Protestant Ethic and the American Dream."[12]

By mid-century, however, this "adulation" was being directed toward what Lowenthal called "idols of consumption" – "the entertainers and sports figures who filled the leisure hours with music, drama, and athletic prowess ... This transition coincided with the development of an entire industry dedicated to creating and selling celebrity."[13] The biographies of such entertainers also changed from "those about serious artists and writers to popular entertainers of one sort or another."[14] So it was the lifestyle choices and spending patterns of these "idols of consumption" that interested readers rather than what their "idols" had achieved.

Implied in any development of Lowenthal's analysis is the evident fact that fame today does not necessarily require any particular talent or aptitude. In fact, one of the most important personal attributes required for celebrity has always been a measure of persistence. The difference today is that this persistence can be allied to no particular ability whatsoever. Thus persistence as a "skill" becomes both a means to an end and the end in itself. Lowenthal died in Berkeley, California aged 92.

Participatory Culture and "We Media"

In the past, newspapers have always exerted a formative influence on the modes and extent of public participation in cultural communication. Radio and later television were in competition with newspapers, but the press often used its pages to denigrate the new broadcast media, both for its news output and for its more general programming. One of the earliest examples was the struggle waged by the black-owned *Pittsburgh Courier* to engender a new respect for African Americans by the community at large and a new self-respect by the African-American community itself. In 1931 the newspaper launched a campaign against the *Amos 'n' Andy* radio show. The show was a hugely popular situation comedy set in the African-American community that ran nightly on Chicago's WMAQ station from 1928 until 1943. Black community leaders, however, felt the show was "crude" and "moronic" and, moreover, the two leading characters were both played by white men! Church ministers were urged to deliver "self-respect" sermons and nearly 750,000 people signed a petition to demand that the show be ended, all however to no avail.[15]

Yet radio held, and still holds, enormous potential for community participation. The talk shows is a good example. The first "call-in" shows in the US date back to 1945. Barry Gray worked for New York's WMCA radio and one day, so the story goes, became bored with playing music and put the phone receiver up to the microphone to talk to bandleader Woody Herman.

This was soon followed by listener call-ins and Gray became known as the "hot mama of Talk Radio." The fact that regular people were invited to have their say represented an important new form of audience participation, and one that was all the more necessary in order to broaden what were perceived as rather restrictive news values. Radio phone-ins suffered from the "screening" decisions of the editorial team about who should be heard and who should not, just as copy tasters functioned in the press, and broadcast journalists applied similar criteria as their print colleagues. However, it was often the live radio or television program that broke through taboos that newspapers still fought shy of. In 1965, for example, British theater critic Kenneth Tynan used the f-word on a late-night television show, *BBC-3*, for the first time. According to a *Daily Express* columnist, "it was … 'the bloodiest outrage' he had 'ever known'."[16]

In the US in the 1970s and 1980s the popularity of high fidelity FM broadcasts with their increased clarity over typical AM music formats meant that many listeners migrated to FM and talk radio began to catch on, especially in the larger cities. By this time television talk shows and news programs with viewer emphasis were also becoming fashionable. Two of the most popular titles on local television news during the 1990s were *On Your Side* and *Working 4 You*.[17] Of course, claiming to be on the side of viewers is not the same as allowing them to participate or air their opinions and television has always been more wary than radio of allowing a voice to an "unreconstructed" public. The most famous exception to this is probably the Oprah Winfrey Show that began in 1986, producing some of the most powerful human interest journalism seen anywhere on television.

In Britain, BBC Radio Four's "first example of the [phone-in] genre, *It's Your Line*" aired in 1970.[18] The first studio guest, labor union leader Hugh Scanlon, attracted over 8,000 calls. The *Daily Telegraph* commented on its shock at "the undisguised prejudice of the callers."[19] And the overall consensus seemed to be how wide was the gap between the "communicators and the public at large."[20] Other programs followed such as *Voice of the People* (1974) but this time the BBC's own Head of Radio Drama, Martin Esslin, was the most vociferous critic. He described listeners' views on Rhodesia (Zimbabwe) as "no more than 'a collection of untested and untestable old wives' tales'."[21]

The very tangible way in which radio phone-ins offered direct audience participation, as well as the shocks they often provided, can be contrasted with the way that most newspaper editors chose to work with assumptions rather than concrete information about their readers. Memoirs of veteran journalists abound with examples of how such assumptions led to the narrowing of news agendas. Walter Cowan, reporter and editor in New Orleans from 1936 to 1979, recalls:

> What happened in the black community wasn't considered news. So the city editor had to know where the blacks lived. Say there was a police calling the 2200 block of Louisiana Avenue. If the city editor knew the street well enough, and he knew Louisiana Avenue was all black ... he would know not to bother sending somebody out on the story.[22]

There have been a number of studies addressing this theme over the years. Most have identified the reliance of newspaper editors in particular on instinctive rather than empirical forms of decision making. One example was the frequent reliance for audience strategy on the concept of "near audience" (colleagues and family) rather than feedback from an "unknown" mass audience whose views may have been represented by market surveys, unsolicited letters, and phone calls but who were nonetheless considered untrustworthy.[23] Unscientific assumptions about audience appeal were guided by a belief that journalists' interests and instincts mirrored those of the person in the street. But as noted above this was something of an illusion, especially for the BBC which discovered with some alarm how wide was the gap between the "communicators and the public at large."

In America, press news values were imprinted on the new technologies of radio and television largely because the news agencies, which had deployed cable technology so successfully, were still a part of the press's sphere of influence. In the early days of radio its news supply was deliberately restricted by the agency and wire services because they wanted to maintain control of bulletin information. In Britain radio news bulletins were allowed only after 7p.m.,[24] and the "Licence of the BBC, which was issued on 18 January 1923, included a clause stating that the BBC should not broadcast any news or information except that obtained and paid for from the news agencies."[25] Finally, the news agencies agreed to supply the BBC with a daily summary of world news between the hours of 6p.m. and 11p.m. The consequential rarity value of radio news prompted the BBC in particular to believe that its appeal was an upmarket one, as restraint meant that the worst excesses of the print tabloids were avoided.

Despite this, however, the BBC often fretted over commercial competition. When the independent "Talk Radio" started broadcasting in February 1995, there was concern that it would undermine Radio Four. But quickly it became "apparent that this newcomer was sufficiently downmarket and under-resourced to offer no real threat."[26] It is not only new forms of media but also rivalry *within* media that often helps to clarify thinking about audience: each produces a competitive environment – which can compel a repositioning of production values, producer decisions, and audience imperatives.

Getting the Audience's Measure

As already suggested, any examination of news media will conclude that audience has moved center stage. Early attempts to define it were necessarily vague. But in the last hundred years our understanding of audience has moved from a simple numbers game to a highly sophisticated analysis based on audited figures from independent organizations like the Audit Bureau of Circulations (ABC) for newspapers and magazines in the UK and US, Radio Joint Audience Research Limited (RAJAR) for UK radio, Broadcasters' Audience Research Board (BARB) for UK television, and Nielsen Ratings, for US radio and television.

Newspaper circulation figures are further broken down for each element of the paper – magazine section, travel section, and so forth, and also into socioeconomic, age, and gender profiles. There is even a figure for Female Main Shoppers that identifies the number of women readers who do a family shop each week. Newspapers also advertise the potency of their pages with regular "puffs" – "*Guardian* readers spent over £423.5 million on furniture in the last 12 months" – appeared in the color *Weekend* section of the Saturday edition under a group of display ads for furniture.[27] For newspapers, however, this is not just a matter of circulation and readership. Although it is accepted that readers are primarily there to be sold to advertisers, a modern newspaper now actually sells its readership twice over. First, it uses circulation figures to lure advertisers – the higher the circulation the higher the advertising rates. But second, it is also busy compiling a database of readers from subscription sales, responses to special offers, and readers' letters – so that it can then market that information database to any organization prepared to pay for it.

To complicate matters still further, there is a continuing argument over what is more important – circulation or readership. In Britain, the National Readership Survey (NRS) carries out regular interviews with people chosen at random to compile its readership figures for newspapers and magazines, which it makes clear are only estimates.[28] The circulation lobby, on the other hand, suggests that readership figures are affected by differing sample sizes and the demographics of both interviewers and interviewees and are thus unreliable. Which is likely to be more accurate? Which should advertisers assume is the correct figure when making decisions about which newspaper to advertise in?

FactFile
Measuring the Audience

Audit Bureau of Circulations – ABC

The practice of inflating circulations was common at the turn of the twentieth century as a means of maximizing advertising income. In a bid to end such practices, a number of advertisers, advertising agencies, and responsible publishers in the US banded together and formed an independent agency to collect and verify circulation data of participating newspapers and magazines. Thus the Audit Bureau of Circulations was formed in 1914. In Britain a similar organization was formed in 1931.

Today there is an international federation of ABCs based in Stockholm, Sweden – all are nonprofit-making associations funded by dues and service fees from advertisers, media organizations, and other subscribers. ABCe was established in 1996 as the "new media" arm of ABC. It verifies and reports on media performance, providing traffic and related data across a broad range of digital platforms.[29]

National Readership Survey – NRS

The NRS provides estimates of the readership of Britain's major newspapers and consumer magazines, showing the size and nature of the audiences they achieve in terms of sex, age, regionality, and many other demographic and lifestyle characteristics. To capture trends in readership, the NRS interviews a large sample of 36,000 adults (aged 15+) each year on a continuous basis.

Interviews are conducted face-to-face in the homes of respondents. The survey covers some 300 newspapers, newspaper supplements, and magazines. Its research methods are jointly agreed by publishers, advertising agencies, and advertisers.[30]

Radio Joint Audience Research Limited – RAJAR

RAJAR was established in 1992 to operate a single audience measurement system for the radio industry in the UK. It is jointly owned by the BBC and RadioCentre, commercial radio's trade body. The methodology is based on a paper diary, which is filled in on a quarter-hour basis for each week by a representative sample of listeners. In a single year, around 130,000 people complete a RAJAR diary. There are currently approximately 320 individual stations on the survey and results are published every quarter.[31]

Broadcasters' Audience Research Board – BARB

BARB is the organization responsible for providing the official measurement of UK television audiences. It commissions specialist companies to provide the television audience measurement service on its behalf – RSMB, Ipsos MORI, AGB Nielsen Media Research, and TNS. Its estimates are obtained from a reporting panel of 5,100 television-owning private residential households to represent the viewing behavior of the 25 million plus TV households within the UK. On average each panel member represents about 5,000 of the UK population. The service covers viewing within private households only.[32]

Nielsen Media Research – NMR

In May 1938, *Time* Magazine printed the following story:

> A 4 in. × 5½ in. box designed and colored to suit the housewife's fancy, was installed last week inside the radio of an average-income family in Chicago. Installer was A. C. Nielsen Co's Executive Vice-President Hugo L. Rusch, who is out to start a new and much better listener survey service for advertisers. Two hundred similar "Audimeters" will soon be placed in private homes and the Nielsen firm, Chicago marketing research organization, expects by the end of the year to have more than 5,000 spotted in radios throughout the country.[33]

> This was the beginning of radio ratings in the US and in 1950 Nielsen moved in to television. The ratings were gathered using both a viewer's "diary," where a target audience self-recorded its viewing habits, and Set Meters connected to televisions which gathered viewing habits in selected homes. The meter recorded what programs the television was tuned to and for how long. It couldn't detect whether anyone was actually in the room, however. In 2005, Nielsen began measuring the usage of digital video recordings such as TiVo.[34]

It is obvious, therefore, why broadcast media in particular are obsessed with quantifiable data on audience. In both Britain and America television followed the pattern already established with radio: a public service ethos in Britain and a commercial ethos in the US. Public service broadcasting uses audience figures to justify a license fee or government subventions. Commercial broadcasters use such figures to justify their advertising rates to commercial sponsors, either for in-program commercial breaks or for actual program sponsorship. As a commercial broadcaster's main source of income was from advertising it wasn't long before the needs of advertisers became paramount and the acid test for television was program popularity. This of course could best be measured by ratings, which became all-powerful both locally and nationally. Indeed, complaints about the reliability of ratings (which could make or break careers within the business) rose to such a level in the early 1960s that Congress decided to investigate.[35]

Ratings systems specifically designed to measure radio listeners were pioneered in the US by Arthur Nielsen with his radio Audimeter, television diaries, and Set Meters (see FactFile above), from the outset clearly intended as a service for advertisers. The danger with such systems – the perception that broadcasters were responding to the ratings battle by what was to become known as the "dumbing down" of content – soon became apparent, however.

Perhaps the most obvious example of the "trivializing" of broadcast content was the growing popularity of the soap opera. "The term 'soap opera' was coined by the American press in the 1930s to denote the extraordinarily popular genre of serialized domestic radio dramas, which, by 1940, represented some 90% of all commercially-sponsored daytime broadcast hours."[36] These programs were sponsored by the makers of household cleaning products, hence the "soap" epithet. But the ideological construction of a soap opera with its mimicry of everyday life facilitated by daily or weekly episodes has meant that right from its beginnings the term has never been value-neutral. The phrase itself "signals an aesthetic and cultural incongruity: the events of everyday life elevated to the subject matter of an operatic form. To call a film, novel, or play a 'soap opera' is to label it as culturally and aesthetically inconsequential and unworthy."[37]

Broadcasters, however, tended to make pessimistic assumptions about what audiences might be interested in and also about their attention span for more in-depth programming and, from a journalistic perspective, their appetite for documentary and investigative stories. As one of the upholders of a public journalism model, Edward J. Murrow responded to this perceived "dumbing down" by asserting in a speech in 1958: "I am entirely persuaded that the American public is more reasonable, restrained and more mature than most of our industry's program planners believe. Their fear of controversy is not warranted by the evidence."[38] Yet respect for viewers did not necessarily mean that the audience–media relationship was one of equivalence. According to ex-CNN editor David Mindich: "The age that nurtured [Walter] Cronkite, [David] Brinkley and [Ben] Bradlee represents a fossilized moment of innocence, when journalists told us the way it was, and we, more often than not, believed them."[39]

But certainly, since World War II, as broadcasters' concern for ratings tended to override worries about quality or "the way it was," so media analysts and scholars developed a renewed anxiety about content. As early as 1958 the influential Japanese writer Soichi Ohya produced a series of essays on the effects of television in which he argued that the medium was the new means of "creating 100 million idiots," the implication being that by reading less and watching more, people were becoming infantilized. And indeed, most concern over content was invariably expressed about children's viewing habits. By 1975, Japanese children aged 10 to 15 years were watching an average of four hours television a day.[40] In the US, those aged 2–11 now watch three-and-a-half hours each day,[41] and these figures are mirrored in UK statistics.[42]

According to Judith Graham, a human development specialist, "Studies show that too much television viewing [by children] can have adverse affects, such as more violent and aggressive behavior, poor school performance, obesity, early sexual activity, and drug or alcohol use."[43] Graham does not specifically reference news programs, no doubt because they are little watched by children. But she goes on to say that "Children aren't engaging in the activities they need to help them develop their bodies and brains when they watch television."[44] For populations at large however, at least according to US statistics, "the overall percentage of Americans reading the papers, watching TV news or listening to news on the radio has changed very little in recent years ... the number of news outlets regularly used by the public appears to be shrinking, more for television news than radio and newspapers."[45] Television news is a declining interest for all age groups and statistics from the Pew Research Center confirm that this decline in viewing numbers goes as far back as 1993, where 60 percent of people in the US said they got their news from TV. By 1996 that figure had already fallen to only 42 percent.[46]

Today this trend is reflected in figures that suggest "growing numbers of Americans are losing the news habit. Fewer people say they enjoy following the news, and ... pay attention to national news only when something important is happening. And more Americans than ever say they watch the news with a remote control in hand, ready to dispatch uninteresting stories."[47] In Britain too while watching television is still the most popular leisure activity for eight out of ten men and women,[48] the consumption of news programming by that crucial demographic, the young, has fallen to only 9 percent in the 16 to 44 age group. In comparison, around 14 percent of people aged 65 and over watched TV news.[49]

Yet if one side of the coin has always been a perhaps understandable broadcaster obsession with measuring audiences, the flip side can legitimately be considered television's ability to initiate and promote debate on the effects of TV output on viewers. Edward J. Murrow in particular produced a principled journalism that had a social purpose frequently lacking in today's television reportage. In his 1960 documentary *Harvest of Shame*, for example, Murrow acted as an advocate for migrant workers as a valuable sector of the unified national audience. The film ends with these words: "The migrants have no lobby. Only an enlightened, aroused and perhaps angered public opinion can do anything about the migrants. The people you have seen have the strength to harvest your fruit and vegetables. They do not have the strength to influence legislation. Maybe we do. Good night, and good luck."[50] Yet even Murrow, despite his reputation, was "compelled to augment the traditional (and often distinguished) journalism he did for CBS with forays into what would prove to be perhaps television's most powerful genre of programming, the promotion and exploitation of celebrity personalities."[51] In his *Person to Person* program (1953–9) Murrow pioneered the TV interview of a celebrity. It went out live and Murrow's relaxed technique and the way many of the celebrities used the show to promote their latest book, film, or music product, have had a lasting effect on celebrity journalism. Similarly, social and political documentaries like Murrow's can still be important because of television journalism's potential to influence policy making.

For some time scholarship, in support of such a position, has suggested that in the case of the coverage of terrorism and of missing children the style of television treatment actually becomes part of the social policy process, to the extent that the public agenda can often be predicted from television coverage.[52] Similarly, it has been implied that after the World Trade Center attacks of September 11, 2001 civil rights policies – the Homeland Security Act and the Patriot Act, for example – were affected not only by the event itself but also by the way it was constantly replayed on television screens in homes across America and around the world.

In some respects, the wider issues of how the medium actually constructs meaning in the "global village" and the inherent dangers of cultural aberrance were addressed by Marshall McLuhan in *Understanding Media* (1964). In his chapter on television he offers the "alleged remark of the Nigerian who, after seeing a TV Western, said delightedly, 'I did not realize you valued human life so little in the West.'"[53] The distinguished Italian semiologist, Umberto Eco, goes so far as to suggest that this "aberrant decoding ... is the rule in the mass media" because "people bring different codes to a given message and thus interpret it in different ways."[54] Eco in his analysis also suggests there is a significant difference not only between people of different countries or cultures in the way they understand media "messages" but also between the producers and the consumers of such messages who actually share the same culture. Thus this shared cultural specificity is still no guarantee against aberrant decoding of a media "message."

Résumé
Marshall McLuhan

Herbert Marshall McLuhan was born in Edmonton, Alberta in 1911. He gained an MA in English from the University of Manitoba and his doctorate from Britain's Cambridge University in 1942. He began teaching communication and culture at the University of Toronto in 1952. With a few breaks he remained at the University until his death.

He is best known for his trio of ground-breaking books, *The Mechanical Bride* (1951), that examined the effects of advertising on society; *The Gutenberg Galaxy* (1962), an analysis of the mass media in European culture, where he coined the phrase the "global village"; and *Understanding Media* (1964), in which he speculated on the relationship between local cultures and global values. He suffered a stroke in 1979 and died in Toronto in 1980.

So cultural specificity, while it maximizes the likelihood of shared understanding, cannot guarantee it and media effects research tends to bear this out. In Britain in the 1980s, for instance, it was found that while current affairs programming contributed to pluralism, fictional programming encouraged "mainstreaming" – audience identification with dominant cultural and social norms that tended towards cultural homogenization – as did heavy television viewing, which was also linked to political centrism.

Earlier research had already supported the hypothesis of cultural homogenization in relation to American society.[55]

However, these effects were found to vary considerably according to the stage of a society's media development and the broader context in which such development occurred, such as a country's physical geography. In developed countries economic productivity resulted in media growth and increased press freedom, whereas in less developed countries the media "tend to be used to facilitate the functioning of the economy and to perpetuate the power of the rulers."[56] The worldwide reach of the major news agencies is an example of the hegemony of Western media as seen through the eyes of the developing world. This domination by America and Europe, whose agencies transmit most of the news between countries within the Third World, is still seen by some leaders and intellectuals as a neocolonialist affront to their national or cultural pride and sovereignty.[57]

Television's growth as a worldwide medium naturally raises questions not only about audience effects but also more specifically about how programming decisions can affect the way media and even countries themselves are perceived by others. For example, is the pursuit of "cultural homogenization" a good thing? Can it be encouraged or discouraged by the kinds of output broadcast media produce? Does such homogenization play well in countries like Great Britain where much store is set by multiculturalism? Is the French ideal of an all-embracing French citizenship a better model for the media to reflect? All such questions are currently part of journalism's *obiter dicta* and as such loom large in a news discourse that now embraces such issues as technological nationalism, technological democracy, and above all the role of technological determinism.[58]

All Wired Up – From Cable To Wi-Fi

Cable television systems and the satellite introduced a multichannel, narrowcasting capability to broadcast television for the first time. Both cable and satellite can operate separately, via fiber optics and wall-mounted dishes, but "it is their *combination* that is of immense significance."[59] Putting together a cable television system and a satellite broadcast system such as Sky TV or CNN "creates a new national or international 'network' instantaneously."[60] Such satellite-delivered cable channels first became a reality in the 1970s, when there was also limited experimentation with interactive television. Before the internet, cable and satellite were dubbed the "new media"[61] and they provided a specific form of communication that empowered sectional interests by transforming "inchoate groups into national but specialized audiences organized around ethnic, occupational, class, religious, racial, and other affiliations and interests.... They served as intermediate mechanisms linking local and partial milieus to the wider national community."[62]

These "specialized audiences" were seen as part of the vanguard that would break the monopoly of the large monolithic audience that television hitherto had catered for. A more progressive future was envisaged with greater access for minorities alongside the greater business potential offered by multichannel platforms. There was even discussion about interactive systems capable of providing a diversity of local programming with information, social services, and news extending the inevitable entertainment provision. Yet, as with all new technologies, there was also the fear, especially among traditional broadcasters in Britain, that the new media's "'wall-to-wall *Dallas*' programming – a term for cheap American imports – would eventually erode the public service tradition in broadcasting and lead to 'lowest common denominator' type programming with no regard to quality, education or information."[63]

Such concerns have, if anything, now been exacerbated by the development of the world wide web and the internet. No other medium has blurred the lines between consumers and producers to the same extent as digital technology and also at the same time blurred the lines of responsibility for choice and quality of news content. Yet despite such anxieties, the internet in its first incarnation during the 1990s generated a new optimism that these technological developments would change the face of journalism. Interaction with the audience became a distinct possibility and the use of multimedia content seemed to offer new opportunities for storytelling.

Yet today the way that newspapers in particular use the interactive facilities of the internet to further their claims of accountability to their readerships may amount to nothing more than a reconfiguration of an older form of audience appeal. Indeed, a number of recent content analysis studies designed to quantify the extent of the audience-oriented "revolution" seem to confirm this. According to Thorsten Quandt in his report on mainstream media websites in the US and Europe: "The revolution did not happen. What unifies the websites analysed here is a similar formal structure, the lack of multimedia content, the missing options of direct interaction with the journalists, a fairly standardized repertoire of article types, missing source/author attributions, a general trend towards the coverage of national events, and the limited scope of the news."[64] But despite such pessimism, the scope for convergence of producers and consumers and the social implications of "we media" and "public journalism" are still to be fully assessed in the longer term. Research continues unabated, however, fueled by the potential of wikis, blogs, and the "semantic web" for audience engagement, involvement, and exploitation.

When the long view of reactions to communications technology is examined more closely however, as Hazel Dicken Garcia has pointed out, considerations about the social implications often come as afterthoughts.[65] It is likely that the full cultural and social repercussions of individuals living "virtually" rather than communicating face to face and collectively in specific localities have yet to be fully understood. However, one implication for journalism and its relationship with audiences is already exercising the minds of practitioners and theorists alike. According to Martin Conboy and John Steel:

> Current trends in newspaper digitalisation allow content to be tailored to the end user that enables them to manage content in ways that best reflect their own personal choices. "News" then becomes the picture of the world that we have some power in creating. This power to filter out content and information that the consumer might deem irrelevant and uninteresting enables the end user not only to have the ultimate power as a consumer – the power to define what it is that they read; it also enables individuals to bracket off information and content that is outside their sphere of interest. In short, the consumer has ultimate power over content."[66]

Clearly, more DIY choices do not necessarily mean that all consumers want to be journalists; therefore participation as amateur or "citizen" journalists is not necessarily an organic extension of, nor should it be confused with, consumer power.

Amateur Reporters and Amateur Standards

As new media increase the potential for freelance contributions to the public sphere, research may well demonstrate that the boundaries between audience and journalist are increasingly fluid, in the way they were before so-called "professionalism" was fully embraced. Historians may well have to revisit some of the assumptions about the "profession." For example, during the eighteenth century and the first half of the nineteenth century, most newspapers did not employ professional "foreign correspondents." Most of their unpaid "intelligence" or foreign news came from amateurs who were living in or visiting the country in question – in many respects the equivalent of today's bloggers. There is also evidence that a monstrous army of women, anonymously and without bylines, supplied regular copy, usually for a pittance, to feed the enormous growth in women's periodicals during the late 1830s and the 1840s in France.[67] Somebody had to supply the mountain of recipes, domestic tips, and knitting patterns, and official records about numbers of journalists only recorded full-time employees, not freelancers or part-timers, who were more likely to be female than male.

Margaret Beetham suggests that up to two-thirds of these contributors to female periodicals were women but "the practice of anonymity meant that readers' names never appeared. They were not paid and even had to cover the cost of postage."[68] On top of this, "the practice of anonymity made it as difficult for contemporaries as it is for modern scholars to discover the gender of writers."[69] In other words, society's standard informational categorization may well have contributed to the work of women in early journalism becoming invisible. And if traditional definitions of journalism are too narrow to cater for all the varieties of work and worker, this inevitably influences our empirical, historical assessment of female journalists on the one hand and the structure and composition of the "profession" on the other.

Journalists today are fast becoming used to short-term contracts and freelance working in a world where editorial staffs are being cut, whether in print or broadcast. "The Internet's power lies in its immediacy, its reach and its ability to give voice to those with no access to mainstream channels of dissemination. Received wisdom says that those who work within its weaknesses and strengths will find themselves better journalists."[70] The logic of this is that "professional" journalists have once again to accept working with amateurs in the way that eighteenth- and nineteenth-century newspaper editors accepted foreign stories filed by amateur reporters who were merely members of the public traveling overseas.

To view an audience as either passive or active has always been a rather simplistic notion (even if such a notion ever existed). Similarly, to describe it as homogeneous or to try to understand each individual member of it is patently absurd. But it is probably reasonable to say that any examination of news media today will conclude that audience has moved center stage. And without doubt this movement has accelerated because of the computer, the internet, the interactive information sharing of Web 2.0 and, in the future, the integrated semantic-led information mining enabled by Web 3.0. Although online journalism is more advanced in the United States where the internet originated, even in its likely Web 3.0 incarnation it should not be seen as some sort of panacea for audience participation.

In general, survey data confirm that the emergence of participatory forms of journalism is influenced by a number of external factors such as technology, economics, and the larger sociocultural frameworks in which people live and work. The Gota survey, a Swedish mail questionnaire project, found that from an audience point of view there was not much interest in creating content on internet news sites. When it came to blogs, those people who wrote them and commented on them saw the activity as recreational rather than as a contribution towards participatory citizenship. The overall conclusion seems to be that "the younger and the higher educated, the more likely you [are to] write. Once more, participation in this sense seems to be decided by the fact that you are an online person. This seems to be far more important than, for example, an interest in society or politics."[71] It appears that only small "active elites" are interested in creating content of their own, "for the masses, interest is above all in giving feedback to content created by someone else."[72] Similarly, in his study of mainstream media's online content in five different countries, Thorsten Quandt speculates: "The websites do not make use of www's potential for new types of writing, producing and interacting – but maybe that's not an issue for the users. It is highly likely that they [users] just want their usual news – fast and reliably."[73]

This would imply that it is the technological or speed aspects of digital media that comprise its greatest appeal for the average user. Whether this is the case or not, it is undeniable that internet news has not only arrived but is attracting key segments of national audiences. But in the process, according to John Nichols and Robert McChesney, "Media today treats Americans as consumers, not citizens. And the theory in the boardrooms is that consumers are attracted by entertainment, rather than information."[74] Media executives, editors, and proprietors therefore encourage audience participation as a means of promoting their products. In this model the democratization of audience is an economic as much as a political phenomenon. This is not to imply that questions about representational inclusion and exclusion are no longer relevant, but it does mean that the boundaries between the audience as consumers (previously relegated to advertisements only) and the audience as citizens (previously the territory of editorial and leader pages) have become increasingly blurred.

What can be said with some authority is that where once audience figures were simply a vindication of success or a reflection of failure, audience and advertising are now inextricably bound together as *the* commercial imperatives that drive news organizations. In attempting to trace the historical roots of this nexus, it is apparent that audiences have invariably been manipulated, flattered, ignored, and analyzed at different times in the long history of journalism but nothing can detract from the underlying fact that audiences are essential. So successful journalism, whether niche or mainstream, understands its audience before all else. Successful journalists appreciate that understanding audience is as vital to their survival as it is to the survival of their media organization.

Notes

1 "The Man of the Moment," *Daily Mail*, February 22, 1896, p. 1. Alfred Harmsworth published a "dummy" newspaper for almost three months before the launch proper of the *Daily Mail* on May 4, 1896. The first dummy issue appeared on Monday February 17, 1896 and what is remarkable about these early issues is that they were nothing like the actual *Daily Mail* launched on May 4. According to Harmsworth biographer A. P. Ryan, these papers "included all manner of grotesque features which were designed to delude rivals into whose hands Harmsworth made certain they fell" – *Lord Northcliffe* (London: Collins, 1953) p. 74. The irony is that this dummy paper had a more modern look and feel to it than the official newspaper that proved so successful.
2 "Dr. Jim," *Daily Mail*, February 26, 1896, p. 4.
3 Attributed to Madonna.
4 Kevin Williams, *Read All About It! A History of the British Newspaper* (London: Routledge, 2010), p. 159.
5 Hamilton Fyfe, *Sixty Years of Fleet Street* (London: W. H. Allen, 1949), p. 221.
6 Edgar Morin, *Les Stars* (Paris: Seuil, 1972), p. 54.
7 Jessica Evans, "Celebrity, Media and History," in Jessica Evans and David Hesmondhaigh (eds), *Understanding Media: Inside Celebrity* (Maidenhead, UK: Open University Press, 2005), pp. 11–56 (p. 14).
8 Morin, *Les Stars*, p. 158; Edgar Morin, *L'esprit du temps* 1. Névrose (Paris: Grasset, 1957), p. 256.
9 Evans, "Celebrity, Media and History," p. 15.
10 Leo Lowenthal, *Literature, Popular Culture, and Society* (New York: Prentice Hall, 1961).
11 Arthur Asa Berger, *Media Analysis Techniques* (London: Sage, 1991), p. 92.
12 Jack Levin, James Alan Fox, and Jason Mazaik, "Blurring Fame and Infamy: A Content Analysis of Cover-Story Trends in People Magazine," *Internet Journal of Criminology* (2005). Available online at http://www.internetjounalof criminology.com/Levin,%20Fox%20&%20Mazaik%20-%20Blurring%20 Fame%20&%20Infamy.pdf, accessed on November 15, 2009.

13   Ibid.

14   Berger, *Media Analysis Techniques*, p. 92.

15   Pamela Newkirk, *Within the Veil: Black Journalists, White Media* (New York: New York University Press, 2000), p. 50.

16   David Hendy, *Life on Air: A History of Radio Four* (Oxford: Oxford University Press, 2007), p. 101.

17   Bill Kovach and Tom Rosenstiel, *The Elements of Journalism* (London: Guardian Atlantic Books, 2001), p. 54.

18   Hendy, *Life on Air*, p. 70

19   Ibid., p. 71.

20   Ibid.

21   Ibid., p. 72.

22   Quoted in Newkirk, *Within the Veil*, p. 51.

23   Herbert J. Gans, *Deciding What's News: A Study of CBS Evening News, NBC Nightly News, Newsweek, and Time* (New York: Vintage, 1980); Michael Jacobs, *The Politics of the Real World* (London: Earthscan, 1996).

24   Asa Briggs, *The History of Broadcasting in the United Kingdom*, vol. I, *The Birth of Broadcasting* (Oxford: Oxford University Press, 1961), p. 121

25   Ibid., p. 122

26   Hendy, *Life on Air*, p. 293.

27   Advertisement, *Guardian Weekend*, September 19, 2009, p. 94.

28   NRS, "Top Line Readership," *NRS Open Access*. Available online at http://www.nrs.co.uk/, accessed on September 14, 2009.

29   Audit Bureau of Circulations. The American website can be accessed at http://www.abc.org.uk/. The UK website can be accessed at http://www.accessabc.com/.

30   National Readership Survey. Its website can be accessed at http://www.nrs.co.uk/lights/index.html.

31   Radio Joint Audience Research Limited. Its website can be accessed at http://www.rajar.co.uk/.

32   Broadcasters' Audience Research Board. Its website can be accessed at http://www.barb.co.uk/about/tvMeasurement?_s=4.

33   "Radio: Audimeter," *Time* Magazine, May 16, 1938. Available online at http://www.time.com/time/magazine/article/0,9171,759696,00.html.

34   Nielsen Media Research. Its website can be accessed at http://en-us.nielsen.com/measurement.

35   Sydney W. Head, *Broadcasting in America: A Survey of Television, Radio and New Technologies*, 4th edn (Boston: Houghton Mifflin, 1982), p. 382.

36   Robert C. Allen, "Soap Opera," *The Museum of Broadcasting Communications*. Available online at http://www.museum.tv/eotvsection.php?entrycode=soap opera, para 1, accessed on November 25, 2009.

37   Ibid., para. 4.

38   Edward Murrow's speech is available online at http://www.rtdna.org/pages/media_items/edward-r.-murrow-speech998.php, accessed on September 3, 2010.

39   David T. Z. Mindich, "That's the Way it Was," *Defining Moment in Journalism Special*, 2, 11(1997), 165–76 (p. 176).

40   Hidetoshi Kato, "Japan," in Anthony Smith (ed.), *Television: An International History* (Oxford: Oxford University Press, 1995), pp. 169–81. Quoted in Jane Chapman, *Comparative Media History* (Cambridge, UK: Polity, 2005), p. 232.

41   Shelly Freierman, "Hours By The Tube," *New York Times*, November 16, 2009. Available online at http://www.frankwbaker.com/mediause.htm, accessed on November 25, 2009.

42   "Television Viewing: By Gender and Age," *Office for National Statistics* (1998). Available online at http://www.statistics.gov.uk/STATBASE/Product.asp?vlnk= 3899&More=Y, accessed on November 24, 2009.

43   Judith Graham, "How Television Viewing Affects Children," *Family Issues Facts*, University of Maine Cooperative Extension. Available online at http://umaine. edu/publications/4100e/, accessed on September 3, 2010.

44   Ibid.

45   "Internet Sapping Broadcast News Audience," *The Pew Research Center for the People and the Press*, June 11, 2000. Available online at http://people-press.org/report/36/internet-sapping-broadcast-news-audience, accessed on November 25, 2009.

46   "TV News Viewership Declines," *The Pew Research Center for the People and the Press*, May 13, 1996. Available online at http://people-press.org/report/127/tv-news-viewership-declines, accessed on November 25, 2009.

47   Ibid.

48   "Lifestyles," *Office for National Statistics*, Taking Part: The National Survey of Culture, Leisure and Sport, Department for Culture, Media and Sport (2006–2007). Available online at http://www.statistics.gov.uk/cci/nugget. asp?id= 1659, accessed on November 23, 2009.

49   "Television Viewing: By Gender and Age," *Office for National Statistics* (1998). Available online at http://www.statistics.gov.uk/downloads/theme_social/st30v8.pdf, accessed on September 3, 2010.

50   Quoted in Al Tompkins, "Advocacy Journalism and the Role of Opinion in the Newsroom," *Communicator*, March 2008 (p. 18). Available online at http://www.rtdna.org/pages/media_items/murrow-special-an-effort-to-illuminate988.php, accessed on November 25, 2009.

51   Leonard Downie Jr. and Robert G. Kaiser, *The News About the News: American Journalism in Peril* (New York: Vintage, 2003), p. 129.

52   David P. Fan, Hans-Bernd Brosius, and Hans Mathias Kepplinger, "Predictions of the Public Agenda from Television Coverage," *Journal of Broadcasting and Electronic Media*, 38 (1994), 163–77; David L. Altheide, "The Impact of

Television Formats on Social Policy," *Journal of Electronic Media*, 35, 1 (1991), 3–21.

53   Marshall McLuhan, *Understanding Media: The Extension of Man* (London: Ark, 1964), p. 319.

54   Quoted in Berger, *Media Analysis Techniques*, p. 24.

55   Anthony Piepe, Peter Charlton, and Judy Morey, "Politics and Television Viewing in England: Hegemony or Pluralism?" *Journal of Communication*, 1, 40 (1990), 24–35; Russell W. Neuman, "Television and American Culture: The Mass Medium and the Pluralist Audience," *Public Opinion Quarterly*, 46 (1982), 471–87.

56   David H. Weaver, Judith M. Buddenbaum, and Jo Ellen Faire, "Press Freedom, Media and Development, 1950–1979: A Study of 134 Nations," *Journal of Communication*, 2, 35 (1985), 104–17.

57   John T. McNelly, "International News for Latin America," *Journal of Communication*, 29 (1979), 156–63.

58   Jane Chapman, *Comparative Media History: 1789 to the Present*, (Cambridge, UK: Polity Press, 2005), pp. 222–3, 232.

59   Ralph Negrine, *Politics and the Mass Media in Britain*, 2nd edn (London: Routledge, 1994), p. 185.

60   Ibid.

61   Ibid., p. 184.

62   James W. Carey, "The Internet and the End of the National Communication System: Uncertain Predictions of an Uncertain Future," *Journalism & Mass Communication Quarterly*, 1, 75, Spring 1998, 28–44 (p. 30).

63   Negrine, *Politics and the Mass Media in Britain*, p. 185.

64   Thorsten Quandt, "A Whole New Journalism: Stuck in the Past?" *Future of Journalism Conference*, unpublished paper, University of Wales, Cardiff, September 7–9, 2007.

65   Hazel Dicken-Garcia, "The Internet and Continuing Historical Discourse," *Journalism & Mass Communication Quarterly*, 1, 75 (1998), 19–27 (p. 24).

66   Martin Conboy and John Steel, "The Future of Newspapers: Historical Perspectives," *Future of Journalism Conference*, unpublished paper, University of Wales, Cardiff, September 7–9, 2007.

67   Jane Chapman, "A Business Trajectory: Assessing Female Influence and Representation in Europe's First Mass Circulation Daily Newspaper," in Angela Kershaw and Maggie Allison (eds), *Parcours de femmes – Twenty Years of Women in French* (Oxford: Peter Lang, forthcoming, 2011).

68   Margaret Beetham, *A Magazine of Her Own?: Domesticity and Desire in the Woman's Magazine, 1800–1914* (London: Routledge, 1996), p. 21.

69   Ibid., p. 20.

70   Elizabeth Weise, "That's the Way it Was," *Defining Moments in Journalism Special*, 2, 11 (1997), p. 160.

71 Annika Bergstrom, "Audience Participation in Publishing," *Future of Journalism Conference*, unpublished paper, University of Wales, Cardiff, September 7–9, 2007.

72 Ibid.

73 Quandt, "A Whole New Journalism."

74 John Nichols and Robert McChesney, *Tragedy and Farce: How the American Media Sell Wars, Spin Elections and Destroy Democracy* (New York: New Press, 2005), p. 7.

Part V

Conclusion: A Future History

We may become the makers of our fate when we have ceased to pose as its prophets.

(*Karl Popper*)

14

Paper Tigers?

In the preceding chapters we have attempted to identify historical precedents for many of the issues that concern journalists, journalism, and the media today. These precedents, however, as is invariably the case, often raise as many questions as they supply answers. So in this final chapter we examine briefly the current media landscape – the "state of play" – through the nexus of such historical precedents with the aim of trying to discover what part, if any, they still play in the genetic makeup of modern journalism. At the same time, "Where are we going?" and similar questions are probably best left to seers, sages, clairvoyants, and other pundits who make a living by being wrong!

In order to bring some clarity to what is inevitably a complex picture, we have identified four themes or directions that more than any others seem to define modern journalism. These four themes offer opportunities as well as threats but the extent to which they may be paper tigers is something posterity alone will decide:

- Personalization
- Globalization
- Localization
- Pauperization.

In the following sections, we have noted where these themes are discussed in previous chapters.

Jane Chapman and Nick Nuttall, *Journalism Today: A Themed History*
© 2011 Jane Chapman and Nick Nuttall. Published by Blackwell Publishing Ltd.

Up Close and Personal

In the week beginning November 26, 1703 more than eight thousand people were killed in Great Britain including "a fifth of the sailors in the British Navy." In the county of Kent alone more than 17,000 trees were toppled.[1] Wind and rain lashed the entire south of England and floods were reported almost everywhere. The Great Storm, as it became known, was the greatest tempest ever recorded in the British Isles. Daniel Defoe, more famous now for novels such as *Robinson Crusoe* and *Moll Flanders*, wrote a lengthy account of the event, entitled *The Storm*. It thus became the earliest weather event recorded as a news story to reach a national audience. Defoe reported how "the Bishop of Bath and Wells was killed along with his wife 'by the Fall of two Chimney Stacks, which fell on the Roof, and drove it in upon my Lord's Bed, forced it quite through the next Flower (floor) down into the Hall, and buried them both in the Rubbish.'"[2] Many journalists today would be hard-pressed to match the evocative and powerful prose of *The Storm*. Defoe's account is a master class in all the journalistic techniques we take for granted today – quotes for authenticity, verification and corroboration of sources, anecdotes to provide human interest, statistics to show the nature and extent of the event, eye-witness reportage by the journalist himself, and simple, clear writing displaying economy and precision.

Defoe's story is considered "a founding text for both journalism and the novel,"[3] and part of its appeal is surely the journalistic "temperament" which imbued it with a slickness and immediacy often lacking in the literature of the period. At the same time the journalist in Defoe was no doubt aware that the sheer scale of the event transcended the generally parochial stories that constituted most journalistic output of the period and any coverage would therefore potentially reach a much larger audience than hitherto (Defoe also had just left debtors' prison when he wrote it and had a young family to support). Together, these factors gave the story its wide appeal and ensured its longevity, which is why it is still in print and still talked about today. The other factor that marked out Defoe's writing was his use of anecdote that personalized the story by giving it a human dimension.

Defoe's writing was certainly prescient. But he could not possibly have foreseen the extent to which the anecdote would be transformed from bit-part player, hauled onto the stage when the action flagged, to protagonist around whom a whole story would be based. The following extract is from Dave Egger's *Zeitoun*, the story of another storm:

> In the car, approaching their school, Nademah turned up the volume on the radio. She'd caught something on the news about the coming storm. Kathy wasn't paying close attention, because three or four times a season, it seemed, there was some early alarmist talk about hurricanes heading straight for the city, and always their direction changed or the winds fizzled in Florida or over the Gulf. If a storm hit New Orleans at all, it would be greatly diminished, no more than a day of grey gusts and rain.
>
> This reporter was talking about the storm heading into the Gulf of Mexico as a Category 1. It was about 45 miles north-northwest of Key West and heading west. Kathy turned the radio off; she didn't want the kids to worry.
>
> "You think it'll hit us?" Nademah asked.
>
> Kathy didn't think much of it. Who ever worried about a Category 1 or 2? She told Nademah it was nothing, nothing at all, and she kissed the girls goodbye.[4]

Eggers's chosen form is literary journalism but it exemplifies the great determining trend in modern news and feature writing: telling a story through character. Here Eggers alludes to the approaching Hurricane Katrina through Kathy, the wife of the central character Abdulrahman Zeitoun. And the whole book is told through character and dialogue rather than just the traditional journalistic techniques of facts, statistics, accredited statements, and quotes. In the process it can be seen that the "humanity" inherent in every story is powerfully present in a way that is often lacking in traditional journalism.

So it should not be forgotten that despite all the talk of democratic deficits, digital technology, ethical anxieties, and how to engage an audience to maximize revenue, at its heart journalism is all about storytelling. That story's subject matter and the manner of its telling are different from Defoe's time but *The Storm* should remind us that this "different manner" is not new in itself – we still remember the Bishop of Bath and Wells crashing through the floors of his house to his death – it's just the scale and intensity that has changed. Today, for example, being unable to interview the bishop, journalists of the tabloid persuasion would more than likely "doorstep" his family and interview neighbors and colleagues about what he was like as a family man, priest, friend. Broadsheet editors would no doubt call for think pieces on his place in the church, arguments about the wrath of God, and issues of fate versus faith. For a moment or two, even in death, he would become something of a celebrity.

These issues of personalization have devolved around the celebrity on the one hand and the human interest story on the other. The Holy Grail of course is the story that combines both. Yet even within the world of celebrity the kind of famous person given news space has changed. Sociologist Leo Lowenthal in "The Triumph of Mass Idols" examined the way coverage of celebrity culture developed and changed between the two World Wars in the United States. He constructed a content analysis of two famous magazines of the period, the *Saturday Evening Post* and *Collier's* to chart the way the "idol" or celebrity had changed over time from an "idol of production" to an "idol of consumption." As noted by Lowenthal, "Only two decades ago people from the realm of entertainment played a very negligible role in the biographical material. They form now [1940], numerically, the first group ... The proportion of people from political life and from business and professions, both representing the 'serious side,' has declined from 74 to 45 percent of the total."[5] This "decline" continued through the second half of the twentieth century.

Chapter 13 examined the relationship between celebrity, journalist, and audience and includes a FactFile on Lowenthal, while Chapters 12 and 13 looked at the development of the interview and its place in a modern journalistic culture. Chapter 11 looked briefly at the work of Richard Sennett in *The Fall of Public Man* and in particular his argument that public and private domains are confused such that modern politicians, for example, in their public role have morphed into political "personalities," who rely on the intimacies and disclosures of the private realm for their legitimacy. This personalization of news agendas is both decried and exalted within the industry, depending on a journalist's individual point of view or the sort of media organization he or she works for.

The World is Their Oyster

Globalization and concentration of ownership are two sides of the same coin. In order to survive and remain viable, a media organization has to achieve critical mass. Generally it is easier to accomplish this by acquisition rather than innovation – the starting of new companies with perhaps untested technologies and untested markets is invariably slower and more prone to failure. For these reasons it wasn't until the latter part of the nineteenth century, with the advent of the news agency, that regular cross-border news distribution became a reality. At the same time the influence of the telegraph on the growth of these fledgling news agencies was critical. Although US agencies remained within continental North America until late in the century, news agencies made the world a smaller place and, arguably, the seeds of globalization were sown.

Résumé
Paul Julius Reuter

Paul Julius Reuter was born in Kassel, Germany, in 1816 and later became a naturalized British citizen. After an unsuccessful attempt at publishing radical pamphlets, Reuter started working in 1848 for Charles-Louis Havas's news agency in Paris, the future Agence France Presse. Havas was the first person to organize news by collecting it and then selling it on just like any other commodity.[6] After leaving Havas, Reuter set up his own news and feature subscription service in the city. However, when creditors seized his assets in 1849, he returned to Germany to start again. He was advised by the pioneer engineer Werner von Siemens to go to London and start a cable agency there.[7] It was good advice: Paris, New York, and Berlin had agencies, but there was none in London, despite the fact that the city was the financial center of the world.

Reuter realized that financial information had a value so he set up his "Submarine Telegraph" office in October 1851 just as the Dover to Calais undersea cable was brought onstream. He also negotiated a contract with the London Stock Exchange to provide stock prices from exchanges in Europe in return for access to London stock prices. These in turn he distributed to stockbrokers in Paris. He ensured that all subscribers to his service received their information at exactly the same time to avoid any allegations of favoritism. This was the basis of his success.

Although most newspapers refused to take Reuter's "intelligence" at first, his aim in every country was to gain recognition for his agency as the preferred outlet for circulating official announcements to the foreign press. Reuter insisted that all newspapers printing his telegrams agreed to carry his name at the end of each published message. This served the dual purpose of making him famous and providing transparency, so that the public knew who was responsible for the information in the message. Thus Reuter was the first person to vouch for the information he distributed in his news dispatches. For 150 years the company has provided one of the strongest international financial news services and the profits from this have helped finance its news wire services. Today it operates in more than 200 cities in 94 countries, supplying news text in about 20 languages.

Paul Reuter died at Villa Reuter in Nice, France, in 1899 and was buried in the family vault at West Norwood Cemetery in south London.

The concept of time and in particular its standardization is pivotal to the development of news systems, and in this respect the telegraph's impact was seminal. Chapter 5 offered an early British example of the way the railway timetable had a similar effect. By the mid-nineteenth century the issue of time was one of the elements that prompted 20 European states to set up the International Telegraph Union in 1865. It dealt with technical issues and later took on the role of international management of the electromagnetic spectrum. During this same period the three major news agencies, Havas, Reuter, and the German Wolffs Telegraphisches Bureau (WTB), agreed "agency treaties" which carved out "spheres of interest" for the collection and transmission of world news outside the United States. According to this nineteenth-century version of a global trade agreement, Havas reported from the French empire and South America, Reuter exclusively from the British Empire with the right to develop further in the Far East, while Wolff covered the territories of Central Europe, Scandinavia, and Russia.

The legacy of these early examples of a developing global news structure is twofold. Firstly, Julius Reuter understood the value of financial information and it is no coincidence that today it is the financial newspapers, particularly the London *Financial Times* and the US *Wall Street Journal*, that have successfully exploited similar circumstances by erecting a paywall around their content on the internet, turning a reasonable profit in doing so, much as Reuter did with his monopoly on stock market prices. As noted by media journalist Peter Kirwan in the *MediaGuardian*: "These developments [paywalls] underline the key selling point about the FT [*Financial Times*], of course. Its stock-in-trade-financial information has a value, unlike most news."[8] Secondly, the other characteristic of Reuter's mission – that the same information should be available to all subscribers at the same time – is also equally crucial today. For as Kirwan continues: "If someone has it faster than you, they could gain direct financial advantage."[9] So in the internet age those rubrics established by Reuter and other news agencies still hold true.

Despite the growing tendency to include news agency copy within their pages, newspapers by and large remained nationally or locally owned and regulated. Their traditional roles were clearly and easily defined, as suggested by journalism academic Warren G. Bovee:

> The responsibilities of local journalistic media begin with their localities, and they extend outward to the country, state, nation, and world, in that order and with decreasing urgency, to the extent that time, space, staff, and finances permit. The responsibilities of national journalistic media begin with the nation, and they extend toward localities or toward the international scene, with decreasing urgency, to the extent that time, space, staff, and finances permit.[10]

This was also the case with broadcast media until the launch of Telstar, the first communications satellite, in July 1962. It relayed the first television pictures, telephone calls, and fax images through space and provided the first live transatlantic television feed. Walter Cronkite in America and Richard Dimbleby in Brussels took part in this first live television broadcast. Dimbleby's first words were, "Hello Walter Cronkite, hello United States," and he signed off with, "Go America, go. Go America, go."[11]

Telstar and satellite broadcasting began to change the whole dynamics of news gathering and distribution. News agendas, especially on television and radio, had to accommodate the greater sense of immediacy that satellites provided. At the same time, when international satellite broadcasting really took off with the launch of the first geostationary and geosynchronous satellites in 1964, the new technology acted as a catalyst for many countries' latent fear about national sovereignty and Western "cultural imperialism." Research into the potential for cross-border satellite broadcasting has found that service providers in Asia, for instance, have to take into account linguistic and cultural differences when establishing their markets. Rupert Murdoch's STAR TV Network was a notable example when in 1994 it removed BBC World Service Television from its network after representations from the government of China which was unhappy with BBC coverage. Despite smacking of censorship, such national hegemony to some extent gives the lie to the more extreme rhetoric of "cultural imperialism." Chapter 8 looked at some of the ramifications of digital technology and how it has affected news gathering and production. It includes a FactFile on Rupert Murdoch's News Corporation and the spread of television reception via satellite.

The notion of a culture suffering from its own media "imperialism" is less discussed, however, but writers such as Edward Herman, Robert McChesney, and Ben Bagdikian, who track media monopoly and ownership, argue that within the United States a communications cartel has come to operate at every step in the mass-communications process, from the creation of content to its delivery into the home. The sheer scale of this cartel production can be appreciated by examining the television output in Washington DC on one day in 2000. It was estimated there were 178 hours of news and public affairs programming, of which about 40 percent were talk shows.[12] Subsequently this has been aided and abetted by the digital revolution, "an influence whose scope and power," according to Ben Bagdikian, "would have been considered scandalous or illegal twenty years ago."[13]

FactFile
The "Net Benefit to Canada" Test

In 1995 the Canadian government tried to assert the primacy of home-produced content in major magazines. Foreign investment guidelines required a "net benefit to Canada" test by specifying the production of a majority of national content. When Time Warner's magazine *Sports Illustrated* announced its intention to publish a "split-run" edition by inserting Canadian advertisements into editorial matter from its US edition, the Canadian government imposed an 80 percent tax on advertising revenues.

As a result the US government called in the World Trade Organization (WTO) which found not only that the Canadian tax measures were inconsistent with GATT (General Agreement on Tariffs and Trade, 1994) but also that *Sports Illustrated's* split-run edition in Canada was "directly competitive and substitutable" for the Canadian news magazine *Maclean's*, even though the content of the two magazines was completely distinct one from the other. In other words, one nation's cultural output was deemed to be substitutable for another.

In Europe similar concerns about cultural imperialism resulted in the 1989 "TV Without Frontiers" Directive of the European Union which provided for 51 percent of screen time to be made up of indigenous European drama/film/documentary.[14] This was one response by nation-states to the dilemma of how to defend cultural creativity and pursue their own cultural policies in the face not only of American TV imports but also of a drive by the WTO to extend free-trade rules to film and television. For instance, in 1985 the United Kingdom had an audiovisual trade surplus with the US of £151 million. Since the advent of cable and satellite channels, this has become a deficit of £403 million, meaning fewer jobs and less indigenous audiovisual creation. By the 1990s, in revenue terms, the overwhelming majority of the world's film and TV production, cable and satellite channel and system ownership, magazine and book publishing, and music production was provided by about 50 companies, many of the largest of which were American. By 2002, for example, the EU–US audiovisual trade deficit had reached $8 billion.

Neighborhood Watch

Britain's media regulator Ofcom in 2006 defined "local" services as "any targeted at geographical communities ranging from a neighbourhood of a few hundred or thousand households to a major metropolitan area with a million or more inhabitants."[15] In these geographical communities local and regional newspapers still tend to dominate and are often the most trusted suppliers of local news. However, the picture is constantly changing as digital media platforms begin to fracture traditional models of news gathering, advertising revenue, and readerships.

History teaches that a vibrant local community tends to be reflected in a flourishing local press; Britain's active mid-nineteenth century political culture demanded a constant flow of information and satisfying this demand enhanced the status of local newspaper offices. Newspaper growth was most rapid in the provinces after the abolition of taxes in 1855; by 1870, 78 new provincial dailies had been established, 13 of which were evening papers. Liverpool and Newcastle each boasted five dailies whereas today Liverpool has only two despite a doubling of its population and Newcastle similarly has two despite a sixfold increase in population.[16] This decline, symptomatic of the country as a whole, is a reflection not only of changing technology and reading habits but also of a shift of political power towards state centralization. The privatization of services, together with central government providing the majority of the funds for health, social services, and education, means that there are fewer grounds for the existence of a local community, resulting in "a restriction of a potential supply of locality-based news."[17]

Although local daily newspapers have faced serious circulation declines in recent years it should also be noted that local weeklies – often serving very small areas – have shown considerable resilience in the face of competition from the internet and regional broadcast media. In local areas which are now "public-information poor" they rely on bulking out their copy with feature stories, human interest, and service journalism. This kind of news agenda is relatively cheap to resource and another response to this has been the meteoric rise in free local weeklies. Yet as noted by Bob Franklin, these have not always had a positive influence: "Undoubtedly the most significant impact of free newspapers has been the extent to which their limited and consumer-focused editorial has tended to influence and diminish both the range and quality of the editorial content of the local weekly press more generally."[18] Few local papers, for example, now cover court proceedings and council meetings in the way they once did.

Local broadcast news output is likewise retreating in the face of falling advertising revenues in commercial television and local newspaper opposition to the BBC public service offerings. In 2007 British ITV (Independent TeleVision) announced plans to cut its regional news budget. "The former controller of ITV Central, Laurie Upshon, said he believed [the] announcement of dramatic cuts to the ITV regional news budget was the 'beginning of the end' for the service."[19] The BBC has suffered long-running frosty relations with local and regional newspaper groups over its BBC News website. Members of the Newspaper Publishers Association (NPA) have long regarded the website as a "barrier to them making substantial advertising or paid content income from their own sites."[20] More recently the BBC's decision that its news and sport output would be "repurposed" for smartphones such as iPhone, Blackberry, and Android cell phones would, according to the NPA, "undermine the commercial sector's ability to establish an economic model in an emerging but potentially important market ... This, over the long term, will reduce members' ability to invest in quality journalism."[21]

In the United States the vast size of the country and the lack of fast travel and communications meant that local newspapers of necessity had an important role to play. Some regional newspapers had circulations of 40,000 when Britain had no daily press outside of London. The fragmented, dispersed, and essentially agricultural nature of nineteenth-century American life was represented in many of the smaller journals and this continued in some parts of the country well into the twentieth century together with developments in chain ownership. William Randolph Hearst, for instance, by 1928 had a nationwide string of 28 newspapers. At the same time, the distance to be covered for effective newspaper distribution (especially for the dailies) militated against the establishment of a national press. This "forced" localism continued as radio and TV began to mimic the development of newspapers across the country. Local newspaper ownership increasingly slipped into the hands of local radio and television networks, prompting court decisions in the 1970s to dismantle local "cross-ownership" of broadcast and print media. The response of press owners was often to swap their local radio and television stations with those owned by newspapers in other cities.[22]

One of the early and long-lasting effects of this localism was that newspaper editors in particular took a highly principled approach to serving their communities. Written communication was accompanied by a sense of mission, sadly lacking according to many commentators in twenty-first-century news environments. It was summed up by the editor of America's *Springfield Republican*, who saw his role as "the high priest of history, the vitalizer of society, the world's great informer, the earth's high censor, the medium of public opinion, and the circulating life blood of the whole human mind."[23] Such sentiments, however, were not so much country-specific as culture-specific. W. T. Stead, editor of the London *Pall Mall Gazette*, voiced similar sentiments in his 1886 polemic, "The Future of Journalism," where he adopts a biblical tone: "A newspaper ... is a daily apostle of fraternity, a messenger who bringeth glad tidings of joy, of a great light that has risen upon those who sit in darkness and the shadow of death."[24]

Many scholars today are convinced that the "shadow of death" does indeed hang over local newspapers – whether city-based, regional, daily, weekly, or "freebie." Many current academic texts talk of "The End of Journalism,"[25] "The End of the Newspaper,"[26] or the slightly less apocalyptic "Newspapers at the Crossroads."[27] At the same time others offer various antidotes to the current malaise. Merrill, Gade, and Blevens in *Twilight of Press Freedom* suggest that "What will be needed in the twenty-first century are localized media, interacting constantly with community members, and reinforcing group values and norms."[28] Most people would agree with such sentiments but where it becomes problematic is when the cultural and political implications of localized media ownership are added to the mix, for not all "localized" media are actually local organizations, controlled by local people.

The transnational media corporation that customizes its output for national cultural considerations only if profit so dictates has now replaced the traditional historical relationship between a locality and its media. This has far-reaching implications for freedom of cultural expression in a world that has been moving toward free trade in the ideological construction of news values and agendas, whatever the national repercussions. The "value" in cultural values thus becomes monetary rather than historical. Yet on the other hand there is evidence that this same process also encourages subnational identities and movements, such as Basque nationalism in Spain, as part of a decline in the importance of national identity. In such instances the global seems to promote the local at the expense of the national, but "glocalized" news, with no attachment to the community it ostensibly serves, may prove an unreliable bedfellow. There is the danger that people lose any sense of connectivity with local government and are consequently less likely to become involved in civic affairs – as activists and advocates, community leaders, elected officials, or simply as informed voters. Chapters 1, 2, 3 and 4 examined the relationship between democracy and journalism, as well as that between local and national media. Chapter 7 looked at the plight of some of the great US newspapers now in serious financial trouble. Chapter 11 examined circulations and readerships while Chapter 13 looked at the history of audience measurement systems.

Brother, Can You Spare a Dime?

Has journalism reached a crossroads? Have personalization, globalization, and localization all aided and abetted the new technologies of the satellite and the internet to undermine the traditional ways of delivering news to audiences and deriving revenue from doing so? Have we indeed arrived at the age of pauperization and if so, is it terminal? As noted in Chapter 5, newspaper circulations have been in decline for many years in both the US and Britain as well as in many European countries. However, according to *World Association of Newspapers* statistics the overall picture is mixed. Newspapers, with 27.5 percent of the market, are the world's second largest advertising medium after television with 38 percent. If newspapers and magazines are added together, however, they become the world's largest advertising medium with a 40 percent market share.

The trend over recent years is one where many developing markets are showing strong circulation gains, particularly the BRIC countries (Brazil, Russia, India, China) while many mature markets are seeing sales decline (see Table 14.1). Between 2003 and 2007 global newspaper advertising revenue was up 9.4 percent and this is clearly a result of the large increases in India, China, Latin America, and to a lesser extent Russia.[29]

As already noted, local newspaper circulation in Britain has been in sharp decline since the late 1980s, yet such newspapers remained profitable

Table 14.1 World Press Trends Survey – 2003–7

Country/Region	Circulation	Advertising revenue
Europe	Down 1.9%	Up 10.1%
United States	Down 8%	Up 8%
United Kingdom	Down 10.1%	Down 5.2%
India	Up 35.5%	Up 64.8%
China	Up 20.7%	Up 49.4%
Brazil	Up 24.9%	Up 55.4% (Latin America)
Japan	Down 2.7%	Down 8.8%
Russia	N/A	Up 17%

because of buoyant advertising revenues and persistent job-cutting of editorial staffs required by shareholders to protect their stock price. This cannot, however, disguise the overall malaise affecting print journalism in all its forms. Two recent examples are symptoms of this wider problem. The London *Evening Standard* was bought in 2009 by Russian billionaire and ex-KGB agent Alexander Lebedev for the nominal sum of £1. Despite being over 180 years old, the paper had apparently in all that time amassed no real value as a company or a brand. Lebedev turned it into a free paper and circulation increased as a result. In 2010 Lebedev also bought the *Independent*, a British national daily launched in 1986 as a serious broadsheet, which seldom sold enough to make a profit. It too was bought for a nominal £1. Lebedev is quoted as saying: "I do not treat newspapers as business. I treat them as my responsibility. I think newspapers are the only instrument which, through investigative reporting, can ferret out everything about international corruption."[30]

Many national titles now are subsidized by other divisions of the media organizations they are part of and it is probably true to say that most national newspapers in Britain would not survive long as stand-alone enterprises. The days when press barons could enjoy flamboyant lifestyles on the back of their newspapers' profits alone are long gone. Information has become too cheap and producing it has become too expensive. This paradox is one of a number that suggests how the traditional models of news media and the press in particular might be on the road to pauperization.

The second paradox is that noted by journalism academic Ian Hargreaves: "We have more news and more influential journalism, across an unprecedented range of media, than at any time since the birth of the free press in the eighteenth century; yet journalism is also under widespread attack, from politicians, philosophers, the general public, and even from journalists themselves." Hargreaves also talks of the "growth in the cultural, political, and economic value of information."[31] Yet the "economic value" of specifically journalistic information would now appear to be too low to sustain a pluralist news media either nationally or locally. According to purveyors of this argument – what might be called the Rupert Murdoch tendency – it is digital technology and the internet that are the main culprits. It therefore makes sense to charge for this information by erecting paywalls around electronic versions of their newspapers.

The contrary argument centers on the mantra often credited to Stewart Brand, editor of the *Whole Earth Catalog* and founder of the Global Business Network, that "information wants to be free." But what this fails to do is distinguish between different kinds of information; for the idea that all information is "equal" regardless of the cost of its production or its socio-cultural, political, or economic impact is clearly not sustainable. Journalists therefore have to carry on making the case for the special status of the type of information they peddle. But what if this special status is also under attack?

This leads us to the third paradox. Here, the type of information is clearly alluded to. Media academic Stuart Allan in *News Culture* quotes the *Economist* magazine: "In this age of globalisation, news is much more parochial than in the days when communications from abroad ticked slowly across the world by telegraph. And here is another [paradox]: that in this information age, newspapers which used to be full of politics and economics are thick with stars and sport."[32] The clear implication is that the quality of the information may not be what it was and in the process of not being what it was it undermines its "special status." Paradoxically it is inferred that journalists are in fact undermining their own profession by peddling information that does not exhibit a "special status."

Finally, the role of digital technology, electronic media, and the internet together produce the fourth paradox of modern journalism. This is elucidated very effectively by business journalist and author Nick Carr. According to Carr, a traditional newspaper was in the business of selling bundles of information to subscribers. At the same time advertisers paid to have their ads included in the bundle. In effect investigative journalism and other hard news (the "special status" information) was "subsidized by the softer stuff" (the *Economist*'s "thick with stars and sport" stuff), but you couldn't really see the subsidization, so in a way it didn't really exist. And, besides, the hard stuff contributed to the value of the overall bundle. That whole model has been slowly unraveling for some time, but the web tears it into tiny little pieces. Literally. The web unbundles the bundle – each story becomes a separate entity that lives or dies, economically, on its own. It's naked in the marketplace, its commercial existence meticulously measured, click by click.[33]

At the same time this changes the dynamics of advertising. Now advertisers don't pay to be seen by large groups of readers but to have their "ads clicked on by individual readers."[34] So advertisers go where the clickthroughs are and clickthroughs are priced individually according to content and traffic.

These new realities are driving what the Project for Excellence in Journalism, in its 2006 annual report on the state of the news media, called "the paradox of journalism" – more outlets covering fewer stories:

> As the number of places delivering news proliferates, the audience for each tends to shrink and the number of journalists in each organization is reduced. At the national level, those organizations still have to cover the big events. Thus we tend to see more accounts of the same handful of stories each day. ... Such concentration of personnel around a few stories, in turn, has aided the efforts of newsmakers to control what the public knows.[35]

This argument is something of a corrective to the "more news" element of the Hargreaves paradox but acknowledges, if for different reasons, that journalism is certainly "more influential." Yet in both cases it is journalism and journalists who seem to come under attack. A more positive reading by sociologist Manuel Castells suggests that advanced satellite technology with new forms of news gathering and modes of dissemination in conjunction with virtual news platforms providing continued updates via RSS feeds, blogs, podcasts, and websites have created a new "news" geography – one which integrates journalism into the communication culture of a world "network" society.[36]

The ultimate challenge for journalism in the twenty-first century could therefore be to discover the "precise nature of the correlation between efficient markets and good journalism."[37] The recurrent danger is that in attempting to monetize the internet news organizations lose sight of the fundamental characteristics of good journalism – the successful integration of democratic values, technological innovation, ethical standards, and respect for audiences. Current trends – multiplatforms, paywalls, PR-dominated news gathering, shrinking editorial staffs, re-evaluation of the "special status" accorded journalists' information – rather than pointing the way are often contradictory, at times ephemeral, and always challenging. Are journalists up to the task? Can they reinvent themselves not as a one-time project but as a constant response to constant change? This is, after all, what makes future journalism exciting and it is an environment that should attract and test the integrity of the most dedicated temperaments and the finest intellects.

Notes

1 Jenny McKay, "Defoe's *Storm* as a Model for Contemporary Reporting," in Richard Keeble and Sharon Wheeler (eds), *The Journalistic Imagination: Literary Journalism from Defoe to Capote and Carter* (London: Routledge, 2007), pp. 15–28 (p. 18).
2 Ibid. (p. 21).
3 Ibid.
4 Dave Eggers, *Zeitoun* (London: Hamish Hamilton, 2009), p. 25.
5 Leo Lowenthal, "The Triumph of Mass Idols," in *Literature, Popular Culture, and Society* (Englewood Cliffs, NJ: Prentice-Hall, 1961), pp. 109–40 (pp. 114–15).
6 Donald Read, *The Power of News: The History of Reuters*, 2nd edn (Oxford: Oxford University Press, 1999), p. 9.
7 Graham Storey, *Reuter's Century* (London: Max Parrish, 1951), p. 2.
8 Peter Kirwan, "No FT, No Paywall Model?" *MediaGuardian*, April 5, 2010, p. 1.
9 Ibid.
10 Warren G. Bovée, *Discovering Journalism* (Westport, CT: Greenwood Press, 1999), p. 140.
11 YouTube, *Telstar, Kennedy, and World Gold & Currency Markets*, a recording of the first TV broadcast over Telstar Satellite between the US and Europe: 1962. Available online at http://www.youtube.com/watch?v=FgplIWibv4Q&feature =related, accessed on April 12, 2010.
12 Bill Kovach and Tom Rosenstiel, *The Elements of Journalism* (London: Guardian Atlantic Books, 2001), p. 138.
13 Ben Bagdikian, *The Media Monopoly*, 5th edn (Boston: Beacon Press, 1997), p. ix. See also Robert W. McChesney and Edward Herman, *The Global Media: The New Missionaries of Corporate Capitalism* (London: Cassell, 1997).
14 "Television Broadcasting Activities: 'Television without Frontiers' (TVWF) Directive," *Europa, Summaries of EU Legislation* (2008). Available online at http://europa.eu/legislation_summaries/audiovisual_and_media/l24101_ en.htm, accessed on April 15, 2010.

15   Ofcom Office of Communications, *Digital Local: Options for the Future of Local Video Content and Interactive Services* (2006). Available online at http:// stakeholders.ofcom.org.uk/binaries/broadcast/reviews-investigations/psb-review/digital_local.pdf, p. 11, para. 1.17, accessed on September 6, 2010.

16   Alan J. Lee, *The Origins of the Popular Press 1855-1914* (London: Croom Helm, 1976), p. 277.

17   Meryl Aldridge, "The Ties That Divide: Regional Press Campaigns, Community and Popularism," *Media, Culture & Society*, 25 (July 2003), 491–509 (p. 493).

18   Bob Franklin, "No News Isn't Good News: The Development of Free Newspapers," in Bob Franklin and David Murphy (eds), *Making the Local News: Local Journalism in Context* (London: Routledge, 1998), pp. 125–40 (p. 125).

19   Colin Crummy, "The Beginning of the End for ITV Local News?" *Press Gazette*, September 27, 2007. Available online at http://www.pressgazette.co.uk/story. asp?storycode=38873, accessed on April 16, 2010.

20   Robert Andrews, "UK Newspapers Want BBC Mobile Apps Blocked For 'Undermining' Them, BBC Disagrees," *paidContent:UK*, February 18, 2010. Available online at http://paidcontent.co.uk/article/419-uk-newspapers-want-bbc-mobile-apps-blocked-for-undermining-them-bbc-dis/, accessed on April 16, 2010.

21   Ibid.

22   Anthony Smith, *The Newspaper: An International History* (London: Thames & Hudson, 1979), p. 165.

23   Francis Williams, *The Right to Know: The Rise of the World Press* (London: Constable, 1969), p. 44.

24   W. T. Stead, "The Future of Journalism," *Contemporary Review*, L (November 1886), 663–79 (p. 670). Available online at http://www.attackingthedevil.co. uk/steadworks/future.php, accessed on September 6, 2010.

25   Ian Hargreaves, *Journalism: Truth or Dare?* (Oxford: Oxford University Press, 2003), p. 13.

26   Kevin Williams, *Read All About It!: A History of the British Newspaper* (London: Routledge, 2010), p. 241.

27   Peter Cole and Tony Harcup, *Newspaper Journalism* (London: Sage, 2010), p. 177.

28   John C. Merrill, Peter J. Gade, and Frederick R. Blevens, *Twilight of Press Freedom: The Rise of People's Journalism* (Mahwah, NJ: Lawrence Erlbaum Associates, 2001), p. 197.

29   Larry Kilman, "World Press Trends: Newspapers Are a Growth Business," *World Association of Newspapers* (2008). Available online at http://www.wan-press. org/article17377.html, accessed on April 18, 2010.

30   "The Independent Bought by Lebedev for £1," *BBC News*, March 25, 2010. Available online at http://news.bbc.co.uk/1/hi/business/8587469.stm, accessed on April 18, 2010.

31   Hargreaves, *Journalism: Truth or Dare?*, p. 2.

32   Stuart Allan, *News Culture*, 2nd edn (Maidenhead, UK: Open University Press, 2004), p. 197.

33   Nick Carr, cited in Karl Martino, "What Will be the Future of Newspapers and Local Journalism?" *Paradox1x* (2006). Available online at http:// www.paradox1x.org/archives/2006/03/what-will-be-th.shtml,   accessed on September 23, 2009.

34   Ibid.

35   The Project for Excellence in Journalism, "Major Trends," *The State of the News Media, 2006, An Annual Report on American Journalism* (2006). Available online   at   http://www.stateofthemedia.org/2006/narrative_overview_eight. asp?cat=2&media=1, accessed on March 12, 2010.

36   Manuel Castells, *The Power of Identity* (Oxford: Blackwell, 1997).

37   Carr, cited in Martino, "What Will be the Future of Newspapers and Local Journalism?"

Index

Entries beginning with numbers are listed as if spelled out. Page numbers referring to major mentions of a topic are in **bold**.